Gareth Southwell is .... curator of Philosophyonline.com. .... *ner's Guide to Descartes's Meditation* .... *yond Good and Evil; Philosophy: Key* .... with Julian Baggini); and *50 Philoso*............................ *Really Need to Know.* He lives in Swansea with his wife and children.

is a philosopher, writer and the ...
... His writing credits include A Beginner's Guide ...
..., A Beginner's Guide to Nietzsche's Beyond ...
... Texts and Philosophy: Key Themes (with ...
...phy of Steven ... You ... Very ...
... him through his website at ...

WORDS OF WISDOM

*Philosophy's Most Important Quotations
and Their Meanings*

Gareth Southwell

First published in hardback 2010 by Quercus Editions Ltd

This paperback edition published in 2015 by

Quercus Publishing Ltd
Carmelite House
50 Victoria Embankment
London EC4Y 0DZ

An Hachette UK company

A CIP catalogue record for this book is available from the British Library

PB ISBN 978 1 78429 072 6
Ebook ISBN 978 1 78087 092 2

10 9 8 7 6 5 4 3

Text designed and typeset by Hewer Text Ltd, Edinburgh
Printed and bound in Great Britain by Clays Ltd. St Ives plc

In Memoriam, AC, who was never short of words, both wise and humorous. With love and fond remembrance.

WORDS OF WISDOM

INTRODUCTION

Just as philatelists love stamps, or philanthropists love humanity, philosophers love wisdom – at least, if we take the literal meaning of the name seriously (Greek: *philo*, 'love of'; *sophia*, 'wisdom'). However, whilst stamp collectors might disagree as to the worth of a specimen, and do-gooders might deliberate as to how best to help others, philosophers aren't all in agreement as to what it is exactly that they're supposed to be loving. In fact, 'aren't all in agreement' is a sizable understatement, for if there is one thing that *is* common to philosophy, it is *disagreement*. If there's a hair to be split, or a call to be questioned, you can be sure that somewhere, sometime, a philosopher has done just that.

In *Words of Wisdom* I have scoured two and a half thousand years to bring you what I think are some of the best quotes, ideas, and theories. However, you shouldn't imagine that you'll find here the sort of helpful and inspirational collection of wise sayings that you will benefit from by applying unquestioningly to your daily life. Certainly, there's undoubtedly a lot here that *is* helpful, inspirational, interesting, etc., but there are also things that you'll disagree with, that may trouble you, or even outrage you. Because philosophy is not a unified discipline, and does not really possess an orthodox creed, I have attempted to do justice to a wide range of philosophical opinion. There are, to be sure, similarities of approach between philosophers throughout its history, and I have tried to connect these and point out common themes and ideas. However, the main benefit to the study of philosophy is not to find a perspective that you like, swallow it whole, and then defend it against all comers, but to develop a critical response – to think for yourself. Accordingly, as well as explaining and commenting

3

on the quotations, I have mostly attempted to briefly suggest possible criticisms. I haven't always done this – some ideas are more complex and require more space to explain, whilst at other times (to vary things) I simply present an idea sympathetically. Hopefully, overall, things balance out – atheism and faith, scepticism and trust in reason – so don't assume that I have a personal axe to grind, or even that the opinions presented are mine. Thus, apart from aiming to be enjoyable and informative, the purpose of the book is to encourage you to think; not to *learn* philosophy, but to *do* it.

In choosing quotes and thinkers, I haven't worried too much about sticking to the standard academically approved lists of those deemed 'true' philosophers, for these are often driven by quite a narrow definition of what philosophy is, and I think no harm is done (and a great deal of good) in showing how different conceptions of philosophy are possible. Therefore, you will find here not just the likes of Plato, Aristotle, Descartes, and Wittgenstein, but scientists, theologians, psychologists, anthropologists, writers, and a number of other sorts of people whom you wouldn't immediately think of as contributing to philosophy. By including such figures, I'm not necessarily suggesting that we should rechristen them as philosophers, but merely that they have, in some way, contributed seriously to issues which we would term philosophical in a slightly broader (and, I think, *healthier*) sense. Also, of course, many thinkers lived in a time where what they were doing – physics, psychology, sociology, economics – *was* still part of philosophy (which is in itself an interesting tale).

Regarding the composition of the book itself, thanks are of course due to the various individuals who have been involved in one way or another. Firstly, my thanks must go to: Julian Baggini, for the generous recommendation; to Seiriol Morgan, for being understanding; to my editor, Slav Todorov, for his help and guidance; and to Nick Hutchins for his diligence and care in preparing the manuscript, and for his generous support and patience. During composition, I relied on many of the usual suspects for their support, feedback and suggestions (in no particular order): Dr Mark, Phill Burton, Dad, Robi Wan, Mike, Vicki Sheridan and Nana Gwen. I was also lucky enough to be able to bother the knowledgeable members of Liverpool University's Philos-L mailing list, who, with the generosity of their time and expertise in response to my often trivial queries, never fail to gladden my heart (the inevitable shortcomings of this work, as the formula has it, are of course all my own). Finally, to my family – Jo, El and Tes – who suffered first-hand the alternately grumpy and exuberant moods of a short-tempered man working on a long-term project – I wish I had wise words to convey my gratitude, but they fail me: thank you.

Gareth Southwell

'Know Thyself'
Unknown

It is perhaps fitting that this famous piece of advice, traditionally the cornerstone of knowledge, be of uncertain origin. Inscribed in the forecourt of the Temple of Apollo at Delphi, Greece, it has been ascribed to various ancient philosophers and sages – Thales, Heraclitus, and even Socrates. However, the most tempting attribution is the most mythic: a pronouncement from Apollo – the Greek god of truth, prophecy and the arts, the patron of philosophy itself – relayed via the Delphic oracle.

But what does it mean? The oracle was notoriously cryptic, and – some have suggested – deliberately so. Consulted by the poor and the powerful on affairs of home and state, her position was sometimes precarious: displeasing news or unwelcome advice to the wrong person might have dangerous consequences. Obscurity was therefore the safest policy: let the questioner interpret the god's will.

Accordingly, philosophers have construed this advice differently. Plato, for example, that we must cherish an intellectual understanding of the true nature of things (for the mind is the true self); much later, René Descartes, that certainty regarding the nature of the mind or soul is the basis of knowledge in general; later still, Friedrich Nietzsche, that analysis of self is essential to an understanding of how we tailor knowledge to our own purposes ('We are all greater artists than we realize').

But it can also have a more humble application. I can know my own limits, flaws and failings; I can know my own mind, what I'm capable of, what I feel or desire. This is a less abstract and philosophical undertaking, perhaps, but arguably a more fundamental and important one: to profess to seek truth is no doubt noble, but if I do not first assess the seeker himself, how can I know that I am properly prepared? If I do not investigate my own motives, how will I know that I am proceeding in the right way? And if I cannot distinguish truth from wish, how will I even recognize it should I find it?

'All things are wearisome, more than one can say. The eye never has enough of seeing, nor the ear its fill of hearing. What has been will be again, what has been done will be done again; there is nothing new under the sun.'

KING SOLOMON c.1011–c.931 BC
Ecclesiastes, 1:8–9 (New International Version)

Ecclesiastes **is a book of the Old Testament** and Hebrew Bible, traditionally attributed to King Solomon, though this is now mostly disputed. Modern textual scholars argue that it either represents the original composition of an unknown, more recent author, or else a transmission of, or possible elaboration upon, views ascribed to the historical Solomon.

But whatever its authorship, the book is *philosophically* interesting for its *pessimism*. Life is seen as inherently meaningless, and accordingly, worldly pursuits are vain and empty. However, whilst life is futile and death may strike at any moment, man should not be downcast, but seek consolation in simple pleasures – marriage and family, companionship, food and drink – not as a hedonistic escape, but out of an appreciation of the few simple benefits that existence affords.

As an outlook on life, *Ecclesiastes* is therefore particularly bleak. God is present, but doesn't seem to mitigate the meaninglessness of existence (though this possibility is not denied). It therefore leaves room for commentators to interpret its gloominess. Some argue that the futility of Earthly life is to be contrasted with that of divine resurrection, and yet this was not an explicit creed of early Judaism. Others draw parallels with Buddhism; life is suffering, and we shouldn't seek Earthly satisfaction or heavenly salvation, but merely to transcend its negative character. Or, even that death is total *oblivion* – no afterlife, no heavenly reward, nothing. Obviously, this latter interpretation seems perilously close to atheism, and its closest modern parallel is perhaps *Existentialism*: faced with absurdity, futility and death, we should count our blessings and muster the courage to shun false hope. It might almost have been written by Sartre.

'Some think that the soul pervades the whole universe, whence
perhaps came Thales' view that everything is full of gods'
ARISTOTLE ON THALES c.624–c.546 BC
De Anima

Thales is considered the first genuine philosopher of the Western tradition. Listed by Plato as one of the traditional Seven Sages of Greece,
he was among the first to seek purely scientific explanations for natural phenomena, previous attempts having intermixed science with
religious or mythological accounts.

However, we should not suppose that there was a clean break
between rational and non-rational thinking. The ancient Greeks did
not suddenly think, 'You know? Thales is right. We should seek
rational explanations for things.' They sowed and harvested their
crops, cooked their food, fought their enemies, and generally conducted their daily affairs with much the same regard for practical
wisdom as we do. Yet, they also honoured the gods, occasionally
seeking out their counsel and help, for they believed too that certain
things were out of our control or beyond our understanding.

Thales was therefore a peculiar mixture of ancient and modern. He
made key discoveries in geometry, astronomy, and meteorology, determined the dates of the solstices, predicted a solar eclipse, and
measured the height of the Egyptian pyramids merely from their
shadows. Mocked for his poverty, he proved his business acumen by
renting all the olive presses in advance of the yearly harvest, thus prof-
iting when the demand came. Yet, on discovering a method for
inscribing a right-angled triangle in a circle, he gave thanks by sacrificing an ox to the gods.

What are we to make of this mixture of religion and science?
Modern philosophers would argue that the scientific spirit was in its
infancy and not yet purged of superstition. But for Thales, all things
were alive ('full of gods'), of which the power to convey motion was
itself a sign; the lodestone could magnetize other objects because it
possessed a 'soul'. Science has no patience with such talk – but has it
thereby rejected dangerous and idle superstition, or lost its soul?

'For it is necessary that there be some nature, either one or more than one, from which become the other things of the object . . . Thales . . . says that it is water'

ARISTOTLE ON THALES

De Anima

And Thales was wrong, of course, but we must be a little charitable with the first scientific theorists, for they are still groping their way. Besides, it is easy to see what he was driving at. If we look about us, most things we see can be described as a solid, a gas, or a liquid, which are the three forms that water can take: ice, vapour, and water itself. The important insight here is therefore that there is an underlying substance out of which all existing things are constituted. We don't really know – since most of what we know of Thales comes from secondary sources such as Aristotle – how literally Thales would have wanted us to interpret this thesis, but it's nice to think that his intentions tended to the metaphorical. Interpreted in this way, Thales' theory is logical and insightful: water isn't a different substance from steam or ice, but merely the same substance in a different form, and so, more generally, there is a 'water-like stuff' that is the basis of matter, and which can be moulded by physical forces into different forms.

Later philosophers would take this insight in different directions. Anaximander, Thales' pupil, proposed the more promising idea that everything originated from a sort of primal chaos, which he called 'the boundless'. *His* pupil, Anaximenes, on the other hand, took a sideways, if not a backward step, proposing air as the primary substance. Of course, these ancient Greeks lacked the technology to fully investigate questions that would not begin to be properly addressed until the turn of the twentieth century. They were, then, in a sense, born too early – before electron microscopes or particle accelerators – but, nonetheless, we can see that they were on the right track: the questions they were asking were the correct ones.

'Epimenides the Cretan said that all Cretans were liars, and all other
statements made by Cretans were certainly lies. Was this a lie?'
BERTRAND RUSSELL ON EPIMENIDES *c.*600 BC
'Mathematical Logic as Based on the Theory of Types'

A paradox is a statement that, if true, must be false, but if false, must
be true. In other words, it contradicts itself. In the above quotation, if
Epimenides is telling the truth, then it's true that he himself is a liar;
however, if so, then Cretans are not liars, and he is telling the truth!

This is known as a *self-referential paradox*, because its contradictori-
ness lies in referring to itself. There are other examples: 'I always lie',
'This statement is false', and (still sometimes found in books and doc-
uments), 'This page left intentionally blank' (which, of course, it hasn't
been!).

Epimenides (c.600 BC) was a shadowy figure, given to poetry and
prophecy, and very much belonging to the early period when philosophy was still finding its way. Some doubt that he intended the phrase
to be paradoxical, and consider the *liar paradox* proper to have been
devised by Eubulides two centuries later, merely employing
Epimenides for this purpose. Either way, the paradox has endured –
but is it any more than a logical curiosity, a trick puzzle with no real
solution? Does it in fact tell us anything?

Paradoxes have always fascinated philosophers. Generally, when an
argument results in paradox, it's a sign that something has gone
wrong – a false assumption, an error of reasoning. So, the fact that a
faulty argument sometimes results in absurdity can be used to test a
hypothesis, a method known as *reductio ad absurdum* ('reduction to
the absurd'). 'You are the Third Earl of Davenport, Sir?! But the Sixth
Earl yet lives, and he is, I assure you, quite ancient! That would not
only make you his great-grandfather, but also – at, I hazard, somewhat
shy of thirty years – a time traveller, the discoverer of the Fountain of
Youth, or, more likely, given the palpable absurdity of these two possibilities, a liar!'

> 'He who knows does not speak. He who speaks does not know.'
> Lao Tzu between 6th and 4th centuries BC
> *Tao Te Ching*

Lao Tzu (sometimes spelt Lae Tse or Laozi) was a *Taoist* sage, even taken by some to be a god, who is thought to have existed sometime between the 6th and 4th centuries BC in China, but about whom very little else is known. He was (allegedly) the author of the *Tao Te Ching*, a title very difficult to translate, but which may be loosely rendered as 'The Great Book of the Way and the Virtue' (where 'virtue' also has an additional sense of potency or personal power). The book presents a collection of enigmatic observations on themes that include moral conduct, the nature of reality, the possibility of knowledge, and religious enlightenment.

Taoism itself is difficult to define precisely, but it may be broadly thought of as a religious/philosophical tradition whose practitioners aim to follow 'the way' (the *Tao*). The Tao itself can be interpreted in various senses: as a moral code, as an attitude to life, or as the life force itself. Perhaps the best way of thinking of it, however, is as a way of living that is in harmony with the universe. Taoists therefore aim at a sort of 'doing-without-doing' – which sounds paradoxical, but merely stems from the idea that action and thought that are in harmony with the Tao don't spring from the individual self, but rather come *through* it, unmediated by self-consciousness. Anyone who is at all familiar with any form of Eastern martial art – which Taoist philosophy has had a massive influence upon – will recognize this approach.

In the quote, Lao Tzu is therefore expressing the conundrum involved in communicating knowledge of ultimate reality: whatever is communicated is an expression of the Tao, and not the Tao itself. The silence of the wise man is not therefore some spiteful refusal to share, but merely a consequence of the nature of such knowledge: as Wittgenstein would later argue, some knowledge is beyond words.

'And once when he passed a puppy which was being whipped they say he took pity on it and made this remark: "Stop, do not beat it; for it is the soul of a dear friend – I recognized it when I heard its voice."'

DIOGENES LAERTIUS ON PYTHAGORAS c.580–c.495 BC
Lives of the Philosophers

There are many stories about Pythagoras, and many things are ascribed to him on insufficient evidence – even the geometrical theorem that now bears his name comes under suspicion. However, his belief in reincarnation – or *metempsychosis*, to give it its Greek name – occurs repeatedly in the secondary accounts of his philosophy (which are all we have). Whilst the term can have different meanings – it needn't, for instance, involve death, or even a human soul – in Pythagoras' case it seems to have involved belief in an immortal essence that, after death, could be reborn in either human or animal form.

It is said that Pythagoras himself could remember his previous incarnations, an ability granted to him in his life as Aethalides, son of the god Hermes (we don't generally accord modern heroes and sages divine ancestry, but it was more common in ancient times). Offered a gift by his father – anything except immortality – Aethalides chose the ability to always remember his incarnations – immortality, perhaps, in a different sense.

Maybe this was a cunning choice: ability to remember former lives might give us a whole new perspective on the current one. We might undertake projects spanning many lifetimes, and death would lose its sting. However, another story relates how Pythagoras once cried on seeing a shield he had formerly borne in a life as a soldier – like recognition of his friend's soul in the dog, an instance of 'uncanny' knowledge or *déjà vu*, perhaps (from the French, 'already seen'). Such knowledge therefore also represents a burden; we would remember the bad as well as the good. Also, of course, we might be reborn an animal – which is itself an argument for vegetarianism, or at least that we should be kinder to our pets.

> '. . . he extended his ears and fixed his intellect in the sublime
> symphonies of the world, he alone hearing and understanding, as it
> appears, the universal harmony and consonance of the spheres, and
> the stars that are moved through them, and which produce a fuller and
> more intense melody than anything effected by mortal sounds'
>
> IAMBLICHUS ON PYTHAGORAS
> *Life of Pythagoras*

Pythagoras was perhaps the first to recognize the importance of number in understanding reality – in fact, to propose that the ultimate nature of reality *is* number. This is the basis of most modern sciences, which are ultimately founded on mathematical principles. Modern faith in mathematics is therefore so strong that if a phenomenon *cannot* be described mathematically, we're more likely to question our understanding than the suitability of employing mathematics.

Pythagoreans venerated the number 10, for it was the sum of the first four numbers (1 + 2 + 3 + 4), thus suggesting a belief in *numerology* (that numbers can have a symbolic significance). Also, famously, Pythagoras thought the structure of the cosmos reflected intervals in music: the so-called *music of the spheres*. An anecdote describes how, passing a blacksmith, he heard different tones ringing out, some of which formed harmonies with each other, and others which did not. On investigation, he discovered that the weights of the blacksmith's hammers were the cause: those that could be related as simple ratios (1:2, 1:3, 1:4, etc.) produced pleasing sounds when struck together; those that could not, didn't. Furthermore, such ratios were also embodied in the cosmic order, and determined the relationships between the planets.

It's ironic, then, that Pythagoras, for whom number reflected divine order, should himself have discovered the existence of *irrational* numbers, which cannot be expressed as a ratio of two whole numbers (such as *Pi*, the relation of a circle's circumference to its diameter). As we now know, whilst repugnant to Pythagoras (because 'inharmonious'), such numbers are very important in understanding reality. Thus, whilst science still dances to the tune of mathematics, it's a melody perhaps closer to Schoenberg than Mozart.

> 'We are what we think. All that we are arises with our thoughts. With
> our thoughts we make the world.'
> GAUTAMA BUDDHA c.563–c.483 BC
> *Dhammapada*

Of all religions, Buddhism perhaps bears greatest resemblance to a philosophical system. Disenchanted with his life of affluence and privilege,
Siddartha Gautama, a prince in a region of what is now Nepal, adopted
the life of a wandering monk, investigating various religious and philosophical traditions for a solution to the problem of suffering. Eventually
– as legend has it – he achieved enlightenment meditating beneath the
Bodhi tree, as it's now known (*bodhi* means 'enlightenment'). From here
on, he assumes the title Gautama Buddha ('the enlightened one'),
preaching his own doctrine advocating a *Middle Way* between self-denial
and sensuous indulgence as a means of realizing true self.

Whilst it's perhaps difficult to view Gautama Buddha in traditional
philosophical terms – he has a semi-divine status in some eyes – his
doctrine is a rational and coherent system. Through the commentaries and diverse interpretations of its many practitioners, it has
evolved into a rich and complex philosophical tradition. It espouses
Four Noble Truths – roughly put:

(1) Life is suffering.
(2) Suffering has a cause.
(3) It is possible to uproot or negate this cause.
(4) We may achieve this through following the Buddhist *Eightfold path*.

In philosophical terms, the first three are obviously the most interesting.
(1) is a form of *pessimism*, most famously mirrored in the West by Arthur
Schopenhauer, who, like Buddha, sees self as the main stumbling block
to happiness – through its *attachment* to things, wanting or being denied
possessions or pleasures, and suffering pain as a result. Thus, by cultivating *selflessness*, we experience freedom from desire and suffering (the
state of *nirvana*), and escape the wheel of death and rebirth (like
Pythagoras – Buddhism believes in reincarnation). But *can* we deny self?
Won't there always be *something* that we are? However, perhaps Buddhism
merely denies our limited *concept* of self, in favour of the desireless, con-
ceptless self that it is possible for us to become.

> 'What you do not wish for yourself, do not do to others'
> CONFUCIUS 551–479 BC
> *Analects*

Kung Fu Tzu, or Confucius, as he is more commonly known in the West, is perhaps the most famous Chinese philosopher. His influence upon subsequent Chinese thought and culture cannot be underestimated, and whilst we know more of his life than – for instance – Lao Tzu, it's perhaps not surprising for such a venerated figure that the facts are entangled with myth and legend.

Confucius is most well known for the *Analects*, which were actually collated after his death by his disciples. This was not a systematic philosophical work, but a collection of sayings and wise counsel for all aspects of life, from matters of personal conduct through to politics. Confucius' main concern was to establish an order in society that reflected that of 'Heaven', which acted as a sort of divine template. As such, he was a conservative, claiming that his teachings were not innovations, but merely the wisdom of the ages compiled and transmitted to present times. It is perhaps fitting therefore that the quotation is a principle that has found expression in almost every religion and culture from ancient Egypt to modern times, and has become known as the *Golden Rule*: 'Do as you would be done by'.

However, Confucius' overriding concern was with order and the rule of law. Whilst his emphasis on discipline, ritual, tradition and strict social codes may not chime well with liberal Western attitudes, its overall purpose should be borne in mind. During this period of Chinese history, social disorder and conflict were prevalent, and strict social codes were therefore a bulwark against anarchy. These roles were dictated by Heaven, and so order and happiness – in the country, the home, and the individual – were achieved by fulfilling one's role: 'Let a sovereign be a sovereign, a minister be a minister, a father be a father, and a son be a son.' So, once Heavenly order was established, it was just a matter of maintaining it.

'To win without fighting is best'
SUN TZU c.544–c.494 BC
The Art of War

Sun Tzu was a Chinese general of the Warring States period, during which China descended into chaos and bloodshed as each state vied for dominance over the others. Like the *Tao Te Ching*, *The Art of War* is written according to the principles of Taoism: all actions should aim at following the *Tao* or 'the Way', which thus ensured that the agent would be in harmony with nature and the universe. As such, it argues that, since the best form of action is *inaction* (a sort of egoless 'doing without doing'), then the greatest victory lies in not fighting. This is not a meaningless paradox, but a practical application of philosophical and spiritual principles.

To illustrate this point, think of a teacher who maintains good order in his classroom. Now, would a good disciplinarian be one who maintained order through administering punishments and reprimands, or one who created an environment where such methods were unnecessary, because the pupils were not tempted to misbehave? Obviously, the answer is the latter. Similarly, then, the greatest military strategist or warrior is one who achieves his objectives with the least expenditure of energy, time and resources; in other words, through peaceful means (clever diplomacy, espionage, and so on).

Of course, this assumes that the military strategist concerned is a rational man who appreciates the benefits of peace. If he is a bloodthirsty maniac, hell-bent on death-or-glory conflict, then the wisdom of *The Art of War* will be lost on him. Like the Italian statesman Niccolò Machiavelli, Sun Tzu thought that war was a costly business – to both loser *and* victor – and should be the last resort, and then only when absolutely necessary, either when victory was guaranteed, or conflict was absolutely unavoidable. Paradoxically, then, the central underlying principle of the art of war is a love of peace and prosperity, of which war is the regrettable but sometimes necessary defence.

'Much learning does not teach thought'
HERACLITUS c.535–c.475 BC
Fragments

Heraclitus was known as 'the weeping philosopher', being generally cynical and pessimistic about human nature, and – some commentators suggest – prone to *melancholia* (depression). He also seemed to be fairly sceptical about the possibility of knowledge, more specifically our ability to achieve it, and wasn't afraid to pass disparaging remarks about the great men of Greek history. His targets included Homer and Hesiod, and even other contemporary philosophers, such as Pythagoras and Xenophanes (at whom the above quotation is directed) and, in fact, anyone else whom he considered to have fallen short of his standards. In this sense, he had much in common with the later *Cynics*, standing on the fringes of society, pricking pomposity and highlighting hypocrisy wherever it arose.

Arguably, the fundamental purpose of knowledge is to improve and enrich life. Philosophy, at times, is in danger of taking itself too seriously, or losing itself in its own footnotes, and can easily forget the reasons why we seek truth and knowledge in the first place. This is not to suggest that all knowledge must have practical applications, but merely that it pays, from time to time, to step back and reassess our motivations. Nietzsche is very perceptive on this point: even if it were possible to perceive the world as it really is, such knowledge would not do us any good, for knowledge is always *for a purpose* (even if that purpose is difficult to define or seems to be hidden from us).

It's not enough, then, to simply study the great minds of the past, imbibe their conclusions, and rehearse their arguments; genuine philosophy involves learning to *think*, to engage with ideas actively and critically, as opposed to merely accepting them with passive admiration. Of course, such a book as this would seem to encourage the latter rather than the former; a buffet of titbits rather than a solid meal. Well, the above dietary advice aside, man cannot live by bread alone, and you shouldn't blame a baker for making cakes.

'You cannot step into the same river twice'
HERACLITUS
Fragments

Heraclitus believed that the primary universal substance is fire. As with Thales and Anaximenes before him, we can recognize here the beginnings of the search for a scientific explanation of the world. However, as before, we should perhaps also acknowledge its broader metaphorical significance. Fire represents constant change, and, like the continuously varying forms that appear and vanish in its flames, nothing in the world has any real or permanent existence, for nothing is immune to the process of change.

This doctrine of impermanence echoes Buddhism, and the Buddha himself would have been a near contemporary of the Greek philosopher (there is no record of influence – though it's not impossible – but the parallels are interesting). Both believed deeper wisdom stems from recognition that all forms are fleeting, and that an underlying oneness pervades the universe. Like a religious seeker, Heraclitus also withdrew from life, rejecting the passions and goals of the multitude, and pursuing a deeper understanding of nature and of himself.

Impermanence also provides an interesting philosophical problem, a famous illustration of which comes from the Roman historian Plutarch, who recounts the tradition that the Athenians preserved the actual ship that Theseus (mythological slayer of the Minotaur) used to return from Crete. Over years, as individual planks decayed and were replaced, there eventually reached a point where more new material existed than old. Was it still the same ship? Heraclitus would say not, and we can perhaps support this view with contemporary science, where, moment-to-moment, each cell and molecule in our bodies is changed or replaced.

But can we logically hold that *everything* is in a state of constant change? If so, Aristotle later argued, then how can we know *anything*? For, even to say, 'This river is not the same', we have to have an idea of the *same* river in order to compare its different states. Without this, the possibility of *any* knowledge collapses – even, perhaps, our knowledge that everything is change . . .

'The path up and down is one and the same'
HERACLITUS
Fragments

As well as cynic, social critic, hermit, and sceptic, Heraclitus was also renowned for his obscurity. Many of his pronouncements resemble the riddling *koans* (paradoxical or seemingly nonsensical statements) of Zen Buddhism, and – judging from the tantalizing fragments of his philosophy that are preserved – he was a man who believed that knowledge should be worked for.

Accordingly, some of his assertions are all but impenetrable: 'The thunderbolt steers all things', 'Death is what we see asleep, sleep what we see awake', and 'Gods are mortal, men immortal, living their death, dying their life.' Occasionally, when studying these, a meaning may jump out at us, or we may glimpse a possible interpretation, but it is often impossible to pin their significance down – in the way that scholars are so fond of – with any real certainty. But these mysterious and enigmatic fragments – together with his more comprehensible comments on nature, science, knowledge and culture – only serve to make him more intriguing. Heraclitus was not some wild-eyed, woolly-headed poet spouting colourful metaphors, but someone with a rational purpose who occasionally chose to veil his meaning – and who, if we only possessed more of his writings, would perhaps represent one of the more substantial and fascinating figures in the history of philosophy.

However, even with these elusive fragments, there are some patterns that emerge. Heraclitus is thought to have proposed a doctrine called the 'unity of opposites'. Everything has an opposite, with which it is in constant strife: 'The death of fire is the birth of air, and the death of air is the birth of water.' Partly, this is a consequence of his already discussed idea that fire (constant change) is the fundamental principle: it is the warring of these opposites, their destruction, union, or transformation, which is the process of life. To understand this principle – as in Buddhist or Hindu philosophy – we must transcend opposition, and thereby approach some fundamental realization about reality and the world. Possibly.

> 'In a race, the quickest runner can never overtake the slowest, since the pursuer must first reach the point whence the pursued started, so that the slower must always hold a lead.'
>
> ARISTOTLE ON ZENO c.490–c.430 BC
> *Physics*

Zeno of Elea – not to be confused with Zeno of Citium, the founder of Stoicism – was a pupil of Parmenides, and evolved a number of arguments in support of his tutor's assertion that the world is really an indivisible whole, which he called 'the One'. So, anything that implies *plurality* (the existence of *more* than one thing) or change, was actually an illusion. Common conceptions of space and time were therefore false, and can be shown to be so because they result in contradiction.

Zeno's paradoxes, as they're known, attempt to reveal such contradictions. Originally 40, only nine are known, since only Aristotle's account of them survives. Of these, the majority concern motion, the best known being 'Achilles and the tortoise'. Imagine, says Zeno, that the famous hero Achilles – an exemplary specimen of Greek athleticism – races against a tortoise. The tortoise has a head start, but – well, it's a tortoise! So, there should be no problem with Achilles overtaking it. If the tortoise's head start is 50 yards, by the time Achilles reaches the tortoise's starting point, it will have advanced further (say, two yards). However, by the time Achilles covers those two yards, the tortoise will have moved on further; and so on, infinitely, the distances getting smaller and smaller. Therefore, concludes Zeno, since the gap between them is infinitely divisible (whatever the distance, Achilles will have to reach where the tortoise *was*, by which time it will have moved on – though a vanishingly small amount), then Achilles will never overtake the tortoise.

Obviously, this is nonsense: of course Achilles overtakes the tortoise – and this is Zeno's point. The assumption that space can be infinitely divisible leads to the conclusion that motion is impossible; therefore, space *isn't* infinitely divisible: it is in reality one *indivisible* thing.

'If there are many, they must be as many as they are and neither more or less than that. But if they are as many as they are, they would be limited. If there are many, things that are are unlimited. For there are always others between the things that are, and again others between those, and so things that are are unlimited.'

SIMLICUS ON ZENO
On Aristotle's Physics

This argues against the notion that the world consists of many things (*plurality*), and is known as the *argument from denseness*. Having read it, you might think it an appropriate title: it's not the clearest argument.

Firstly, if the world consists of many things, there must be a definite number of them, because there cannot be an infinite number of separately existing things. Furthermore, the existence of a definite number of things presupposes that each of them is finite: so, if you had ten boxes, one of them can't contain 'infinity'! Therefore, plurality implies a definite number of limited things.

However, plurality also implies the existence of an infinite number of other things. For instance, suppose there's a row of things: what separates one thing from its neighbour? There must be *something else in between* (even just air – which is a 'thing' of sorts), otherwise we couldn't tell where one thing ends and the other begins. But, if so, then the thing in between *also* needs things to separate it from *its* neighbours. And so on, becoming infinitely densely packed.

Therefore, plurality leads to contradiction: there are both a finite *and* infinite number of things. So, as with motion, plurality must be an illusion: everything is one.

There are obvious objections: Why suppose a *finite* number of things? Couldn't there be an *infinite* number? Why do we need a further 'thing' to separate things? Couldn't this be done with a vacuum (i.e. 'nothing')?

However, the argument is difficult to interpret, and it's possible that Zeno means something else. It's also possible, of course, that I'm just a bit dense.

'Man is the measure of all things'

PROTAGORAS OF ABDERA c.480–411 BC

in Sextus Empiricus, *Outlines of Pyrronhism*

The *sophists* were somewhere between private tutors and hot-shot law-yers. They taught a range of subjects considered essential to the education of ambitious young men – public speaking, argument, pol-itics and philosophy – and were popular with the wealthy sons of aristocrats (or whoever could afford their substantial fees). However, 'sophistry' survives into modern times only in a derogatory sense, being a term for ingenious forms of deceptive and dubious argument. One of the main advantages of a sophist education was that it taught you how to use logic and rhetoric for your own benefit. Therefore, whereas earlier philosophers were concerned with truth, the sophists merely focused on winning – in modern terms, 'Truth is what you can get away with'.

However, such opportunism was not always shallow. Prominent sophists such as Protagoras held philosophical reasons for their cyni-cism: man is the measure of all things, because truth is a human concept, and is merely a reflection of human concerns. So, why *shouldn't* I seek to put my own case in the 'best possible light'?

But is this philosophically grounded attitude any different to mere cynical opportunism? Famously, Protagoras is known to have sued his pupil Euathlus for non-payment of tuition fees. The deal had been that Euathlus would pay for his education once he had won his first court case. However, the training finished, Euathlus never won a case, so eventually, in an ingenious move, Protagoras took him to court: if Protagoras won, he would get his money; if Euathlus won, then Protagoras would also get his money, because Euathlus would have won his first case.

This anecdote perhaps best illustrates sophism. It is a self-serving, 'win at all costs' philosophy, which legitimizes any strategy in service of one's own interests. And yet, in doing so, it also undermines itself: if truth is merely a matter of 'what you can get away with', why should we respect any of the sophist's arguments?

'Nothing exists; even if something exists, it cannot be known; and even if it could be known, this knowledge could not be communicated to others'

GORGIAS c.485–c.380 BC
in Sextus Empiricus, *Against the Professors*

Talk about being thorough! Gorgias, alongside Protagoras, forms the first rank of sophist philosophy. A skilled orator, he similarly professed the ability to argue for any position, and therefore his views on knowledge reveal a corresponding 'flexibility'. It's difficult to tell, however, whether this scepticism (extreme doubt) is genuine or merely a professional pose. It may only be a parody of other positive theories concerning knowledge, intended to show that we can just as easily prove that we cannot know anything as that we can.

Taking the statements at face value, what do they mean? The first concerns the true nature of reality: What lies beyond sense experience? Physical matter? One underlying substance? Many? These are *metaphysical* questions.

The second doubts our ability to acquire knowledge: can we ever guarantee our senses are trustworthy, or that our reasoning is sound? Questions concerning knowledge and how to acquire it are matters of *epistemology* (*episteme* is Greek for 'knowledge').

Lastly, he highlights the pitfalls of language. When I tell you something, how do I *know* you understand the words similarly? Even agreeing terms, it is possible we possess different concepts. Of course, we *hope* any misunderstanding would eventually become apparent ('Oh! *That* dog!'), but it is logically possible it won't.

Considering these doubts, we should note that over 2,500 years have not vanquished them. We can make *some* headway: it seems self-contradictory to say that we *know* nothing exists – doesn't that imply knowledge? But the sceptic always has a comeback: 'I didn't say that I know nothing exists, merely that it's possible!' Philosophical pride has caused much ink to be wasted in fighting extreme scepticism. Like the inability to lick your own elbow, perhaps it's a limitation we just have to accept. Isn't it just better to ignore it, and pursue more fruitful topics? (Perhaps if I dislocated my shoulder . . .)

'I do not think I know what I do not know'
SOCRATES C.469–399 BC
in Plato, *Apology*

Socrates is possibly the greatest philosopher never to leave posterity his own written record of his ideas (what we know comes from his pupil Plato). The Delphic oracle famously declared him the wisest man in Athens, and this seems to have played a key role in the development of his celebrated method of philosophical enquiry. How, he asked himself, could he – who knew nothing – be wisest? But knowledge of our own ignorance is the beginning of wisdom. Like Pythagoras before him, Socrates believed in reincarnation, and more specifically that our souls are impregnated with divine knowledge before we are born. Wisdom therefore lies not in adding information, but in bringing out what is already latent – the true origin of the word 'education'.

In testing the oracle's claim, Socrates plagued the Athenian populace, in search of the one person that knew more than he. A peerless orator, he mercilessly interrogated his opponents, trapping them in the snares of their own slippery logic, exposing and dissecting their unexamined assumptions with surgical precision. The medical analogy is apt: Socrates often styled himself the doctor to their moral and spiritual ills, to whom some submitted willingly, others with ill grace. But to a doctor, all bodies are alike, and it was this lack of deference to authority and privilege that eventually fostered powerful enemies, and ultimately brought about his own downfall.

To a modern ear, his arguments can seem contrived and pedantic – artful and ingenious, perhaps, but more verbal trap than unassailable logic; closer, in fact, to the sort of clever way-with-words that he himself criticized in his contemporaries. Assessing the portrait that Plato presents in his dialogues, one may sympathize with the hapless victims of this elaborate game. As Nietzsche later observed, Socrates was just too crafty for the simple, 'noble Athenians', who as men of breeding and instinct, 'were never able to supply adequate information about the reasons for their actions'. Can any of us?

'The unexamined life is not worth living'
SOCRATES
in Plato, *Apology*

Eventually, Socrates' enemies caught up with him, bringing him to account on trumped-up charges: corrupting the youth of Athens, advocating atheism, and – preposterously, given his long-standing opposition to Sophism – making the worse cause appear the better. Accounts of Socrates' 'apology' can be found in both Plato and Xenophon, differing slightly, but agreeing on main points. The term originates in Greek law, whereby the defendant presented his defence (*apologia*), consisting of a justification of his actions (not an admission of guilt or remorse, as the modern use of the term implies).

In defending himself against the charge of corruption, Socrates protests that he has never set out to harm anyone; against that of impiety, he responds that he has rather been divinely inspired to seek out knowledge and expose ignorance; and against amorality, he reminds the jury of occasions where he has risked his life to stand alone against injustice. How, then, can they find him guilty?

But, by narrow majority, they do find him guilty (as Socrates expected), and sentencing is considered. Socrates cannot, he says, afford a large fine, imprisonment would make his life a misery of physical servitude, and exile would require him, for his own safety among strangers, to censor his opinions – something he has never done. They should really honour him as they do Olympian champions, but since the wheels of injustice are in motion, perhaps, he suggests, a moderate fine? However, Meletus, his chief persecutor throughout these proceedings, is adamant: Socrates must be put to death. The jury agrees.

He accepts his fate calmly. Since he cannot live a life of philosophical enquiry, it is better to die. Before consuming the draft of poisonous hemlock, he condemns those who have chosen to execute an innocent man – history will judge them harshly – but consoles his friends that death should not be feared: either it will bring everlasting unconsciousness, or a better existence – from which postmortem perspective, perhaps, our lives can only be truly judged.

'Crito, I owe a cock to Asclepius; will you remember to pay the debt?'
SOCRATES
in Plato, *Phaedo*

After his trial, Socrates' execution was delayed by a month. The Athenian state galley had not yet returned from its annual pilgrimage to Delos (to commemorate Theseus' slaying of the Minotaur), and no executions were to be carried out whilst it was away. Conventions such as this perhaps seem strange to us, and remind us that the world view of the ancient Greeks, for all its rationality, was very different from the contemporary Western one.

Sometimes, when reading the dialogues – with their sophistication, conversational realism, humour and vivacity – we can forget that they were written almost two and a half millennia ago. But, neither Socrates nor Plato was rational in the modern sense. For all his sceptical questioning, his search for reasons and intellectual explanation, Socrates' rationalism is tempered by what some moderns would now term the *irrational* – belief in gods and spirits, in divine inspiration and prophecy, in reincarnation – and it is perhaps ironic that some should see the culmination of the philosophical enterprise he helped set in motion in *atheistic materialism*.

It is in light of these observations that Socrates' last words should be understood. He spent his last month in conversation and philosophical discussion with friends and family, providing justification of his refusal to escape and consoling and allaying their fears. He faced death – not, as the *Existentialists* later would, with a bleak courage divorced from hope or expectation, but rather in modest trust that a better world awaited, and that true courage lay not in facing death, but rather in living a virtuous life. Only the immoral need fear death.

His final words concern a perceived debt to Asclepius, the god of healing. It was traditional to make a sacrifice to him either in hope of a cure, or in thanks for a successful recovery. In either case, Socrates is therefore implying that death is the remedy for all ills, a cure that deserves our gratitude.

> 'By convention sweet is sweet, bitter is bitter, hot is hot, cold is cold,
> colour is colour; but in truth there are only atoms and the void'
> DEMOCRITUS C.460–C.370 BC
> in Sextus Empiricus, *Against the Mathematicians*

Known for his cheery disposition, humility, and simple tastes, Democritus was called 'the laughing philosopher'. He travelled widely, sought out scholars throughout Greece, Egypt, India and even Ethiopia, produced works on many subjects, but possessed a particular interest in *natural philosophy* (science). It is his *atomism*, which he apparently shared with his mentor Leucippus, for which he is now best known, and he is considered a founding father of modern scientific theory.

Atomism proposes that the universe ultimately consists of tiny, indivisible particles – *atomos* is Greek for 'uncut' – and usually accompanies a *materialist* view of reality, where physical matter is the only existing substance. Materialism often also involves *mechanism*, or the idea that all things are related in terms of cause and effect. This view, which treats the universe as a sort of gigantic machine, reached its culmination in the views of Isaac Newton, and held sway up to the beginning of the twentieth century, when everything in physics started to go crazy.

Of course, modern 'atoms' are neither indivisible nor the smallest known particles, but continuing research in *sub*-atomic physics (such as the enormous Large Hadron Collider at Cern in Switzerland) suggests that most modern scientists remain 'atomists' in the sense that they are still looking for the fundamental 'building blocks' of the universe. However, these *elementary particles* – wonderfully entitled entities as *quarks* and *leptons* – do not behave in the orderly and predictable way that Democritus would have hoped: they pop in and out of existence, merge with each other, or even appear in two places at once. The world of quantum physics is therefore a strange and unsettling one, which is quite ironic given that one of the fundamental goals of materialism was to provide certain, clear, natural explanations. It's just as well that Democritus had a sense of humour.

> 'But how will you look for something when you don't in the least know
> what it is?'
>
> PLATO C.428–C.348 BC
>
> *Meno*

Commentators have long debated whether, or at which points, the Socrates as he appears in the work of his pupil Plato is a faithful portrait of the man and his ideas. However, most agree that by the middle to late *dialogues* (Plato wrote in dramatic form), the figure we see has become a mouthpiece for Plato's extension and elaboration of his tutor's philosophy – for *Platonism*. One sign of this, perhaps, is the growing presence of mysticism and metaphysics, and an increasingly systematic approach to questions that the 'early' Socrates was content merely to show that we are in truth ignorant about.

A good example of this shift can be seen in *Meno*, a middle-period dialogue which picks up on an old theme: what is virtue, and can it be taught? After dismissing Meno's attempted definitions, Socrates proposes that, perhaps, it's not a question to be decided by reason. But without a clear definition, how can we know what virtue is? It would seem to be a paradox, for to know something you would seem to need to already possess an idea of what it is so that you recognize it when you find it! But if so, how do we come to know anything at all?

Plato's solution (to what has become known as *Meno's paradox*) is to suggest that we are *born* with innate knowledge, implanted in the soul from before birth, and which we simply *remember* in appropriate situations. Socrates illustrates the point by leading an uneducated slave boy toward an understanding of certain principles of geometry – something he has not already been taught, and which Socrates has therefore simply provided the catalyst for him to remember. Perhaps, then, virtue isn't *learnt* but *recalled*.

In stepping beyond the teachings of his master, Plato thereby finds a new use for Socratic method: no longer merely a tool for unmasking disguised ignorance, but also a method for unveiling hidden knowledge.

'We have seen that there are three sorts of bed'
PLATO
The Republic

Like Goldilocks, for Plato there was only one true bed: whether water, double, bunk or king-sized, all beds must have something in common – otherwise, why call them beds? This illustrates one of the oldest philosophical chestnuts: the problem of *universals* (the existence of general properties or ideas). The features that beds share could not belong to just another bed – there is no *International Bureau of Beds* in Paris that ensures that all beds are in compliance with its 'standard' bed. Therefore, what they must have in common is the idea or *form* (as Plato termed it) of the *real* bed. Such an idea was separate from all existing Earthly beds (which were mere 'copies' of that idea), and represented the original template that existed in a realm of pure thought: God's bed, if you will. Next to it, all other beds were knock-offs: the carpenter's bed was a mere copy, and the artist's representation – a copy of a copy – was furthest of all from the true idea (one reason why Plato banished all artists and poets from his ideal society, because they were mere peddlers in third-hand illusion, drawing people away from truth).

Of course, as for beds, so for more abstract concepts, such as truth, beauty, goodness, and justice. An individual act could be kind, or generous, or pleasurable, but that is not what makes it good or just: it may be kind, in a sense, not to punish wrongdoing, or stealing may result in pleasure, but these qualities do not justify those actions. The forms, then, are independent guides that help us understand that, sometimes, goodness or justice must be harsh or painful. Such guides need to be separate and distinct from desire, sensation, or – in fact – any Earthly standard, and it is only through these perfect ideas (universals), which can only be perceived by the intellect, that we can know truth, justice, goodness . . . and the perfect bed.

Plato's **'allegory of the cave'** is justly famous, and philosophy examiners everywhere are consequently sick of it (*so* well-known, in fact, that if you haven't heard of it, then you've probably been living in . . . um . . . some remote, dark, underground place). Imagine yourself – since childhood – a prisoner in a dark cave, chained up with other prisoners, and forced to face a wall. On the wall appear shadows, which, unbeknown to you, are caused by the passage of various individuals along a raised walkway above and behind you, as variously shaped statues, vases, etc., are carried in front of a large fire. Your only knowledge of the world therefore consists of the strangely shaped shadows cast by objects and people, and occasional noises and snatches of speech. (A bizarre scenario, admittedly, but it's not a film treatment for some Hollywood blockbuster, so only needs to make sense on an allegorical level.)

Next, imagine being freed from your bonds; staggering towards the cave entrance, seeing the object bearers, the statues, the fire, and gradually starting to reinterpret your previous experiences. Eventually, led out into the daylight, you come face to face with the Sun. Though initially blinded, as you adjust you come to realize that your whole worldview has been completely wrong.

Plato then interprets his own metaphor: the Sun represents the truth, the source of goodness and wisdom, and the cause of everything (the *forms*), which can only be directly apprehended by the understanding, or approached via rational enquiry; the statues, etc., represent physical things, about which we form beliefs based on sense experience; and the shadows represent unexamined opinions or assumptions, which frequently prove illusory.

When returned to the cave, the philosopher is an outsider: he knows, but struggles to communicate his knowledge; he has seen, but few believe him, or think his journey worthwhile. A stranger to his friends, to his former self, he desires only to return to the light.

'It is better to suffer wrong than to do wrong'

PLATO

Gorgias

In a number of places, Plato argues against what might be thought of as conventional wisdom – or at least, against the sort of practical, everyday concern for oneself that motivates most of us most of the time. Faced with the choice of committing an immoral act, or of permitting an immoral act to be committed against us, it is natural – if somewhat cynical – to assume that many would choose immorality. However, Plato reverses this: it is in fact more prudent to be the *target* of wrongdoing than its agent.

But surely, the coward who deserts his unit at least lives to fight another day, whilst the courageous martyr leaves nothing but a heroic and fleeting memory; it is the understandable, if not wholly excusable logic of Shakespeare's Falstaff; of the undiluted instinct to survive. So, in what way could it be 'better' to suffer? An immoral man not only commits wrongs against others, but also against himself, for the desire to commit immoral and selfish acts stems from a disease of the soul. 'Better', then, that the immoral man submits to punishment for his misdeeds, for – in Plato's medical analogy – it is the chastisement that is the treatment for the illness. Consequently, a good man cannot truly be harmed, for, whilst he may suffer physical ills, his soul escapes the more grievous injury caused by immorality.

And what of kings, or tyrants, who may do completely as they please, fulfilling their least desire unopposed? Are such men also wretched? In *The Republic*, Socrates' interlocutor, Glaucon, cites the legend of the ring of Gyges, which was believed to make its wearer invisible (and which, perhaps, was the basis of Tolkien's symbol of temptation and power). Would not the bearer of such a ring behave with impunity? Perhaps, concedes Socrates, but such a man would be utterly miserable. For what could be worse than be at the mercy of one's own desires with no hope of a cure?

> 'Is that which is holy loved by the gods because it is holy, or is it holy because it is loved by the gods?'
>
> PLATO
>
> *Euthyphro*

What is goodness? How do we know which actions are moral? Religious believers mostly argue that such things are defined by God. This is *divine command theory*: stealing is wrong because God says so. But this leads us into a difficulty: are moral actions good *merely* because God says, or is there some quality that good actions possess that makes them good? If we deny the latter, it seems that goodness is completely arbitrary, and God could have chosen *any* moral standard – or might even one day change his mind. But surely this is absurd: could it have been, or might it yet be the case, that murder is 'good'? However, if God values those actions that already possess good qualities, then God is not ultimately responsible for goodness, which calls into question his omnipotence (his power to decide the nature of goodness).

Religious believers therefore face a dilemma – more specifically, the *Euthyphro dilemma*, as it is known, from the dialogue where it appears. It is meant to show that such a religious account of morality is incoherent, and that we should instead seek a *natural* interpretation (a *utilitarian* one, perhaps). Also, of course, it is an attack upon the coherence of the notion of God, implying that if it were possible that he exists, then such questions wouldn't arise.

However, we don't in fact need God in order for the dilemma to exist, for we may couch it in strictly human terms: do we consider certain actions 'good' because we have always done so, or have we always done so because they are good? Of course, the atheist will argue that this does not let God off the hook, but it does give him some breathing space: if we cannot yet understand morality in human terms, then how can we criticize God on the same basis?

Plato thought the ideal society should be founded on a 'noble lie' – a myth that legitimizes social order and justice. Plato's myth states that there are three types of individual, corresponding to three psychological aspects – desire, spirit, and reason – which Plato symbolizes as bronze or iron, silver, and gold. The bronze/iron type, the commonest and lowest class, were ruled by desire, and destined for manual labour or skilled trades. The silver, in which spirit predominated, were ruled by courage and honour, and were therefore the ideal soldiers. However, the highest class of man, the gold, was ruled by reason, which – in Plato's famous analogy – kept in check the other aspects like a charioteer reigning in two unruly horses. Since reason should rule the individual, so should it govern society, and a man ruled by reason was fit to govern others.

The gold and silver types were the guardians of society, forbidden to breed outside their class, and from whose ranks the rulers – the philosopher kings, the most 'golden' – were chosen. The first task was therefore to sift out these types and allot them their proper fate, but this was not easy: a 'gold' baby might be born to 'bronze' parents, or vice versa, so careful watch was needed to ensure early identification. To facilitate this, child-rearing duties were held in common, thereby underlining the fact that children belonged, and owed their primary allegiance, to the state.

However, some critics have found this ideal society troubling. Austrian philosopher Karl Popper thought it a template for totalitarianism, putting power in the hands of an unelected and self-perpetuating intellectual elite. In the words of the Roman satirist Juvenal, 'Who watches the watchmen?' Who ensures that rulers do not fall prey to corruption or self-interest? Plato argued that, through training and education, the guardians could regulate themselves – that, effectively, they would believe the noble lie: their own 'golden' nature ensures their selflessness. But, being the brightest of the bright, mightn't they eventually see through this?

'He whom love touches not walks in darkness'
PLATO
Symposium

The word 'Platonic' survives today – outside of its philosophical context – when referring to a non-sexual friendship: 'We get on really well, but it's just Platonic'. As such, it describes a relationship that falls short – for whatever reason – of the fuller communion of romantic sexual love. However, for Plato, the opposite was the case: true love went beyond mere sex or physical attraction and, at its highest, love partook of spiritual ecstasy.

Plato discusses love in the *Phaedrus*, where he characterizes it as a sort of madness, presenting arguments both for and against it. However, it is in the *Symposium* that we find the doctrine of love that is now known as Platonic. The dialogue takes the form of a discussion over a meal – or, rather, a drinking party with food (which is what the Greek word *sympotein* originally refers to). Each of the guests gives a speech in praise of love. Famously, the poet Aristophanes recites a myth where human beings were originally split in half, thereby creating sexual desire as the one half was driven in search of its 'soul mate' (which is most probably the origin of the idea).

However, when Socrates comes to speak, the notion of love takes on the broader sense of a desire to possess and delight in beautiful things. So, whilst a young person might learn about this initially from the appreciation of a beautiful body (male or female – the Greeks didn't mind), a deeper understanding of love involved looking beyond mere physical appearances; an old or ugly person might possess a beautiful personality or mind. From there, the lover could progress, by gradually divorcing beauty from the physical and individual, to recognizing it in increasingly abstract things, such as actions, customs, and ideas. Eventually, the true lover exchanges beautiful things for beauty itself, experiencing love as a force, intermediary between mind and matter, which pervades the universe.

Platonic love, it seems, is not what it once was.

'Stand a little less between me and the sun'
DIOGENES OF SINOPE C.412–323 BC
in Plutarch, *Life of Alexander*

There were many notable Diogenes – a number of whom were philosophers, it seems – but only one who lived in a barrel. It was quite a large barrel, often depicted lying on its side, providing shelter overhead but otherwise open to the elements. Diogenes was one of the founders of *Cynicism*, an unpretentious philosophy that stripped man back to his fundamental state, achieving happiness through living in harmony with nature. Cynics lived on the fringes of society, eschewing wealth and status, and were often called 'dogs' due to their lack of concern for social niceties. However, their social position allowed them to observe and pass critical commentary on the hypocrisy and immorality of polite society. For instance, Diogenes is reported to have walked the streets with a lamp in daytime, searching for an honest man – he didn't find one. The word 'cynic' in its modern sense is therefore not so very far from this original meaning, for it retains a sense of focusing on the worst interpretation of human motives.

As monks and ascetics of all ages agree, living a simple life of minimum requirements we find out what man really is, what is necessary or superfluous to his happiness, and – free of compromise – can live a virtuous and honest life. True Cynics were immune to flattery and uncowed by wealth or power. One anecdote has Diogenes visited by Alexander the Great, who asks whether there is anything that he can do for the philosopher; 'Yes. Stand a little less between me and the sun.' Some interpret this as a comment on freedom – the would-be ruler of the world 'blocking out' what should be the entitlement of every man – whilst others cleverly point out that the sun was the symbol of Macedonian royalty. But we might equally interpret the story at face value, as a celebration of simple pleasures: it's nice to lie in the sun, and a shame when someone spoils it.

> '. . . that some should rule and others be ruled is a thing not only necessary, but expedient; from the hour of their birth, some are marked out for subjection, others for rule'
>
> ARISTOTLE 384–322 BC
> *Politics*

As Plato's pupil, the respect of Aristotle for his teacher didn't stop him disagreeing with him on almost everything. The primary difference is his emphasis on empirical investigation. Abstract theorizing was all very well, but true scientific knowledge requires data, which we can't get sitting in an armchair. Therefore, science owes Aristotle a lot: his biological theories provided a foundation for later forms of classification, and his division of philosophy into separate disciplines eventually helped establish the sciences as independent fields of study.

This said, we must also recognize that some of his ideas are completely mistaken – thinking takes place in the heart, heavy objects fall faster than light ones – whilst others are deeply embarrassing. Chief of these, perhaps, is his contention that slavery is *natural*. Not that *all* people who find themselves enslaved are deserving: *legal slaves* were often taken in war, where, through sheer bad luck, even the best could find themselves enslaved. However, *natural slaves* were a *type* of people that, as stated above, 'from the hour of their birth . . . are marked out for subjection'.

But what marks them out? For Aristotle, man is essentially rational. Thus, the *most* rational should rule over the *less* so. Just as the rational soul rules the body, so human rules animal, man rules woman, Greek rules barbarian, and master rules slave. This hierarchy of dominance is difficult to apologize for – though some have tried. Perhaps, some suggest, Aristotle was not sexist, racist and inhumane, but was being ironic: perhaps he was simply laying out society's flaws before criticizing them. This is possible: we only possess his brief lecture notes, so he may have gone on to expound his ideas differently. However, given that Plato held similar views, a more likely explanation is simply that he was a product of his time, and a slave to common prejudice.

'Any one can get angry – that is easy – or give or spend money; but to do this to the right person, to the right extent, at the right time, with the right motive, and in the right way, that is not for every one, nor is it easy'

ARISTOTLE
Nicomachean Ethics

For Plato, wrongdoing was based on ignorance. A man could not deliberately, in full conscious knowledge, undertake a bad act, for that would be illogical: people seek what is good. The only answer then was that he commits an immoral act without full knowledge of what the good is.

In contrast, Aristotle thought morality requires cultivating certain virtues and developing your character (what is termed *virtue ethics*). There aren't, necessarily, fixed notions of what's right and wrong in any particular situation, but rather morality is a skill that we learn. Like all skills, of course, there are times where we don't get it quite right. Like learning to dance, we are going to step on a few toes before we trip the light fantastic.

Also, there are many things that influence the morality of an action. For instance, being selfless might commonly be seen as 'good', but it may not always be appropriate: if someone has a destructive drug habit, then generously gifting them money may not be the wisest thing. Learning what is good therefore takes time and experience.

However, Aristotle suggested, we may apply a rule of thumb: most inappropriate actions involve an imbalance of sorts – being too rash or too fearful, too extravagant or too miserly – so perhaps, as a general guide, moral actions strike a balance, a *golden mean* between opposites. However, since this isn't a hard and fast rule, we are therefore free to deviate from it. Of course, what is a 'mean' will depend upon the context of the situation: being brave is as likely to involve remaining calm under pressure as it is rushing into battle. So, the right course isn't always the middle way, but it's a reasonable place to begin.

> 'Suppose that a tool, e.g. an axe, were a natural body, then being an axe
> would have been its essence, and so its soul; if this disappeared from
> it, it would have ceased to be an axe, except in name'
>
> ARISTOTLE
> *On the Soul*

For Aristotle, any object has four 'causes'. Firstly, a *material cause*, what it's made of (an axe might be made of wood and metal). Secondly, a *formal cause*, its shape (axes are obviously 'axe shaped'). Thirdly, its *efficient cause*, what brought it into existence, which is how we generally use 'cause' (the axe maker). Fourthly, a thing's *final cause* or *telos*, its reason for being, its essence or 'soul' (the axe chops wood – we'll ignore its occasional use in maniacal killing sprees). Of course, axes can be anything we want them to be, and, unlike natural objects, don't have a 'final cause' independent of the use we prescribe. Man-made objects are therefore to be contrasted with, for example, trees or some other object in the natural order.

Considering these different causes, modern thinking can probably find a place for three of them: when analyzing what something *is*, we still think in terms of its material, its shape, and what caused it to exist. However, the fourth and *final* cause is problematic, for we tend now *not* to think everything possesses an *essence* or reason for being. For example, what is the true nature of a stone? Aside from the fact that it can have all sorts of social uses (paperweight, projectile), it is questionable as to whether it has any *natural* purpose. However, biological objects are different, and we are much more likely to consider, for example, that the purpose of the eye is 'to see'.

However, there is a problem even with this, for Darwinian evolution has no room for purpose. Eyes evolve not because they have a job to do, but in reaction to blind forces; if not through chance as such, then certainly not in fulfilment of anyone's plan: ironically, sight has a *blind* cause.

'Man is the rational animal'
ARISTOTLE
Metaphysics

Aristotle thought that man's essence lay in his rationality. This springs from the idea that there are different souls or essences for the different levels of life. So, for instance, plants possess a *vegetative soul*, capable only of reproduction and growth; animals, however, possess both a vegetative and a *sensitive soul*, permitting the additional capacity for sensation and movement; humans, however, not only possess both these, but also a *rational soul*, allowing rational thought. The essence of man, therefore, lies in the essential activity of his most evolved and distinctive quality: his reason.

These ideas were instrumental in placing man at the top of the natural order, above animals and below angels, an intermediary between the divine and natural worlds. It also dovetailed neatly with Christianity, which accorded man a special, central place in the world. This idea of man's distinctness was for so long unchallenged that we have to wait until Darwin before any real shift in opinion even begins to be possible (and it's still controversial).

But *are* we different? The modern trend has been to question human rationality: such thinkers as Schopenhauer, Nietzsche and Freud, for example, attacked the notion that our actions are always consciously controlled, and also doubted the degree to which we can ever be completely rationally motivated. A cursory glance at history, its wars, genocides and cruelties, would seem to support this. As American novelist Mark Twain put it:

'Man is the only animal that deals in that atrocity of atrocities, War. He is the only one that gathers his brethren about him and goes forth in cold blood and calm pulse to exterminate his kind.'

And yet, despite all this, man does seem distinct. Whilst dolphins or apes can display certain linguistic or cognitive skills, man outstrips them by many leagues. Furthermore, it's curious: why *is* there such a gap? If rationality is the trump card in evolutionary survival that it undoubtedly is, why have no other animals even come close?

> 'He who is unable to live in society, or who has no need because he is sufficient for himself, must be either a beast or a god'
>
> ARISTOTLE
>
> *Politics*

For Aristotle, man was not only a rational animal, but also a political and social one. People need people. Anthropologists and psychologists agree: sharing a genetic predisposition for communal living with the apes we have evolved from, and giving birth to vulnerable young who need protective care much longer than any other animal, humans who choose or find themselves in isolation are at much greater risk in all sorts of ways.

Most philosophers also agree. Firstly, socialization is arguably necessary for acquiring language in the first place. It might be tempting to argue – as A. J. Ayer did – that someone growing up on a desert island could develop their own words and signs for things, but this seems unlikely. The fact that different cultures can evolve different ways of classifying things (colours, plants and animals) suggests that community plays an important role in developing the way we speak and think. However, without anyone to speak to, how could such concepts evolve? So, an isolated individual might not only fail to develop language, but also rational thought. This is borne out by studies of feral children (who grow up without human contact), who display few distinctly human traits, but acquire them quickly when reintroduced into human society.

Another problem is morality. A person living alone is cut off from social standards. So, even assuming that they had already acquired a moral code, there is the added difficulty of not being able to check it against society's norms. This is problematic because we don't swallow a moral rulebook at birth, but rather learn through interacting with others in society.

Add to this the increased psychological vulnerability to irrational fears and beliefs that isolation fosters, and we can see Aristotle's point: isolation *dehumanizes*. So, anyone who *can* survive would either have excelled the normal human, or reverted to his animal nature.

'Nature abhors a vacuum'
UNKNOWN

And so, for centuries, did science and philosophy. Whatever the origin of the phrase, the idea originated with Aristotle, but also had the support of many pre-Socratic philosophers, who argued that 'nothing' could not be 'something', a conclusion Plato shared. It still held sway almost 2,000 years later, when Descartes argued that 'Space is identical with extension', meaning that for something to exist it must possess length, breadth, and height – but how could 'nothing' have dimensions?

Vacuums, then, were a contradiction in terms – perhaps God could create one, if he chose; or perhaps they could exist *outside* the universe, but not *inside* it. The alternative was *plenism* (from the Latin for 'full'), the view that every part of space contained something. You might think this would lead to chronic congestion: wherever an object moves it displaces other things, but where do *they* go? This leads ultimately to questions of the size of the universe. Imagine a packed concert: no one can move, and the stewards are being really strict, not letting anyone over the barriers. If plenism were true, and the universe were a fixed and finite size, everyone pushes and jostles against everyone else, and any space is quickly filled. In fact, there *could be* no free space; nothing could expand or contract, for that would involve creating space somewhere else. The world is therefore like a bag of footballs, and in the gaps, tennis balls, and in the gaps between *them*, marbles, and so on, to infinity. But it is a world without *friction*: plenism requires everything to glide around without effort; introduce friction, and the whole thing grinds to a halt.

But if there is true 'nothing', then things can expand *into* it without displacing anything (if Archimedes had taken a bath in 'nothing', there would have been no 'Eureka!'); the stewards can move back the barriers, and everyone can breathe. Praise be, then, for nothing, which gives us all some space.

> 'Once Chuang Chou dreamt he was a butterfly, fluttering here and there just as if he was a butterfly, conscious of following its inclinations. It did not know that it was Chuang Chou. Suddenly he awoke; and then demonstrably he was Chuang Chou. But he does not know now whether he is Chuang Chou who dreamt he was a butterfly or a butterfly dreaming he is Chuang Chou.'
>
> CHUANG CHOU c.369–c.286 BC
> *The Book of Chuang Chou*

Chuang Chou was a 4th century BC Chinese philosopher in the *Taoist* tradition. As with Lao Tzu and other philosophers of this period, we do not know very much about Chunag Chou (also sometimes written Zhangzi or Chuang Tzu), and there is even some doubt that he is the author of the text that now bears his name. However, whoever its author is, *The Book of Chuang Chou* presents a broadly sceptical approach to human knowledge, applying the principles of Taoism to point out that the human view of life is merely one possible perspective among many. The dream of the butterfly is therefore to be taken in this spirit: whilst reality may take different forms, no one form represents the ultimate truth, and all are resolvable to a single underlying unity.

The passage also highlights the intractable nature of *scepticism* (that we can doubt everything). In the *Meditations*, French philosopher René Descartes argues that it is possible to distinguish reality from a dream, for the two experiences are characterized by different features: dreams are disjointed, unpredictable and incoherent; waking reality is ordered by fixed laws, and our experiences fit into a coherent narrative. However, as Chuang Chou points out, whilst the two realities may be different, this doesn't prove *which one* is more fundamental – if, in fact, either of them is. For it's as logical an interpretation of my experience to say that I'm a butterfly dreaming that I am a Chinese philosopher, as it is to argue that I'm a Chinese philosopher who has just dreamt that I was a butterfly.

'Death is nothing to us, since when we are, death has not come, and
when death has come, we are not'
EPICURUS 341–C.270 BC
in Diogenes Laertius, *Lives of the Eminent Philosophers*

These days, an *epicure* is someone who appreciates the finer things –
fine wine, classical music, gourmet cooking – but the original
Epicureans were comparatively simple souls. Named from the Greek
philosopher Epicurus, Epicureanism emphasized simplicity, courage,
honesty and moderation.

Like Democritus before him, Epicurus pictured the world as consisting ultimately of colourless, indestructible physical atoms, in a
constant state of unpredictable change. This meant that the things of
the physical world – ourselves included – had a fleeting existence, for
they were merely passing forms in the universal flux.

This, perhaps, influenced the Epicureans' attitude toward death. As
materialists, they thought the spirit or soul did not survive into an
other-worldly afterlife: death is the end. And yet, consequently, we also
have nothing to fear, for how can we fear that which it is impossible to
experience? It is as if we were to fear being cremated or buried; these
are things which happen to 'us' once we are forever unconscious –
once, in fact, there is no more subjective experience. What, then, have
we possibly got to fear?

However, whilst Epicureanism itself was not a bleak philosophy –
encouraging pleasure in moderation and avoidance of the extremes of
passion and physical excess – its ultimate message nonetheless provides stark comfort. Subsequent philosophers have argued that, even
if it is true that we cannot experience death and there is no afterlife, it
is what we think and feel prior to our demise that is important. Will I
suffer? Who will care for my family? Will my memory live on? So,
whilst it may be true that after my death none of these things can
matter to me, they may yet distress me whilst I am still alive. Hurtling
in our car toward a brick wall, is it any comfort that the crash will kill
us instantly?

> 'Epicurus' questions are yet unanswered. Is [God] willing to prevent
> evil, but not able? Then is he impotent. Is he able, but not willing?
> Then is he malevolent. Is he both able and willing? Whence then is
> evil?'
>
> DAVID HUME ON EPICURUS
> *Dialogues Concerning Natural Religion*

There is some debate as to whether this argument actually stems from
Epicurus. Certainly, though a materialist, he never admitted to any
form of atheism, merely arguing that the gods were far away and disinterested in human affairs. This in itself makes the attribution less
likely, for it would suggest a solution to the problem: the gods do not
do anything, because they don't care or aren't aware. Also, the traditional monotheistic conception of God, whereby he is omnipotent
(all-powerful), omniscient (all-knowing) and omnibenevolent (all-
good), suggests a later source for the argument, perhaps as a response
to the growth of Christianity.

But whether or not Epicurus held these opinions, the problem has
an old pedigree. Writing in the 18th century, Scottish philosopher
David Hume is therefore simply pointing out that it remains unre-
solved. If God is all-good, all-powerful, and all-knowing, then why is
there evil? 'Evil', incidentally, does not here just refer to malevolent
spirits or intentional immorality – though it may include these – but
also so-called *natural evil*, such as earthquakes and disease. *Moral evil*
– the actions of human agents – is easier perhaps to defend: God gave
us free will, and the occasional evil act or person is outweighed by the
greater expression of goodness that such freedom allows. Not everyone
is convinced by this: couldn't God have created good 'robots'? What
about the suffering of innocents – is this all in God's 'calculation'?
However, it is natural evil that represents the greater objection: what
greater good results from ovarian cancer or from a tsunami that kills
thousands?

We could, of course, abandon one of the three traditional qualities
of God: Perhaps he is unaware? Perhaps he is indifferent? Perhaps he
cannot do anything? However, would such an amended concept still
be God?

'As a person puts on new garments, giving up old ones, similarly, the soul accepts new material bodies, giving up the old and useless ones. The soul can never be cut into pieces by any weapon, nor can he be burned by fire, nor moistened by water, nor withered by the wind.'

VYASA C. 2nd century BC

Bhagavad Gita

The *Bhagavad Gita* ('Song of the Lord') is a central text of *Hinduism*, forming part of the larger *Mahabarata*, an epic poem chronicling the history of ancient India. Its authorship is disputed, though it's traditionally assigned to Vyasa, a semi-mythical sage. The date of its composition is also uncertain, but scholarly consensus places it in or after the 2nd century BC.

The text is a dialogue between Arjuna, an Indian prince, and Krishna, an *avatar* (incarnation) of the Indian god Vishnu, disguised as Arjuna's charioteer. Arjuna's armies are preparing to face his cousins in a war for the throne, and the *Gita's* themes are therefore life and death, reincarnation, the true nature of self, and the bearing of these questions on moral action (*karma*). As with *Taoism*, Krishna preaches a form of 'non-action', allowing man to act blamelessly (not incurring *karma*) by following a path of selfless duty (*dharma*). Thus, as Arjuna worries at the rightness of fighting his own kinsmen, Krishna reassures him: 'How can a person who knows that the soul is indestructible, unborn, eternal and immutable, kill anyone or cause anyone to kill?' Thus, Krishna's advice comes from the transcendent standpoint of the true self (*Atman*), which, since it is immortal, represents a refuge from all Earthly suffering.

It is interesting to note the parallels also between Krishna's advice and the philosophy of Sun Tzu. Both see military action as possible if conducted in a certain way – by following the *Dharma* or *Tao* respectively. But does this excuse violence? Yet perhaps the deeper question here isn't what excuses it, but what makes it *necessary*? In following the *Dharma*, was Arjuna's battle *fated*?

'. . . in the one living and true God there were two supreme and primary powers – goodness [creative power] and authority; and that by his goodness he had created every thing, and by his authority he governed all that he had created; and that the third thing which was between the two, and had the effect of bringing them together was reason [*logos*], for that it was owing to reason that God was both a ruler and good'

PHILO OF ALEXANDRIA 20 BC–AD 50
On the Cherubim

Philo was a Jewish philosopher and Platonist, who sought to synthesize Hebraic and Greek thought. He lived in Alexandria, Egypt, which at the time was a conflux of many cultures and ideologies, and therefore a formative influence on his thought.

Philo distinguishes between the Absolute (God as supreme creator of the universe), and *Logos*, that aspect of God human beings may relate to (the 'first-born of God', as Philo terms it). Philo equates this with the Platonic notion of the world of pure *forms* or perfect ideas, the *Logos* being their origin or common source. In making the connection between Greek philosophy and Judaism, Philo is attempting to move away from the *anthropomorphic* concept of divinity in the Hebrew Bible: God *speaks* to his prophets, is *angry* or *pleased*, etc. However, in Philo's vision, the language is more impersonal and abstract – in keeping with Platonism, more rational and philosophical. *Logos* is the divine 'word' or rational principle – the mind of God – that exists as a point of harmony between the twin extremes of divine creativity and authority.

There are obviously parallels here with Christianity, particularly the Gospel of John. Since man is incapable of directly relating to the power and glory of God, the true nature of the divine is beyond our understanding; the *Logos* – just as Christianity would see Jesus Christ as doing – therefore mediates between man and God. However, unlike Christianity, Philo's communion is *intellectual*: we have an affinity with the *Logos* because we partake of the divine *mind*. It is our *reason* that makes us divine.

SENECA 5 BC–AD 60
On the Shortness of Life

It's relatively common among philosophers, poets, writers in general, and – well, just about anyone, really – to complain of the shortness of life. It therefore comes as a mild shock when someone says that, actually, life is quite long enough, thank you. Seneca the younger was a Roman *Stoic*, contemporary with (unfortunately for him) two of history's greatest sociopaths, the Emperors Caligula and Nero.

Stoicism contends that the greatest virtue lies in acceptance of, and indifference to, the misfortunes of life, for, whilst we aren't completely powerless, we cannot ultimately change or avoid fate's decree. So, one's attitude to life (and death) should therefore reflect this by acceptance of natural limits, and determination to make the best of our allotted span. Accordingly, Seneca identifies two principal drains on our time: pleasure and work. Above all, one should be master of oneself; of one's desires, and choices. The great and the powerful – those you might expect to possess most command over themselves – were frequently the worst offenders. Seneca cites Emperor Augustus, who, even in retirement, 'longed for leisure'; this, he ironically observes, 'was the prayer of the man who could grant the prayers of all mankind'. The ultimate aim was to rise above the whims of fortune; not to *control* one's fate – who can do that? – but be unmoved by it; to choose meaningful, achievable goals; and forge a life free of regret.

Finally, the fittest reward for a life well lived is the power to choose when it ends. For Stoics, suicide wasn't a sin against nature or God, but, when undertaken with the right mental attitude and for a genuine reason, a human right. Therefore, on being informed that Nero was to have him executed for treachery, Seneca calmly took his own life. There was no need to drag things out: he had achieved all that he wanted to achieve, and had no regrets – life had been long enough.

'Men are disturbed, not by things, but by the principles and notions
which they form concerning things'

 EPICTETUS AD 55–135

The Enchiridion

A Stoic, Epictetus thought we have little say in what happens to us.
Born into slavery, half his life under the dominion of others, we can
trace the cause of this fatalism. Powerless to alter his situation, he
concentrated instead on what he *could* control: his reaction to events.
He could do this because 'there is nothing good or evil save in the will'
– that is, save our decision to view things as good or bad, how we
choose to react to the inevitable. As Hamlet puts it: 'there is nothing
either good or bad, but thinking makes it so'.

In psychology, this is a tenet of *Cognitive Behavioural Therapy*,
which concentrates on changing patterns of behaviour by addressing
habitual thinking. CBT argues that we sabotage our own endeavours
with negative reinforcement – 'I'm useless at this', 'No one is interested in my opinion' – and so all we need do is change the way we
think. Thought is powerful: only an eighth of people involved in a
catastrophic event develop Post Traumatic Stress Disorder – why not
all? It's down to individual perspective.

Taken to its extreme, however, 'you are what you think' leads to
dangerous self-deceit. Consider the variously self-deluded hopefuls
that pepper reality-TV-driven talent shows: there comes a point where
the correct response to setback is not to believe harder, but to reassess
one's goals. Faced with a brick wall, we should prefer the brake to the
accelerator. Epictetus agreed:

> 'Some things are in our control and others not. Things in our
> control are opinion, pursuit, desire, aversion, and, in a word,
> whatever are our own actions. Things not in our control are
> body, property, reputation, command, and, in one word, what-
> ever are not our own actions.'

Certain things (especially physics) should be respected. We may therefore complement Hamlet's words with contrary advice: 'Thinking so
don't make it so.' Wisdom, it seems, consists in judging when each
one applies.

'. . . do what comes to hand with correct and natural dignity, and with humanity, independence and justice. Allow your mind freedom from all other considerations. This you can do if you will approach each action as though it were your last . . .'

MARCUS AURELIUS AD 121–180
Meditations

Roman emperor and prominent Stoic philosopher Marcus Aurelius forged an attitude to life that married the active and the contemplative. In fact, he managed this so well that in addition to being considered one of the foremost Stoics, he is also deemed one of the great Roman emperors (even meeting Machiavelli's exacting standards for ideal statesmanship. Add to this that his thoughts on moral and spiritual matters anticipated and influenced Christianity, then it's no wonder that we still find him fascinating.

The Stoics are famous for their attitude to death. As a natural and inevitable event, we should not fear it, but let its inevitability shape our lives and inform our actions. Even a long life is relatively short, and might any day be cut shorter by the inscrutable will of fate – a power over which we have no control. We do, however, have control over our attitude to life, and so we should concentrate on perfecting that.

Whilst death is a sobering fact for anyone, the realization of its unavoidability may not itself be a cause of courage, wisdom and equanimity. Treating each action as our last can mean different things for different people, as is illustrated by the phrase 'it was the last act of a desperate man'. Imminent death is therefore as likely to give rise to panic, rage, or apathy as it is calm acceptance and wise employment of one's time.

And yet, there does seem to be a general consensus that facing death makes one honest; in common law the 'death-bed confession' still possesses greater evidential power than other types of declaration: why should the dying lie? To protect a loved one? A reputation? I suppose what ultimately governs our attitude to our last actions is what we consider to lie beyond them.

> 'For as it certainly is in the power of a mother to give strong food to her infant, [but she does not do so], as the child is not yet able to receive more substantial nourishment; so also it was possible for God Himself to have made man perfect from the first, but man could not receive this [perfection], being as yet an infant'
>
> ST IRENAEUS C. AD 130–200
> *Against Heresies*

One question the problem of evil often provokes is why, if moral evil stems from human free will, God did not make us perfect to begin with? St Irenaeus, a bishop in what is now Lyons in France, argued that it wasn't because he *couldn't* (God can accomplish anything), but because man wasn't ready. You wouldn't feed a newborn baby solid food; God wouldn't give full spiritual perfection to an immature soul. Man is made in the image of God, but is not exactly like him, so must strive through his own free will to achieve this.

This view is developed by English philosopher John Hick, who argues that the spiritual immaturity that Irenaeus cites as the reason for our imperfection can also be seen as the reason for the existence of evil in general: if God had created a perfect world, then we would never develop, just as someone who never exercises will never become physically strong. Therefore, suffering is an 'obstacle course' that allows us to develop spiritual maturity and perfection.

However, not everyone gets an equal go on the assault course, and some never even get going. An infant's short life of abuse and neglect provides little conscious opportunity to learn, and what is 'developing' about a sudden and painful death? Hick's answer is that such disproportionate *dysteleogical suffering* (as he calls it) is, perhaps, part of a process that extends *after* death, where the soul may contemplate its Earthly experiences. Obviously, we cannot know if this is true or not – except of course when our own time comes, and maybe not even then . . .

'And the Son of God died; it is by all means to be believed, because it is absurd. And He was buried and rose again; the fact is credible, because it is impossible.'

TERTULLIAN C. AD 160–C.220

De Carne Christi

Tertullian is a shadowy figure in the history of the early Christian Church. Born in Carthage, in Roman North Africa, he converted to Christianity in his late thirties, and spent much time in writing *apologetics* – that is, defending Christian doctrine against other forms of thought and belief. In doing so, he proposed the *rule of faith*, taking the scriptures as authoritative and beyond question: if the Gospels say that Jesus rose from the dead, then he rose from the dead, and that's that.

This attitude therefore not only draws a line between Christian and non-Christian thought, but makes reason somewhat redundant. Philosophy, since it stemmed from paganism (in the general sense of being outside monotheistic religion), was simply to be rejected: 'What indeed has Athens to do with Jerusalem? What has the Academy to do with the Church?' he argues. As such, Tertullian is seen as the epitome of anti-intellectualism and an example of *fideism*: faith does not require reason, and truth may be independent of it. The assertion that the absurdity or impossibility of a belief is a sign of its truth is therefore merely an expression of his antagonism toward reason in matters of religion. It is faith that decides such things, not their rational likelihood.

But if faith is irrational, then isn't it an 'all or nothing' affair? There can be no little steps toward it, or indeed rational defence of it. For it is one thing to say that the tendency to rationalize gets in the way of genuine religious understanding, and quite another to propose that reason can play no part in religious belief. The one simply attempts to make room for what perhaps cannot be fully explained; the other is *carte blanche* for the worst excesses of irrationalism, where any action may be condoned.

> 'But I forsee that, in times to come, clever intellectuals will mislead the minds of men, turning away from pure philosophy'
> HERMES TRISMEGISTUS 2nd or 3rd centuries AD
> The *Corpus Hermeticum*

The collection of writings which has become known as the *Corpus Hermeticum* is a collation of various ancient texts written in Greek, Latin and Coptic, purporting to be authored by an ancient Egyptian sage, Hermes Trismegistus, or 'Thrice Great Hermes', and to date back to 3000 BC. Subsequent scholarship has shown the more likely date of composition to be around the 2nd or 3rd centuries AD. But it remains possible that the texts represent the attempts of more recent pagan philosophers to reformulate the teachings of the old Egyptian mystery traditions, or, failing that, to produce a synthesis of Christian, Jewish and Neo-Platonic thought. So, whatever the case, the texts themselves are still uniquely interesting.

The influence of the *Hermeticum* has been immense. Even before its introduction into Europe via the translations of Marsilio Ficino its ideas were influential upon strands of Middle Eastern thought, and it would go on to interweave with alchemy, its ideas imbibed by some of the greatest minds of Western culture – Leonardo da Vinci, Shakespeare, Copernicus and Newton.

The texts themselves generally take the form of a dialogue between Hermes and his pupil, and range over a number of mainly religious themes – the nature of God, the creation, the place of man in the universe, and so on. Where it touches on philosophy, however, it is quite scathing: much contemporary philosophy is idle speculation, the pursuit of pointless controversy and subtle but trivial distinctions. It's a criticism that philosophy is always vulnerable to, for, left to its own devices, rational discourse is apt to become nitpicking. It is on this basis that Hermes distinguishes cleverness from wisdom: reason is but a tool, an instrument of divine aspiration, but used for any other cause philosophy becomes an idle endeavour. True philosophy serves God.

'But if any one desires to see many bodies filled with a divine Spirit, similar to the one Christ, ministering to the salvation of men everywhere, let him take note of those who teach the gospel of Jesus in all lands in soundness of doctrine and uprightness of life . . . there are many christs in the world, who, like Him, have loved righteousness and hated iniquity . . .'

ORIGEN AD 185–254
Against Celsus

With these words, Egyptian Christian theologian Origen betrays his unorthodox Christianity. Like Philo, Origen was influenced by the many interweaving strands of cultural life in Alexandria, also seeking to combine Greek philosophy with religion (Christianity). As such, his ideas are close to *Neo-Platonism*: like Pythagoras and Plato, he believed in reincarnation; like Plotinus, in the hidden transcendence of the *Absolute*, or God; and like Philo, in the intermediary role played by the *logos*, which Origen equated with the Christ and considered a cosmic force distinct from the man Jesus. This therefore explains his assertion that there are 'many christs', who are similarly 'anointed' (*christos*) by God.

However, Origen wasn't greatly different to other Church Fathers; Platonism had also influenced Augustine, but for whom scripture outweighed philosophy. Furthermore, Christian doctrine was diverse until the Council of Nicea in AD 325, where Emperor Constantine, keen to unify state religion, pressured factions into agreement. It's here that Origen's teachings were questioned, a process ultimately resulting, in the Church council of AD 553, in his being declared *anathema* (subject to major excommunication) and a heretic.

Some doubt these *anathemas* were ever officially ratified, and it's possible the heretical beliefs concerned were actually those of later followers. Whatever the case, it's certainly true that no mainstream forms of Christianity now hold to, for example, reincarnation. Might they have done? Regarding Church history, believers see the will of God guiding events towards truth, whilst historians trace chance occurrences that might easily have taken another path. According to the former, Origen went astray; according to the latter, he was merely unlucky.

> 'His mind must be dull and sluggish in the extreme . . . who, in seeing
> all the beautiful objects of the sensible world, all this symmetry and
> great arrangement of things, and the form apparent in the stars . . .
> does not venerate them as admirable productions of still more
> admirable causes'
>
> PLOTINUS AD 204–269
> *Enneads*

Those influenced by Plato's thought emphasized different aspects, expanding and adapting his ideas in new directions. Even his famous Academy, which continued for 800 years after his death, eventually embodied a *sceptical* philosophy far from Plato's own. The more distinct and independent offshoots of his thought are therefore known as *Neo-Platonism*, to distinguish them from the views of his interpreters and close followers.

The foremost Neo-Platonist was Plotinus, an Egyptian-born philosopher who, on moving to Rome, found great success as a teacher, numbering emperors among his pupils. Plotinus emphasized the other-worldliness of Plato's philosophy, developing his concept of *ideal forms* into a more systematic and mystical vision. In this, Plotinus was influenced by *Zoroastrianism*, a Persian religious philosophy that pictured two supernatural principles – one good, one evil – at constant war for dominion. The evil principle was embodied in matter, and the means of salvation therefore lay in turning one's back on the physical and striving to realize the divine reality residing behind and beyond the world. Thus, for Plotinus – who's said to have been somewhat contemptuous of his physical body, and erased his personal history (never celebrating his own birthday, never talking of his past) – philosophy was a means to ascend, through greater and greater abstractions, to a contemplation of divine reality: the One. Thus, all lower manifestations, being closer to matter, were also closer to illusion.

However, as our quote suggests, the physical world isn't to be despised, because it is – though far removed – an expression of the One. But, is there still an element of world-denial in Plotinus? A disappointment with a world that doesn't live up to his ideals?

'Therefore do not seek to understand in order to believe, but believe
that you may understand'
ST AUGUSTINE AD 354–430
Homilies on the Gospel of John

Born to a pagan father and a Christian mother, St Augustine sampled
numerous belief systems before settling with Christianity. However,
in doing so, he also brought with him some of the central tenets of
Platonism, thus complementing Christianity's simple ethical and
spiritual teachings with Plato's more complex and rational philosophical outlook. This partly reflects Augustine's obvious enthusiasm for
intellectual studies; he was never someone (e.g. Tertullian), who
thought that faith should enslave and dominate reason, or that the
intellect should not seek to be satisfied in relation to religious questions. However, even so, faith had the upper hand over philosophy: the
role of reason was to reinforce and illuminate what was *already*
believed, not to establish reasons *to* believe.

The modern rational mind finds this view difficult to accept, and,
as noted with Tertullian, it comes close to *fideism*, or the idea that only
faith can provide religious truth. In its most undiluted form, this
seems a dangerous doctrine: a religious extremist could justify almost
any act based on the merely personal conviction that *his* interpretation
of scripture was correct. However, there is a milder version, which
simply proposes that reason is *inadequate* for achieving religious revelation, and that, to an extent, doubt and concern for rational proof
should be suspended before any true knowledge can be obtained.

This latter view is more attractive, for it merely asks that we open
ourselves up *emotionally*, inviting truth in on a level that bypasses
reason. However, herein also lies a danger, for how do we know to
trust emotion as a guide to truth? What is there to guarantee that we
will not be deluded by wishful thinking?

It's difficult to decide this question. There are many philosophers,
perhaps most, for whom truth can only ever be rational. For those,
suspending reason is tantamount to turning one's back on philosophy
– and thereby, perhaps, admitting that philosophy has its limits.

'Grant me chastity and continency, but not yet'

ST AUGUSTINE

Confessions

During his philosophical and religious wanderings, Augustine was also, it seems, greatly interested in sex. For many years of his youth he was torn between a deep and genuine desire for spiritual fulfilment, and a hedonistic libertinism. At the height of this conflict, and wishing to postpone the strictly spiritual life a bit longer, he uttered the above prayer: 'Lord, make me a good person – only not yet . . .'

After his conversion to Christianity, Augustine seems to identify sexual desire as symptomatic of a more general *concupiscence* (desire for a certain object or experience), which was itself the root of sin. Adam and Eve, having been foolish and disobedient enough to ignore God's commandment not to eat from the tree of knowledge, were therefore seen ever after to be polluted by their indiscretion – they were 'wounded' by it – and so certain activities involving desire, most notably copulation, would forever be tainted by sin.

It is interesting to note here that original sin was not native to Christianity, but sprang from other teachings. Most likely, the doctrine is inherited from Augustine's previous involvement with *Manichaeism* (a religion built around the Persian 3rd century mystic Mani), which strictly divided the universe into spirit (good) and matter (evil). Since sex was primarily a physical activity, then it was therefore evil, and consequently to be avoided.

However, if it is the broader sin of concupiscence that's at fault, then might there be a form of sex that is not sinful? Since concupiscence involves desiring or enjoying possession of an *object*, then it seems that the obvious sin involved lies in valuing something more highly than God (in a sense, setting up a false idol). Some modern forms of Christianity therefore try to redress this past imbalance by promoting sex as a natural and beautiful act that *celebrates* God. For, after all, if sex is a natural act, and nature, created by God, is good, then shouldn't sex be also?

'God works in the hearts of men to incline their wills wherever He wills, whether to good deeds according to His mercy, or to evil after their own deserts; His own judgment being sometimes manifest, sometimes secret, but always righteous'

St Augustine
On Grace and Free Will

An enduring problem for believers is to reconcile God's omniscience with human free will: if God knows what we will do, then some are destined to sin and suffer damnation, and others (the *elect*) to live righteously and obtain salvation. Aren't we then just 'going through the motions'? If our actions are predestined, what's the point of anything?

Augustine tries hard to disentangle this: humans *do* possess free will, but cannot by their own efforts be genuinely good. This is a consequence of original sin, whereby all our actions are necessarily tinged by selfishness; genuine goodness requires *divine grace*. This cannot be deserved or worked towards – God is as likely to accord it to an abject sinner as a devout believer – and to 'earn' it would make it no longer free, but payment for our behaviour (and, as the word implies, grace is a *gratuity*, or free gift from God). Thus, whilst we may behave as we wish, whether we receive grace or not (and therefore salvation or damnation) is not up to us.

But if God also influences 'the hearts of men', their desires and choices, how then can grace be freely sought, or punishment deserving? I cannot be open to grace if God has closed my heart. So, whilst Augustine provides one solution – we have free choice, but cannot choose a genuinely selfless motivation – with the other hand, he takes it away. God decides what our hearts desire, even influencing us to commit evil. His motives in this are inscrutable and 'secret' – we don't know why he accords or withholds grace – which is perhaps fair enough (he *is* God, after all). And yet, the threat of hell makes us bridle: shouldn't I at least have a say as to where I end up?

> 'What then is time? If no one asks me, I know what it is. If I wish to explain it to him who asks, I do not know.'
>
> St Augustine
>
> *The Confessions*

What is time? This question is difficult enough, but there is an additional problem for religious believers: if God is eternal (timeless), how can he act *within* time? There's a paradox: either God is outside time (but unable to engage with temporal events), or inside it (and not eternal).

But what *is* time? It consists of past, present, and future – but what are *these*? If nothing changed or finished, there would be no past; if nothing came into being, there would be no future; and if nothing existed, there could be no present. And yet, both past and future have no real existence except as they are related to our present experience: when we remember things, we are not *in* the past, but in the present (otherwise we could not be conscious in order to remember). When we anticipate things, we are not *in* the future, but once again in the present, awaiting whatever is to come. But what, then, is the present? If it were just one continuous moment, then it would really just be eternity, and time itself would not exist. There must be change in order for time to exist. Augustine concludes that the nature of the present – the nature of time – is that 'it tends not to be'. In other words, it is forever moving from *being* to *not being*. Time is therefore our subjective awareness of this process: it is the consciousness of change.

God, then, who is changeless, must also be timeless. Since God has no beginning or end, everything takes place in his eternal present: God is *always* creating the universe. This arguably doesn't clarify things greatly – which isn't necessarily a criticism of Augustine, but may simply indicate that time is so embedded in our thinking that trying to understand anything 'beyond' it may be . . . a waste of time?

> 'Reserve your right to think, for even to think wrongly is better than
> not to think at all'
> HYPATIA OF ALEXANDRIA C. AD 370–415
> in Ada Alder, *Suidae Lexicon*

Hypatia was a Neo-Platonist philosopher based in Alexandria, Egypt. She had been raised by her father, Theon, a Greek scholar and mathematician, who fostered her scholarly ambitions and inculcated in her a love for the pagan intellectual tradition. As a result, she eventually became head of the Platonist school of Alexandria, teaching Plato and Aristotle both there and in Athens. Her main academic contributions seem to have been to the mathematical theories of the time.

Hypatia is particularly notable in that she is a rare woman in the history of premodern philosophy, a discipline which seems, like so many others, to have been dominated by males up until the most recent times. However, she is now best remembered for her violent and horrible death, a pagan martyrdom of sorts, which some see as marking the end of the classical period of thought. As a committed rationalist in the Greek mould, she found herself in the way of the increasing Christianization of the empire. Refusing to convert, but retaining a popular following – even among certain Christians – she was seized by a mob, dragged to a church, dismembered and finally burnt. 'After this,' Bertrand Russell wryly notes (*History of Western Philosophy*), 'Alexandria was no longer troubled by philosophers'.

Whether this incident did indeed signal the end of classical antiquity is moot, but the incident does take place somewhere near the transition to the *Dark Ages*. However, the point of no return in this decline is usually reserved for the Emperor Justinian's closing of the Neo-Platonic Academy (a revival of Plato's earlier institution) in AD 529. From this point on, pagan thought was actively repressed, and philosophy in general was stifled for most of the next millennium – in effect, all but revoking the right to think.

> 'No man can injure the rational mind, or cause it that it should not be
> what it is'
> BOETHIUS C. AD 480–525
> *The Consolation of Philosophy*

Anicius Manlius Severinus Boethius was a Roman philosopher, best known for *The Consolation of Philosophy*, which presents his thoughts as a dialogue between himself and a female personification of philosophy itself. It was written whilst Boethius was imprisoned and awaiting execution, having served as a minister to Theoderic the Great, ruler of the Ostrogoths and later of Italy, but who had come to suspect Boethius of plotting against him. Thus, similar to Plato's account of Socrates' philosophical courage in the face of death, Boethius attempts to convince us (and no doubt himself) that no matter what our fate, a man's rational mind is untouchable. Boethius illustrates this by the case of a Roman nobleman who, under torture, bites off his tongue and spits it at his persecutors rather than give up the information they seek.

But is reason immune to influence? We are, perhaps, more sceptical of this proposition than previous ages. The ideas of Freud have shown that the rational ego is not 'master in its own house'. In *Stockholm syndrome*, a kidnap victim can, through stress, come to identify with his captors. In Stanley Milgram's famous 'shock machine' experiment, volunteers were encouraged to administer (unknown to them, fake) 'fatal' electric shocks to strangers. All this indicates that rationality and morality are often heavily influenced by context. We act as we are *expected* to act. The behaviour of Nazi concentration camp guards is therefore far closer to the capacity of the average human being than we'd like to think.

The notion of a private, impervious self has therefore been undermined by both psychology and neuroscience. There are now subtler ways to bypass the rational will, and the modern torturer has a much greater range of distasteful and ingenious means at his disposal than his medieval colleague. So, whilst it would be nice to agree with Boethius on this point, it has become much harder to do so.

> 'Unless the hand acts according to the will of reason, it acts in vain.
> How much nobler, then, is the study of music as a rational discipline
> than as composition and performance!'
>
> BOETHIUS
> *The Fundamentals of Music*

Philosophers may be grouped according to their attitude to music. There are those, like Wittgenstein, to whom music was an essential part of life, and Nietzsche even went as far as to state that 'Without music, life would be a mistake'. It would seem natural therefore to interpret this appreciation of music as the recognition that there are certain truths or experiences that music conveys that are either beyond reason, or express philosophical truths perhaps more fully than mere words can.

However, this isn't the only possible philosophical attitude, and there exists an opposite extreme whereby music is seen in purely rational terms. The origin of this view can perhaps be traced to Pythagoras, who saw the harmonies of music as expressing the fundamental mathematical ratios that governed reality – the 'music of the spheres'. True musical appreciation is therefore an intellectual exercise, an enjoyment of form and order as opposed to emotion and sensation.

Reflecting this tradition, Boethius identifies three types of music: *mundana* (the Pythagorean music of the cosmos), *humana* (the physical and spiritual music of the human being), and – least important – *instrumentalis* (the music of instruments). Boethius does admit that feeling plays a role in music – we *instinctively* appreciate it – but the highest appreciation comes from reason not sense; not because we *feel*, but because we *understand*.

Much of this goes against our modern view, which takes music to be largely a language of emotion. To appreciate it intellectually, therefore, whilst possible, seems something reserved for academics and music professionals. However, Boethius argues that reason is required to *correct* the mistakes of sense, just as Plato and Descartes believed that the senses mislead us. But if music is considered as *feeling*, then can we be *misled* by our own emotions? Don't we just enjoy them?

> 'Directly pointing to one's own soul, my doctrine is unique, and is not hampered by the canonical teachings; it is the absolute transmission of the true seal'
>
> BODHIDHARMA AD ?–535
> in D. T. Suzuki, *Introduction to Zen Buddhism*

Zen is an offshoot of Mahayana Buddhism that originated in China in the 6th century AD (records are vague), later spreading to Japan (*Zen* is the Japanese translation of the Chinese *Chán*, meaning 'meditation'). Its founder, Bodhidharma – the *First Patriarch* – first brought Buddhism to China from Southern India, where, on arrival, he seems to have been influenced by *Taoism*, imbibing its love of paradox and emphasis on the inexpressibility of ultimate truth. Biographical accounts blend the few known facts with surmise, allegory and myth – meditating for nine years uninterrupted facing a wall, and sailing across the Yangtze River on a blade of grass – and yet this too is characteristic of Zen, which eschews veneration of personality or historical exactitude: everything is a teaching opportunity, and a potential door to realization.

Zen isn't doctrinally different from Buddhism, merely a change in emphasis and method. Bodhidharma stressed that the essence of Buddhism ('the true seal') lay in realizing truth (*dharma*) at instinctive and emotional levels, not just intellectually. However, to achieve this, we must somehow bypass the mind's tendency to rationalize – to see truth in a detached, abstract way. Zen masters therefore traditionally do anything to help their pupils 'wake up', confounding their intellectual curiosity with riddles and paradoxes, and even striking them. However, these riddles (*koans*) – such as the famous 'what is the sound of one hand clapping?' – aren't meant to have a determinate answer, but are designed to provoke a spontaneous realization: *satori* (enlightenment).

This is beautifully illustrated by a conversation between Bodhidharma and his pupil Huike (who became the *Second Patriarch*). Huike admits to his master that his mind is not at peace. Bodhidharma replies, 'Bring me your mind; I will put it at peace.' Huike complains that he cannot find his mind anywhere; Bodhidharma responds, 'Then I have put it at peace.'

> 'The entire universe is truly the Self. There exists nothing at all other than the Self. The enlightened person sees everything in the world as his own Self, just as one views earthenware jars and pots as nothing but clay.'
>
> ADI SHANKARA c.788–c.820
> *Atma Bodha*

Adi Shankara was a Hindu philosopher in the *Advaita* tradition of *Vedanta* (following the portion of the Hindu scriptures – *Vedas* – known as the *Upanishads*). Unlike the *Bhagavad Gita*, which sees *atman* (self or soul) and *Brahman* (God, the cosmic spirit) as separate, Shankara sees them as one – the soul, in its deepest essence *is* God. As such, his philosophy is a form of *religious monism* or *non-dualism*: there is only one truly existing thing, and that is God (*a-dvaita* literally means 'not dualist', distinguishing it from the *Dvaita* or dualist school of Vedanta). This obviously has parallels with Buddhism and Plotinus in denying the existence of a personal self or soul.

Philosophically, Shankara's thesis leads him to propose that the *apparent* nature of the world, in which things appear to have a separate and independent existence, is actually illusory (*maya*). However, since realization of this truth is not possible for everyone, then there is also a 'lower' level of truth, represented by doctrines which bear closer resemblance to the everyday experience of the average person (the *Bhagavad Gita*, which proposes a unique individual self, would be an example of such an approach).

As a result of this monism – God and self are in everything – God himself can have no attributes. But what, then, is the essence of the divine? It is, Shankara argues, the eternal 'I' – self-consciousness. But isn't there a paradox involved in trying to be conscious of self whilst also transcending or denying it? Doesn't the notion of 'I' need to be distinguished from other things – such as 'not I' or 'you'? But Shankara, like Buddha, is not interested in pinning down a *concept* of self, but in transcending *all* concepts: it's the *experience* of 'I' which is essential, and which represents a *non-conceptual* truth. Is this possible?

> 'For authority proceeds from true reason, but reason certainly does not proceed from authority. For every authority which is not upheld by true reason is seen to be weak, whereas true reason is kept firm and immutable by her own powers and does not require to be confirmed by the assent of any authority.'
> JOHANNES SCOTUS ERIGUENA c.815–877
> *The Division of Nature*

The misleadingly named Johannes Scotus, or John the Scot (not to be confused with *Duns* Scotus), was an Irish-born philosopher ('Scotus' then referred to Irishmen, and 'Eriguena' means 'Irish-born'). During the fall of the Roman Empire in the 5th century AD, whilst the marauding German tribes that sacked Rome devastated the established cultural institutions, they respected the Church, allowing it to become the unifying cultural force of the new order. However, as the Church grew, it neglected or abandoned the philosophical traditions which had once influenced and merged with it, inaugurating the period of cultural decline referred to as the *Dark Ages*. So, whilst St Augustine had imbibed the concepts of Plato and the later Neo-Platonists to bolster Christian theology, philosophy now only survived in the writings of earlier Church Fathers such as himself.

Accordingly, the appearance of Johannes Scotus is all the more surprising, until we realize that Ireland had originally provided ideal refuge for those fleeing the growing intolerance and anti-intellectualism of the continent. A 9th century Irishman with knowledge of Greek and professing a form of Neo-Platonism was therefore perhaps not such a strange thing after all. That Scotus survived unscathed, however, is quite surprising, for his ideas would have seemed to the contemporary Christian clergy (raised on respect for authority and dogma) utterly fantastic, and highly heretical. In contrast to Augustine, and in accord with Plato, Scotus argued that reason was the *supreme* guide to truth. Ideally, faith and philosophy should sing from the same hymn sheet, but where they did not, reason should win out over dogma. Belief was not enough.

> 'Imagine a man flying in a void. His organs would not register any sensation, and perhaps he would not feel like a three dimensional being. But he would be aware of not experiencing his body, which means that the soul is a spiritual reality.'
>
> IBN SINA (AVICENNA) c.980–1037
> *The Book of Healing*

Abu-Ali Ibn Sina, or in the Latinized form by which he is better known in the West, Avicenna, was a Persian philosopher, scientist and doctor, who – like Omar Khayyám – possessed a great reputation for learning in a bewildering array of subjects. Thus, he was a leading light in what is often considered the golden age of Islamic thought, during which the study of philosophy and science blossomed, and existed in harmony with theology and religious practice.

Avicenna's reputation permeated Europe as a commentator and interpreter of Aristotle, and his *Canon of Medicine* was required reading in most medieval universities. However, one particular thought experiment of his is also well-known. The 'floating man', as it's called, envisages someone falling or flying through space, without bodily sensation of any kind, and deprived of sensory information (blind, deaf, etc.): would he not, in such a situation, still be aware of himself? Therefore, if he is unaware of his body, he must therefore be essentially a mind or soul.

This bears some similarity to Descartes, especially his *conceivability argument*: I can conceive of myself without a body; therefore, I'm not essentially a body, but a mind. The floating man therefore similarly argues from conceivability to actuality. And yet, as with Descartes's argument, it relies upon an idea that conceivability means something in the actual world. Like the ontological argument, it attempts to argue from idea to reality – but can it?

However, what if I *can* conceive of sensory deprivation *without* feeling compelled to conclude that I am not the body? Or even – using a floatation tank, perhaps – experience 'bodilessness'? But this merely proves that we may free the imagination by quieting the senses, doesn't it? Conceivability, it seems, isn't everything.

'... the fool has said in his heart, there is no God ... but ... this very fool, when he hears of this being of which I speak – a being than which nothing greater can be conceived – understands what be hears, and what he understands is in his understanding; although he does not understand it to exist'

ST ANSELM 1033–1109
Proslogion

St Anselm was an Italian monk who rose to become Archbishop of Canterbury. Like St Augustine, Anselm held that faith preceded reason, and that we must believe in order to understand. However, he also thought reason could bolster faith by adding proofs for God's existence; a heart closed to God might reject them, but an already open one might find greater understanding and support for faith.

The fool in Anselm's quote (from *Psalms* 14:1) has an idea of God, but rejects it. Anselm therefore makes a distinction between *understanding* an idea, and an idea merely being *present* in the understanding. There's an idea of Einstein's theory of relativity 'in my understanding', but I don't understand it! We must therefore show the fool how the mere existence of the *idea* of God entails his existence.

We can conceive of the greatest being ('than which none greater can be conceived'). If this were merely an idea, it wouldn't be the greatest conceivable being; it would be greater, however, if the being *also* existed in reality. Since we have such an idea, and that idea implies existence, then the being (God) must exist. This is known as the *ontological argument* (from the Greek, *ontos*, 'being').

Many people feel tricked by this argument. Is there some logical 'sleight of hand' at work? Perhaps the most telling criticism is Kant's: existence isn't a *quality* that things possess (or don't); rather, it is a statement about the world (whether something exists or not). So, a being isn't greatest *because* it exists, but because – *if* it exists – it possesses certain qualities. It would certainly be 'great' if the money we dreamt of having in our sleep really existed, but there's nothing about the *idea* of the money that would make it so.

'Myself when young did eagerly frequent
Doctor and Saint, and heard great argument
About it and about: but evermore
Came out by the same door where in I went.'
OMAR KHAYYÁM 1048–1131
The Rubáiyát (Edward Fitzgerald translation)

Omar Khayyám was a Persian philosopher, mathematician, astronomer and doctor, among other things, renowned for contributions to algebra, but most remembered for his *Rubáiyát* ('verses') due to the immensely popular translation by English poet Edward Fitzgerald (1809–1883).

Fitzgerald's interest reveals something of the nature of Khayyám's message. A friend of poet Alfred, Lord Tennyson, Fitzgerald shared his religious doubts, was a lapsed Christian, and at least agnostic. Khayyám's evocation of impermanence and the dubious consolations of philosophy therefore struck a chord with Fitzgerald, whose loss of a friend early in life deeply affected him. In Khayyám, therefore, Fitzgerald recognizes a kindred spirit.

Or does he? There are differing interpretations of the *Rubáiyát*, and Khayyám is respectively claimed as atheist, agnostic and mystic. He shares some of the *pessimism* of Schopenhauer, and the author of *Ecclesiastes*, whose advice to 'eat, drink and be merry' in the face of life's transience is mirrored in Khayyám's own: 'Ah, make the most of what we yet may spend, / Before we too into the Dust descend'.

Khayyám's advocacy of sensual pleasure – of women, wine and song – make him an unorthodox Muslim, but we shouldn't judge on the *Rubáiyát* alone (some parts of which are of dubious authenticity). Furthermore, Fitzgerald's translation is very free, and sometimes inaccurate, creating perhaps his own Khayyám, not unveiling the true one. Perhaps, therefore, Khayyám has most in common with the mystic *Sufi* poets, who often employed sensuous metaphor – we experience 'union' with the 'beloved', we savour the 'wine' of divine knowledge – suggesting that a true philosopher must love wisdom with *all* his being.

> 'The existence of God and other like truths about God, which can be
> known by natural reason, are not articles of faith, but are preambles to
> the articles; for faith presupposes natural knowledge, even as grace
> presupposes nature and perfection the perfectible'
>
> ST THOMAS AQUINAS 1225–1274
> *Summa Theologica*

St Thomas Aquinas was an Italian monk and the foremost proponent of *Scholasticism* (embodying the teachings of the Catholic schools), which sought to bring philosophy and religion into accord. Aquinas is interesting in this respect, claiming that, whilst there are aspects of faith that stretch beyond reason (such as knowledge of the Trinity), reason is an important guide to truth, and is in fact sufficient in itself to prove the existence of God. Faith was therefore the crowning of natural reason, merely moving slightly further down the path indicated.

The Scholastic period follows the philosophically barren *Dark Ages*, and constitutes a reaction to the influx of ideas from the East stemming from the *Crusades*. Unlike the West, Islamic culture had preserved the works of the Greek philosophers, Aristotle in particular, and the prolonged conflict paradoxically provided an opportunity for a reintroduction of his philosophy.

Threatened by Aristotle's sophisticated intellectual system, the Church survived by adapting it to support Christian dogma. In this way, the marriage of Aristotle and Christianity provided a new philosophical orthodoxy: there was no need to think, because Aristotle had already done it for you. Thus the union that scholasticism aimed at – and that Aquinas was instrumental in bringing about – eventually became a highly restrictive one (a straightjacket that philosophy would only begin to escape during the 15th century through the *Renaissance*).

Scholasticism illustrates the difficulties faced in reconciling reason and faith. Whilst he shuns Tertullian's anti-intellectualism, Aquinas makes philosophy the handmaiden of religion. His respect for philosophy therefore only goes as far as it supports faith – he has *faith* in reason to reach the same conclusions as revelation (trust which now seems perhaps misplaced). Fundamentally, of course, tension arises because philosophy needs room to breathe – without which, is it really philosophy?

'. . . whatever is moved must be moved by another. If that by which it is moved must itself be moved, then this also needs to be moved by another, and that by another again. But this cannot go on to infinity . . . Therefore it is necessary to arrive at the first mover, moved by no other; and this everyone understands to be God.'

ST THOMAS AQUINAS
Summa Theologica

Aquinas presented five proofs for the existence of God – what are known as his 'five ways'. The first of these (quoted above) deals with motion, but the other four involve causation, contingency, goodness and design, respectively. The first three of the five ways are therefore similar, and basically argue from the fact of the existence of the universe; the fourth argues that morality must have a moral source, and the last is basically a version of the *teleological argument*. I deal with versions of the latter two elsewhere, so let's look at the first three.

The idea that God is required to provide some aspect of the universe, or even the universe itself, goes back at least to Plato, and is called the *cosmological argument*. It basically takes the form: x exists; x cannot have come from nothing; therefore, something produced x. Obviously, whether x stands for 'all motion in the universe', or just 'the universe', the cause needs to be capable of producing such an effect. So, the argument goes, that cause must either be God (the 'first' or 'prime mover'), or something very like God.

Scientific evidence would seem to support some sort of Big Bang theory (the universe exploded from a point of infinite density), and if so then God isn't the only explanation. But even science starts to sound a bit surreal here, and its 'explanations' equally mythical. It's difficult then for the layman to choose: between an intellectual account that he does not comprehend, and a divine mystery that 'passeth all understanding'. Both seem quite far-fetched.

> 'In order for a war to be just, three things are necessary.
> First, the authority of the sovereign. Secondly, a just cause.
> Thirdly, a rightful intention.'
>
> St Thomas Aquinas
> *Summa Theologica*

At the time of writing, Tony Blair had just given what's been described as 'a robust defence' to the Iraq war inquiry in London, stating his primary justification for invasion, and the deposition of Saddam Hussein:

> '. . . if there was any possibility that he could develop weapons of mass destruction we should stop him.'

Of course, no evidence of such weapons has been found, and it's now a moot point whether he actually had – or might have – developed any. *Was* the war justified?

Firstly, we must distinguish just *conduct in* war from just *cause for* war. Codes have always existed governing acceptable military practice (ceasefire, treatment of prisoners, etc.), but whilst a just cause for war is now a matter of international law, Aquinas considered it a matter of *conscience*: was it a sin against God?

He thought not – providing three conditions were met. Firstly, *individuals* shouldn't wage war; armies mustn't settle the personal grievances of powerful men. Secondly, justification: what are the enemy's crimes? Retaliation for unprovoked aggression – or, in Blair's case, to avoid the *threat* of such – is perhaps permissible. Thirdly, motivation: war shouldn't stem from a cruel desire for revenge, or for profit (for oil, perhaps . . .), but from an aim of 'securing peace, of punishing evil-doers, and of uplifting the good'.

To modern eyes, Aquinas' standards seem too broad and proactive. Whilst we might *like* to 'punish evil-doers' – the problem of defining 'evil' aside – is it any one country's job to act as an international police force? Also, any benefit must be weighed up against resultant suffering (the inevitable civilian casualties, the ensuing anarchy). Arguably, more long-term good may be accomplished by peaceful persuasion – aid, trade, security – thus encouraging countries to realize the value of peace and consensus. However, these controversies aside, one thing is certain: even a *just* war can only ever be the lesser of two evils.

'Entities are not to be multiplied beyond necessity'
WILLIAM OF OCKHAM C.1288–C.1348
Opera Philosophica et Theologica

William of Ockham was an English Franciscan friar, hailing (probably) from Ockham in Surrey. Whilst not a 'bad boy' as such, he seems to have been of a wilful and independent temperament, falling out with Pope John XXII over whether Jesus and the apostles actually owned any property (they didn't!), and landing himself with a charge of heresy. Steering clear of Rome as a consequence, he spent the remainder of his days in Germany, mulling over the abuses of papal power.

Philosophically, he is one of the more substantial and enduring medieval figures. His writings range through logic, theory of knowledge, natural philosophy (theoretical science), and political theory, and, like any self-respecting medievalist, he weighed in on the question of whether universals (general abstract ideas) actually exist (they don't!).

However, he is now almost universally remembered for his doctrine of 'ontological parsimony', or – as it is more commonly and friendlily known – *Ockham's razor*. Faced with two competing explanations of the same thing, both explanations providing a full account, one should favour the simpler. An example is provided by the history of science, where for centuries scientists and philosophers argued over the existence of the so-called *aether* (a sort of subtle substance that filled space and was thought by some to be necessary as a medium through which light travelled, or gravitational force was effected). However, physicists ultimately rejected this explanation, because competing theories provided a simpler and more elegant account. Therefore, whilst it may have been (or might still be) possible to resurrect *aether* theory by tweaking it in certain respects, why should we, when a simpler theory (with fewer 'entities' – substances or things) suffices?

But the problem here is that there is no necessary connection between simplicity and truth. For all we know, complexity is closer to truth, and – since theories to which the principle applies are otherwise equal – favouring simplicity may just be an arbitrary preference on our part – a choice.

> 'Come and see: there is a garment visible to all. When those fools see
> someone in a good-looking garment they look no further. But the
> essence of the garment is the body; the essence of the body is the soul!
> So it is with Torah.'
>
> MOSES DE LÉON C.1250–1305
> *Sefer ha-Zohar*

The *Zohar*, or 'Book of Radiance', is a founding text in *Kabbalism*, a
mystical tradition considered to embody the secret teachings underlying Judaism. The *Zohar* offers an esoteric commentary upon the
Torah (the Pentateuch, or first five books of the Old Testament, attributed to the prophet Moses). Moses de Léon, a Spanish Jew, claimed to
have found it in a cave, its true author being Shimon bar Yochai, a
famous 2nd century Rabbi. However, as with the *Corpus Hermeticum*,
most textual scholars suspect a more recent author, namely Moses de
Léon himself.

The *Zohar's* main premise is that the words of the Torah have various levels of meaning. Aside from the literal meaning, there are
three, increasingly profound levels of interpretation: allegorical, metaphorical, and mystical. The simple message is merely an 'outer
garment' hiding secret doctrines from the profane and unworthy.

The *Zohar* sees creation as a 'Tree of Life' containing ten *sephirot*
('emanations'), each expressing a divine principle. Ranging from the
highest expression of godhead, the *sephirot* trace the path of creation
to its lowest manifestation in the physical world. Paralleling
Hermeticism's doctrine of 'as above, so below', the cosmic structure
reflects the constitution of individual man. Thus, divine reason,
mercy, justice, etc., has its corresponding expression in man's faculties, and man – a *microcosm* – reflects the divine in as much as he
activates and balances these different aspects, an evolutionary process
taking many lifetimes (like Hermeticism, Kabbalah believes in
reincarnation).

Kabbalah has spread beyond Judaism (e.g. Pico della Mirandola,
but most orthodox Jews consider it heretical. Perhaps the most fundamental objection is that it undermines the message of transparency
and equality: would God really hide his message from all but the
select?

> 'Philosophy . . . is the ascent of the mind from the lower regions to the highest, and from darkness to light. Its origin is an impulse of the divine mind; its middle steps are the faculties and the disciplines which are described; and its end is the possession of the highest good. Finally, its fruit is the right government of men.'
>
> MARSILIO FICINO 1433–1499
> *Letters*

Italian philosopher Marsilio Ficino was a formative influence upon the Renaissance. Sponsored by the renowned Medici family, he was the first translator of Plato's complete works into Latin, and further translations of, and commentaries upon, Plotinus and the *Corpus Hermeticum*, helped formulate an alternative to Aristotelian Scholasticism, a synthesis of ancient thought that inspired such artists as Botticelli, Raphael and Michelangelo.

However, Ficino was more than just a philosophical popularizer and synthesizer, though he is often seen as such – a reason, perhaps, for his relative neglect. Another factor perhaps is his emphasis on the practical uses of philosophy, which led him toward astral magic, whereby the influence of the planets and stars could be drawn into our life by conscious means – typically through use of images, music, scents, types of food and drink, etc. However, we should not dismiss his ideas merely as a crude form of astrological superstition – Ficino was subtler than that: 'The important thing', he says, in *The Book of Life*, 'is to hold on correctly to whatever spirit, whatever force, or whatever powerful thing it is that these planets signify.' In other words, his intentions are largely psychological: the man born under the influence of Saturn – as Ficino himself was (and, he claims, as are most 'men of letters') – should seek to lighten his natural gloominess by Jovial and solar influences, such as wearing bright colours, early rising, working only during daytime, frequenting airy and well-lit places, and so on.

Some of this is common sense, but Ficino's virtue lies in tying together disparate strands – psychological, philosophical, moral and spiritual – into a unified and coherent system: a living Platonism.

> 'It would be good for religion if many books that seem useful were destroyed. When there were not so many books and not so many arguments and disputes, religion grew more quickly than it has since.'
>
> GIROLAMO SAVONAROLA 1452–1498
> in Jacob Burckhardt, *The Civilisation of the Renaissance in Italy*

Savonarola was an Italian Dominican priest who came to prominence in Florence for a brief period, preaching hellfire sermons, and advocating a return to ascetic simplicity. This led to the so-called *Bonfire of the Vanities*, whereby the citizens of Florence were encouraged and even forcibly persuaded to give up their superfluous and irreligious possessions (*vanities*), which included clothes, jewellery, ornaments, games, musical instruments, pagan books and works of art (many cultural treasures were lost during this period). These were then collected and burnt in the public square.

Whilst praised in some quarters, Savonarola's puritanism is in direct opposition to the spirit of the *Renaissance*. The three-year period during which he ruled Florence therefore represents a partial return to the *Dark Ages*, where unquestioning faith was once again asserted over the dictates of natural reason, and philosophy was reviled as an irreligious and superfluous activity:

> 'The only good thing that we owe to Plato and Aristotle is that they brought forward many arguments which we can use against the heretics. Yet they and other philosophers are now in hell.'

In hindsight, Savonarola owed his brief dominion to the coincidence of his apocalyptic message with the various misfortunes that beset Florence in the 1490s (deprivation arising from the French-Italian war, culminating in the invasion of Charles VIII; the spread of syphilis). Fortunately, for the growth of science and knowledge, Savonarola's influence was short-lived and didn't spread beyond Florence. Ironically, having consigned so many things to the flames, he refused the challenge of a *trial by fire* from a Franciscan friar, the public began to turn against him, and he was eventually imprisoned, tortured, and executed – burned alive on the very spot where the *bonfire of the vanities* had taken place.

DESIDERIUS ERASMUS C.1467–1536
Adagia

Desiderius Erasmus was a Dutch scholar, theologian and priest who argued that the study of classical philosophy and literature was compatible with Christianity. His scholarly and popular writings prepared the way for critical reassessment of Church teachings, and influenced the Reformation. But, whilst a life-long critic of religious intolerance and hypocrisy, he preferred to reform the Church from within.

Erasmus is often considered a founding father of *humanism*, a worldview that places humanity at its centre. However, whilst many modern forms of humanism are atheistic and secular, Erasmus was humanist in the sense that he promoted the study of 'human' subjects that complemented Christian thought, stating that, 'Wherever you encounter truth, look upon it as Christianity.' This therefore opened up the world of classical (Greek and Roman) literature and thought, and encouraged focus on *human* (as opposed to divine) subjects, such as logic, grammar, history, and rhetoric (the basis of the *humanities*). However, whilst he considered such studies important, he was also sceptical about the power of the intellect to arrive at truth unaided, and so proposed that we also require faith and reliance upon Church teaching. In this sense, he adopts a middle way between faith and reason, between Church and the needs of society.

Accordingly, Erasmus was impartial in his criticism, attacking both conservative and liberal. His view was cosmopolitan: we could not but benefit from extending our search for knowledge to areas beyond the limits of our own tradition, and from recognizing truth wherever it was found. The famous proverb, quoted above, may therefore be taken as both an admission of the limitations of human reason, and as an encouragement to gain what understanding we can: where ignorance is widespread, even a little knowledge is better than none. To rely *only* on faith, or *only* on reason, to side with one sect or tradition over another out of prejudice, is therefore to blind ourselves unnecessarily – and we see poorly enough as it is.

'We have set thee at the world's centre that thou mayest from thence more easily observe whatever is in the world. We have made thee neither of heaven nor of earth, neither mortal nor immortal, so that with freedom of choice and with honour, as though the maker and moulder of thyself, thou mayest fashion thyself in whatever shape thou shalt prefer.'

PICO DELLA MIRANDOLA 1463–1494
Oration on the Dignity of Man

These words, spoken as if by God to Adam, represent the vision of the Italian philosopher Giovanni Pico, count of Mirandola. Pico was a protégé of fellow Neo-Platonist Marsilio Ficino, but his influences extended to Arabic and Jewish philosophy, synthesizing Platonic and Aristotelian thought with such diverse elements as *Kabbalah*, *Hermeticism*, Zoro-astrianism and Chaldean theology. Unsurprisingly, this cosmopolitan mix didn't impress Christian orthodoxy, and the 900 theses (points for discussion) that he published (and which the *Oration* was meant to support) occasioned direct conflict with the Church.

The *Oration* proposes that what makes man special is his free will: he may indulge his animal appetites, and so revert to the level of beasts, or develop his reason and spirit, and soar with the angels. This is one point of conflict with orthodoxy, for in emphasizing personal choice and potential for unlimited development, Pico undermines reliance upon faith and the mediation of Christ. A second point of controversy concerns Pico's attitude to pagan and other non-Christian beliefs, for he maintained that religious and philosophical truth wasn't confined to one particular religion, but could be found in many different traditions. Wisdom therefore lay in rejecting what was false in these different approaches, and combining the separate truthful elements into a unified whole.

Perhaps disconcerted by his brush with heresy, Pico renounced his philosophical studies under the influence of the Dominican priest Savonarola. However, since he died soon after (only 31) – poisoned, probably by the Medici family (Savonarola's opposition) – we can never know whether his 'conversion' would have been as short-lived as Savonarola's reign.

'A prince . . . should not deviate from what is good, if that is possible,
but he should know how to do evil, if that is necessary'
NICCOLÒ MACHIAVELLI 1469–1527
The Prince

Whilst Raphael, Michelangelo and Leonardo vied to celebrate the beauty of the human form, others were busy dismembering it. It is often overlooked, amid the flowering of philosophy, literature, art and science, just how bloody and turbulent a time the Renaissance was.

This was especially true in Italy, where Machiavelli's Florence was just one of a number of independent city states, weaving loose affiliations and constantly shifting alliances against the backdrop of the imperial ambitions of France and Spain. Machiavelli was a high-ranking diplomat, well-placed to observe the intricacies of statecraft at close quarters. This intimate acquaintance with power made him cynical about human nature, but above all a realist: 'men ought either to be well treated or crushed, because they can avenge themselves of lighter injuries, of more serious ones they cannot'. In other words, politics is no place for Christian sentiment, for we cannot assume that others will share it, and since wounded enemies are most dangerous, then – regrettably – the most effective course of action may also be the most brutal.

Thus is Machiavelli's name a byword for cynicism, manipulative cunning and amorality. But is this fair? The picture of human nature that emerges from *The Prince* is indeed bleak, but – arguably – one that is borne out by experience. Machiavelli was not irreligious, but merely thought that, since, historically, 'all unarmed prophets have been destroyed', words of peace should be backed by the threat of steel. The ideal leader should possess the courage of a lion, but also the cunning of a fox. Today, his diabolical reputation seems less deserved, and his views less exceptional. It is tempting, in fact, to see his early critics as most offended by his honesty – that he wrote, as Francis Bacon says of him, of 'what men do, and not what they ought to do'.

> 'At rest, however, in the middle of everything is the sun. For, in this most beautiful temple, who would place this lamp in another or better position than that from which it can light up the whole thing at the same time?'
>
> NICOLAUS COPERNICUS 1473–1543
> *On the Revolutions of the Celestial Spheres*

Copernicus was a Polish astronomer who was the first (in modern times, at least) to provide a systematic account of the order and movement of the planets. Under the system proposed by the Roman astronomer Ptolemy (c. AD 90–c.168), and accepted as supported by Biblical orthodoxy by the Catholic Church, the Earth was the centre of the universe, orbited by the seven 'planets' (which included the Sun and the Moon) against the backdrop of the 'fixed' stars. Obviously, this did not make for the neatest fit with astronomical observations, and the complex system became increasingly unwieldy as more observational knowledge was amassed.

For instance, to account for the *apparent retrograde motion* of Saturn and other planets, which appeared at times to stop and move backwards across the sky, Ptolemaic astronomy proposed the notion of *epicycles*. Thus, whilst describing a general circular orbit (the *deferent*) around the Earth, the planet in question would also move in a smaller, circular orbit (the *epicycle*). What's more, the deferent's centre of orbit was not even the Earth, but a separate point (the *equant*).

Copernicus replaces the arcane complexity of Ptolemy's system with a more coherent and logical fit with the known data, resulting in a victory for empirical science and observation over superstition and dogma – or is it? Like Isaac Newton, Copernicus was also a keen student of *Hermeticism*, and even quotes from the *Corpus Hermeticum*: 'the Sun is the visible God'. Also, the idea of a *heliocentric* (Sun-centred) universe was itself ancient – it can be found in Aristarchus (310–c.230 BC) and Pythagoras, among others. Therefore, some suggest, Copernicus saw himself not as enthroning a new science, but as restoring an ancient wisdom.

'They wonder much to hear that gold, which in itself is so useless a thing, should be everywhere so much esteemed, that even men for whom it was made, and by whom it has its value, should yet be thought of less value than it is'

SIR THOMAS MORE 1478–1535

Utopia

Sir Thomas More was an English lawyer, friend of Erasmus and humanist philosopher. He's most famous as Lord Chancellor for opposing the establishment of the Church of England, and for Henry VIII's self-proclamation as its head. His resolution in this matter, for which Henry had him executed, is widely admired, and eventually led to his canonization by the Catholic Church.

More's *Utopia* is a philosophical account of an ideal society, and is the origin of the modern use of the word (echoing the Greek for 'no place' and 'good place', thus suggesting, perhaps, that such an ideal community cannot exist). As in Francis Bacon's similar work, Utopia is an island chanced upon by a traveller. The community combines elements of tolerant Christianity with what we would now call *communism*. There is a strong element of state control and enforced equality, though the leaders are elected or rule by merit, serving only to administer its laws. There's no personal property or wealth, no one can profit from private enterprise, and everyone must engage in the same amount of work (thus allowing everyone to work less overall). There's a standard form of dress, towns and residences are identically and pragmatically designed, and, to avoid 'keeping up with the Joneses', everyone moves house periodically. Other progressive ideas include female and married priests, state welfare, euthanasia, divorce, and a broadly tolerant attitude to religion.

However, other aspects of More's paradise aren't so appealing. Utopia uses slavery as a means of penal servitude, and those who have engaged in adultery or other crimes are made to perform menial and unpleasant tasks. Ultimately, though, its enforced material equality, and its imposition of communal values, make it somewhat oppressive – and, perhaps, a little dull.

FRANÇOIS RABELAIS C.1483–1553
Gargantua

Philosophers are not especially known for their humour, which is a shame, for no discipline is in greater need of light relief. Seeking perhaps to redress this, French doctor, writer, satirist and humanist philosopher François Rabelais lampooned the religious and philosophical attitudes of his day, and without the protection of influential friends might have suffered the fate of other heretics and free thinkers.

Rabelais' main works consist of a series of novels, *Gargantua and Pantagruel*, which describe the adventures of two giants, father and son, and bear much in common with Jonathan Swift's *Gulliver's Travels*, the fantastic action providing a pretext for political and religious satire. However, Rabelais is also renowned for his bawdy sense of humour, and part of his satirical method – like Chaucer's – is to prick pomposity and hypocrisy through earthy jokes and innuendo.

However, there is a more serious purpose. Most famously, during his satire of monastic life at the 'Abbey of Thélème', Rabelais embarks on a defence of humanist principles founded on personal conscience. The monastery's inhabitants live by one rule: 'Do What Thou Wilt'. However, this isn't moral anarchy, but an expression of faith in the inherent decency of man, because

> 'people who are free, well bred, well taught, and conversant with honourable company, have by nature an instinct – a goad – which always pricks them towards virtuous acts and withdraws them from vice. They called it Honour.'

This view opposes the authoritarianism of the 16th century Catholic Church, which saw man as fundamentally corrupt (due to *original sin*) and needing to be constantly monitored, guided and kept in check. The bawdy humour, too, has a purpose, for even that which is crude and 'base' is natural, and thus stems from God. To be reminded of such things is therefore to take ourselves less seriously, and to move toward true humility. Laughter is therefore important, for it is an aid to truth. Which leads us to a very interesting theological question: does God laugh?

'Nature being the Universe, is one, and its origin can only be the one eternal Unity. It is an organism in which all natural things harmonize and sympathize with each other. It is the Macrocosm. Everything is the product of one universal creative effort; the Macrocosm and man (the Microcosm) are one.'

PARACELSUS 1493–1541
Philosophia ad Athenienses

Phillippus Aureolus Theophrastus Bombastus von Hohenheim was a Swiss philosopher and physician, commonly known as *Paracelsus* (in reference to his reputation having surpassed that of the renowned Roman physician *Celsus*). His philosophy blended alchemy, magic, astrology, and *Hermeticism*, though his general outlook was *Neo-Platonist*, sharing something with near contemporary Marsilio Ficino.

Paracelsus considered man (the *microcosm*, 'little world') to be a reflection of the universe (the *macrocosm*, 'big world'), and health to consist in maintaining the harmony between both. This idea springs from ancient Greek philosophy, but Paracelsus uses it to identify substances for medical treatment. This cosmic harmony allowed the compilation of a table of correspondences – between minerals, plants, metals, organs of the body, moods, planets, and so on. For instance, possession of a short temper might suggest treatment with some substance rich in iron, the metal corresponding to Mars, which is associated with anger (thus curing like with like).

Obviously, such 'treatments' could kill or cure (quicksilver being a common remedy), and whilst some were effective and innovatory, others were dubious or dangerous. As with alchemy (which pioneered chemistry), Paracelsus' ideas represent a dual legacy: whilst certain ideas and practices foreshadow modern medicine, his general philosophy and method is now considered outmoded superstition. Interestingly, though, his philosophy lives on in homeopathy, which, taking up his idea that 'like cures like', treats symptoms with minute quantities of the substances thought to produce them – poison is simply a matter of dosage. Were homeopathy scientifically proven to be effective, there might be new respect for Paracelsus. However, as things stand, he illustrates a stage in the history of medicine's struggle from the grasp of superstition.

> 'There is (gentle reader) nothing (the works of God only set apart)
> which so much beautifies and adorns the soul and mind of man as
> does knowledge of the good arts and sciences'
>
> JOHN DEE 1527–c.1609
> Preface to Billingsley's English translation of Euclid

John Dee was an English mathematician and philosopher in the *hermetic* tradition, whom history has largely consigned to the margins of philosophy. However, in his time, he was considered one of the foremost minds of Europe. He possessed one of its greatest libraries, and was consulted on all manner of things – from the most auspicious date for Elizabeth I's coronation (to whom he had been a tutor), to the possibility of establishing a trade route via the *Northwest Passage* (linking the Atlantic and Pacific Oceans). He was also, reputedly, Elizabeth's spy, adopting the codename '007' (which Ian Fleming borrowed for James Bond), and the inspiration for Shakespeare's Prospero in *The Tempest*.

However, despite his renown, Dee was always held in suspicion, and popular prejudice considered him a sorcerer, leading to the ransacking of his house and library. From a modern perspective, many of his interests seem unbecoming of a 'man of science': hermeticism, numerology, *Kabbalah*, and astrology. Also, not content with abstract learning, he combined his interest in practical science with practices which science looks askance upon.

In collaboration with Edward Kelley, reputed alchemist and psychic, Dee conducted experiments spanning years, during which Kelley claimed to contact angels. Fascinated by the prospect of divine knowledge, Dee was drawn in (or *duped*, most suggest), as Kelley claimed to relay the principles of the original language Adam had used to name all things, now termed *Enochian* (from Dee's claim that the Biblical figure Enoch was the last descendent of Adam to use it).

Setting aside the question of whether Dee's substantial intellect was ultimately undermined by his own desire for knowledge, we may ask: would angels *need* a special language? As spiritual beings tasked with relaying divine messages to peoples of all cultures and ages, mightn't it prove a hindrance?

'The only thing certain is nothing is certain'
MICHEL DE MONTAIGNE 1533–1592
Apology for Raymond Sebond

At the age of 38, having served as a courtier and diplomat, Montaigne retired from public life to his family castle in Bordeaux, and to devote the remainder of his life to writing. These numerous essays produced at this time, on topics as diverse as cannibalism, repentance and thumbs, are what he is now best remembered for. The essays' accessible and conversational style, peppered with anecdotes and stories, ensuring not only that they would be hugely popular, but hugely influential, impressing great minds such as Shakespeare, Pascal, and Nietzsche.

Montaigne was fundamentally a sceptic – not the life-denying, nit-picking sort, but one that allowed his doubt to liberate him from dogma and narrow-mindedness. His personal motto was, 'What do I know?' and he used his professed ignorance as the basis upon which to challenge hypocrisy, prejudice and oppression. On many subjects, his views were refreshingly down to earth: 'Kings and philosophers defecate, and so do ladies'; 'No man is a hero to his own valet.' In this sense, without being irreligious, he was a humanist, for whom man was as much the product of natural forces as of the divine.

One of the most important consequences of man's humanity is, of course, his proneness to error: he cannot know anything with absolute certainty, and belief supplies conviction but not proof. Therefore, this fallibility has consequences: we should be tolerant of the differing opinions and customs of others, especially in matters of ethics and religion, where disagreement can provoke conflict; we should base our judgements upon what seems to be borne out by experience, because this is our main guide to knowledge; we should strive for self-knowledge, since it is only through self-examination that we can hope to understand our nature and needs, and so be happy and fulfilled; but most of all, we should be humble, for we do not know where we might be wrong.

> '*Are we not brutes to call the act that makes us, brutish?*'
> MICHEL DE MONTAIGNE
> *Essay on Virgil*

For the ancient Greeks and Romans, 'obscene' was a theatrical term. Events unfit for public witness took place literally *ob scenus*, 'off stage'. Oedipus re-enters having blinded himself in the wings, a practice still honoured in Shakespeare's *King Lear* some 2,000 years later, where Regan and Cornwall cruelly put out poor Gloucester's eyes ('Out, vile jelly!') out of sight – but not earshot – of the audience. (That we cannot see, but only hear Shakespeare's lurid description, perhaps heightens the horror more than if it were actually portrayed.) So, the obscene was that which would otherwise have drawn attention away from dramatic *meaning*; hidden not out of squeamishness (consider the violent spectacles that both ancients and Elizabethans enjoyed outside of the theatre), but rather a concern for artistic expression. Perhaps, in fact, graphic violence might simply have provided too enjoyable a distraction!

But when did sex become obscene, and the word acquire its specific modern application to sexual acts, or depictions of acts, which are by nature debased and distasteful? For, as Montaigne argues, there is nothing obscene about sex itself, for it is only our attitudes that make it so.

> 'How is man wronged by the genital act, which is so natural, so necessary and so just, that he should not dare to speak of it but with shame, and should exclude it from serious and gentle conversation? Shall we say boldly: kill, rob, betray, but that – only in whispers?'

Thus, we may speak of all manner of terrible acts, but not, it seems, the most natural and joyful of them.

The obvious villain here is the sort of prudery that is often termed 'Victorian'. Gradually, through human history, guilt and shame became grafted onto thought and experience of the sexual act, a pall that the West is still struggling to lift. Montaigne's enlightened scepticism – his questioning of received attitudes – is therefore an early chink of light.

'If in the eyes of God there is but one starry globe, if the sun and moon
and all creation are made for the good of the earth and for the welfare
of man, humanity may be exalted, but is not the Godhead debased? . . .
the earth is but a planet, the rank she holds among the stars is but by
usurpation; it is time to dethrone her'

GIORDANO BRUNO 1548–1600
On the Infinite Universe and Worlds

Bruno was an Italian Dominican monk who rebelled against Catholic
orthodoxy in favour of Copernican *heliocentrism* (the Earth orbits the
Sun), combined with a form of *hylozoism* (all physical matter is imbued
with life). His views brought him into direct conflict not only with the
Church, but also with the prevalent *Scholastic* philosophy, based on
Aristotle, and he spent most of his life wandering through Europe,
before the Inquisition finally caught up with him. He was burnt at the
stake for heresy in 1600.

As is obvious from the quote, Bruno was not just against *geocen-
trism* (the Earth is the centre of the universe), but also against
anthropocentrism: man is not the centre of creation, but merely an
aspect of it. However, whilst this was heretical in orthodox Christian
terms, Bruno saw it as liberating us to appreciate the true wonder of
creation. Everything was alive – even the stars and planets, which, like
'animals', possessed a form of conscious life. Thus, the same divine
spirit pervaded the universe, unifying all its creatures into one being.
To give up the illusion of our privileged position was therefore actually
a 'promotion', for in doing so we share in the totality of everything –
every blade of grass, every planet and supernova: 'Dwellers in a star,
are we not comprehended within the celestial plains, and established
within the very precincts of heaven?'

Inspiring as this vision is, it's easy to see how it got Bruno into
trouble. In his exotic fusion of mysticism, magic and science, the vestiges of orthodox Christianity are all but lost.

> 'For it is hardly possible at one and the same time to gaze with
> admiration upon authors and to excel them, knowledge being like
> water, which does not rise higher than the level from which it
> descended'
> FRANCIS BACON 1561–1626
> *The Great Instauration*

Son of the Lord Keeper, and nephew of the Lord Treasurer, it was only natural that Francis Bacon should aim high. Not content with law and politics, Bacon announced, 'I have taken all knowledge to be my province', and set about revolutionizing philosophy. He is now remembered for his attempts to provide a philosophical underpinning to science, which, even if modern scientists don't exactly follow his prescribed methods, can consider him a founding father.

The problem, Bacon thought, involved how philosophers approached knowledge. Firstly, men of theory contented themselves with merely summarizing and annotating past thinkers (commonly, Aristotle). This is the meaning of the water simile: however profound Aristotle's reservoir of knowledge, merely drawing from this source prevents us ascending higher (we'll ignore the fact that steam rises!). Furthermore, abstract theorizing was all very well, but, in Bacon's famous phrase, 'Knowledge is power': philosophy should ultimately be useful. Secondly, men of invention, though occasionally happening upon useful discoveries, lacked the discipline to establish principles that would allow ordered progress. What was needed was to marry theory to practice.

Bacon's proposed solution was 'true induction'. *Induction* draws a general conclusion from particular observations. So, we see apples, balls, arrows, etc., fall to Earth, and conclude that some force is working on them (gravity). However, induction may also reach incorrect conclusions, especially if we are too hasty in reaching them. Rather than haphazard enthusiasm, or dogmatic abstract theorizing, *true* induction therefore preached patience: as much data as possible should be collected, compared, and analyzed; that data, used to form testable hypotheses, generated new data; and so on. This would shed new light on controversies, and allow us to move toward truth gradually. In short, true induction would help establish 'natural philosophy' (science's old title) on new foundations. Science had begun.

> 'There is a great difference between the idols of the human mind and the ideas of the divine mind . . .'
>
> FRANCIS BACON
>
> *Novum Organum*

Bacon identified four common obstacles to knowledge, termed 'idols'. As the Israelites sinned by worshipping false idols instead of God, so philosophers erred by accepting *mental* idols instead of truth.

Through *Idols of the Tribe*, the human mind, 'like an uneven mirror', 'distorts and corrupts the nature of things by mingling its own nature with it'. Astronomers once assumed planetary orbits were circular, because the mind prefers the more perfect or regular. Unusual events seem more significant than they are: a friend phones when you are thinking about her – but what of all those times you thought of her and she *didn't* phone? These false tendencies are therefore natural assumptions common to all the *tribe* (mankind).

Idols of the Cave spring from limited personal experience and character traits (the 'cave', after Plato, is the human mind). A proud individual is reluctant to admit he is wrong; someone allows personal dislike to influence evaluation of another's opinions; an idea is attractive because it echoes already cherished beliefs. Here, personality gets in the way of the truth.

Idols of the Market-place concern language (our 'trade' in opinions), and the assumption that words truly reflect reality. Words can suggest the existence of illusory things ('phlogiston', 'aether'), or can prove vague or misleading. Confusion results when we use language carelessly: many arguments spring from a simple failure to agree definitions.

Finally, *Idols of the Theatre* denote mistaken theories that have taken root in the common understanding. For example, 'old wives' tales': 'Carrots help you see in the dark', perhaps spread in the Second World War to disguise the fact that the British airmen's excellent night vision stemmed from the invention of radar! However, it primarily refers to false religious or philosophical opinions, where, like an uncritical theatre audience, we become lost in 'imaginary worlds'.

Rejecting these false idols, we are then free to . . . read the mind of God?

> 'We cannot command nature except by obeying her'
> FRANCIS BACON
> *Novum Organum*

Bacon has been attacked by certain feminist academics, who see in him the origin of science's alleged disrespect for nature. Animal testing, ozone depletion, mass deforestation – aren't these all signs of arrogant male contempt for 'Mother Nature', another 'female' to be exploited and dominated? Science sees nature as an organic machine it may tinker with at will.

Central to their case is Bacon's perceived chauvinistic language: nature must be 'hounded as a slave', 'put on the rack', 'raped', her secrets revealed by 'torture':

> 'you have but to hound nature in her wanderings, and you will be able when you like to lead and drive her afterwards to the same place again. Neither ought a man to make scruple of entering and penetrating into those holes and corners when the inquisition of truth is his whole object.'

But this is just a hunting metaphor. As Alan Soble observes:

> 'I suppose that a man who made no scruple of penetrating holes (and corners?) might be a rapist, but he also might be a fox-hunter, a proctologist, or a billiard player.'

Aside from this passage, with its Freudian suggestiveness, scant evidence exists to back feminist claims. 'Nature on the rack' is Leibniz writing *about* Bacon, but for whom 'rack' didn't mean 'torture'. Similarly, nature as machine (*mechanism*) originates with Descartes, whilst Bacon believed nature contained *vital force* or spirit.

Furthermore, as our main quote suggests, Bacon's writings reveal great respect for nature. Man is nature's 'servant and interpreter', whose subtlety 'is far greater than that of the sense of the understanding'; furthermore, using force is pointless because it consequently 'maketh nature more violent'. Bacon occasionally talks of 'pursuing', winning 'victories' over, or 'dissecting' nature, but his writings don't mention 'slave' 'rape', or 'torture' in this context.

Few are unworried by scientific advance, and the feminists may have a point. But their interpretation of Bacon would seem – at best – uncharitable; at worst, a wilful distortion.

> 'A little philosophy inclines man's mind to atheism, but depth in philosophy brings men's minds about to religion'
>
> FRANCIS BACON
> *Of Atheism*

Atheists naturally deny this. Isn't the opposite true? Little thought fosters gullibility and superstition, but careful consideration leads to the logical conclusion that God doesn't exist.

Obviously, terming oneself *a*-theist explains as little as calling oneself *theist*, for as there are different sorts of belief, so there are many possible forms of *un*-belief. An atheist might find religion 'mystifying codswallop', something that simply 'doesn't make sense'. But this isn't really a philosophical position, merely a personal reaction, like saying: 'Other people rate him, but Dickens does *nothing* for me.' If we combine this with the type of thing troubling to the simpler sort of religious believer – the existence (or not) of Adam's navel, a stone so heavy that God can (or can't) lift it – then we can appreciate Bacon's point: it's easy to cobble together an unexamined, half-baked antipathy to religion, based on gut feeling, and call it 'atheism'.

Bacon is himself an interesting case; no run-of-the-mill Christian, but certainly someone whose genuine and deep faith didn't apparently conflict with his scientific and philosophical pursuits. Is this possible today? A recent survey of professional philosophers reveals that almost 73% of respondents accepted or 'leant towards' atheism, whilst only 14% leant the other way (the remainder agnostic).

God no longer plays a direct role in philosophy. Berkeley and Descartes relied heavily on God, and their conclusions fail without him. However, Bacon thought certain questions better left to the theologians. Philosophy is rational, but faith requires going *beyond* reason: 'the more discordant, therefore, and incredible, the divine mystery is, the more honour is shown to God in believing it, and the nobler is the victory of faith'.

Bacon therefore undoubtedly contributed to God's philosophical exile. However, if representative, the survey shows that most philosophers haven't just stopped involving God in argument, they have stopped involving him *altogether*. 'Depth in philosophy' has brought men's minds to atheism.

> '. . . among the excellent acts of that King, one above all hath the
> pre-eminence. It was the erection and institution of an order, or
> society, which we call Saloman's House, the noblest foundation, as we
> think, that ever was upon the earth, and the lantern of this kingdom. It
> is dedicated to the study of the works and creatures of God.'
> FRANCIS BACON
> *New Atlantis*

Published just before his death, the *New Atlantis* represents Bacon's partial vision of an ideal society (it remained uncompleted). However, unlike Thomas More's *Utopia*, Bacon's island of Bensalem is governed by an organization dedicated to scientific advancement, and as such was an inspiration behind the *Royal Society*, and a template for the modern university.

In many respects, Bacon's proposed researches are eerily prescient. He describes a process similar to genetic engineering, creating all manner of creatures where 'we know beforehand of what matter and commixture, what kind of those creatures will arise'. He also describes the utilization of independent energy sources, possessing 'heats, similar to the sun's and heavenly bodies' heats'; refrigeration for preservation of food and other organic material; something similar to genetically modified (GM) crops; communications technology; projected images and holograms; aeroplanes and submarines . . . The list goes on.

Of course, it's easy to accord these 'predictions' greater credibility through hindsight. And yet, it's also difficult *not* to be taken aback by them. It's as if, waking from a dream of the future, Bacon has made some rough notes. However, there is another possibility. Whilst, as some have pointed out, modern science didn't advance in strict accordance with Bacon's prescribed methods (though it followed them in spirit), it is clear from the *New Atlantis* that Bacon clearly understood the *potential* of science. So, whilst his own scientific knowledge was rudimentary (by modern standards), he understood the way science *could* work, and thus what it was capable of. He was therefore confident – enough to petition parliament for funding – that incredible things were within our reach, if we only proceed methodically, with an open mind, and put in the necessary legwork.

'I do not feel obliged to believe that the same God who has endowed us with senses, reason, and intellect has intended us to forgo their use and by some other means to give us knowledge which we can attain by them'

GALILEO GALILEI 1564–1642
letter to Grand Duchess Christina, 1615

Italian renaissance philosopher, astronomer, and arguably the father of modern science, we are indebted to Galileo not only for his many individual discoveries (both theoretical and practical), but also for his overall championing of empirical investigation. If we are to understand the world, he said (as the above quote suggests), we must trust the evidence of our senses in line with the guidance of our reason.

This said, the degree to which he actually relied on practical experiment is disputed: the famous instance where he was supposed to have dropped cannon and musket balls from the top of the Leaning Tower of Pisa (thereby disproving Aristotle's assertion that heavier objects fall faster than lighter ones) arguably never took place. Rather, he seems to have relied on much smaller workshop-based experiments involving balls and slopes, and – less practically – imaginative thought experiment (which isn't in itself 'unscientific', for it is a tool that even such modern greats as Einstein was very fond of. However, to whatever degree, the shift in emphasis that Galileo helped bring about seems based on a greater courage to accept evidence over dogma and pre-conceived opinions.

However, there is also a prevalent misconception here: prior to Galileo, it is not as if no one paid attention to sensory evidence. The practice of detailed astronomical observation went back thousands of years, and Galileo wasn't the first to look up with a critical and puzzled eye. Rather, such discoveries as that the Earth went around the Sun were simply signs that certain people were ready to attempt a parallel shift in *their own* centre of gravity: faith and trust in authority, though they gave meaning and security, were no longer enough; people, as individuals, needed to know *for themselves*.

As adopted children trace their birth parents, or American politicians
the village in Ireland where their great-great-grandfather grew up,
man desires to establish context and pedigree for his existence. In this
spirit, Irish Archbishop James Ussher calculated the creation of the
world occurred as evening fell on 23rd October 4004 BC (710 according
to French scholar Joseph Scaliger's dating system – obviously, Ussher
thought Scaliger was wrong!).

Ussher used Biblical reference: Babylonian King Nebuchadnezzar
died 3442 years after creation, historical records dating this in 562 BC.
Therefore, 3442 + 562 = 4004 BC. The 23rd of October is the Sunday
closest to the Autumn Equinox, the beginning of the Jewish New Year,
and therefore the most likely point for time to begin.

Passing over the trustworthiness of Ussher's Biblical scholarship,
historical records, or even the Biblical account itself, the main argument against *creationism* (as it's known) is its contradiction of
biological, geological, and astronomical evidence. Contemporary science declares, judging by the gradual formation of landmasses, that
the Earth is 4,500 million years old. The oldest fossil records suggest
life began 1,000 million years later, with *Homo Sapiens* originating
200,000 years ago. Finally, astrophysicists argue the Big Bang happened over 13 billion years ago, an event that is still causing the
universe to expand.

Denying this not only disregards scientific consensus, but questions why, like a furniture maker *antiquing* a piece of furniture, or a
forger replicating the *craquelure* effect on oil paint, God has created an
artificially aged world, complete with dinosaur fossils, billion-year-old
rock formations, and other 'false trails'. Whilst some creationists
aren't so inflexibly literal, all face the same problem: isn't it simpler to
admit that religious doctrine was never intended to provide a *scientific*
account of the world?

'In such condition . . . the life of man [would be], solitary, poor, nasty, brutish, and short'
THOMAS HOBBES 1581–1679
Leviathan

The above quotation from the English philosopher Thomas Hobbes is often misconstrued. Hobbes was not arguing that this is what life *is* like, but rather that it is what life *would* be like *if* man lived in a 'state of nature' (that is, prior to the formation of civilized society with its laws and institutions). In other words, without a society in which the populace are protected from each other by the enforcement of just laws, there would be anarchy – a 'war of every man against every man'. So, whilst Hobbes was pessimistic about human nature, this was simply part of his argument for the need for a powerful state. This is the *leviathan* referred to in the title of his major work, an all-powerful and autocratic ruler or government that would ensure peace and security, and would protect the members of society both from outside aggressors, and from themselves.

Of course, the problem with this social model is all too obvious: what if the 'just ruler' turns out to be a tyrant, or the duly elected government becomes a fascist regime? What, then, are the people to do? This is a difficulty for Hobbes, because the ruler is meant to be obeyed, and the only occasion on which civil disobedience is justified is if the ruler proves to be weak or ineffective. So, if the government fails to protect its people, or allows social unrest or lawlessness, then a revolution may be the only course to get society back on track. But isn't this a circular argument? Hobbes is basically saying that civil disobedience is justified . . . if there is civil disobedience! To justify a revolution, all we therefore need to do is to start one! Hobbes' view of human nature therefore comes through in the end: the strongest will rule, and if they are overthrown, then they were not truly the strongest, and were not fit to rule in the first place.

'Suppose [someone] had a basket full of apples and, being worried that some of the apples were rotten, wanted to take out the rotten ones to prevent the rot spreading. How would he proceed? Would he not begin by tipping the whole lot out of the basket? And would not the next step be to cast his eye over each apple in turn, and pick up and put back in the basket only those he saw to be sound, leaving the others?'

RENÉ DESCARTES 1595–1650
from the 'Seventh Replies' to the *Meditations*

Doubt is generally considered a terrible thing – crippling alike for the groom before the altar, the candidate for holy orders, and the hacksaw-wielding surgeon – but it actually proves a very useful *philosophical* tool.

French philosopher René Descartes recognized that most of our beliefs are a hodge-podge of unexamined assumptions, half-digested experiences, and half-baked opinions, and set out to put this right. His approach has become known as the *method of doubt*, whereby – as indicated in the above 'basket of apples' analogy – we tip out all our ideas and opinions and examine them one by one. Some, we will find, are 'rotten', infected by the possibility of falsehood, and should be removed lest they infect the rest; others, however, are sound, and we should set these aside, both as examples of what good healthy ideas should look like, and as foundations for the other types of knowledge that we hope to acquire afterwards.

These 'foundational ideas' are immensely important, for without them we are subject to the ravages of *global scepticism* – that is, that *all* of our ideas might be false. Sense impressions can mislead us, we may be dreaming, and – to update Descartes's example somewhat – we may even be purposely deceived by some evil scientist, maintaining our disembodied brain in a vat of chemicals, whilst force-feeding us a computer-simulated *virtual* reality. Is nothing, then, immune to doubt? What is it that makes a philosophical apple sound and healthy? Read on . . .

'I think, therefore I am'
René Descartes
Discourse on Method

The above words – or, in the Latin in which they were originally published, *cogito ergo sum* – are perhaps the most famous in Western philosophy. But what do they mean? In his search for those all-important foundational ideas on which to establish certainty, Descartes reaches his final and most extreme expression of doubt: perhaps there exists an 'evil demon' who, combining God's omnipotence with a diabolical malevolence, has set out to deceive him as to the nature of everything that he perceives (or, according to the modern equivalent just considered, an evil scientist keeping his brain in a vat). And yet, it is in this most philosophically bleak of places that Descartes discovers his one indubitable truth: if I am deceived, then it is at least true that I exist, for to be deceived *implies* existence.

Let's put this another way: doubting is a form of thought; to think, one must exist in some way (it would be inconceivable *not* to exist in some form *whilst* also thinking); therefore, doubting that I exist, since it involves a form of thinking, is a contradiction in terms. We might, Descartes concedes, doubt that the physical world exists, or even – since it is part of the physical world – that our own body exists. But we cannot use the very organ of doubt (our conscious mind) to doubt its own existence.

But *what* exists? Subsequent commentators have questioned Descartes's right to claim the existence of a unified self. David Hume argued that we can only ever experience our thoughts and impressions, and not their cause, and Nietzsche pointed out that there is no guarantee that it is the *same* self that thinks from moment to moment. Science has also weighed in: study of so-called 'split brain' patients (where the connection between the two hemispheres is severed) has revealed that there are at least two 'selves' which can act independently. Perhaps, then, the *cogito* is not the foundation that Descartes thinks it is.

> '[Therefore,] it is certain that I, that is to say my mind, by which I am
> what I am, is entirely and truly distinct from my body, and may exist
> without it'
> RENÉ DESCARTES
> *Meditations*

Following the *cogito* argument, Descartes is now certain that he's 'a thinking thing'. That is, his essence – what makes him what he is – consists in the activity of thinking. He may *have* a body, but he is not *essentially* a body. He knows this because he can conceive of himself without a body, but not without the capacity for thinking, for that would be simply not to exist (which is, really, what the *cogito* attempts to prove).

Matter, then, is a completely different type of *stuff* to that of mind: it has dimensions (length, breadth, height), mass, and objective existence. Mind, on the other hand, is dimensionless, has no physical properties, and is subjectively experienced (exists for each individual). This view, that reality consists of two *substances*, is known as *dualism*.

One problem, which Descartes's contemporaries highlighted, is how this purely immaterial, thinking thing could in fact fulfil the role of the mind as we know it. A mind that is 'entirely and truly distinct from the body, and may exist without it' thereby has no physical parts – but then how does it affect physical nerves and muscles? Receive impressions from the senses? A physical effect requires a physical cause, doesn't it? But if all interaction is physical (as science argues), then there can be no interaction between physical (material) and mental (immaterial) substances. Descartes's self is therefore a ghostly thing, a passive and ineffectual passenger in an otherwise concrete world.

The *problem of interaction* – aside from how such a ghostly entity can be said to exist in the first place – is the main stumbling block for dualism. And yet, as any casual survey of contemporary philosophy of mind will show you, the problem is still a live one. For whilst it seems inconceivable that a 'ghost' can affect matter, it seems equally perplexing that a lump of physical stuff can be conscious.

'The idea, I say, of a being supremely perfect, and infinite, is in the highest degree true; for although, perhaps, we may imagine that such a being does not exist, we cannot, nevertheless, suppose that his idea represents nothing real . . . It is likewise clear and distinct in the highest degree, since whatever the mind clearly and distinctly conceives as real or true, and as implying any perfection, is contained entire in this idea.'

RENÉ DESCARTES
Meditations

Though Descartes claims to have found an absolutely certain truth in the *cogito*, it doesn't get him very far – what about the external world? How can he arrive at a true picture of it, or even know that it exists and is not some dream or illusion?

Descartes's answer is God: if he exists, and is – as traditionally conceived – a good and wise being, he would not make us subject to constant deception – would he? Judging by the evidence of my senses, perhaps the world actually exists more or less as I perceive it, and the odd error (optical illusions, mirages) is actually due to me, not God. Therefore, if God exists, he would seem to guarantee knowledge of the world.

But how does Descartes know that God exists? He actually employs two arguments: a variation of St Anselm's *ontological argument*, and what is known as the *trademark argument* (that we possess the idea of God as a sort of 'trademark' or signature left by the 'craftsman' that made us). But, leaving aside the details of these arguments, how does he know that they are true? In other words, how can he trust his own reason? Descartes's answer is that some ideas are more 'clear and distinct' than others: by virtue of certain qualities they possess, they supply their own proof. But how can he trust that those qualities are real, or that his mind perceives them correctly? Well, because God is good and would not deceive us . . . hang on: isn't he using God to guarantee reason, and reason to guarantee God? Isn't he *arguing in a circle*?

> '. . . were there such machines exactly resembling in organs and outward form an ape or any other irrational animal, we could have no means of knowing that they were in any respect of a different nature from animals . . .'
>
> RENÉ DESCARTES
> *Discourse on the Method*

For Descartes, animals were just machines, whilst humans possessed a rational soul. So, whilst human and animal bodies shared similar physical 'mechanisms', humans were distinguished by virtue of their power of *reason*, which was not natural, but rather a gift from God. Conversely, animals, lacking such a soul, were mere clockwork; the product of God's ingenious craftsmanship, but nothing more.

Animals did not possess reason, nor did they possess genuine speech: their 'language' was merely a succession of behavioural grunts and emotive cries. This was in fact proof that they lacked thought, for otherwise they would surely have evolved a way of communicating it, and humans would have developed a way of understanding it. However, neither appears to be the case, therefore they were mindless 'automata', and we could treat them accordingly.

For these views, Descartes has rightly become the *bête noire* of animal rights. Whether or not animals possess cognitive or linguistic skills (and there is some evidence to suggest that some of them – certain apes and dolphins – actually do), there is good reason to recognize (as Jeremy Bentham later argued) that they can *suffer*. However, their treatment aside, the question of their nature remains: are animals machines?

The problem with this view is that, if they are, then so are humans (at least physically). Descartes would have concurred: it was the soul that made humans special. However, given that (a) a great deal of common ground exists between animal and human behaviour, and (b) the physical brain manifestly affects the workings of the mind, it seems that we cannot so neatly distinguish either between animals and humans, *or* between mind and body. Is the distinction between human and animal therefore not one of *kind*, but of *degree*?

> 'I have discovered a truly remarkable proof of this theorem which this
> margin is too small to contain'
> PIERRE DE FERMAT 1601–1665
> notes written in a copy of Diophantus' *Arithmetica*

Rationalist philosophers have always liked maths. In an uncertain
world, mathematical proof is the epitome of certainty. So, Descartes
and Spinoza patterned the structure of their philosophy after Euclid,
the ancient Greek father of geometry, constructing knowledge upon
secure first principles. However, as Gödel and Russell have shown,
maths itself isn't the embodiment of surety that it's been taken to be.
But even if it *were* – and we *could* found maths on rational principles
– there's another problem.

In the margins of a book, French mathematician Pierre de Fermat
briefly noted that he had a proof for a particular theorem, but – unfortunately – no room to outline it. This claim, known as *Fermat's Last
Theorem*, drove mathematicians mad for centuries, and was only
established in 1995 by an extremely long and complex proof.

Briefly, Fermat's theorem takes Pythagoras' famous theorem – $a^2 +
b^2 = c^2$ – as only being true if the numbers are *squared*. There are
numerous sets of numbers (*Pythagorean triples*, as they're called) that
satisfy the equation ($a = 3, b = 4, c = 5$, or $a = 5, b = 12, c = 13$), but no
known numbers that will satisfy (for instance) $a^3 + b^3 = c^3$, or $a^4 + b^4 =
c^4$, and so on.

Having eluded mathematicians for centuries, it's therefore unlikely
that Fermat possessed a correct proof. But since proofs are now so
complex, how do we *know* they're correct? As Keith Devlin, Stanford
Professor of Maths, observes ('What Do Mathematicians (Usually)
Mean by Proof?'), some modern proofs are so long that no one person
could check them in a lifetime. So, has 'proof' changed? 'Would we
say,' he asks, 'that something was a novel if no person could ever read
it?'

This reflects a more general philosophical problem: in an increasingly information-saturated world, with little time to check things,
aren't we more than ever taking things on trust?

'The heart has its reasons of which reason knows nothing'
BLAISE PASCAL 1623–1662
Les Pensées

The French philosopher, physicist and mathematician Blaise Pascal possessed a prodigious intellect and devout faith, but his academic pursuits were always at odds with his religious temperament. Having made important contributions to mathematics and physics at a young age, he was tormented by what such achievements represented: the independence of man from his creator. It was this independence of will which had caused the fall in Eden, and Pascal saw the same temptations in the quest for intellectual truth: reason provided its own basis for knowledge, and thereby took a step away from faith. It also led to the sin of pride, further setting man apart from God: 'Look,' it seems to say, 'at what *I* have achieved.'

At 31, Pascal underwent a mystical experience, causing him to completely turn his back on science, severely limit his mathematical investigations, and confine his philosophical speculations to strictly religious matters. His writings from this point on – *Les Lettres Provinciales* and *Les Pensées*, for which he is now best known – are a popular treatment of religious topics, ranging from arguments in support of religious belief, to attacks on the contemporary abuses and hypocrisy of the Catholic Church.

It is in these latter writings that we find the above quotation. He continues:

'It is the heart which experiences God, and not the reason. This, then, is faith: God felt by the heart, not by the reason.'

Has reason no role to play in faith? Perhaps, but only to clear a path for faith, and not as a cause of faith itself, which is a gift from God. But Pascal also argued that reason alone was insufficient for any aspect of life, for many things are logically possible which are not in fact true – how then to decide between them? 'We know truth, not only by the reason, but also by the heart': to recognize truth, we must also feel it.

> 'Belief is a wise wager. Granted that faith cannot be proved, what harm will come to you if you gamble on its truth and it proves false? If you gain, you gain all; if you lose, you lose nothing. Wager, then, without hesitation, that He exists.'
>
> BLAISE PASCAL
> *Les Pensées*

Reason cannot prove God's existence; faith is needed. Without faith, one must wait for a change of heart; it cannot be forced, but must come of its own accord. However, reason can encourage faith, preparing the ground so that, if or when it arrives, it has reason's backing.

Let's look at this through gambler's eyes. Your stake: your immortal soul/your Earthly happiness; your winnings, your eternal reward/the consequences of choosing aright. You have four options: don't believe, he doesn't exist, and you maximize a life chasing earthly pleasures; don't believe, he *does* exist, and – depending on how earnestly you chased those earthly pleasures – you reap an eternity of suffering; believe, he doesn't exist, but since (let's assume) no God equals no afterlife either, you have no opportunity to regret your dull and pointless life of religious conformity; finally, believe, he *does* exist, and you hit the jackpot. This last choice has the greatest reward and the least risk. If you didn't bet on this, and it turned out to be true, then you have maximum losses – for what is eternal reward next to a single life's pleasure and pain? You gambled your soul and lost. And if it were *not* true? Well, at least you played the odds!

Critics point out that gambling isn't really a good basis for faith. What sort of person would accept such a wager, and how would God judge such a person? Others focus on Pascal's dismissal of the godless life: why can't an atheist's life be equally noble and meaningful? However, others take issue with the odds themselves: given the many different religions, and therefore many gods, which should we gamble on? And if we choose incorrectly . . .?

> 'In regard to intellect and true virtue, every nation is on a par
> with the rest, and God has not in these respects chosen one
> people rather than another'
> BENEDICTUS DE SPINOZA 1632–1677
> *Theological-Political Treatise*

Born Baruch de Spinoza, his Sephardic Jewish family had fled persecution in Portugal and sought refuge, like many freethinkers and
victims of religious persecution (John Locke would later do so), in the
liberal protection of Amsterdam. However, his unconventional ideas
brought him into conflict with the Jewish religious community there,
and, at 23, he was declared *cherem*, as is the Hebrew term, and effectively excommunicated. However, in the traditional formula used for
the pronouncement, Spinoza was also cursed:

> '. . . cursed be he by day, and cursed be he by night; cursed be he
> when he lieth down, and cursed be he when he riseth up; cursed
> be he when he goeth out, and cursed be he when he cometh
> in . . .'

Which, I think you'll agree, just about covers everything. However,
more significantly, he was also shunned by all other members of the
Jewish community, who were not to

> 'communicate with him verbally or in writing, nor show him any
> favour, nor stay under the same roof with him, nor be within four
> cubits of him, nor read anything composed or written by him.'

Isolated but undaunted, he changed his name to 'Benedictus' (the Latin
equivalent of Baruch, meaning 'blessed'), and continued to develop
unconventional philosophical and religious views. In his *Theological-
Political Treatise* he condemns religious intolerance, criticizes the narrow
mindedness and superstition of organized religion, and advocates secular government. At his untimely death (aged 45), he was in the process
of translating the Old Testament into Dutch, with a view to bringing a
more historical and scientific attitude to scriptural scholarship.

And yet, whilst heretical to both Jews and Christians, Spinoza's
philosophy was really an attempt to combine religion and philosophy.
He therefore remains an enigma to his modern admirers, both religious and secular, of which there are a growing number.

> 'Individual things are nothing but modifications of the attributes of God, or modes by which the attributes of God are expressed in a fixed and definite manner'
>
> BENEDICTUS DE SPINOZA
>
> *Ethics*

Spinoza's fellow rationalist, Descartes, also sometimes found himself in opposition to Church teachings. It's little wonder then that Spinoza, wandering much farther and more daringly from the paths of orthodoxy, should have caused greater controversy.

Firstly, Spinoza identifies an 'asymmetry' in Descartes's thought. Descartes's world had two substances – mind and matter – plus God. However, whilst Aristotle thought that each individual thing – 'Nigel', 'that tree' – was itself a substance, Descartes argued that all physical things were part of the *same* physical stuff. So, just as all things made out of clay are essentially clay, so physical things are just differently shaped examples of the same substance. However, since Descartes – as nature is said to – abhorred a vacuum, then empty space was really an illusion. In reality, physical stuff extends over *every* part of conceivable space – matter was itself space. Physical objects were really individual shapings of one universal clay possessing no true individuality, and which might be 'remoulded' into a different 'shape' at any moment. All matter was *one*.

However, Descartes's mental stuff didn't pervade the universe, but was packaged into individual minds. Intrigued by Descartes's bold concept of physical stuff, Spinoza asked why we couldn't do the same for mental stuff (thus making our conceptions of mental and physical stuff *symmetrical*): what if each mind is not separate, but actually a manifestation of one *unifying* consciousness? What if, furthermore, 'mind' and 'matter' are not distinct substances at all, but merely different aspects of the *same* substance? And what if this were God?

So, there are no individuals, physical or mental; no duality of substances, only one: God. This is called *panentheism*. Unlike *pantheism* (which Spinoza is sometimes accused of), where God is nature, panentheism sees God as present *in* the world (*immanent*), but also beyond it (*transcendent*). Thus, humans merely experience *two* of his aspects, which are in fact infinitely many.

> 'The mind has greater power over the emotions and is less subject
> thereto, in so far as it understands all things as necessary'
> BENEDICTUS DE SPINOZA
> *Ethics*

Spinoza was a determinist, for whom human freedom was an illusion. We think we have conscious, rational choice, but are actually driven by emotion. Furthermore, the only thing that can overcome an emotion is another emotion: compassion might overcome anger, for example. However, we've no control in this process either, so are we merely puppets in an empty show?

We can never achieve mastery of emotion, because it is the effective cause of action (it's how action is motivated and produced), in relation to which rational thought is a powerless bystander. However, we have a degree of freedom in relation to how we choose to *react* to our emotions. In understanding and accepting emotions, we switch from experiencing them as passive victims, to identifying with them as active agents: I *am* my emotion, and it is necessary that I feel this way at this particular moment.

There's something of the Eastern sage about Spinoza. We aren't wholly conscious, rational agents, nor are we in fact separate individual selves. Realizing this therefore gives us freedom from illusion. It's as if we're the passenger in a car: we aren't driving, so we sit back and trust that the driver knows the way. But if all things are *necessary* (cannot be any other way), then doesn't that also include my thoughts, and therefore my ability to come to terms with my emotions? So, trusting the driver, and accepting the route we take, would seem to be as much out of our control as the movement of the car itself.

However, we shouldn't be too hard on Spinoza here: any attempt to combine free will and determinism is fraught with paradox. And yet, we seem to require both: without belief in causation, life would be unintelligible; without free will, unendurable. Perhaps, then, we should just accept the paradox. But is even *this* within our power?

> 'For to imprint anything on the mind, without the mind's perceiving it, seems to me hardly intelligible. If therefore *children* and *idiots* have souls, have minds, with those impressions upon them, they must unavoidably perceive them, and necessarily know and assent to these truths, which since they do not, it is evident that there are no such impressions.'
>
> JOHN LOCKE 1632–1704
> *An Essay Concerning Human Understanding*

Like Francis Bacon, John Locke juggled his philosophical interests with a career in politics. However, his political affiliations eventually forced him into hiding, providing time to dedicate to philosophy.

Locke's philosophical contribution is on two main fronts: politics and theory of knowledge. The second is perhaps the most important of these, marking a radical break with tradition. Many philosophers held that at least some of our knowledge was *innate* (present from birth). Descartes, for instance, claimed we have an innate idea of God, and even Bacon, who stressed the importance of experience in acquiring knowledge, held that seeds of certain ideas were inherent.

Locke, however, considered the mind a *tabula rasa* ('blank slate'), upon which experience 'writes' simple 'ideas' (sense impressions). The mind then works upon these to form more complex concepts. Thus, Locke re-established *empiricist* philosophy, and, with Bishop Berkeley and David Hume, is considered one of the *British Empiricists*.

Locke's argument is simple: if such innate ideas exist, then children, who haven't been taught them, and 'idiots' (in the non-politically-correct sense of lacking general intelligence – for whatever reason), would be aware of them; they aren't, so such ideas don't exist.

We could argue (with Plato) that children and 'idiots' simply haven't yet received the right experiences to trigger these ideas. However, there's a deeper problem: can our minds contain an idea of which we are not – and never have been – aware?

> 'The state of nature has a law of nature to govern it, which obliges every one: and reason, which is that law, teaches all mankind, who will but consult it, that being all equal and independent, no one ought to harm another in his life, health, liberty, or possessions'
>
> JOHN LOCKE
>
> *Two Treatises of Government*

Unlike Hobbes, Locke thought human beings fundamentally rational and decent. However, in a 'state of nature' (without government), they tended to selfishness, especially in matters of property and trade. Locke therefore echoed Hobbes' call for a *social contract*: government agrees to uphold the law, punish wrongdoers and protect citizens, in return for civil obedience.

Locke's political ideas were hugely influential, forming the basis for much of Western democracy, and inspiring the American Constitution and the French Revolution. He argued that all humans possess three *natural rights*: to life; to liberty, or freedom of action (so long as it doesn't affect anyone's right to life); and to property, legitimately obtained (so long as it doesn't infringe on anyone's rights to life or liberty).

It's interesting to note, firstly, how close Locke's ideas are to the US Declaration of Independence's rights to 'Life, Liberty, and the pursuit of Happiness'; and secondly, how an earlier draft of the Declaration was even closer to Locke, including a right to 'the means of acquiring and possessing property'. Why change it?

The substitution of 'happiness' for 'property' *may* reveal a desire to put moral and spiritual concerns above material ones; however, more cynically, we might observe that a government that protects a man's right to acquire property might also find itself in the awkward position of having to regulate trade, protect wages, etc., *so that* he can do so – otherwise, a man who works all hours for a pittance might have difficulty acquiring *anything*. However, this would undermine a fundamental capitalist principle: the right to become rich at the expense of others. After all, it wasn't called the *Starship Happiness* was it?

> 'If any man err from the right way, it is his own misfortune, no injury
> to you; nor therefore are you to punish him in the things of this life
> because you suppose he will be miserable in that which is to come'
>
> JOHN LOCKE
> *A Letter Concerning Tolerance*

Hobbes and Locke also disagreed about how governments should deal with religious diversity. Whereas Hobbes thought religious differences provoked unrest, Locke disagreed: what provoked unrest was *intolerance*. If different religious persuasions are allowed to coexist, a government need only ensure that they don't interfere with one another. Locke therefore also believed in *disestablishment*, or separation of Church and State. He believed that religion shouldn't dictate law, and government shouldn't prescribe religious doctrine, for an official State religion could lead to religious persecution ('Truth, not tolerance', as a recent bumper sticker puts it, which isn't really a recipe for social harmony).

Interestingly, this protection did not extend to atheism, which Locke saw as undermining social practices in general (how could anyone ever swear on a Bible if they didn't believe it meant anything?), or Roman Catholicism, which was more due to political pragmatism (what if the Pope stirred up France or Spain to attack Britain on some religious crusade: which side would British Catholics choose?).

However, whilst dated in certain respects, Locke's principles of tolerance are otherwise extremely liberal. No human can be the judge of another's beliefs because this is an area where we all rely on faith (which might be wrong). Also, not only would attempting to enforce a single faith result in greater unrest, but you cannot force someone, in his heart, to change what he believes; and even if he is wrong, that is his own affair.

In modern times, where radicalism and fundamentalism can manifest not only in unrest but terrorism, some might question Locke's advocacy of tolerance: if we allow complete freedom of belief, won't extremists abuse this? Well, yes, and this is why Locke also proposed one limitation: a belief should itself be tolerant.

> '... whatever has the consciousness of present and past actions, is the
> same person to whom they both belong'
> JOHN LOCKE
> *An Essay Concerning Human Understanding*

What is a person? A body? A mind? An immaterial soul? If the body, then we might imagine a Frankenstein scenario with a patchwork individual consisting of different body parts: *which* person is he? A new one? A composite? Perhaps the mind or soul is the answer. But here we hit a parallel problem: if consciousness requires a substance as its basis, then what happens when that substance enters a different body? This is the same for 'brain transplant' scenarios (if we are materialists) as it is for 'metempsychosis' (the soul inhabiting a different body).

Locke's answer is to concentrate not on *what* a person is made of, but what *makes* a person in the first place: his *consciousness*. Locke therefore distinguishes between *man* (or *human being*), and *person*. A man with someone else's brain is still a man, but that man would now be 'Dave' not 'Nigel'. The reason for this is that he can remember being 'Dave', and Dave's memories provide links from his present to his past experiences. Being the same person is therefore merely a matter of having the right memory connections.

But what if you forget distant memories, or – as sometimes happens – lose recent memories but retain childhood ones? In such cases, the bridge is gone, as is any justification for thinking yourself the same person that your body suggests you've always been. But perhaps there's a workaround: if you can remember yesterday, and *yesterday's* 'you' could remember the day before, and so on, then you have lots of little interconnected bridges into the past.

However, there's a more fundamental problem: how do you know that these are *your* memories? They might be false, fantasy, or even (a futuristic possibility) implanted (as in the film *Total Recall*). In other words, the whole argument assumes what it wants to prove: that you *are* the same person.

> 'You find yourself in the world, without any power, immovable as a
> rock, stupid, so to speak, as a log of wood'
> NICOLAS MALEBRANCHE 1638–1715
> *Dialogues on Metaphysics and Religion*

As we've seen, Descartes's *dualism* saw mind and body as completely different *types* of substance – but how then do they interact? As a follower of Descartes, and similarly keen to safeguard the existence of the soul, Nicolas Malebranche also accepted dualism. However, whereas Descartes's solution to mind-body interaction had been somewhat vague – *somehow*, mind and body 'intermingle', or perhaps interact in the brain – Malebranche proposed a different solution: there isn't any.

But not only is there no interaction between mind and body, there isn't any between physical objects, or indeed between mental ones (thoughts). So, causation is not what we think it is: I think that, when I decide to reach for something, it's my individual thought and volition that cause my hand to move. However, what's actually happening is that, through his omnipotence, God produces the various interactions, linking together what we have come to think of as 'cause' and 'effect'. So, when I want to pick something up, God moves my hand to the object in question. However, more broadly, God also moves each physical thing in its interaction with other physical things – so, in effect, what we think of as the laws of nature are actually the actions of God.

This view is known as *Occasionalism*, for God intervenes on each *occasion* that interaction is necessary – which, since the laws of nature are always in operation, would seem to be all the time. However, not only would this be difficult for non-believers to accept, it was also controversial in its day. Firstly, it seems more straightforward to simply assume that there *is* some interaction: why should we believe that God merely 'choreographs' mind and body like two synchronized swimmers? Secondly, it would seem to leave us without free will, for God causes everything. But then, isn't God responsible for *all* human actions, including evil ones?

> 'I have not been able to discover the cause of those properties of gravity from phenomena, and I frame no hypotheses; for whatever is not deduced from the phenomena is to be called a hypothesis, and hypotheses, whether metaphysical or physical, whether of occult qualities or mechanical, have no place in experimental philosophy'
>
> SIR ISAAC NEWTON 1643–1727
> *Mathematical Principles of Natural Philosophy*

For Isaac Newton, the universe was a grand mechanism, working according to fixed principles and laws. His account went unchallenged right up until the time of Einstein, and laid the foundation for the scientific revolution. However, unlike the French mechanist, Pierre-Simon Laplace, Newton did indeed find room for God – in his life, at least, if not explicitly in his theories.

Newton's laws of motion and universal gravitation didn't require the postulation of mysterious or 'occult' forces, but merely explained how things – whatever their true nature – interacted with one another. In contrast to Descartes, who looked to build up knowledge from first principles, Newton concentrated on what could be shown through experiment and mathematical proof. So, it did not really matter, for scientific purposes, whether matter and spirit were separate substances, or – in Newton's case – exactly what gravity *was*, for progress could be achieved by mathematical description of the laws that govern reality. Of course, we can still investigate how reality is constituted, but the greater importance and practical benefit lay in a purely *mechanical* understanding of how things fit together, and the laws that govern them.

Most intriguing, in light of this, were Newton's religious beliefs. Often described loosely as an 'unorthodox Christian', Newton's enthusiasms actually included alchemy (he had his own alchemical laboratory), astrology, numerology, and attempts through Biblical textual analysis to predict the end of the world (AD 2060 was one date). Newton's reluctance to deal with metaphysical issues therefore works both ways: on the one hand, it allowed science to progress unhindered by pointless controversy; on the other, it left room for views that both Church and science would have found heretical.

'. . . it is not possible for two things to differ from one another in respect of place and time alone, but that it is always necessary that there shall be some other internal difference'
GOTTFRIED WILHELM LEIBNIZ 1646–1716
On the Principle of Indiscernibles

Leibniz's Law, or the *principle of indiscernibles*, claims that two things can't possess *exactly* the same properties. Thus, exact clones, identical to the last molecule, can't exist, for they would only be *externally* different (concerning their circumstances) – something German philosopher Gottfried Wilhelm Leibniz considered impossible. Therefore, seemingly identical things must be in some way *internally* different (possess different *qualities*), for it's the difference between our qualities that makes us distinct in the first place. The fact that I have brown hair and you have blond hair distinguishes us, not that we live in different countries.

However, is this a logical principle, or a belief about the nature of the universe? There doesn't seem to be anything that *forbids* me from hypothetically assuming that qualitatively identical things can exist. Physicists might point out that tiny particles may only differ in terms of their position. However, Leibniz rejects this version of atomic theory: such particles *must*, he says, be different in some respect. But why?

Leibniz argues that the precondition of things having a separate existence, or being in a different place or time, is *that* they are qualitatively different. In other words, in order to occupy a separate space, time, etc., my clone must first differ *qualitatively*. Perhaps we can illustrate Leibniz's point this way: you draw two circles that look identical on a piece of paper. However, since the qualities of the paper differ (due to minute imperfections), then the circles are minutely different. Therefore, the only way they could be identical is if they were drawn in the same place – and therefore be the same circle.

Also, of course, some qualities *can* only be possessed by one thing – 'the world's best golfer', perhaps, or God: the existence of two 'bests' or two 'infinite substances' undermines such concepts. There can't be two Absolutes, can there?

> 'If there were no best among all possible worlds, God would not have created one'
>
> GOTTFRIED WILHELM LEIBNIZ
>
> *Théodicée*

One of the strongest objections to the existence of God is the problem of 'natural evil': the devastating Indian Ocean tsunami of 2004, the 2010 earthquake in Haiti. Unlike moral evil, which requires a human agent, natural evil has no human cause: it is an act of God. How, then, can religious believers excuse it?

Leibniz's famous attempt takes the following form: if God exists, and is all-good, omniscient, etc., then he will necessarily have created the best world possible. We can assume, therefore, that such terrible events have an ultimately benign purpose. In other words, it is either 'all part of God's plan', or else an unavoidable evil in an otherwise perfect world, but either way we can be assured that the world in which we live contains the minimum possible evil.

This view was mercilessly ridiculed in Voltaire's *Candide*, where blithe Leibnizian optimism is embodied in the attitude of Dr Pangloss, who greets a catalogue of catastrophes and disasters merely with the comment that 'all is for the best'. Noses are conveniently shaped for spectacles, pigs are perfectly constituted to be eaten, and stones are extremely handy for building houses. Terrible events must therefore have some hidden purpose, and could not have been any other way: 'if there is a volcano at Lisbon', Pangloss declares, 'it could not have been anywhere else'.

In Dostoevsky's *The Brothers Karamazov*, Ivan questions the explanation that some evil is the necessary cost of the good we have. Why must innocents suffer?

> 'If all must suffer to pay for the eternal harmony, what have children to do with it, tell me, please? It's beyond all comprehension why they should suffer, and why they should pay for the harmony.'

If the suffering of even one innocent is the price of entry to God's world of 'divine harmony', then, Ivan concludes, 'I most respectfully return him the ticket.'

'The nature of peoples is first crude, then severe, then benign, then delicate, finally dissolute'
GIAMBATTISTA VICO 1668–1744
The New Science

The ideas of Giambattista Vico ran very much counter to the intellectual trends of the time, where Descartes's project to provide a rational basis for science and philosophy was still hugely influential. However, whilst for Descartes knowledge should be based on indubitable, 'clear and distinct' truths, Vico saw human knowledge as limited by its origins: reason is not some impartial tool of objective discovery, but has rather developed out of the *irrational* foundations of human culture. In other words, reason is only *human* reason, built upon (and serving) human prejudices and needs.

This also contradicts the idea that civilization continuously progresses in an upward-sloping line from caveman to computer. Whilst not against the idea of progress, Vico viewed history as cyclical, moving in an upward spiral of repeating stages: the age of Gods, of Heroes, and finally Men. Originally, societies were theocratic, ruled by religious decree; then emerged kings and conquerors, and physical conflict; finally, men evolved rational laws to ensure freedom and equality. However, this final period – the goal of the 17th and 18th century *Enlightenment* movement – was fragile, likely to regress back into barbarism. And so the process began again – but at a higher level, building gradually upon the lessons of the past.

Vico's ideas are therefore a warning against imbalance and overreaching: rationalism is a fine goal, but should we consider objectivity and knowledge as worthy goals *in themselves*, even where they seem to rob life of meaning? This is a real danger, but not one that is widely recognized: as certain elements in society become more rational, attacking what they see as 'irrational' and 'superstitious', there's a correspondingly hostile reaction. People don't like to be told that their traditional beliefs are deluded, especially where the alternative seems to be *nihilism* (belief in nothing). Perhaps, then, we are not as securely on the path of relentless progress as we think: perhaps, in fact, we teeter on the brink of decline.

'I refute it thus!'
DR SAMUEL JOHNSON ON BERKELEY'S IDEALISM 1685–1753
in James Boswell, *The Life of Samuel Johnson*

Unlikely as it now seems, Irish philosopher Bishop George Berkeley saw himself as returning common sense to philosophy. Philosophers such as Descartes and Locke had proposed that we do not perceive the world directly, but merely representations of it – *ideas*, in an older and broader sense of the term. But, if we can never directly perceive the 'real' world, how do we know that it exists? Thus, we open the door to scepticism.

Berkeley's answer was simply to make *ideas* the true reality (hence *idealism*). Consequently, there was no such thing as 'matter', because this would represent an unperceivable substance (and hence something to be sceptical as to the existence of). In his famous Latin phrase, *esse est percipi*, 'to be is to be perceived', everything that exists must be perceived by someone. Berkeley's favourite proof was to question the ability to think of something that could exist independently of being perceived. Of course, as soon as we think of something, we are – in Berkeley's sense – perceiving it (i.e. forming an *idea* of it). But what about the existence of things when we are not perceiving them? Does the chair on which I am sitting cease to exist when I am not perceiving or thinking about it? Berkeley's response was to call in God, whose eternal awareness of all things guarantees that they do not pop in and out of being.

Unsurprisingly, few appreciated this solution. In his biography of the cantankerous man of letters, Dr Samuel Johnson, James Boswell recounts a discussion of Berkeley's idealism. Irritated with what he saw as abstract nonsense, Johnson kicked a large stone: 'I refute it *thus!*' However, this merely illustrates a prevalent misconception: Berkeley didn't argue that the world consists of wisps of airy nothing, but simply that 'solidity' is itself merely another type of *idea*. A sore toe, or any other test of 'materiality', is therefore no refutation at all.

> 'If a tree falls in the forest, and there is no one there to hear it, does it
> make a sound?'
>
> UNKNOWN

It's still quite common to hear this quotation (the precise source of which is unknown) – often in the form of a riddle, or an unanswerable question. Sometimes, when someone finds out that you are interested in philosophy, it is repeated as a piece of wisdom, or else proof of philosophy's profound nature. But few seem to know what it actually means.

As previously explained, Berkeley believed that to exist is to be perceived, and that nothing exists which is not in some sense the object of perception. In Berkeley's idealism, God perceives everything, so *he* hears the sound. However, with other forms of idealism – which reject God's role – the answer is less clear.

Firstly, sound, as commonly conceived, is a human construct, for what a dog, a bat, or a human hears, will all be different. However, whilst most people admit this, they also seem to assume that there is still *something* that exists independently of any hearer – whether animal or human. What if we were to put a sound recorder in the forest? Yes, but then we would listen to it (we would be there by proxy). Could we measure sound vibrations using some sort of audio-sensitive device? But is that really 'sound', or just a set of vibrations? And we still need humans to identify those vibrations as 'sound' – to 'translate' the measurements. Slowly, it begins to dawn on us that, whilst *something* seems to happen when no one is there, we can only really call it 'sound' in relation to our actual or hypothetical presence – if I *were* there, then I would hear it.

Of course, this doesn't just apply to sound, but to all our sense impressions and concepts – the colour of the tree, its size, smell and texture. Are these features of the tree as it exists, or merely *constructions* that the human mind has assembled?

> 'What is tolerance? It is the consequence of humanity. We are all
> formed of frailty and error; let us pardon reciprocally each other's folly
> – that is the first law of nature.'
> VOLTAIRE 1694–1778
> *Tolerance*

Voltaire was the pen name of François-Marie Arouet, one of the leading intellects of the *Enlightenment*. A French writer, critic and philosopher, Voltaire championed free speech and religious tolerance, his ideas forming a cornerstone of Western democracy. He was also a biting critic of religious hypocrisy and dogmatism, and is perhaps most famous for *Candide*, his satirical attack on Gottfried Leibniz's philosophical optimism (that this is 'the best of all possible worlds'.

However, as much as this might seem to make him a forerunner of atheistic rationalism, Voltaire was in fact what is termed a *Deist*, believing in a deity whose existence and nature was compatible with the dictates of reason, and who was independent of any one religion. This approach is known as *natural theology*, to distinguish it from *revealed theology*: knowledge of God is arrived at through reason, and not solely based on scripture, which may accordingly be viewed as the product of *human* hands, and therefore not free from error or bias. So, if dogma contradicts reason, then reason should win out.

This obviously has benefits: deists are not obliged to believe in anything 'irrational' or without proof – miracles, or spiritual visitations, perhaps – so science and religion can coexist (more) happily; also, different faiths may find a common ground of core beliefs, thus promoting tolerance. However, there are also dangers: that something does not comply with reason does not mean that it is false. Therefore, if we use rational principles to vet our religious beliefs, then there is a real risk that we end up with 'religion lite', a handy pocket-sized edition that doesn't take up any metaphysical space in our rational belief system, but which is fundamentally a distortion. For if the 'God of the philosophers' does not, in some sense, 'passeth all understanding', then is he really God?

'The human body is a machine which winds its own springs'
JULIEN OFFRAY DE LA METTRIE 1709–1751
Man a Machine

La Mettrie was a French philosopher and physician, now famous for his *mechanism*: man isn't, as Descartes thought, a soul in a body, but an organic machine that regulates itself ('winds its own springs') through nutrition, exercise and rest. Thus, when the springs finally wind down, the 'soul' expires. As such, La Mettrie was one of the first atheistic materialists. Ironically, whilst one of Descartes's main motives was to reinforce faith with philosophy, his division of mind and body, and especially his view of the latter as a purely mechanical organism, made it easier than before for materialists to formulate a non-spiritual view of man.

La Mettrie's materialism was highly controversial during his day, and he published most of his works anonymously or under a pseudonym. Even so, his books were burned, and he was even at one point forced to flee Holland (then known as a bastion of tolerance). And yet, all La Mettrie was really arguing for was the unity of the individual. His other well-known work – *Man a Plant* – reveals that it was not so much the *mechanical* aspect of materialism that interested him, but the absence of mysterious entities (soul, spirit), and the possibility that science and medicine might better comprehend – and therefore treat – a purely physical organism. He postulates, 'Man is so complicated a machine that it is impossible to get a clear idea of the machine beforehand'; accordingly, all purely *a priori* (theoretical) speculation is pointless: knowledge lies in investigation.

No one would disagree with this, but – and this is the general problem with *positivist* science – we should not mistake a method of enquiry for an account of what exists. As Korzybski later argued, 'the map is not the territory'. In other words, simply because science may best proceed by sensory evidence – treating things in terms of mechanical cause and effect – it doesn't mean that *this is all there is.*

> 'It cannot be truly said, according to the ordinary use of language, that a malicious man, let him be ever so malicious, cannot hold his hand from striking, or that he is not able to show his neighbour kindness . . . In the strictest propriety of speech, a man has a thing in his power, if he has it in his choice, or at his election; and a man cannot be truly said to be unable to do a thing when he can do it if he will.'
>
> JONATHAN EDWARDS 1703–1758
> *Freedom of the Will*

Schooled in the Puritanism of John Calvin, but drawn also to the rational and scientific ideas of Locke and Newton, American theologian Jonathan Edwards sought to blend aspects of both. This is most apparent in his famous treatise, *Freedom of the Will*, which argues that *determinism* is compatible with divine judgement.

If we're predestined to sin, and our will is 'depraved' or ineffective without divine grace, doesn't God destine sinners to damnation? Edwards attempted to wriggle out of this by distinguishing between 'natural inability' to do something, and 'moral inability'. Natural inability represents something that cannot be changed – we cannot fly unaided, or hold our breath for an hour; but moral inability is related to will – the violent man and the drunkard can reform if they choose.

However, having suggested a resolution, Edwards seems to undermine it by attempting to account for moral action in terms of *causation*. So, we do *x* because it is caused by our 'strongest motive', the result of habit and previous choice. But weren't those previous actions *also* based on the 'strongest motive'? But we cannot both *choose* our strongest motive *and* be influenced by it!

This seems to paint Edwards into a corner – or does it? Like Augustine, he argues that whilst we need God for salvation, our actions are our own. This is because will is linked to *understanding*, which isn't subject to causation: in apprehending goodness, and allowing that to form our choices (not habit), we may therefore willingly seek God's grace.

'If we take in our hand any volume; of divinity or school metaphysics, for instance; let us ask, Does it contain any abstract reasoning concerning quantity or number? No. Does it contain any experimental reasoning concerning matter of fact and existence? No. Commit it then to the flames: for it can contain nothing but sophistry and illusion.'

DAVID HUME 1711–1776
An Enquiry Concerning Human Understanding

I love a good book burning! 'Divinity' refers to theology, and 'school' to medieval philosophy (*Scholasticism*), both, for Hume, prone to unverifiable *metaphysical* assertions. 'Metaphysics' here has, perhaps for the first time in philosophy, a negative sense. Previously, it merely described things beyond experience: the soul, God, true reality. But if *beyond* sense experience, and not matters of science or logic, isn't it just *nonsense*?

This distinction is called *Hume's Fork*. 'Relations of ideas' concern logic and mathematics (triangles have three sides, $2 + 6 = 8$, nothing is simultaneously true and false). Such observations are certain, but not especially informative, for they merely tell us how ideas *relate*. 'Matters of fact', however, *are* informative, but depend on sense experience (which may be doubtful or inconclusive). As an *empiricist*, Hume believed most knowledge requires sense experience, and together with logic, constituted the whole of philosophy and science. What else is there?

Logical positivism later adopted this as the *verification principle*: statements are only meaningful if *verifiable* by actual or possible sense experience, or according to the meaning of their terms. So, 'All bachelors are unmarried' is true from the meanings of 'bachelor' and 'unmarried'; 'There is a chair in the corner', if I can see it, feel it; but 'Murder is wrong', or 'God loves us like a father' are not purely logical truths, and what evidence could establish them?

However, even if true, 'nonsense' seems too strong. Many things fail Hume's test, so perhaps it's just too strict. Besides, the distinction seems to suffer at its own hands: the observation isn't either matter of fact or empirical observation – is it, then, *nonsense*?

> 'The man who has fed the chicken every day throughout its life at last wrings its neck instead, showing that more refined views as to the uniformity of nature would have been useful to the chicken'
>
> BERTRAND RUSSELL ON HUME'S PROBLEM OF INDUCTION
> *The Problems of Philosophy*

How often something happens increases our expectation of its continuing to happen – the neighbour walking his dog at 7 am, the purple car always parked outside number 6. However, as with Russell's chicken, things may suddenly change: the neighbour walks his dog at 6:30 am, or moves away; the purple car owner buys a pink one, or invests in a bike.

We call this *inductive* knowledge – based on the process of *induction* – which establishes a general conclusion based on particular observations. You will see that none of the examples given above involve certainty, because things can change. However, what about science? We arrive at scientific laws by induction, performing experiments to discover the laws that underlie various phenomena. Isn't *this* knowledge certain?

No. Originating with Hume, this is known as the 'problem of induction': it might *appear* inconceivable that certain 'laws' might change (gravity ceases to operate, the Earth spins the other way), but these things are not *impossible*, merely, given past experience, *improbable*. So, even if nature is uniform (its laws are fixed and unchanging everywhere), our knowledge of them depends on experience, which can change. It's always amusing to hear scientists dismiss some newly alleged fact or theory on the basis that it would 'contravene the laws of nature!' Well, no, it wouldn't: whatever the new phenomenon (walking on water, perpetual motion), it would only contravene *our knowledge* of those laws.

We do not, as Hume put it, experience the fixed and unchanging 'necessary connection' between causes and effects, but merely their 'constant conjunction' (their repeatedly appearing together); things happen again and again, and we expect them to keep happening. 'Laws' then are merely hopeful predictions that currently fit our experience. We are, it seems, no better than the chicken.

'It is not contrary to reason to prefer the destruction of the whole world to the scratching of my finger'

DAVID HUME
A Treatise Upon Human Nature

Not contrary to reason, perhaps, but contrary to most sane people's preferences. Hume's point is that morality is closer to desire and emotion (what he termed the 'passions') than to reason. So, whilst it isn't technically *irrational* to prefer world destruction to an injury that requires a small plaster, it would go against most people's natural instincts and desires, which are the basis of morality.

Hume drew a 'sharp' distinction – what some call *Hume's Guillotine* – between descriptive, factual statements, and *prescriptive*, moral ones. So, 'Compassion is good', really says two separate things: firstly, that compassion is *generally considered* good (*describing* that moral attitude); secondly, that you ought to be compassionate (*prescribing* that act).

Suppose you like cakes. You pass a bakery, and your friend says, 'Look: they have cakes. You should buy one.' Now, it's a fact that you like cake, but does that mean you *should* buy one? Perhaps you are dieting, or allergic to certain ingredients. So, the fact that you like cake doesn't *oblige* you to do anything; as for cake, so for morality.

This is termed the 'is-ought gap', existing between '*x is* good', and 'you *ought* to do *x*'. Since Hume identified it, philosophers have tried to bridge it. For instance, John Searle argues that certain moral statements automatically imply an obligation: if you say, 'I promise to do *x*', then – to be factually correct, consistent and rational – you must actually fulfil your promise.

However, what if the meaning of the word 'promise' were to change? Perhaps it comes to mean, 'something we don't always have to fulfil' (which is probably how most people treat it anyway!). In which case, it is not irrational or inconsistent *not* to fulfil it. So, I promise to go to the cinema, but don't. You know, I *wanted* to, I really did, but I had this scratch on my finger . . .

> '. . . when I enter most intimately into what I call *myself*, I always
> stumble on some particular perception or other, of heat or cold, light
> or shade, love or hatred, pain or pleasure. I never can catch *myself* at
> any time without a perception, and never can observe any thing but the
> perception.'
>
> DAVID HUME
> *A Treatise of Human Nature*

Hume therefore concludes that the self is 'nothing but a bundle or collection of different perceptions'. This 'bundle theory' of self is a direct consequence of Hume's empiricism: knowledge requires sense impressions; when I try for an impression of myself, I only ever receive impressions of *other* things (heat, light, love, pain); therefore, perhaps there *is* no self.

The same, of course, can be said of the world: I *try* to gain an impression of the chair itself, but all I ever get are shades of colour, texture, light and shade, and so on. Philosophers call this the *veil of perception*: if we could draw back the veil, perhaps we would see things as they really are? However, it doesn't make sense to say that we can have an *impression* of things as they are *beyond our impression* of them! Similarly, then, what would an impression of the self look or feel like? It would look and feel like being conscious. But of what? Of thoughts and feelings. Therefore, just as it doesn't make sense to have an impression of a world beyond our impressions, it doesn't make sense to talk of having an impression of the thing *that has* impressions!

Eastern philosophies tend to have a better and more practised grip on these slippery questions. As a Zen poem puts it, the self is

> 'Like a sword that cuts, but cannot cut itself;
> Like an eye that sees, but cannot see itself.'

'Self', then, may be a process, not a thing. We may catch glimpses of it in action (when self-aware, or analyzing perceptions), but we are like a cat chasing its tail. A Manx cat, maybe.

'When anyone tells me, that he saw a dead man restored to life, I immediately consider with myself, whether it be more probable, that this person should either deceive or be deceived, or that the fact, which he relates, should really have happened'

DAVID HUME

An Enquiry Concerning Human Understanding

Long experience establishes knowledge of causes, but miracles, by definition, are extremely rare. So there will always be more plausible interpretations of such events. A witness may be lying, or himself the victim of deception, or he may be drunk, drugged, over-tired or have experienced a 'trick of the light'. Or he may merely be mistaken about certain facts. The phenomenon in question may have unknown but *natural* causes, or represent a rare occurrence of *known* natural ones. In short, *anything* is more likely than a miracle.

Whilst Hume doesn't explicitly say, 'miracles aren't possible', he does seem to imply that, if they were they would have been established by now. And yet, the traditional definition of a miracle – a supernatural event originating with God – would appear to entail a *suspension* of natural laws. So, someone is raised from the dead, walks on water, cures blindness – these are not due to unknown principles or laws, but rather the direct intervention of God. In other words, Hume's advice is probably sound when considering whether something is a law of nature, but a miracle will never be part of that order.

Another problem is that Hume's approach decides likelihood, not truth. Certain interpretations will always be more *likely* than others, merely because history has proven them most often correct. However, such an attitude is as likely to *conceal* the truth as reveal it. Some events are, by their nature, rare. Halley's Comet passes the Earth every 75 years, and sightings of it were for a long time discounted as unreliable. Hume would no doubt reply, 'Yes, but it was *repeated* sightings which ultimately confirmed its existence!' True, but what of even scarcer events: are we to conclude that something, only ever witnessed once, didn't happen?

'Man was born free, and everywhere he is in chains'
JEAN-JACQUES ROUSSEAU 1712–1778
The Social Contract

History may be viewed as *progress* or *decline* (well, also as *cyclical*, *unchanging* or *chaotic*, I suppose, but admitting that robs me of a neat opening). Religions and myths picture a *Golden Age* of innocence, peace, and goodness from which we have fallen; science favours progress, a long hard slog out of primitive slime towards the distant lights of reason and civilization. Rousseau was in the former camp: originally a peaceful, self-reliant and relatively solitary individual, a 'noble savage' who endured hardship for the sake of freedom, man has been morally corrupted by civilization, which forces us to live in uncomfortable proximity to our neighbours, jealously guarding the comfort and possessions that we have exchanged for true liberty. Consider, he said, the caged animal that will rather crack its head against the bars trying to escape than remain in incarcerated ease: this is the instinct that man subdues, to the detriment of his true nature.

Typing at my laptop, sipping tea, and occasionally wondering whether I can justify an Apple iPad as a work-related expense, I consider Rousseau's point: it is true, I have never caught or grown my own food, mended a roof, or fought off an intruder. However, though technological progress distances us from life's sobering realities, and smothers us with over-indulgent comforts (who really needs a six-blade battery-powered wet razor?), where would we be without penicillin, or the telephone, or the countless benefits that come with the increase in knowledge that civilization fosters?

Technology is a double-edged sword, but whatever our problems, to hark back to a rose-tinted heyday seems ill-conceived: as Pandora discovered, once you let things out of the box, it's difficult to get them back in. Rather than turning our back on modern civilization altogether, wouldn't we be better employed turning its acquired knowledge to our advantage? 'Progress' may seem overwhelming at times, but it's surely not a problem solved by born-again ignorance.

> 'In order then that the social compact may not be an empty formula, it tacitly includes the undertaking, which alone can give force to the rest, that whoever refuses to obey the general will shall be compelled to do so by the whole body. This means nothing less than that he will be forced to be free . . .'
>
> JEAN-JACQUES ROUSSEAU
> *The Social Contract*

Freedom can be paradoxical. If defined as the right to follow our desires, we might argue we aren't free at all: I want to eat cake because my greedy instincts *compel* me. On the other hand, a man in a jail cell isn't 'free' just because he *doesn't* feel compelled to go anywhere.

Since, unprotected, society's members don't play well together, Rousseau agreed with Hobbes and Locke: there must be a *social contract*. However, there would be no Hobbesian 'Leviathan' or absolute ruler ensuring compliance, but a republic of equal members. This would ensure freedom and justice, for the laws protecting all would express the common interest – the *general will*. This isn't necessarily the view of the democratic majority, which could theoretically oppress minorities, but rather an identification of what would be to the benefit of all. Thus, whilst all citizens possess the freedom to express their opinion as to what the common interest resides in, in reality, 'the common good makes itself so manifestly evident that only common sense is needed to discern it'.

However, such faith in an inherent ability to recognize the common good seems idealistic, there being no practical measures in place to resist a *tyranny of the majority*, whereby the *general will* merely expresses *the norm* (what most people believe). Consequently, Rousseau's theory takes on a sinister aspect: those in disagreement with the general will must be forced to comply. Of course, forced compliance has its place: children stealing others' toys should be made to return them. However, in a world of increasingly diverse opinions and values, enforcement of what 'common sense' takes to be the common good edges uncomfortably close to totalitarianism.

'We are born weak, we need strength; helpless we need aid; foolish we need reason. All that we lack at birth, all that we need when we come to man's estate, is the gift of education.'

JEAN-JACQUES ROUSSEAU
Émile

The above quotation might seem to support any form of education – we know nothing, so we need teaching. However, Rousseau actually has in mind a very different idea of child development from the traditional notion of pouring knowledge into empty vessels.

Reflecting his views on nature and society, *Émile* presents Rousseau's ideal account of the education of a young boy. Rousseau thought that children should be encouraged to develop their natural powers of reason, not merely force-fed with facts: 'We should not teach children the sciences; but give them a taste for them.' In this sense, his views are progressive, and bear some resemblance to later educational theorists, such as John Dewey and Maria Montessori, who both stressed the natural curiosity of the child given the right environment and stimulus. For Rousseau, therefore, education seems to have consisted of supplying the child with the right kind of experiences and opportunities to develop in appropriate ways. A key aspect of this was therefore the fostering of independence: not only in terms of rational enquiry, but also practical skills and self sufficiency (literally: Émile actually learns a trade). Perhaps most interestingly, considering our modern emphasis on either practical or academic skills, Rousseau proposes that the child should be taught *sentiment*, or to develop the appropriate emotional responses (love, sympathy, respect). In broad terms, then, Rousseau's central goal is to foster *self government*.

However, Rousseau's views on the education of women are less progressive. In a notorious passage, he contrasts the qualities of the sexes: men should be 'active and strong', possess a powerful will and be generally capable of meeting the demands of life; women, however, being 'passive and weak', need only 'put up little resistance', since 'woman is made specially to please man'. Indeed.

> 'All the members of these learned societies are more than is needed for a single object of human science; all the societies together are not sufficient for a science of man in general'
>
> DENIS DIDEROT 1713–1784
> 'Philosophy', *L'Encyclopédie*

French philosopher, art critic, playwright, novelist, and general man of letters, Denis Diderot was the driving force behind the *Encyclopédie*, the first modern encyclopaedia. Whilst the idea of a book which brings together knowledge from different fields goes back to ancient times, *L'Encyclopédie* was distinctive in that it invited contributions from various authors possessing particular expertise. It also sought to broaden its appeal so as to provide not just an academic reference book, but a source of artistic, scientific and historical knowledge to the general public.

As such, *L'Encyclopédie* had a definite political slant. Diderot was a friend of Rousseau, and the publication promoted the ideals of the *Enlightenment* (the rational and democratic force behind the French Revolution): in short, it was a dangerous book. Realizing, as Francis Bacon said, that 'Knowledge is power', the ruling French aristocratic regime therefore attempted to suppress its publication, and Diderot's efforts were hampered by censorship, legal injunction, and even police surveillance.

It seems surprising now that a mere encyclopaedia can have been so controversial, but this was a time where most knowledge was concentrated in state-sponsored and -monitored academies. However, as Diderot observes, not only does this stifle free thought, but it also slows the advancement of knowledge: so, whilst academics were plentiful, their knowledge was not. However, if the knowledge of the libraries of the world were opened up to non-academics, and they in turn could contribute their findings on subjects ignored by academia, human knowledge as a whole would benefit.

Diderot's ideas are therefore very relevant to today. The encyclopaedic website *Wikipedia* – whilst it has its critics – has much in common with *L'Encyclopédie*. Both see the importance of the *democratization of knowledge*, and the danger of academic exclusivity. If knowledge is power, shouldn't power be shared?

'It is not from the benevolence of the butcher, the brewer, or the baker that we expect our dinner, but from their regard to their own interest'

ADAM SMITH 1723–1790
On the Wealth of Nations

Economic philosopher and friend of David Hume, Adam Smith provided the cornerstone of capitalist theory, arguing for division of labour, free trade, and private ownership of property.

Underlying these principles is pursuit of self-interest. Division of labour is vital to a nation's wealth and productivity: a baker who grew his own grain, milled his own flour, etc., wouldn't bake many loaves. However, if the farmer grows, and the miller grinds, the baker is free to bake, and we shall have plenty of bread. Thus, in the pursuit of his self-interest, society in general shall benefit – aside from baking, the baker may take on staff, providing jobs and livelihood for others. However, as an incentive, he must be allowed to keep his profits and own private property – the fruits of capitalism.

But won't self-interest simply foster greed, and concentrate wealth in the hands of the few? Not if market forces keep people honest: when produce is overpriced, people will shop elsewhere; when workers are underpaid, they will seek other employment. Furthermore, rich people's wealth trickles down, feeding the families of jewellers, Ferrari dealers and estate agents, who in turn pass on their profits in similar ways. Thus, unfettered by government legislation, self-interest is an 'invisible hand', regulating economic behaviour to everyone's benefit.

In practice, Smith's optimism seems idealistic: employers often form *cartels* to keep wages low, leaving nowhere for low-paid labour to go; modern industry divides production into individually meaningless, repetitive tasks, thereby de-skilling workers. But Smith foresaw these and other problems. In fact, many who now invoke his support exemplify the abuses he feared – protection of trade secrets, corporate domination, erosion of workers' rights – and he did not, as some think, oppose all restriction. So, has capitalism failed, or just failed to read Adam Smith?

> 'I do not, therefore, need any penetrating acuteness to see what I have to do in order that my volition be morally good. Inexperienced in the course of the world, incapable of being prepared for whatever might come to pass in it, I ask myself only: can you also will that your maxim become a universal law?'
>
> IMMANUEL KANT 1724–1804
> *Groundwork of the Metaphysics of Morals*

'Inexperienced in the course of the world' could itself describe Kant, who spent his whole life in the Prussian town of Königsberg. Good humoured, witty, and sociable, he was nonetheless a confirmed bachelor and stickler for routine (you could set your watch by his afternoon walks), who even devised schedules for topics of dinner conversation (though most guests left happy, for he never lacked dining companions).

So, perhaps significantly, Kant thought morality springs solely from reason. We don't learn to be moral (as Aristotle thought), but come to recognize, through application of logic, that certain actions imply an inescapable duty. Morality is full of imperatives: 'Do *x*!', 'Don't do *y*!' However, if such imperatives were merely *hypothetical* – we could do them *if* we felt like it, or *if* we wanted something – then this wouldn't really be morality (people would behave erratically and inconsistently). So, moral commands must be *categorical* – there must be no choice in the matter.

But *which* maxims must be followed categorically? The ones that may be *universalized*: what if *everyone* were to act that way? If, for instance, I steal something, then I am basically saying, 'It is OK if everyone steals.' However, in that case there would be no such thing as property, for ownership would have no meaning, and neither would stealing! So, certain immoral principles have self-contradictory results.

This is Kant's famous *categorical imperative*, but it is not without problems. What if I universalize, 'I shall steal only on my birthday'? This isn't self-contradictory. Also, what if two duties conflict – could I steal food to feed my children? Like Kant himself, the categorical imperative seems somewhat inflexible.

'Act in such a way that you treat humanity, whether in your own person or in the person of any other, always at the same time as an end and never merely as a means to an end'

IMMANUEL KANT
Groundwork of the Metaphysic of Morals

Kant actually gives three formulations of the *categorical imperative* – not changes of mind, but differing perspectives. The second formulation (quoted above) is particularly interesting: moral duty consists in acknowledging others' *rational autonomy*; their possession of free will and their own rational goals. This has wide-reaching consequences, implying that we only have a strict duty to other members of our moral community. If your employer pays you poorly, then he treats you merely as a means to serve his own ends (financial profit); but if he pays you a decent wage, then he is treating you fairly out of respect for you as an individual. However, if you are *not* a rational being (an animal, a fetus, a coma patient, brain damaged), you may not possess the mental capacity for rational goals or free will, and aren't a member of the moral community; therefore, I don't injure your autonomy by treating you as a means to an end (for testing, stem cells, organ donation, etc.)

Kant sidesteps this problem by arguing that I still have an *indirect* responsibility to such beings, which springs from the effect that certain actions may have upon the person who performs them; abusing animals may deaden me emotionally, encouraging others to behave similarly, thus *discouraging* compassion in general.

However, many dislike here how rationality becomes a ticket to a special club where members get special moral treatment. Also, should we allot such a secondary role to emotion? For Kant, good actions can only be based on the correct sort of rational motivation, but this means that one may be good *and* a completely 'cold fish'. But don't we question just those moral actions which are cold pieces of logic? Has Kant left the heart out of morality?

'It is precisely in knowing its limits that philosophy exists'
IMMANUEL KANT
The Critique of Pure Reason

We do not see the world as it *is*, but as it *appears* to be. This is a key realization. Certain aspects of reality are *in us*, not *in the world*. A table appears brown because of the particular constitution of my visual apparatus; a species that could, for instance, visually process a wider range of light waves (infrared, ultraviolet) would see it differently.

And not just colour, but space, time, cause and effect, and numerous other aspects of reality – what Kant termed 'categories' of experience – determine how we experience the world. Without these innate categories, our experience would merely be a chaotic jumble.

Whilst imposing order, the categories also impose limits on our experience, determining what we can know. For instance, we can seek causal explanations regarding our everyday experience – Who put that box here? What made that sound? But there are certain things to which causal explanations cannot be applied, such as the question of human free will, or the origin of the universe, and seeking answers to such questions often results in what Kant terms *antinomies* (two equally rational but mutually exclusive possibilities). For instance, it seems equally inconceivable to our boggled brains that the universe at one time didn't exist, as the contention that it has and will always do so. Similarly, it appears at once plausible that humans possess free choice and that every effect has a determined cause. Such contradictions, Kant concludes, imply that these are things that the limits of reason forbid us from understanding. Kant's view is therefore known as *transcendental idealism*, in that whilst we only ever experience our own perceptions (*idealism*), there is a reality that exists beyond (*transcends*) them.

Kant's ideas are as important as his writings are difficult. He described himself as a philosophical Copernicus, relocating philosophy's gravitational centre, but in some ways he is closer to Ptolemy: *we* are the creators of reality, not some external source.

'The moral law commands me to make the highest possible good in a world the ultimate object of all my conduct. But I cannot hope to effect this otherwise than by the harmony of my will with that of a holy and good Author of the world.'

IMMANUEL KANT

Critique of Practical Reason

Kant rejected traditional arguments for the existence of God. As we've seen, he argued that existence isn't a necessary part of the idea of God (the *ontological argument*), for ideas don't 'possess' the quality of existence. He also agreed with Hume that we cannot argue from *effect* to *cause* – that the world was designed (the *teleological argument*, or must have a definite origin (the *cosmological argument*) for this is to argue beyond the limits of reason. Instead, Kant argues that we need God to make sense of morality.

Moral acts aim at the *summum bonum* (the highest possible good), which has two aspects: moral justice and happiness. So, whilst good acts won't always provide happiness, in an ideal world the two would coincide: helping an old lady across the road is both good *and* gives you a warm fuzzy feeling inside. However, whether moral acts result in happiness or not, morality necessarily implies a duty to strive for this perfect state of affairs – and doesn't duty imply possibility? In other words, if you *ought* to help the old lady, then that's because you can do it. So, if it's possible that moral acts *can* result in happiness, then that's because God must have linked morality and possibility in this way – something that a man-made or natural morality could not achieve (if the *summum bonum* were merely 'pleasure', then moral justice would fall apart).

But *must* we seek the *summum bonum*? Must happiness ideally accompany virtue? Furthermore, even if Kant is right that man cannot have created a disinterested morality – good for goodness' sake – this assumes 'moral' actions *are* disinterested. But perhaps (as *utilitarianism* argues) morality *is* just about seeking happiness – in which case, morality doesn't need a divine explanation, and cannot in turn act as divine proof.

> 'Women will avoid the wicked not because it is unright, but because it is ugly; and virtuous actions mean to them such as are morally beautiful'
>
> IMMANUEL KANT
> *Observations on the Feeling of the Beautiful and the Sublime*

As with other forms of judgement, Kant thought our aesthetic sense (our ability to appreciate art and beauty) was inherent. So, the beauty of a statue or a flower resides not in the object itself, but in our reactions to it: it is, in the well- known proverb, in the eye of the beholder.

However, this doesn't make beauty merely a matter of personal taste – remember that Kant thought truth and knowledge were also, in a sense, *in us*, because they're determined by the structure of our own mental faculties. This means that aesthetic opinions are, firstly, *subjective*: they spring from sensation and pleasure, residing in the *subject* (person) not the object; secondly, they're *universal*, for everyone should share similar reactions.

For Kant, beauty is about *form*: an arrangement of certain structural properties (composition, proportion), and not merely pleasing qualities (thus, interestingly, colour is irrelevant). Kant therefore distinguished between beauty or the sublime (true for everyone), and the merely *agreeable* (individual taste, such as partiality to a particular food).

But if aesthetic opinions are universal, aren't they a guide to truth? As English poet John Keats put it: 'Beauty is truth, truth beauty'. This is – in somewhat chauvinistic fashion – what Kant seems to suggest in the quote: *moral* actions are also *beautiful*, and *immoral* ones *ugly*. Therefore, whilst ladies struggle to appreciate moral principles, they may approach moral truth *aesthetically*.

I don't think Kant wants to push this parallel too far, and it would be misleading to suggest that a life lived by aesthetic principles (such as, perhaps, Oscar Wilde's) would also be a moral one. And yet, it's interesting to note how often beauty is taken as a sign of *other* things – health, status, trustworthiness. But perhaps we should remember here that Socrates was famous for his ugliness: truth can also lie far beneath the skin.

'People will not look forward to posterity, who never look backward to
their ancestors'
EDMUND BURKE 1729–1797
Reflections on the Revolution in France

The French Revolution divided 18th century opinion greatly: was it the
progress of reason and democracy over corrupt privilege and tyranny,
or a mistaken step toward anarchy? Whilst thinkers such as Thomas
Paine and Mary Wollstonecraft would go on to applaud it, Irish-born
politician Edmund Burke was among the first neutrals to present a
sustained attack on the revolution.

Initially undecided, Burke came to see that the revolution had not
just overthrown the monarchy, and its elitist apparatus of wealth and
privilege, but had disrupted and destroyed the very institutions that
make society function. So, the Church, army, law, business, manufacture, the arts, were all to varying extents victims of a sort of will to
destruction. Gone was the hope – which Burke had at first shared –
that French society would be made more rational, democratic and fair,
as the monarchy was replaced with a 'ferocious, bloody, and tyrannical
democracy', which seemed bent on destroying all vestiges of the previous order – at whatever cost.

The consequences of the revolution therefore confirmed Burke in
his *conservatism*: meaningful social change couldn't be accomplished
instantaneously without thereby destroying what previous generations had achieved. Rather, progress required *conserving* what was
good about the past, which entailed largely preserving a country's
institutions, laws and practices, and seeking gradually to improve
them through lawful means. Accordingly, Burke praised what he
termed 'prejudice', or the tendency to maintain opinions gained from
past experience (one's own or others), which, since it had survived
from previous generations, was likely of some use, and should not
therefore be given up lightly merely because it *is* prejudice. Burke also
criticized the *social contract* theory, for, though such a contract did
exist, it wasn't merely between living members of society, but also past
and future ones. Tradition was therefore the means whereby wisdom
was handed down from age to age, and we ignore it at our peril.

> 'He that rebels against reason is a real rebel, but he that in defence of reason rebels against tyranny has a better title to "Defender of the Faith", than George the Third'
>
> THOMAS PAINE 1737–1809
>
> *The American Crisis*

Thomas Paine was an English writer and political activist whose contribution to American independence has led some to call him 'The Father of the American Revolution'. Early on, Paine worked in numerous forms of employment, including corset-maker and customs officer, and it was a chance meeting with American Founding Father Benjamin Franklin that drew him into political affairs. Under Franklin's patronage, he emigrated to Philadelphia, where he set about garnering popular support for independence from British rule.

Paine's chief merit was as a popular pamphleteer, couching complicated abstract concepts into common language. As such, his most famous work, *The Rights of Man*, is a distillation of ideas to be found in Rousseau, Voltaire, and especially John Locke. Written in response to the French Revolution, and as a counterblast to the conservative criticism of Edmund Burke, the book primarily concerns political reform, and the idea that revolution is legitimate when a government fails to protect the rights and interests of its people. Published in 1791, on the heels of revolution in America and France, it is therefore easy to see it as a direct call for a British revolution in the same mould. Alongside proposals for an American-style constitution, Paine also proposed tax reforms to alleviate poverty, the abolishment of hereditary titles, heavy taxes on wealthy landowners, and reforms to support universal access to education.

The book caused such a storm in England that Paine was forced to flee to France (which did not stop him being tried and convicted of treason in his absence). Ultimately, the popular British revolution Paine hoped for never occurred, but his ideas influenced popular reform movements which in turn gradually brought about some of the changes he desired – perhaps, in fact, in a manner that Burke himself might not have disapproved of.

'Happiness lies only in that which excites, and that which excites is crime'
MARQUIS DE SADE 1740–1814
Aline et Valcour

French aristocrat the Marquis de Sade inspired the term *sadism* (enjoyment of cruelty to another, especially in sexual contexts), doing his best to populate the list of prohibited books. However, whilst no saint, and more than partial to the sort of activities to which he gives his name, the exploits of Sade's literary characters far outstrip his own, and represent a determined attempt to catalogue the worst crimes imaginable – rape, murder, incest, torture – interspersed with observations on philosophy, religion, society and ethics. It is these latter qualities which perhaps rescue his work from being the perverse drivel of a deranged mind.

Why was such an intelligent, cultured individual driven to concoct such disturbing material, and to what purpose? Firstly, it must be observed that most of his works were written in prison (where he spent most of his adult life), and therefore are partly motivated by boredom and revenge. However, this aside, a general world view does emerge. Firstly, Sade is a committed atheist, but has no truck with the 'halfway house' of pseudo-religious *humanist* ethics prevalent in his day. For Sade, no God means no morality either; man is just an animal, and as such is subject only to Nature. However, since it's almost impossible to outrage or offend Nature (which seems to 'condone' any act), we are free to indulge our passions – in fact, *duty bound* to transgress, for how else can we combat the absurdity of life and the hypocrisy of social convention?

Sade is *amoral*, *hedonistic* and *egoistic*: he exists only for himself, and only *his own* sensations are real: 'The strongest pain in other people is certainly nothing to us, but we are affected by the slightest tickle of pleasure that touches us.' But why should this justify cruelty? Sade's views, despite the sympathy of later *existentialists*, never fully evolve beyond a justification of his own nature – a nature which few share, and his outlook is perhaps more psychological symptom than philosophical system.

'In crossing a heath, suppose I pitched my foot against a stone, and were asked how the stone came to be there: I might possibly answer, that for any thing I know to the contrary, it had lain there for ever: nor would it perhaps be very easy to show the absurdity of this answer. But suppose I had found a watch upon the ground, and it should be inquired how the watch happened to be in that place; I should hardly think of the answer which I had before given, that for any thing I knew, the watch might have always been there.'

WILLIAM PALEY 1743–1805
Natural Theology

The *teleological argument*, as it's known, goes back to Plato. However, it is the nineteenth-century analogy of English philosopher and theologian William Paley that has become most famous: just as, upon finding a watch on a beach, we would assume the existence of a watchmaker, so, on considering the complexity and order of the natural world, we conclude that it has not originated by chance.

Of course, no word is more guaranteed to give Richard Dawkins apoplexy: evolution by natural selection, the main alternative to divine design, is not 'chance', but rather the application of simple, naturally occurring principles. One argument against Paley is therefore that – applying *Ockham's razor* perhaps – evolution is a simpler theory that fits better with other scientific views.

But, Darwin vs. Design aside, let us assume that the world *is* designed: what does it tell us about the designer? Mischievously, Hume proposed that – for all we know – the world is the first, abandoned attempt of some 'infant deity'; a poor production of some 'second-rate' God; or even the creation of some doddering, geriatric divinity. From our one world, with no other to compare it to, *we simply cannot know.* Nor, however, can we infer the designer's moral character, or even whether he (she?) had help. We cannot argue from *effect* to *cause*: from the watch, to the watchmaker.

Of course, this still doesn't mean that there isn't one.

'Habits form a second nature'
JEAN-BAPTISTE LAMARCK 1744–1829
Philosophie Zoologique

Darwin did not invent the idea of evolution, but merely provided what seems to us now to be the best explanation of the mechanisms involved (i.e. *natural selection*). Before Darwin, therefore, various evolutionary theories abounded, the most prominent of which was that of French naturalist Jean-Baptiste Lamarck. Unlike Darwin, Lamarck believed in a vital force within living organisms that was responsible for the growing diversification and complexity of life (he was what is termed a *vitalist*). However, since some of these complex developments were useful to the organism and some were not, it was habit which decided which features were retained and strengthened, and which atrophied and died out.

The most often cited of Lamarck's examples is the giraffe.

'this animal . . . is known to live in the interior of Africa in places where the soil is nearly always arid and barren, so that it is obliged to browse on the leaves of trees and to make constant efforts to reach them. From this habit long maintained in all its race, it has resulted that the animal's fore-legs have become longer than its hind legs, and that its neck is lengthened to such a degree that the giraffe, without standing up on its hind legs, attains a height of six metres.'

So, through habit, the giraffe's neck is lengthened, and this trait is then passed on.

However, there's some debate as to the accuracy of this picture. Evolutionary biologist Stephen Jay Gould criticized this common caricature of Lamarck, pointing out that the doctrine of *inheritance of acquired traits* was actually the common intellectual property of various evolutionary theorists, not Lamarck's alone. Furthermore, he argues, the reduction of Lamarck's work to this sole theory distorts and marginalizes his overall contribution to evolutionary theory, which was actually quite substantial.

Whether this is true or not, it's perhaps difficult now to combat the tendency to perceive Lamarck in this way: the habit is too strongly ingrained, and the caricature is just too useful.

> 'It is the greatest good to the greatest number of people which is the measure of right and wrong'
> JEREMY BENTHAM 1748–1832
> *Rationale of Reward*

Initially, in terms of human history, what is good is decreed by God, or the gods. However, with technology and civilization, man comes to trust more in himself and less in the divine – at least regarding the explanation of natural phenomena. So, natural explanations come to supplant supernatural ones, and Vulcan gives way to vulcanology, but can we also apply similar methods to morality?

Utilitarianism is just such an attempt. The good is what makes us happy through the natural goodness of pleasure. But individuals are constituted differently, so what do we do when our pleasures conflict? On a car journey, you want to listen to classical music, and I want to hear a documentary on the rarely spotted, Lesser-Spotted Lithuanian Tree Lizard – who should get what he wants? English philosopher Jeremy Bentham would argue that it should be judged on the *quantity* of happiness produced: if there is a third person in the car who favours one or the other, then that would swing it. Or, if one person's choice would generate a much greater amount of pleasure than the other two combined – to listen to their favourite song, perhaps – then that should win out. So, as you can see, utilitarianism need not be a strictly democratic method, for it is the overall quantity of happiness produced that counts and not the number of people that feel it (at least, in *act utilitarianism*, as Bentham's form is known).

But can we quantify happiness in this way? Bentham thought so, and even devised what he called a *felicific calculus*, a mathematical formula to help determine the correct action in any circumstance. Today, a 'happiness calculator' seems artificial and unworkable: would we rate our own happiness? Utilize brain scans? However, there are deeper problems: what if someone were to receive the greatest pleasure from an immoral act? If the whole of society enjoyed witnessing torture, perhaps? Does *this* explain the existence of reality TV?

Today, those who wish to argue for animal rights often do so on the basis of empathy. A dog, monkey, or chicken does not possess the same mental or linguistic faculties as a human, but is no less sentient; it feels pain and distress just as we do. However, until Bentham made this point, philosophers – such as Descartes and Bacon – had focused mostly on the differences between humans and animals: animals could not speak because they did not possess reason, and lacked reason because they lacked a rational soul. Therefore, animals were a fundamentally different order of being, were not moral agents, and consequently did not possess rights.

Bentham thought the notion of natural human rights to be 'nonsense on stilts', but his concern for animal welfare was based on fellow feeling. Just as we can sense another person's discomfort, because our common biology allows us to discern his pain or pleasure, so too with animals. A monkey's pain is no different to a human's, and we cannot – as Descartes notoriously argued – treat its cries as merely the unconscious and automatic responses of a biological machine.

Furthermore, if we adopt reason and communication as criteria for possessing rights, then we are faced with an uncomfortable consequence: some humans will fail this test, and some animals will pass. As Bentham puts it, 'a full-grown horse or dog, is beyond comparison a more rational, as well as a more conversable animal, than an infant of a day or a week or even a month, old'. In addition, some brain-damaged humans will *never* develop the capacity for reason or language – are we then to treat them as animals? Use them for medical experimentation or organ donation? Humanity should not be a club from which we exclude the undeserving, but a standard to which our actions aspire.

'We may regard the present state of the universe as the effect of the past and the cause of the future. An intellect which at any given moment knew all of the forces that animate nature and the mutual positions of the beings that compose it, if this intellect were vast enough to submit the data to analysis, could condense into a single formula the movement of the greatest bodies of the universe and that of the lightest atom; for such an intellect nothing could be uncertain and the future just like the past would be present before its eyes.'

PIERRE-SIMON LAPLACE 1749–1827
A Philosophical Essay on Probabilities

Astronomer and mathematician, the contributions of Pierre-Simon Laplace to science earned him the reputation 'the French Newton', who was his contemporary. Like Newton, Laplace argued for a mathematical and mechanical understanding of the universe. Therefore, since the universe was merely a vast machine, a sufficiently vast mind, furnished with all available data, could describe the course of all events past and future. Such a mind, since termed 'Laplace's Demon' (possessing a supernaturally powerful intellect), would no doubt now be a computer – perhaps 'Deep Thought', from Douglas Adams' *Hitchhiker's Guide to the Galaxy*, which is tasked with finding the meaning of life.

Unlike Newton, who continued to pursue somewhat unorthodox religious beliefs, Laplace was an atheist. An anecdote records his meeting Napoleon: why, the emperor enquired, hadn't he once mentioned God in his book on astronomy? 'I had no need of that hypothesis', Laplace replied. God, then, is superfluous to a mechanical universe.

What is peculiar here is how theology and mechanism coincide. Mechanism ultimately leads to *determinism*: since everything results from fixed laws of cause and effect, everything is decided in advance, free will is illusory, and the world a meaningless piece of mechanical theatre. However, we reach the same conclusion theologically: an omniscient God already knows everything that will ever occur, including everything we will ever do. Either way, things are predestined.

You may be forgiven if you find neither 'choice' particularly inviting.

'Tell me what you eat, and I will tell you what you are'
JEAN ANTHELME BRILLAT-SAVARIN 1755–1826
The Physiology of Taste

Jean Anthelme Brillat-Savarin was a French politician, lawyer, and writer, famous for his *Physiology of Taste*, which established him as a founding father of modern *gastronomy*. A *gastronome* is interested in the relationship of food to culture; the significance it has in people's social lives. Other gastronomic topics include the science of nutrition or taste, the history of food growth and production, its relation to trade and economy, to moral and ethical issues, etc. But can we have a *philosophy* of food?

Doubters observe that the philosophically interesting things about food are already covered: the ethics of food production comes under moral philosophy, as does the role played by pleasure in our concept of moral action (e.g. *utilitarianism*; the cultural significance of food forms part of a more general philosophical concern with social theory, where it sits alongside other social concerns such as sport or film. And yet, there is 'philosophy of film' and 'philosophy of sport', so why *not* food? We can of course put 'philosophy of . . .' in front of almost anything, but perhaps our reluctance to do so with food (or sex?) is a sign of a guilty conscience: *surely*, we shouldn't be allowed to take such enjoyable things *seriously*?

But, as Brillat-Savarin notes, food can tell us so much about a person: his attitudes and opinions, his character, etc. As such, like our attitude to other fundamental things, food indicates how we view the fundamental questions of life. Is it worth living? Should we, as *Ecclesiastes* advises (viii.15), 'eat, drink and be merry', for Earthly life is otherwise meaningless and empty? Or should we exercise restraint and self-denial? Perhaps, as the Epicureans proposed, simple pleasures in moderation are best. We can see then that food, whilst not a fundamental philosophical issue, is no less interesting and important a way into the deeper questions than other established sub-topics. Can't we therefore do philosophy *and* enjoy ourselves?

> 'I must create a system or be enslaved by another man's; I will not
> reason and compare: my business is to create'
> WILLIAM BLAKE 1757–1827
> *Jerusalem*

William Blake was an English poet, artist, printmaker, and philosopher, who rejected the principles of the *Enlightenment*, and set imagination and creativity above reason and science. Accordingly, he is a forerunner of *Romanticism*, a broad movement stemming from art, music and literature that aimed to redress the bias toward rational thought, and mend the neglect of emotional and imaginative expression. Blake therefore terms *scientific materialism* 'Newton's sleep', claiming that 'Imagination is the real and eternal world of which this vegetable universe is but a faint shadow.' Reason, therefore, can never fully capture true reality, because it's merely 'the bound or outward circumference of Energy'. It's the latter, then, the world of spirit, emotion, and imagination, which is true life.

Whilst, as the quote suggests, Blake evolved his own system, he's not really a *systematic* thinker – at least, not in the traditional philosophical sense. This, of course, is part of his rebellion against rationalism, and whilst there are themes and continuities within his work, these spring more from the unity of his overall vision than from any strict underlying rational principles.

Yet Blake wasn't anti-intellectual, merely contending that reason should be kept in check by other faculties. Therefore, his opposition to Enlightenment principles wasn't total, and, like many other Enlightenment and Romantic thinkers, he supported the French Revolution, but became repelled by the bloody chaos its high ideals descended into.

However, Blake's outlook is fundamentally religious and mystical. He cares little for artistic and literary conventions, his writings echoing the form and tone of religious scripture, and his meaning is sometimes obscure. This has led some to doubt its worth, the English Romantic poet William Wordsworth even considering that there was 'no doubt that this poor man was mad'. Thankfully, subsequent critics have rescued Blake's reputation, and revealed that, more than method in his madness, there was an extraordinary, intense and highly creative (if eccentric) genius.

> 'Taught from infancy that beauty is woman's sceptre,
> the mind shapes itself to the body, and roaming round its gilt cage,
> only seeks to adorn its prison'
> MARY WOLLSTONECRAFT 1759–1797
> *A Vindication of the Rights of Woman*

Whilst as concerned with the rights of man as contemporary Thomas Paine, Wollstonecraft thought that the rights of women represented a special case. Similar to Paine, and other *Enlightenment* thinkers such as Locke, Wollstonecraft proposed that behaviour should be governed by reason, that republican government was the most beneficial form of society, and that education would allow individuals to play equal roles in society. However, she also believed that society was male dominated, and that women were encouraged to be docile, sweet and innocent, to concentrate on domestic chores, idle pleasures, and looking pretty. What was needed, she argued, was sexual equality.

As such, Wollstonecraft is often considered the first modern feminist. Despite their high regard for rational thought, many Enlightenment thinkers did not extend its principles universally. So, even Rousseau could, whilst decrying slavery, propose that women should be educated differently, because their job was merely 'to please man'. However, Wollstonecraft argued that it was exactly this educational inequality that kept woman 'in her place', stopping her fulfilling her natural potential. Given the *same* opportunities, woman could be as rational as man.

And yet, woman was also the problem: encouraged by male flattery, she turns her back on rational pursuits in preference to trifles and trivialities, fashion and gossip. In contrast, Wollstonecraft's own life was packed with incident and drama. She supported herself producing novels, children's stories, translations, and reviews. She worked as a governess; documented the French Revolution at first hand; conducted love affairs with artists, soldiers, and anarchists, conceiving children by two different fathers (one daughter, Mary Shelley, went on to write *Frankenstein*). All this was achieved by the mere age of 38 when she died following complications in childbirth. Of course, in relation to this, most lives would seem somewhat dull and domestic.

THOMAS MALTHUS 1766–1834
An Essay on the Principles of Population

Thomas Malthus was an English clergyman and political economist
whose theories on population growth influenced both Charles Darwin
and Alfred Russel Wallace's independent development of the theory of
evolution. Contrary to contemporary thought, Malthus didn't think
society was capable of progressing toward utopia. Firstly, he believed,
human nature was unchanging (future generations wouldn't be less
wasteful or sexually active than previous ones). Secondly, population
growth always outpaces food production. This is because population
increases *exponentially* (by doubling: if every person has two offspring,
and *they* have two offspring – 2, 4, 8, 16 . . . etc.), whereas food supply
increases *linearly* (if one acre yields ten bushels, each additional acre
will only produce the same amount – so: 10, 20, 30 . . .).

Therefore, whilst utopia might come about if we change human
behaviour (decrease birth-rates), or consume fewer resources (or else
find an endless supply), neither is likely, so population is curtailed by
natural checks, such as war, famine, and disease. In fact, Malthus
thought God *planned* it this way to force humanity to be industrious
and ethical.

In a world running out of fossil fuels, living space, and polar ice,
Malthus is as relevant today as he ever was. Unaddressed, current
trends in world population growth and resource consumption are
driving us to a *Malthusian catastrophe* of unimaginable severity,
whereby we would be forced to adopt *subsistence-level* standards of
living (the barest possible to survive). The most salutary illustration
here is perhaps the fate of the inhabitants of Easter Island. Eventually,
having deforested their island in the process of moving and erecting
their statues of giant heads, they found themselves with a dwindling
supply of wood for boats, houses, and fuel. Ultimately, miles from
anywhere (the nearest landmass is over 1200 miles away), with no
other means of survival, they turned to cannibalism. We don't even
know how close the nearest habitable planet is. Let's hope Malthus
was wrong.

'The Idea, as unity of the Subjective and Objective Idea, is . . . the
absolute and all truth, the Idea which thinks itself'
GEORGE WILHELM FRIEDRICH HEGEL 1770–1831
The Shorter Logic

Bertrand Russell considered German philosopher G. W. F. Hegel 'the
hardest to understand of all the great philosophers' (*History of Western
Philosophy*) – and when even Russell says this, the rest of us perhaps
ought to worry. However, beneath the obscure prose and complicated
terminology sit a number of key ideas that exerted massive influence
upon subsequent strands of philosophy.

Hegel thought that the world was one thing (a brand of *monism*),
what he termed *the Absolute Idea*, which we might think of as a sort of
universal force, spirit, or God, uniting all opposites and driving the
evolution of the world. However, we tend not to notice this underlying
unity, but concentrate instead on its parts or individual aspects –
objects, people, ideas. However, just as any part can only be fully
understood through its role in the whole machine, so separate aspects
of reality can only be understood in relation to the Absolute. Failure to
understand this leads to contradiction and confusion.

In fact, Hegel argues, it is this very incompleteness of the parts that
proves the existence of the Absolute. For instance, if we propose that
only matter exists (*materialism*), then we seem to struggle to account
for consciousness; on the other hand, if we assume only the existence
of mind or spirit (*idealism*), we have difficultly explaining how objects
seem to exist independently of perception. Ultimately, Hegel argues,
the attempt to make the part stand for the whole results in a
contradiction.

But does this prove that there is an underlying unity? It is true that
the history of philosophy is littered with attempts to reduce reality to a
set of certain principles, often distorting it at the expense of a fuller
understanding. However, such failures might not reveal the existence
of some absolute unity, but merely a limitation in our understanding:
perhaps the human mind is simply not up to the job.

'The History of the world is none other than the progress of the consciousness of Freedom'
GEORGE WILHELM FRIEDRICH HEGEL
Lectures on the Philosophy of History

Hegel proposed a dialectic view of history. Unlike Spinoza or other monist philosophers, Hegel saw the underlying unity of the world not as fixed, but rather as dynamic and evolving. Consequently, history was not just a random string of events, or the same cycles repeated, but the unfolding of a deliberate purpose.

This ultimate end was conscious freedom. For Hegel, a man was free when his needs reflected those of his society, but for this to true both must embody principles of rationality, equality and justice. It is a high ideal: societies often sacrifice freedom for order, or liberty for equality and justice. However, Hegel argued, such attempts were merely steps toward an absolute goal. History was therefore a struggle between opposing elements – individual and state, science and religion, reason and emotion – moving forward through a process of conflict and resolution.

This process represents a sort of argument which the Absolute is having with itself through time. Hegel thought of this in terms of a *triad* or three-fold progression: a certain view emerges; this provokes a conflicting view; the conflict ultimately results in resolution, whereby a new view is produced which rescues certain aspects of both approaches; the process begins again.

This is a simplification, but you get the general idea: history is progressive. However, whilst this view has been greatly influential (especially on Marxism), it is controversial: is humanity really becoming more rational and liberated? Critics warn that we should not confuse technological progress with greater rationality: the atom bombs dropped on Hiroshima and Nagasaki prove that. But, aside from the question of *whether* we have progressed, might we not question whether we *can*? Perhaps, ultimately, progress is an illusion: there is no 'better' only 'different'. Whilst this is a pessimistic view, it does ask an important question: if there is a goal to existence, who or what decided it?

> 'To romanticize the world is to make us aware of the magic, mystery and wonder of the world; it is to educate the senses to see the ordinary as extraordinary, the familiar as strange, the mundane as sacred, the finite as infinite'
>
> NOVALIS 1772–1801
> unpublished fragment

Novalis was the pen name of Georg Philipp Friedrich Freiherr von Hardenberg, a German philosopher and writer, and a key figure in early *Romanticism*. Whilst he published few works before his untimely death from tuberculosis, he left behind a mass of notes and fragments (from which our quote is taken) on subjects as diverse as philosophy, politics, science and law.

Romanticism was chiefly a reaction to the industrial revolution, the Enlightenment emphasis on rational thought, and the progress of science. It's characterized by a return to nature, which is seen as embodying higher truths than those reason can access, and which therefore requires inspiration and emotional insight. However, for Novalis, poetry and philosophy should enrich one another, and among his unfinished projects was a 'Romantic encyclopaedia', bringing together the arts, sciences and religion. However, like Blake, he also thought that a world ruled by reason alone was missing something, and what was required was something to awaken the senses that had been dulled by familiarity and habit, an approach he christened 'magic idealism'.

In his short life, Novalis is also emblematic of another Romantic theme: the fleeting nature of life. The stereotype of the flighty, otherworldly Romantic poet, eulogizing beauty as he expires of consumption (tuberculosis) or engages on some fantastic but doomed exploit, isn't so far from the truth in many cases, and we don't have to look very far – Byron, Shelley, Keats – to find examples that fit the myth. And yet, in Novalis' case, the myth obscures a subtler picture. Tragic as his early death was, it ended a life as dedicated to science and philosophy as it was to poetry and nature. Novalis aimed at a reunification with reason; reinvigorating it, possibly transcending it, but not denying it.

> 'The primary Imagination I hold to be the living power and prime
> agent of all human perception, and as a repetition in the finite mind of
> the eternal act of creation in the infinite I AM'
>
> SAMUEL TAYLOR COLERIDGE 1772–1834
> *Biographia Literaria*

Samuel Taylor Coleridge, an English poet, writer and philosopher, was
a founder of *Romanticism*. Influenced by *German idealism*, especially
Kant, this in turn inspired Emerson and *American Transcendentalism*.

In privileging imagination over reason, Coleridge is typically Romantic: reason alone can only give us knowledge of an aspect of reality, and
relying solely on reason we risk negating life itself. As Coleridge's friend
and fellow poet William Wordsworth put it ('The Tables Turned'):

> 'Sweet is the lore which Nature brings;
> Our meddling intellect
> Mis-shapes the beauteous forms of things:–
> We murder to dissect.'

Though Coleridge and Wordsworth stressed the importance of
imagination, they also differed. For Wordsworth, 'the inward eye' saw
'into the life of things'; for Coleridge, imagination is the creative principle itself, and thus also the source of the fantastic: of dreams, visions
and nightmares. Thus whilst, for both poets, imagination is (as Kant
argued) an aspect of our inherent *aesthetic* sense, allowing us to appreciate beauty intuitively, the objects of Coleridge's interest are less
worldly. Like Blake, Coleridge goes further: imagination is an alternative source of philosophical and spiritual truth.

This opinion is interestingly shared by such a seemingly unlikely
person as Francis Bacon: imagination wasn't only a servant of memory
and reason, but also a portal for truths with a non-rational source – for
both inspiration and revelation. However, there's increased danger
here, for in turning our attention inward we thereby exclude the
normal external tests of truth (the opinion of others, correspondence
with physical reality). Perhaps, however, some ideas are more 'real'
than others – marked with the stamp of truth. Or is truth, like beauty,
in the inward eye of the beholder?

German philosopher Arthur Schopenhauer was a pessimist, meaning simply that, for him, life had a negative value. Unlike Leibniz, with whom he is often contrasted, Schopenhauer thought that this was not the 'best of all possible worlds', because even man, often lauded as the pinnacle of creation, was irredeemably flawed, doomed to a life of suffering. Was this the work of an omnibenevolent and omnipotent God? No. Rather, life is driven by a fundamental *will*, serving nature's purposes, not man's. The natural impulses we inherit are therefore fundamentally at odds with our rational morality, leaving us tormented, guilty, frustrated and miserable.

Whilst not Christian, or even theist, Schopenhauer has much in common with certain forms of Christianity: life was a burden to be borne, existence itself a form of sin. He differs, however, in his idea of 'salvation': no heaven awaits, only a release from suffering, something we can achieve in this life only by self-denial. In denying pursuit of happiness and pleasure, we thereby escape the reach of pain and suffering. Also, under certain circumstances, suicide becomes permissible, for what is death but a merciful release? There are also obvious similarities with Buddhism and other Eastern schools of philosophy (though Schopenhauer denied direct influence, but was in fact quite pleased at the coincidental agreement).

Schopenhauer's pessimism has been hugely influential in the arts – in music, poetry, drama, and literature in general – and, though it is not always designated 'pessimism', can often be found to underlie a standard 'realistic' world view in philosophy and science. It especially appeals to the already tormented and miserable: a philosophical justification perhaps of a truth intuitively felt. But is it justified? Is life essentially suffering? Some would argue (such as Nietzsche later did) that we have a choice. The glass may be half-full after all.

'After your death you will be what you were before your birth'
ARTHUR SCHOPENHAUER
'On the Indestructibility of Our Essential Being by Death'

Despite conceiving of the world as a place of suffering, Schopenhauer was not – as you might consequently expect – a traditionally materialistic atheist. However, neither was he religious, so we must be careful in assessing his position. He opposed traditional religion – the idea of a God-made world designed with man in mind – and instead proposed that the primary force of the world was *will*, which manifested itself through nature's blind biological imperatives.

However, whilst *will* governed our physical existence, our desires and physical needs, a certain peace was possible through realizing our true nature. The intellect was a secondary thing, arising with our physical bodies, and thus was the basis for the notion of ourselves as separate entities – as 'I', as 'Arthur' or 'Martha'. This personal self was transitory and dependent, only existing whilst our bodies did. Schopenhauer scoffed at Christianity's concern for the preservation of this 'I', and its promises for personal immortality: no such thing was possible, for the body, and with it the senses and physical brain through which we were aware of time and space – the basis of personhood – no longer existed. A heaven where my everyday self persisted was therefore inconceivable.

Many would take this as a basis for materialism: before-life and after-death are both states of non-existence. However, Schopenhauer believed that the essence of our being – or rather, since individuality was an illusion, of being *in general* – was beyond death. In this sense, his vision of a transcendent, non-personal universal consciousness is close to that of Buddhism. Similarly, he believed in *palingenesis* – not reincarnation, as such, but a continual process of rebirth whereby the eternal, non-personal consciousness of the world manifested itself bodily through individuals, before reabsorbing the personal, intellectual consciousness through death. Death, therefore, both was *and* was not the end: that which had and would always exist, persisted; that which was born, died.

> 'Since compassion for animals is so intimately associated with
> goodness of character, it may be confidently asserted that whoever is
> cruel to animals cannot be a good man'
>
> ARTHUR SCHOPENHAUER
> 'On the Basis of Morality'

Animals do not possess the intellect that humans do, but share the
same basis of experience, for their lives are likewise an expression of
the same fundamental natural *will*. Both are driven by natural desires,
checked or encouraged by pain and pleasure. The similarities are
therefore greater than the differences, and we should acknowledge
our kinship with them from the mere fact of their fellow suffering.

Schopenhauer's views find an almost exact correspondence in 'To
A Mouse' by Scottish poet Robert Burns. The poem describes his reaction on disturbing a mouse's nest whilst ploughing a field. Both
mouse and man are driven by the urge to survive, and are similarly –
or should be – part of 'Nature's social union'. However, having
concluded that we should live in harmony with nature, and that, if we
treat its resources with respect, there is enough for both man and
mouse, Burns proceeds to distinguish the human from the animal:

> 'Still, thou art blest, compar'd wi' me!
> The present only toucheth thee:
> But Och! I backward cast my e'e,
> On prospects drear!
> An' forward, tho' I canna see,
> I guess an' fear!'

The mouse does not possess the intellect, the sense of self and time,
to relate itself to past and future; to be tormented by painful memories,
or made anxious by its ignorance of what might come.

Similarly, Schopenhauer argues that the capacity for pain and
pleasure increases with the capacity for knowledge. So, pain capacity
reaches 'its zenith only where, by virtue of the existence of reason,
there also exists the possibility of denial of the will'. In other words,
were it not for the human capacity for reason, which allows us to deny
our desires and transcend self-interest (and all the pain thereby
caused), life would be but 'aimless cruelty'.

'They are *sexus sequior*, the inferior sex in *every* respect: one should be indulgent toward their weaknesses, but to pay them honour is ridiculous beyond measure and demeans us even in their eyes'

ARTHUR SCHOPENHAUER

'On Women'

Schopenhauer's *On Women* is outrageous, anachronistic, and highly entertaining; something a Victorian patriarch might have mined for advice before dispatching his son on the Grand Tour. 'Woman is not intended for great mental or for great physical labour', they are 'childish, silly, and short-sighted', 'inferior to men in respect of justice, honesty, and conscientiousness', and are so prone to 'falsity, unfaithfulness, treachery, ingratitude' that 'it is questionable whether they ought to be allowed to take an oath at all.'

Sexism is never just sexism, springing perhaps from fear, ignorance, or desire for control. The origin of Schopenhauer's is debateable, but some of his views do importantly anticipate modern *evolutionary psychology* in suggesting a biological basis to human nature. Woman, he says, is enslaved by her instincts, obsessed with reproduction, providing for her children, and fulfilling nature's role for her in perpetuating the human race. Such views have a different footing to those of previous misogynists, and would deserve more sympathy were they not so one-sided and blinkered. Firstly, men are 'objective' and 'rational' because less biologically programmed (which, modern research suggests, is untrue: the imperatives are just *different*). Secondly, he underestimates the extent to which woman's under-representation in arts and sciences, her lack of participation in government and administration, has a *social* basis. Educated differently, given limited employment opportunities, and generally treated as inferior, then *of course* inequities will persist.

The debate is ongoing. Biological differences undoubtedly influence how the sexes think and behave, but do they completely determine us? Schopenhauer proposed complementary gender roles: woman, flighty and carefree, soothing man's brow as he momentarily sets aside the serious burden of running the world. We laugh, but there is a serious issue here: faced with biological imperatives, but also choice, is our duty to ourselves, to nature, or to each other?

'On two occasions I have been asked, – "Pray, Mr. Babbage, if you put into the machine wrong figures, will the right answers come out?" . . . I am not able rightly to apprehend the kind of confusion of ideas that could provoke such a question.'

CHARLES BABBAGE 1791–1871
Pages From the Life of a Philosopher

It's reassuring – but, perhaps, mildly depressing – to note that a failure to understand the principles of their design has dogged computers from the very beginning. As the term itself suggests, computers were originally meant as a mechanical replacement of human activity. 'Computers' were literally people who 'computed' – using their wits, pen and paper, or else that most ancient of reckoning tools, the *abacus*. However, the point isn't that machines are *better* at calculating than humans, merely that they can perform such calculations faster, for longer, and with fewer errors. What's more, those errors will result from design flaws or malfunction: thus, even the computer's mistakes are really of *human* origin. As the modern computer programmer puts it: 'Garbage in, garbage out' – a computer is a *tool*, and only as good as its designer, programmer and operator.

English inventor, mathematician and philosopher Charles Babbage is often considered the father of the computer. However, none of Babbage's various designs were fully constructed (though a later project by the London Science Museum shows that his *Difference Engine* would in fact have worked), and he wasn't even the first to conceive of such a possibility. Nevertheless, Babbage's importance lies in detailing how complex *mental* processes could be modelled mechanically, and that – as the design for his *Analytical Engine* suggests – the application of such machines was theoretically limitless.

The *Analytical Engine*, if built, would have been more powerful than the first prototype electronic computers, possessing memory, CPU (the modern computer's 'brain'), and even a form of printer. However, that it wasn't built (mainly due to the great expense involved) suggests that Babbage's contemporaries didn't fully grasp its potential. Had they done, it would have changed the course of human history – or at least, much earlier than it has done.

> 'Love not Pleasure; love God. This is the EVERLASTING YEA, wherein all contradiction is solved; wherein whoso walks and works, it is well with him.'
> THOMAS CARLYLE 1795–1881
> *Sartor Resartus*

Thomas Carlyle was a Scottish philosopher, writer, historian and satirist, whose promotion of *German Idealism* influenced the Romanticism, and was a formative influence upon *American Transcendentalism*.

He first came to prominence with *Sartor Resartus* ('The Tailor Retailored'), a somewhat strange and eccentric book, which combines a satirical account of a German 'philosopher of clothes' (the first half), and a sort of thinly-veiled spiritual autobiography (the second half). Clothes here are a metaphor for the 'external' aspect of the world – the 'fashions' of ideas and opinions, and of material reality in general. Seeking to go 'behind' outer appearances, the book's hero first denies the conventional wisdom of the world, and contemplates rejecting existence as meaningless (thus adopting *pessimism* the 'Everlasting No'). However, he moves from this to an attitude of detachment from the world ('the Centre of Indifference'), and finally reaches a positive affirmation of the value of life (the 'Everlasting Yea').

In part, Carlyle's book is therefore a critique of *empiricism*, or the belief that we must base our knowledge on the evidence of the senses, and therefore also of *utilitarianism*, which sees the 'good life' as one whose chief aim is the maximization of pleasure. In contrast, however, Carlyle argues that seeking pleasure, and avoiding pain, cannot lead to a truly meaningful life; rather, we must seek an ideal that makes sense of this – 'wherein all contradiction is resolved'.

As well as with Romanticism, Carlyle also shares something with Nietzsche, whose *Übermensch* was perhaps influenced by Carlyle's later ideal of the Hero: the man of genius, such as Shakespeare or Oliver Cromwell, driven by a guiding passion or vision. Thus, seeking to maximize pleasure and avoid pain, to make ourselves 'more comfortable' or 'better' (the aim of progress), were in themselves meaningless unless serving some greater ideal; without which, such concerns were merely empty fashions . . .

French scientist and philosopher Auguste Comte is the father of both *sociology* and *positivism*. Comte was concerned by the disparity between the natural sciences (biology, physics, etc.) and what are now known as the *social* sciences (political philosophy, psychology, etc.), for whilst the former involved measurable results and testable hypotheses, the latter generated widely differing and subjective theories. What was needed therefore was a method of studying social phenomena that allowed for greater precision and objectivity.

Comte firstly proposes a form of *relativism*: 'the only absolute is that everything is relative'. Thus, comprehending social behaviour and institutions requires an understanding of their historical development. This is because there are no absolute values *outside* of human society – no *theological* (God) or *metaphysical* values (e.g. Platonic ideals) – so the only values are those that society evolves itself. Human development – as described in our main quote – therefore gradually moves away from absolute, universal values, toward greater scientific understanding of how morals, institutions and social practices originate.

Here we arrive at positivism's central tenet: scientific theories should be based on the evidence of sense experience: what can be observed and *positively* verified. This was not a new doctrine (it was foreshadowed by Francis Bacon), but Comte applied it as a general principle for the acquisition of knowledge. This reaches its extreme in the philosophy of *logical positivism*, which considered non-verifiable statements meaningless – and herein lies the general danger of positivism. We may distinguish between that which sensory evidence can prove, and broader (moral, religious) claims that it's arguably impossible to conclusively verify, but does that make the latter meaningless? In his later career, Comte himself proposed a pseudo-mystical positivist surrogate for traditional religion – a 'religion of humanity'. Yet in doing so, doesn't this suggest that he sensed that a purely positivist outlook was missing something?

'The sun illuminates only the eye of the man, but shines into the eye
and heart of the child. The lover of nature is he whose inward and
outward sense are still truly adjusted to each other; who has retained
the spirit of infancy even into the era of manhood.'

RALPH WALDO EMERSON 1803–1882
Nature

Ralph Waldo Emerson was an American philosopher and writer who
founded the movement of *American Transcendentalism*. Graduating
from Harvard Divinity School, Emerson became a Christian pastor,
but this led to a growing dissatisfaction with orthodox religious attitudes and forms of practice, and ultimately to his resignation.

Transcendentalism therefore develops out of Emerson's desire to
reinvigorate religious belief. In *Nature*, perhaps his most famous
work, Emerson criticizes the contemporary tendency to experience
God through dogma, and the opinions and attitudes of past generations. Rather, he proposed, we should seek to realize the truths of
divinity through direct experience, especially through the natural
world. In doing so, Emerson rejected the notion that Jesus was divine,
considering him merely an exemplary man whose spirit and wisdom
we could follow. Such attitudes, however, led Emerson into controversy, and some even branded him an atheist.

Firstly, by 'nature' Emerson means everything that is 'NOT ME':
'both nature and art, all other men and my own body'. Thus, we can
experience the wonder of creation in people and created objects as
well as trees and sunsets. This is a vision in sympathy with the
Romanticism of Coleridge, whom Emerson met and was influenced
by, and Emerson's call for us to regain the innocent spirit of the child
is parallel to Coleridge's advocation of imagination as the primary
instrument for the apprehension of truth.

However, whilst *Nature* certainly isn't atheistic, it's a large step
from doctrinal Christianity – closer to *pantheism*, seeing God as *immanent* (present) in, and identical with nature. However, Emerson's
nature-worship was tempered by *Platonic idealism*, which makes him,
like Spinoza a *panentheist*: nature was merely the outward form of
divine truth, an expression of the thoughts of God.

> 'The divine being is nothing else than the human being, or, rather, the human nature purified, freed from the limits of the individual man, made objective – i.e., contemplated and revered as another, a distinct being. All the attributes of the divine nature are, therefore, attributes of the human nature.'
>
> LUDWIG FEUERBACH 1804–1872
> *The Essence of Christianity*

Nineteenth century German philosopher Ludwig Feuerbach, anticipating Sigmund Freud, saw God as a projection of human attributes. The Greek god Zeus was the strongest, most virile of the gods, because strength and virility were valued in Greek culture; his strength was, in effect, a glorification of *human* strength.

However, Feuerbach wasn't merely proposing that we clothe the divine in human concepts due to its *ineffable* nature (what is termed *anthropomorphism*), but simply arguing that God doesn't exist; he is a fiction, a mere externalization of our own ideals. Feuerbach called this process *alienation* (a term later borrowed by Karl Marx to describe the capitalist worker's relationship to his labour): human qualities are unconsciously projected onto an 'external' fictional being. Realizing that – for instance – we conceive God in our own image, or that we cannot fully describe the qualities of God, is therefore, for Feuerbach, merely a step towards the fuller realization that, beyond these projected qualities, there *is* nothing. Human culture could therefore progress by re-empowering itself, reversing the process of alienation, and re-assuming those qualities it had projected onto God at the cost of undermining its own self-esteem.

But does this disprove God's existence? Feuerbach points out that the more sophisticated and abstract the notion of God, the more hazy his actual existence, until religion ultimately entails faith in an abstract principle (whereas once it had embodied tangible ideals – strength, wisdom, courage, etc.). However, this process doesn't necessarily imply the gradual historical realization that God doesn't exist, and may only signify that our concepts of the divine are *evolving*. Once, man's ideas of divinity were anthropomorphic, *now* they're conceptual. So, that our ideas of God are projections isn't itself decisive: it supports both conclusions.

'The divine is God's concern; the human, man's. My concern is neither the divine nor the human, not the true, good, just, free, etc., but solely what is mine, and it is not a general one, but is – unique, as I am unique. Nothing is more to me than myself!'

MAX STIRNER 1806–1856

The Ego and its Own

Max Stirner was the pen name of Johann Kaspar Schmidt, a German philosopher who, along with such philosophers as Karl Marx, Friedrich Engels, and Ludwig Feuerbach, was early on associated with the *Young Hegelians* – a group of thinkers influenced by G. W. F. Hegel. Like Marx, Stirner, broke away and established his own ideas in opposition to aspects of Hegel's teachings.

Stirner's philosophy combines elements of *anarchism, individualism*, and *nihilism* (the view that life has no inherent or objective meaning). However, the underlying basis of his philosophy is the contention (similar to Feuerbach's) that all concepts and ideologies deprive us of what is rightfully ours – that is, our self. So, the ego owes no allegiance to God (who does not exist), country, society, community or family, nor to any abstract moral or social cause, nor ethical or philosophical ideal. Furthermore, by withdrawing our adherence from such external forces, we dispel the illusions that govern us.

However, paradoxically, such illusions also include the ego itself, which Stirner considered a 'creative nothing'. In abandoning all belief systems, we therefore make the world *and* our self 'nothing'. This concept of the self, perhaps, owes something to Schopenhauer or Buddhism. The self is not a name or a concept, but nor can our experience itself be denied. Stirner's position therefore differs from the straightforward sort of *ethical egoism* that individualist philosophies often espouse. We are not so much driven by personal motive to seek personal gain, but rather compelled to overcome the illusions that beset us. So, there is a tension here, for isn't this an almost *religious* ideal?

> 'It is better to be a human dissatisfied than a pig satisfied; better to be
> Socrates dissatisfied than a fool satisfied'
> JOHN STUART MILL 1806–1873
> *Utilitarianism*

In the classical version of utilitarianism, Jeremy Bentham had made no distinction between types of pleasure. Famously, he had argued that 'push-pin is as good as poetry' – that a simple child's game of the time was, in terms of its ability to provide happiness, equal to the works of Milton, Keats, Shakespeare, *et al.* But he was not arguing that there is *no* difference between types of pleasure – he acknowledged that there would be those more sophisticated types that would not be satisfied with such simple things – merely that we should not take this into account when assessing courses of moral action.

Whilst agreeing that pleasure was the chief good that moral acts aimed for, English philosopher John Stuart Mill argued that we must also make a distinction between higher and lower forms of pleasure. If we could choose between a sensually gratified, but mentally 'untroubled' life, such as an animal or ignorant person might lead, and a life of greater intellectual and cultural fulfilment, but accompanied by keen awareness of the many drawbacks of human existence, then we should still choose the latter. Therefore, higher, more sophisticated pleasures should be valued above lower ones.

In *Futurama*, the cartoon series developed by *Simpsons'* creator Matt Groening, the Professor invents a hat that turns its wearer into a genius. But the monkey he uses as a test subject isn't happy, for he now has enough intelligence and awareness to make him realize that he's now a freakish, lonely and excluded monkey genius. Should he continue wearing the hat and remain unhappy but intelligent, or remove it and return to blissful ignorance? His dilemma is eventually resolved when the hat is slightly damaged, causing him to be less intelligent, but therefore happier. Perhaps, then, happiness resides in having just the right amount of intelligence: not a satisfied pig, perhaps, but a monkey wearing a slightly-squashed, genius-making hat.

'The social subordination of women thus stands out an isolated fact in modern social institutions; a solitary breach of what has become their fundamental law; a single relic of an old world of thought and practice . . . as if a gigantic dolmen, or a vast temple of Jupiter Olympius, occupied the site of St. Paul's and received daily worship, while the surrounding Christian churches were only resorted to on fasts and festivals'

JOHN STUART MILL
On The Subjugation of Women

Mill's point is simple: whilst society has developed in equality and justice, the continuing inequality of women represents a blind-spot. Once, inequality in all manner of respects was the norm – racial, cultural, etc. However, whilst some of these (by Mill's time) have been addressed, sexual inequality has not. But why not?

Firstly, Mill rebuts prevalent arguments against sexual equality. We can't debar women from activities and occupations on the basis of incapacity, for it may be such restrictions that *cause* the inability. That is, if we let all women be soldiers, politicians, lawyers, etc., we'd find out how capable they are.

Also, we shouldn't judge woman's potential based on her current qualities, for 'What is now called the nature of women is an eminently artificial thing – the result of forced repression in some directions, unnatural stimulation in others.' Since there's never been a Country of Women, we don't know what women would be like free of the yoke of male dominance.

Mill then points out the benefits of sexual equality, such as increased companionship between the sexes, who would then have more in common – no more need for men to retreat into the drawing room for port and cigars, perhaps – the women could join them! Of course, this would benefit society as a whole, and competition would spur on both sexes.

Whilst valid and laudable, Mill's arguments now seem somewhat patronizing. The irony is, of course, that this is a result of their success, and how far feminism has come: their truths are now so obvious, we find the need to present such arguments tiresome – don't we?

> '. . . the only purpose for which power can be rightfully exercised over any member of a civilized community, against his will, is to prevent harm to others'
>
> JOHN STUART MILL
> *On Liberty*

The *harm principle,* as it is known, argues that governments should basically leave people alone, so long as their actions are not harming anyone. So, if, after a gruelling day in the House of Commons, I like to don a nappy and be fed, burped, bathed and bedded by 'Nanny', then – as long as no one is harmed – I should be free to do so. 'What a man does in the privacy of his own home, etc.' (By the way, this isn't . . . never mind.)

However, individuals incapable of 'self-governance' – children, the mentally ill or deficient, and (more controversially) members of less 'civilized' societies – may not benefit from the harm principle. This therefore means that their actions may be legitimately regulated and prescribed so that we can protect them from themselves and others.

Underlying the apparent freedom of Mill's liberalism is therefore a standard of rational behaviour. Children, the insane, and 'primitives' have not – and may never – achieve that standard. But also, creeping in through the back door, is a definition of 'sane' behaviour. For instance, if someone decides that it will improve their appearance immensely to put a spike through their nose, or lop off one of their limbs, are they rational? To be 'rational', in one sense, merely means, 'to have reasons'. But *who* decides a 'good' reason from a 'bad' one?

What is 'irrational' or 'harmful' are not absolute standards, but merely describe what most people take to be so. We evolve these standards as a community, not as individuals, so rationality is not some independent touchstone by which we can test personal tastes, but merely another expression of the majority's views (what society considers 'rational'). This means that it is not so easy to distinguish between what we disapprove of and what we find irrational. Will Nanny have to find another job?

'Owing to this struggle for life, any variation, however slight and from whatever cause proceeding, if it be in any degree profitable to an individual of any species, in its infinitely complex relationship to other organic beings and to external nature, will tend to the preservation of that individual, and will generally be inherited by its offspring'

CHARLES DARWIN 1809–1892
On The Origin of Species

Faced with the overwhelming complexity and intricacy of nature, and the extraordinary order that it seems to exhibit, it would seem that any explanation should at least be equally complex. And yet, Darwin's theory of evolution by *Natural Selection* is remarkably simple: faced with a battle over limited resources, organisms possessing appropriate characteristics will survive, procreate, and pass those successful features on.

A good example of this is Darwin's own *Eureka* moment, involving finches on the Galapagos Islands. Given a place aboard the HMS *Beagle*'s voyage to South America, Darwin was to catalogue and collect specimens of the various flora and fauna. However, whilst on the Galapagos, he noticed that the finches possessing larger beaks, more suited to cracking nuts, existed on the island where those nuts were to be found, whereas those with finer beaks, suited to seeds, existed on an island with seeds. The conclusion struck him: the birds had simply thrived on the island where their characteristics were most suitable for survival.

This picture is not complete, for Darwin still had no way of accounting for how original variations came about, and only modern genetics fills in the theory completely. However, the process of Natural Selection remains a central cog in the mechanism of evolution.

Evolution is now often accompanied by atheism, and yet this was never a position that Darwin explicitly advocated. Perhaps he just thought it prudent to keep quiet, but I think it equally likely that he was a man disturbed by his own findings: that, having provided the means to undermine conventional faith, he simply found himself as much at a loss as everyone else.

'I put my face close to the thick glass-plate in front of a puff adder in the Zoological Gardens, with the firm intentions of not starting back if it struck at me; but, as soon as the blow was struck, my resolution went for nothing and I jumped a yard or two backwards with astonishing rapidity. My will and reason were powerless against the imagination of a danger which had never been experienced.'

CHARLES DARWIN
The Expression of the Emotions in Man and Animals

In linking man and animal, Darwin does more than establish a fact of genetic history. As his later work shows, animals and humans share a common behavioural and emotional inheritance. To illustrate this, Darwin pointed to the appearance of the same facial expression of basic emotions – fear, surprise, pain, etc. – in both humans and chimps.

The most interesting consequence of this is that it suggests human emotions are *universal*. Just like Darwin's fearful reaction at the puff adder's strike, primal emotions are genetically pre-programmed. Phobias such as fear of snakes or spiders also illustrate Darwin's point: these are often triggered at an unconscious level, and not by a particular traumatic event, as with other phobias (though, of course, they *can* be caused in this way). If true, this might begin to account for the general similarity between the moral and social codes of societies the world over.

However, Darwin's views are only gradually finding acceptance (e.g. through Paul Ekman's work, a resistance which is perhaps due to fear that such universalism might support a restrictive notion of what is 'natural'. The opposite, and for many years orthodox view is embodied by anthropologists such as Margaret Mead, whose famous study of adolescents in Samoa claimed to prove that the sort of difficulties faced by Western adolescents aren't universal. Underlying this was the assumption that behaviour and emotion is learnt and therefore variable between cultures. Darwin and Ekman's work suggests, however, that, whilst superficial customs vary, humans are much more similar than their apparent differences suggest.

> 'What I really lack is to be clear in my mind what I am to do, not what
> I am to know'
> SØREN KIERKEGAARD 1813–1855
> *Journals*

Often cited as a forerunner of *Existentialism*, Danish philosopher Søren Kierkegaard rejected Hegel's grand rationalist system and proposed instead that philosophy should concentrate on the individual. However, this return to the self was not like Descartes's attempt to secure a basis for knowledge of the world, but rather an effort to address the emotional burdens that accompany our everyday personal choices.

Central among these choices was the question of the existence of God. All rational proofs for God – the teleological argument, the ontological argument, the cosmological argument, and so on – were arguably inconclusive. This is because, Kierkegaard says, reason cannot ultimately supply the answer to such a question, for reason is always accompanied by doubt, and the possibility that we are wrong; a genuine relationship with God cannot be built upon abstract thought, but rather requires an *irrational* 'leap of faith'.

Kierkegaard illustrated this by the biblical story of Abraham. Called upon by God to sacrifice his only son, Abraham was faced with a choice: to perform an act which not only went against his own deepest wishes, but was also contrary to God's own commandments; or, to defy a direct decree from God himself. Of course, as we know, God was just testing Abraham, but the situation summed up for Kierkegaard the sort of personal choices we are faced with. Abraham would have felt, to use a more modern expression: 'I'm damned if I do, and I'm damned if I don't!' (Well, literally!) The effect was, therefore, like some Zen *koan*, paralyzing Abraham's reason so that the only thing which might save him is a choice based on faith.

It is curious to note that Existentialism proper (Sartre, Camus, de Beauvoir) rejected Kierkegaard's theism – possessing no religious beliefs to be torn by the paradoxes of reason, they preferred atheism – whilst honouring his general insights. But can the two be so clearly divorced?

'To be a philosopher is not merely to have subtle thoughts, nor even to found a school, but so to love wisdom as to live according to its dictates, a life of simplicity, independence, magnanimity, and trust'
HENRY DAVID THOREAU 1817–1862
Walden

Thoreau was an *American Transcendentalist* philosopher who attempted to put into practice some of the ideals he shared with his friend and mentor Ralph Waldo Emerson. Turning his back on worldly ambitions, Thoreau sought to get closer to Nature and the divine reality embodied therein, and his working life consisted of a succession of odd jobs (working in his family's pencil factory, as a tutor to Emerson's children) whilst he pursued his main goals of writing and self-sufficiency. These latter were combined in two years spent on the shore of Walden Pond, in Concord, Massachusetts, in a house that he had built himself.

The resulting account – from which our quote is taken – presents his thoughts on a range of topics – nature, solitude, neighbours, education, spirituality – yet all reinforce his central theme: society, in its growing emphasis on money and possessions, is in danger of obscuring the true value of life, which can be appreciated by anyone, given enough space and time. The desire to 'better oneself' through owning a bigger house or getting a higher-paid job was therefore delusory:

'This spending of the best part of one's life earning money in order to enjoy a questionable liberty during the least valuable part of it reminds me of the Englishman who went to India to make a fortune first, in order that he might return to England and live the life of a poet.'

Thoreau's outlook should not therefore be mistaken for a form of monkish asceticism; whilst it may seem Spartan to live in an isolated cabin, farming his own food and earning his own crust, it was not a show of self-denial. Rather, it illustrated that the fineries of affluent society were superfluous and distracting: in ourselves, in the glories of nature, we have all we need.

'That government is best which governs not at all'
HENRY DAVID THOREAU
'Civil Disobedience'

Thoreau's idealism and independence made him sceptical of traditional democracy, and wary of government's tendency to marginalize individual interests. On occasion, this led him into direct conflict with the law, and in such situations Thoreau believed that it was permissible to transgress those laws in order to defend one's principles. For instance, at one point he was imprisoned for refusal to pay his taxes, citing as his reason his opposition to the Mexican- American War and the continued legality of slavery. Thoreau's argument was simple: why should he continue to support a government (in obeying its laws) that ceased to represent his views?

The practice of *civil disobedience* is a contentious one. Some reason that, where the laws of society are established by democratic process, we should respect them – even where we disagree with them – and register our discontent by established legal means (e.g. petitioning one's political representative, engaging in peaceful protest). However, others see this attitude as favouring the majority, arguing that one has no obligation to obey a law which one disagrees with, for matters of individual conscience should not be decided by democratic vote.

Thoreau is in this latter camp. He is, foremost, an *individualist*. If the government ceases to represent my views and interests, then I will cease to obey its laws. However, this comes dangerously close to *anarchy*, and to contravening the *social contract*. The point is, critics argue, not that we should only obey those laws that we agree with, but that we should respect the democratic process, for, even though we may disagree on certain points, society's members generally benefit from the state's protection. But, Thoreau argued, this is the problem with democratic government: whether it serves the majority of my interests, or the interests of the majority, it ignores minority concerns, and disregards individual conscience. So, the ideal government was none at all, or – since this was perhaps an impractical ideal – one which respected the individual, and facilitated his self-expression.

'The history of all hitherto existing society
is the history of class struggles'
KARL MARX 1818–1883 AND FRIEDRICH ENGELS 1820–1895
The Communist Manifesto

Though agreeing with aspects of Hegel's view of history, German philosophers Karl Marx and Friedrich Engels realized it was basically conservative. Society *should* pursue increased rationality and freedom, but this wouldn't occur naturally, without disobedience to the state; it required revolution. They also rejected Hegel's religious framework: history isn't a mystical unfolding of a single God-like absolute spirit, but a tale of *economic inequality*, and the resulting struggle between different social classes. This may *appear* as a conflict between different ideologies and philosophies, but in reality it stemmed from material differences between classes. For example, people in power – landowners, aristocrats – favour beliefs which justify and maintain their position, as exemplified by the Victorian hymn, *All Things Bright and Beautiful* (1848): 'The rich man in his castle, / The poor man at his gate, / God made them high and lowly, / And ordered their estate.' Atheism might therefore be seen as a reaction to 'divinely ordained' poverty.

So, Marx and Engels developed a *materialist dialectic* of history. In the beginning, *primitive communism* existed, where simple tribes banded together for survival. This evolved into *slavery*, where tribes conquered other tribes, and conquerors became aristocrats. Next came *feudalism*, where aristocratic landowners exacted enforced labour from *serfs* in return for protection and rights. Then *capitalism*, where middle-class landowners (the *bourgeoisie*) exploit the proletariat for economic profit. But this was not the end of the dialectic process. A future stage advocated revolution as the proletariat reclaim the *means of production* (factories, farms, mines, etc.) from the hands of the bourgeoisie; this *socialist* period is transitional, where social inequalities are ironed out in preparation for *communism*: a classless, stateless society.

And they lived happily ever after. Not. Debate still rages as to whether the communist *ideal* has failed, or merely its *implementation*. Apologists point out that the totalitarian regimes of Russia and China are not true communism, but were hijacked by corrupt and power-hungry elites. True, but then doesn't communism's flaw lie in its failure to allow for this?

'*Religious* suffering is, at one and the same time, the *expression* of real suffering and a protest against real suffering. Religion is the sigh of the oppressed creature, the heart of a heartless world, and the soul of soulless conditions. It is the *opium* of the people. The abolition of religion as the *illusory* happiness of the people is the demand for their *real* happiness. To call on them to give up their illusions about their condition is to call on them to *give up a condition that requires illusions*.'

KARL MARX

Contribution to the Critique of Hegel's Philosophy of Right

This is so well-known that it barely needs commentary. And yet, as sociologist Andrew McKinnon points out ('Reading "Opium of the People" '), there are a number of possible associations with 'opium' here: as medicine, as dangerous sedative, as emblem of social conflict, as source of visions or delusions. Which does Marx mean? It may well be all of them, but the main gist is clear: opium is not a good thing. It might 'help you through the day', but it has some unwelcome side effects (bad dreams, delusions), and it only seems necessary whilst the situation which produces the need for it exists. Therefore, let's kick the habit, go cold turkey, and look for real solutions.

Marx sees people's need for religion as a remedy for the pain of living. However, religion treats the symptom, not the cause – in fact, it works hand in hand with the cause, helping to ensure that workers continue to face the meaningless drudge of their existence. It is, then, merely an agent of social control.

But is this true? Well, we shouldn't assume that, just because religion *can* be used in this way, it has no other purpose. Domestic murders frequently involve kitchen utensils, but there is no call to ban *them*, because they also have a legitimate use (i.e. cooking). The point therefore isn't necessarily about the *truth* of religion (though Marx was atheist), but its *use*: shouldn't we reject or reform a religion that condoned such inequality?

> 'Ethical ideas and sentiments have to be considered as parts of the phenomena of life at large. We have to deal with man as a product of evolution, with society as a product of evolution, and with moral phenomena as products of evolution.'
>
> HERBERT SPENCER 1820–1903
> *The Principles of Ethics*

English philosopher Herbert Spencer famously applied Darwinism to society and ethics (*Social Darwinism*) and coined the phrase 'survival of the fittest'. However, 'fittest' isn't 'strongest' or 'most powerful', but simply 'most fit for survival within its environment' – a slow-moving, peaceable animal with good camouflage might prove the 'most fit'.

However, applied to human society, it's become synonymous with 'might is right', 'law of the jungle', and a general lack of compassion. This perhaps distorts Spencer's views, but he certainly believed we should help not hinder social evolution, and if this entailed the death or 'deselection' of weaker elements, then so be it.

Yet natural selection hasn't any conscious goal, and certainly not Spencer's 'progress' – a belief in humanity's moral and physical perfectibility. Darwinian evolution doesn't recognize individuals; man is no more precious than moss. Also, Spencer argued, society evolves *via* passing on acquired moral and knowledge-based traits, which is actually *Lamarckism*, a theory that Darwinism rejects. 'Social Darwinism' is therefore a misnomer: it isn't Darwinian at all.

Talk of social/genetic engineering also rings alarm bells. However, concern for genetic inheritance and 'progress' isn't the sole preserve of Nazis or mad scientists, and we must distinguish between *means* and *purpose*: Plato's philosopher guardians were selectively paired to foster qualities ideal for rulership, and modern genetic screening can help limit inheritance of incurable diseases. Unlike nature, we may consciously choose, and 'letting nature take its course' is effectively a euphemism for neglect: we either value life for its own sake, or not. But if we do, in choosing to help those who might not otherwise survive we say two things: we cannot put a value on another's existence, and nor can we say who might prove essential to human progress.

> 'Theory of the true civilization. It is not to be found in gas, or steam, or table-turning. It consists in the diminution of the traces of original sin.'
>
> CHARLES BAUDELAIRE 1821–1867
> 'My Heart Laid Bare', from *Intimate Journals*

Like Oscar Wilde, French poet and writer Charles Baudelaire rejected Romanticism's nature worship in favour of *aestheticism*: art and culture hid us from the world's grim realities. However, unlike Wilde, Baudelaire focused on these darker, underlying truths, scoffed at technological and social progress, and fads such as *spiritualism* ('table-turning'). As such, he is a *Decadent*, originally a disparaging term, but accepted by Baudelaire with pride.

When younger, he had pursued the Wildean ideal of the *dandy* – dressing expensively, running up debts, dining extravagantly – eventually leading to physical and financial ruin: he contracted gonorrhoea and syphilis; became addicted to opium, alcohol, and hashish; and squandered all his inheritance (leaving him practically penniless).

Baudelaire illustrates what happens when the dandy's aesthetic pose is undermined by circumstances. Whilst, 'Style is character', his eventual inability to support this style, hampered by hardship, illness and laziness, embittered him against polite society. But this bitterness and cynicism – famously expressed in his collection of poetry, *Les Fleur du Mal* ('the flowers of evil') – make him the ideal social critic. Like Diogenes, he sits on the fringes, perfectly placed to discern the true human motives beneath the surface – thus anticipating Freud and Nietzsche. So, whilst polite society pities and despises his wretchedness, he holds a mirror up to it: 'Hypocrite reader – my likeness – my brother!'

So, the good citizens, would they admit it, are driven by the same forces, but merely more fortunate – and self-deceiving – than he. And yet, for all his cynicism and seeming amorality, Baudelaire isn't (arguably) an atheist: rather, in his dark assessment of human nature, he merely recognizes the gap between reality and the religious ideal.

> 'The consciousness of brutes and men would appear to be related to
> the mechanism of their body simply as a collateral product of its
> working. And to be as completely without any power of modifying that
> working as the steam whistle, which accompanies the work of a
> locomotive engine, is without influence upon its machinery.'
> T. H. HUXLEY 1825–1895
> *On the Hypothesis that Animals are Automata*

Philosophers and neuroscientists are still struggling with the question
of how our subjective mental experiences relate to neurological brain
processes. In the 19th century, in terms coloured by the industrial
revolution, English biologist T. H. Huxley argued that consciousness
played no causal role in the physical workings of the brain, but was
merely a sort of 'steam' or by-product of the 'mental machine'.

Grandfather of novelist Aldous Huxley, and best known as *Darwin's
Bulldog* from his championing of evolutionary theory, Huxley's *epiphe-
nomenalism* (as the view is now known) was influenced by his biological
views. Similar to Descartes, he believed that biological organisms
were merely machines. However, whilst consciousness was not an
objective, measurable 'stuff' that could influence the brain's functioning, it must exist in some sense. It was, therefore, an ineffectual
by-product – like noise and smoke from an engine. But if so, then
control and free will are an illusion – in fact, a *delusion*, for it would be
like watching a film where we think we control the actors' behaviour!
However, since humans and animals are merely machines, then this
is not a problem for Huxley's theory.

But there are inconsistencies that any modern advocate of epiphe-
nomenalism (of which there are some) would need to address. For
instance, how can consciousness exist, but not possess any physical
influence? Aren't existence and physical reality the same thing? Also,
whilst it is only a simile, the model of the steam-producing machine
seems inadequate: not only can by-products affect the running of a
machine (by clogging up workings, etc.), they are also physical. So,
perhaps, far from being a solution to the mind-body problem, epiphe-
nomenalism is merely another illustration of it.

'From the Hierophants of Samothrace, Egypt, and the initiated
Brahmins of the India of old, down to the later Hebrew Rabbis, all
preserved, for fear of profanation, their real *bona fide* beliefs secret.'
H. P. BLAVATSKY 1831–1891
Key to Theosophy

Helena Petrovna, or *Madame* Blavatsky, was a Russian writer, philosopher, and proponent of *Theosophy*. She travelled widely throughout
Europe and as far as India, Mexico and Tibet (claiming to have been
made a Buddhist initiate there), ending up in New York, where she
established herself as a medium and clairvoyant. Investigating her
alleged powers (as a journalist with a reputation for unmasking spirit-
ualist frauds), Colonel Henry Steel Olcott was won over, to the extent
that, shortly after, Blavatsky, Olcott and others founded the *Theosophical
Society*.

The key message of Theosophy – a central tenet of the *New Age*
movement – is that all religions share the same source, variously
termed 'the secret doctrine', 'the perennial philosophy', or 'occultism'
(which simply means 'hidden'). Religions therefore had *exoteric*
(external) and *esoteric* (internal) aspects; the former representing the
face presented to the profane, the uninitiated, and the idly curious; the
latter constituting the inner, secret truth known only to its adepts. In
this sense, the formation of the Theosophical Society as a public
organization that anyone could join, was a break with this tradition:
the truth was now accessible to all.

Despite this, Theosophy still preserves a mysterious element,
namely Blavatsky's claim to be guided by 'Hidden Masters', enlightened beings who had transcended conventional human limitations,
mastering miraculous abilities – telepathy, teleportation, longevity. It's
easy to mock this as fanciful, even fraudulent. However, counter-
sceptics point to the evidence collected by Olcott, a sceptically-trained
professional debunker, including items left by the Masters (clothing,
letters), and signed affidavits of witnesses. Is this enough? As William
James argues, proof can be relative: what's incontrovertible to one is
circumstantial to another, and even direct experience can be doubted.
Is even evidence a matter of faith?

> '"When I use a word," Humpty Dumpty said in rather a scornful tone,
> "it means just what I choose it to mean – neither more nor less." "The
> question is," said Alice, "whether you can make words mean so many
> different things." "The question is," said Humpty Dumpty, "which is to
> be master – that's all."'
>
> LEWIS CARROLL 1832–1898
> *Through the Looking Glass*

Lewis Carroll was the pseudonym of English mathematician and logi-
cian, Reverend Charles Lutwidge Dodgson. Despite these
contributions, it's for the *Alice* books that he's most fondly remembered. However, as Martin Gardner's *Annotated Alice* reveals, whilst
primarily written for children, they contain a wealth of subtle allusion
to philosophical and logical doctrines.

For example, in *Through the Looking Glass*, Alice's conversation
with Humpty Dumpty, the egg-shaped victim of the 'great fall', recalls
a controversy concerning whether words have a definite meaning, or
whether they can mean whatever we want them to. The former position is called *conceptual realism*, the latter *nominalism*. Realism, which
Plato held to, argues that words invoke *real ideas* (what he termed the
forms; so, meaning isn't arbitrarily decided, but springs from its association with one of these general ideas.

Nominalism, on the other hand, argues just the opposite. Like
Humpty Dumpty, nominalists (such as William of Ockham, and A. J.
Ayer) reject the existence of meaning independent of use, and so it's
use that defines it. Thus, when Alice complains that he misuses 'glory',
Humpty Dumpty defends his right to make a word mean anything.
Interestingly, it's a position which Carroll himself held (quoted in
Gardner): 'any writer of a book is fully authorized in attaching any
meaning he likes to any word or phrase he intends to use.'

However, nominalism has its problems: if we define our own
meaning, how can we ever communicate with anyone? To understand
what Humpty Dumpty means by 'glory', he needs to tell Alice using
other words – whose meaning in turn must be explained . . . and so
on. Thus, we may *never* understand him (no great loss there,
perhaps . . .).

'First, you know, a new theory is attacked as absurd; then it is admitted
to be true, but obvious and insignificant; finally it is seen to be so
important that its adversaries claim that they themselves discovered it'
WILLIAM JAMES 1842–1910
Pragmatism's Conception of Truth

William James hailed from a cultured and cosmopolitan background
(his brother was the novelist Henry James), and pursued a broad
variety of interests, even qualifying in medicine, before finally settling
on psychology and philosophy. Such wide-ranging curiosity informed
his philosophical outlook, and its most striking features are its
open-mindedness, its lack of cast-iron dogmas, and its unpretentious
and accessible style.

These are often characteristics of *pragmatist* philosophy. The dogmatic philosopher looks for indubitable truths on which to found
knowledge, but the pragmatist focuses on the potential *usefulness* of
beliefs. So, whilst those following Descartes mire themselves in an
arguably fruitless search for first principles, the pragmatist says, 'Well,
you know, *this* seems to have worked for me so far, and, whilst it *might*
ultimately prove false, it is a good working hypothesis.' In this way,
whilst not discounting the possibility that there *are* fixed and indubitable truths, it nonetheless recognizes that we may make more ground
if we aren't so concerned with absolute certainty. In a way, then, this
encourages a more empirical, 'rule of thumb' approach to
philosophy.

Also, of course, it proposes that *this is what people generally do*. I do
not seek absolute proof before sitting on a chair to eat my breakfast,
and, arguably, this isn't even something that I *could* possess; many of
my everyday beliefs – even those I'd never *entertain* denying – are
equally 'shaky' in this sense. Rather, as our main quote suggests, truth
sneaks up on us: it begins as an idea, gradually forms into a hypothesis, which is in turn tested and borne out – though maybe not
unquestionably proven – by experience; like a stranger who becomes
an acquaintance, and turns out to be a best friend: we feel like we've
always known him.

WILLIAM JAMES
The Will to Believe

Having described how level-headed and sensible pragmatism can be, we come across a statement which seems to suggest that we can believe what we like! Well, this isn't *quite* what it says.

Since many beliefs are merely working hypotheses, we don't necessarily adopt them because they are *true*, or even because they *might* be true, but for other reasons. James therefore identified various criteria that people commonly use to decide their beliefs.

Firstly, when presented with two options, do we consider both equally possible? Deciding between *fruitarianism* (only eating fruit) and *veganism* (consuming no animal products) may be equally unappealing (*dead*) to you. However, buying only organic food or not may be a decision you feel you can make (they are *live* options). Secondly, can we avoid choosing? Do I believe in God, or not? Well, I feel pretty healthy now – I'll decide another day. However, on my deathbed, I may feel differently. So, decisions are either *avoidable* or *forced* upon us. Finally, choices are *momentous* or *trivial*. Do I want tea or coffee? Does it matter? Will I marry you? Well, um . . . can I think about it? Some decisions come once in a lifetime. As well as the above, we're also driven by two warring principles: *desire* to know and commit, and *fear* of error and regret.

Belief, then, is not a matter of having enough evidence, but of having *living, momentous* choices *forced* upon us. Facts play a part, but aren't decisive: a shaky faith may only require a chance comment to topple it; a devout one may withstand rigorous evidence in refutation of every article.

Many criticize this approach for suggesting that truth is relative. But James is arguing that we may adopt beliefs with little evidence, because of their overall positive effect on our lives. This doesn't mean they're completely immune to falsification, merely that believing them may eventually open up new paths of knowledge and understanding.

> 'My first act of free will shall be to believe in free will'
> WILLIAM JAMES
> diary entry, 1870

You're out walking, and come to a fork in the road: Which way? Left or right? Either will lead you home, so it's just a matter of preference. You choose left. But *could* you have chosen right? *Determinists* say no. Like Laplace's omniscient demon, if we had all the facts, then we could predict every event, for everything is linked by fixed laws of cause and effect. Therefore, your apparently free choice was determined by your personal history, likes and dislikes, biology, environment, and so on. However, this means that our experience of choice is illusory.

Libertarians disagree: we have free will because we experience deciding to do or not do something. However, libertarians need to somehow account for cause and effect, so they sometimes argue that rational, conscious decision-making is *outside* of physical causation. Descartes's notion of an immaterial soul is an example of this. But how does an immaterial thing affect material processes?

Or, perhaps there's *no* determinate cause (*indeterminism*): things *aren't* fixed. But this doesn't provide choice, merely chance. If things aren't caused, then they're random, not free.

A fourth option (*compatibilism*, or *soft determinism*) combines aspects of determinism and libertarianism. So, we have our cake and eat it. It's an appealing view, if only because it allows us to give credence to our own experience of free choice without undermining science. This isn't completely satisfying – we are still left wondering how both can be true – but it does provide a commonsense middle-ground.

As with other philosophical issues, James held that we often believe things that seem contradictory or lack evidence. The problem of free will is such a case. For a while, James was himself determinist. However, he came to realize that, whilst it was still problematic, it might yet be *possible* that free will and determinism were compatible. And if so, given his experiences, why should he not *choose* to believe that?

> 'Scientific theories are organically conditioned just as much as
> religious emotions are; and if we only knew the facts intimately
> enough, we should doubtless see "the liver" determining the dicta of
> the sturdy atheist as decisively as it does those of the Methodist under
> conviction anxious about his soul. When it alters in one way the blood
> that percolates it, we get the Methodist, when in another way, we get
> the atheist form of mind.'
>
> WILLIAM JAMES
> *The Varieties of Religious Experience*

As soon as science and medicine realized and began to chart the connection between physical and mental processes, there sprang up the popular pastime of 'pin the malady on the mystic'. Thus, St. Paul's vision on the road to Damascus was 'nothing but' epilepsy, resulting from 'a discharging lesion of the occipital cortex'; St. Teresa's mystical experiences were merely the delusions of 'an hysteric'; and George Fox, founder of Quakerism, wasn't 'pining for spiritual veracity', but merely suffering from 'a disordered colon'.

However, James points out, this cuts both ways: if thought and behaviour have a physical, organic cause, then this is as much true of 'rational', 'normal' thought as it is of religious ecstasy. Is the atheist therefore suffering from a dysfunctional liver? The nihilist from a grumbling appendix? *Medical materialism*, as James calls it, commits the error of assuming that spiritual experiences are false because they can be traced to a certain physical cause. And yet, the fact that our physical organism plays a similar role in our genuine *everyday* experiences, does not mean that *those* are false. It might just be that, when mystics have visions, their brain behaviour looks like epilepsy, just as hallucinating and actually seeing share similar features of brain activity (to an extent).

James' point then is that physical origin by itself does not tell us anything. This is known as the *genetic fallacy*: tracing something to a 'lowly' origin (Jesus was *just* a carpenter) does not make it unreal. Everything must start somewhere.

> 'Common sense says, we lose our fortune, are sorry and weep; we meet a bear, are frightened and run; we are insulted by a rival, are angry and strike. The hypothesis here to be defended says that this order of sequence is incorrect . . . we feel sorry because we cry, angry because we strike, afraid because we tremble.'
>
> WILLIAM JAMES
> 'What is an Emotion?'

In other words, do physical reactions cause emotions, or emotions cause physical reactions? As James points out, it seems most commonsensical to think that emotions – sorrow, fear, anger – cause bodily sensations such as weeping, trembling, lashing out. However, if the other way around, emotion becomes secondary.

This shouldn't perhaps be very surprising, especially in light of recent studies into the speed of conscious reaction. For instance, presented with alternative choices, subjects whose brains were being monitored showed that brain activity associated with a particular decision (yes or no) occurred some time before the decision registered at a conscious level. So, if I had a brain scanner, I could predict what decision you might make!

Determinists and materialists seize on this type of information to argue that we aren't in fact in conscious control of our actions. Nietzsche, for instance, argued that a 'free' action is merely one that happens to correspond with our desires: an action happens, we like it, and call it 'free'. So, if the *James-Lange theory of emotion* (as it's called) is correct, then it merely removes another supporting strut from our illusory picture of the conscious rational self.

But need we see it this way? Firstly, not everyone agrees with James' analysis, and there are still other theories: the *Canon-Bard theory* reasserts the commonsense view, whilst the later *Two Factor theory* aims at a sort of compromise. But even if James *is* correct, must this entail determinism? My body is as much 'me' as my emotions, my unconscious processes as much mine as my conscious ones. Is the problem then that we separate them in the first place?

'Mutual aid is as much a law of animal life as mutual struggle'
PYOTR KROPOTKIN 1842–1921
Mutual Aid

And not only animal life, but human too. One of the main influences on both Darwin and Wallace's accounts of evolution was Thomas Malthus' theories regarding population growth. Societies that favour equality and fairness are always running out of resources: need outstrips the ability to satisfy it. However, animals are not governed by ethical principles, which leads to constant conflict over limited resources – the 'survival of the fittest' (the 'most fit' or best suited to prevailing conditions, not necessarily the strongest or fastest).

Some saw in this 'law of the jungle' a model for human society that has become known as *social Darwinism*, where the strongest, most virile members rise to the top, whilst its weakest decline and perish. Furthermore, we should not oppose this natural process, but work with it to facilitate human evolution.

But why take nature as a model for society? Humans need not dominate and exploit, because they can communicate and cooperate. However, is this really a true picture of the natural world? Birds and insects pollinate flowers, and animals spread in their droppings the seeds of the fruit they eat. Furthermore, nature is rich in colonies, packs, flocks and other forms of social organization, suggesting that, whilst life involves struggle, it is one that is best faced together.

When it came to human society, Russian philosopher Pyotr Kropotkin identified nature's lesson as the need to cooperate to exist. His *anarchist communism* therefore proposed that all laws are decided democratically ('anarchy' means 'without leaders', not 'without laws'), the means of production should be local and communally owned, and the results of labour are shared (therefore, no one goes without).

Maybe Kropotkin overstated the degree of cooperation in nature – but no more than, perhaps, capitalists selectively interpreted it as continual struggle. Nature may support both models. Therefore, the deeper question is why we need such natural evidence to support our choice of society.

'As a man Sacher-Masoch cannot lose anything in the estimation of his cultured fellow-beings simply because he was afflicted with an anomaly of his sexual feelings. As an author he suffered severe injury so far as the influence and intrinsic merit of his work is concerned, for so long and whenever he eliminated his perversion from his literary efforts he was a gifted writer, and as such would have achieved real greatness had he been actuated by normally sexual feelings.'

RICHARD VON KRAFT-EBING 1840–1902
Psychopathia Sexualis

Masochism (**sexual pleasure** from submission and degradation) is named after Austrian writer Leopold von Sacher-Masoch (1836–1895), a respected and popular author whose own 'Masochism' briefly surfaced in *Venus in Furs*. As such, Kraft-Ebing argued, whilst his predilections were incidental to his talent, it would have been greater without them – wouldn't it?

Richard von Kraft-Ebing was a German psychiatrist who pioneered *Sexology* (the study of sexuality). His landmark work, *Psychopathia Sexualis*, coins many still-used terms – 'heterosexual', 'masochism', 'sadism' – and helped recast sexual deviance in medical language – as 'perversions' requiring treatment, rather than 'sins' or 'crimes'. He's also the first to propose a biological basis for homosexuality, which therefore isn't a mental illness.

But, Kraft-Ebing argues, since the proper object of sex is procreation, all other aims are deviant. So, if he could have overcome his masochism, Sacher-Masoch would have been an even greater writer, for deviant sexuality diverts energy that would otherwise benefit health and self-fulfilment. But there's an assumption here that nature determines what is correct sexual behaviour. And yet, as the range of 'normal' sexual preferences suggest, whilst nature provides the imperatives, it's culture that fills in the details. So, perhaps what defines *illegitimate* perversion (rape, paedophilia) is not so much 'Is it *natural*?' but 'Is it *moral*?' Since Sacher-Masoch's 'perversions' were harmless, shouldn't we say 'live and let live'? As British actress Pat Campbell famously put it: 'Does it really matter what these affectionate people do – so long as they don't do it in the streets and frighten the horses!'

> 'Much will have been gained for aesthetics once we have succeeded in apprehending directly – rather than merely ascertaining – that art owes its continuous evolution to the Apollinian-Dionysian duality, even as the propagation of the species depends on the duality of the sexes, their constant conflicts and periodic acts of reconciliation'
>
> FRIEDRICH NIETZSCHE 1844–1900
> *The Birth of Tragedy*

The first published work of German philosopher Friedrich Nietzsche was an unusual affair, combining ideas on aesthetics, Greek tragedy, music, philosophy and history. It wasn't well received by his colleagues at the University of Basel (where he was a professor of philology), and as such marks a transitional point before his transformation from salaried academic to stateless philosopher.

However, whilst *The Birth of Tragedy* doesn't sparkle with the wit and insight of the later Nietzsche, it lays the groundwork for much of his mature philosophy, its chief contribution, perhaps, being his distinction between two types of psychological impulse: the *Apollonian* and *Dionysian*. Named after the Greek Sun god Apollo, patron of poetry, the arts, and philosophy itself, the Apollonian seeks to mould experience into a definite form – through images, words, rational ideas and logic. In contrast, Dionysus, the Greek god of wine and ecstatic celebration, embodies emotional and physical involvement, and a desire to experience reality on its own terms. As such, the two aspects – both equally an expression of who we are – work at cross purposes. The history of art and culture can therefore be seen as a constantly tilting balance between these two forces as they vie for dominance.

In later works, Nietzsche abandons these terms, but is still concerned with the principles in question. In one sense, his philosophy is an attempt to redress what he saw as the contemporary *imbalance* towards the Apollonian – through the *Enlightenment*, through Kant and the rationalists – which valued reason above all else. However, as Nietzsche's philosophy shows, our supposed rationality is really based in instinct and irrational desire. Nietzsche therefore styled himself a 'disciple of Dionysus', undermining these rational assumptions and reuniting philosophy with its irrational brother.

'. . . if the lambs say among themselves: "these birds of prey are evil; and whoever is least like a bird of prey, but rather its opposite, a lamb – would he not be good?" there is no reason to find fault with this institution of an ideal, except perhaps that the birds of prey might view it a little ironically and say: "*we* don't dislike them at all, these good little lambs; we even love them: nothing is more tasty than a tender lamb"'

FRIEDRICH NIETZSCHE
On the Genealogy of Morals

Nietzsche's most infamous doctrine, which draws a distinction between *master* and *slave* moralities, has suffered by association with Hitler's 'master race', which it probably influenced, but shouldn't be confused with. Nietzsche argued that every being has *will to power*, the desire to express itself to the fullest extent. But the form this takes depends on the creature: a lion succeeds through strength and power; a snow fox by guile and camouflage. Will to power, then, is not the same as 'might is right'.

For humans, however, morality must embody the highest expression of human strength, health and vitality. This doesn't mean that the highest ideal should be brutish or savage, but merely that we should not turn our back on our own nature. Originally, the *master* morality was therefore merely the code that governed the aristocracy – in its truest sense (Greek, *aristos*, 'best') – those clever and strong enough to rule. Such a ruler *might* be magnanimous, or compassionate, but out of *abundance* – an overflowing of wealth and health – *not* out of pity.

However, the morality of the 'lambs' springs from what Nietzsche termed *ressentiment*: born of powerlessness and envy, it *inverts* traditional virtues; the 'good' are humble, meek, and passive; compassion is required because we're all equally weak or miserable; the proud, strong, healthy, man becomes the 'evil' tyrant.

Hitler therefore drew selectively from Nietzsche (if he read him at all), but in scapegoating Jews and other minorities, isn't he rather 'lamb' than 'bird of prey', blaming others for his powerlessness?

> 'What does not destroy me, makes me stronger'
> FRIEDRICH NIETZSCHE
> *Twilight of the Idols*

Faced with the likelihood of disease, disappointment and general hardship, we are limited in our choice of responses: denial, acceptance, or avoidance. Most, it is fair to say, choose the latter option. In never adopting a consistent philosophy of life, we simply deal with things as they arise, thanking our lucky stars or cursing their ill influence as the occasion dictates.

Philosophers are generally more systematic. Leibniz, famously satirized in Voltaire's novel *Candide*, argued that we live in 'the best of all possible worlds', thereby denying the reality of its apparent evils; all would eventually work out for the best. Schopenhauer, not blessed with such a blithely sunny disposition, argued that, actually, the opposite is true: we live in the *worst* of all possible worlds, for only the slightest of changes – a rise in the Earth's temperature by just a few degrees, a relatively small rock hurtling from space – would leave no world at all. Hence, we constantly teeter on the very precipice of annihilation – how much worse could it get?!

Nietzsche considered these two extremes equally unproductive: to deny the reality of pain and suffering was self-deluding; to allow it to have the final say, self-defeating. But what if we welcome it? Not as a trial for a heaven yet to come (where everything is balanced out), nor out of some perverse need to revel in our own misery, but rather as a test of true *positivity*.

Imagine that a demon came to you one night, and offered you the following deal: you can live for all eternity, but only so long as you live the *same* life – exact in every detail – over and over again. What would you say? Most would be horrified: every *joy*, yes – but every *sorrow*? Every *pain*? And all repeated *endlessly*? But, Nietzsche argues, wouldn't a person who could say 'yes' to such a life – accept it unreservedly, with all his heart – be the highest example of joy and strength?

> 'The world itself is will to power – and nothing else!'
> FRIEDRICH NIETZSCHE
> *The Will to Power*

Diary of a Superman

At the bus stop a herd of people stood in line like sheep. Realising my destiny, I barged to the front – 'Make way! *Übermensch* coming through!' Murmurs from the cattle – one old crone carped, 'There's a queue, you know! It's not right!' 'Ha! *Fear* is the mother of morality!' I thundered, and kicked her tartan shopping trolley from under her, flooring her and scattering a bag of satsumas, two packs of digestive biscuits, and a copy of *Heat* magazine. 'Good God, man!' a genetically inferior specimen protested, 'Have pity! She's an old lady!' 'Pity preserves that which is ripe for destruction,' I spat, 'and thwarts the law of evolution!' I ground my heel into a wandering satsuma for emphasis. 'And *man* is that which must be overcome!'

At the police station . . .

At bottom, Nietzsche argued, we are afraid; of ourselves, and of others. We fear that, if people acted without constraint, untold horrors would result. So, we need morality as an external form of restraint and justification: why be good? Because we *must*. What *is* 'good'? It is defined for us – by God, or some otherworldly ideal.

But what if morality is an expression of our deepest instincts and values? What if these instincts could explain *all* life and behaviour? A common misinterpretation of Nietzsche is that 'will to power' means 'might is right'; that we must discard sensitivity and compassion, letting loose the beast within. But this is at best a half-truth: he *did* claim that every creature seeks to impose its will upon others, but this is as true of Jesus as it is of Hitler. He thought morality should embody strength and health, and we turn our back on these at our peril. However, we craft *our own* principles: the ideal *Übermensch* (superman) transcended conventional morality to a higher, self-defined code. Would such an ideal *really* condone the psychotic tyrant, the amoral sociopath, or the geriatric-bashing, satsuma-squashing queue-jumper?

'The madman jumped into their midst and pierced them with his eyes. "Whither is God?" he cried. "I will tell you. *We have killed him* – you and I. All of us are his murderers." '

FRIEDRICH NIETZSCHE
The Gay Science

'**God is dead**' is the atheist's t-shirt slogan, but there is seldom understanding of what Nietzsche meant by this, or any appreciation of his complex attitude to religion. Firstly, as our main quote states, *we* are responsible for the death of God, and it is by no means clear that this is an unequivocally *good* thing. The passage in which the phrase occurs tells a parable: a madman goes looking for God with a lit lantern in the daytime (recalling Diogenes, perhaps; laughed at, ridiculed, he turns on his mockers and pronounces their guilt – but they do not understand him.

The parable concerns the shift in the world-view that has come about through the growth of reason and science. As yet, most people do not fully grasp the Godsized hole that scientific explanation has created. Religious belief persists, but it is an empty show – the churches have become 'the tombs and sepulchres of God' – and his death has left us rudderless, without meaning.

The thing that the madman – and Nietzsche – understands, and the people do not, is that we must now create our *own* meaning. This is as true of our time as it was of Nietzsche's. Science gives us knowledge and technology, but takes away the simpler, unifying picture of an orderly, meaningful universe. What, then, is the answer? Having lost our innocence, we must grow up: having performed the terrible deed, 'Must we ourselves not become gods simply to appear worthy of it?'

Whilst compatible with atheism in some regards, there is a spirit here which, like Kierkegaard's existentialism, is not in itself irreligious (and which therefore has appealed to certain religious believers): in the modern world, where science and scepticism call all dogmas into question, it is *we* who must take responsibility for our values and beliefs, not God.

> 'You are visiting women? Don't forget your whip!'
> FRIEDRICH NIETZSCHE
> *Beyond Good and Evil*

Nietzsche's views on women seem so close to Schopenhauer's, one might be forgiven for thinking that he had never actually met one, but – as with some exotic species of bird – contented himself with the account of a more seasoned traveller. Schopenhauer had, admittedly, more mileage in this respect – he had fathered an illegitimate son, conducted love affairs – whereas Nietzsche's experiences seem confined to one brothel visit and two rejected marriage proposals. Given the alleged misogyny both philosophers share, it is tempting to attribute one's to bitter experience, the other's to frustration at lack of it.

Nietzsche's case at least is more complex. The brothel visit is contested: depending on whom you believe, he either contracted the syphilis that drove him insane, or simply played the piano and left. The would-be love of his life was Lou von Salomé, a fellow intellectual, later famous for pioneering psychoanalysis alongside Freud, the lover of the poet Rilke, and one of the first to write an in-depth study of Nietzsche. A photo taken with him and their friend Paul Reé shows her seated in a cart, holding a whip, the two men standing ready to be harnessed. Salomé later rejected his advances in favour of Reé's, and we can imagine that this image stayed with Nietzsche; reminding him who truly had the 'whip hand', and how he would like it to have been.

Some trace Nietzsche's misogyny from here: retiring from romantic life after Salomé, seeking revenge against all women, his comments are obvious psychological compensation (*ressentiment!*). But contemporary personal accounts reveal him to have been a charming, polite and thoughtful companion around women. Once asked about the whip comment, he replied, 'But that is only a joke!' Was it? It is difficult to say, for even once we get behind the popular caricature – misogynist, anti-Semite, proto-Nazi, Anti-Christ – we face other masks – well-mannered professor, lonely visionary, bitter social critic. Was misogyny merely another mask, worn for effect?

> 'Refusal to believe until proof is given is a rational position; denial of
> all outside of our own limited experience is absurd'
> ANNIE BESANT 1847–1933
> *Annie Besant*

Annie Besant was one of those rare personalities that seems more a force of nature than a human being. Social reformer, advocate of birth control, campaigner for women's rights, supporter of Irish home rule and Indian independence, female Freemason – the list goes on. In a long, committed, and often controversial life, she embodied the sort of intensity and drive that we slugabeds can only look upon with a sort of lackadaisical awe.

In 1889, she converted to *Theosophy*, an occult religious organization with Buddhist leanings, after interviewing its founder, H. P. Blavatsky. Numbering among its doctrines belief in clairvoyance, reincarnation, and the existence of a hierarchy of 'Secret Masters', Theosophy was a far call from the sort of pragmatic, socially progressive societies that she had until that point been associated with. How would she tell her secular friends, such as atheist Charles Bradlaugh, with whom she had once faced prison for promoting birth control? She delivered a series of lectures, later appearing as a pamphlet, 'Why I Became a Theosophist', setting out her reasons for accepting beliefs that many of her atheist *and* religious acquaintances would no doubt consider ridiculous.

Her main point was clear: logic is but a tool, and science merely a method; we should not confuse our current understanding of reality with a dogma that we dare not deviate from, nor treat consensus opinion as the final word on possibility. She reminds her critics of Giordano Bruno, the Italian Renaissance philosopher burnt at the stake for suggesting the possible existence of other inhabited worlds: yet, if we judge on the prejudice of received opinion, aren't we guilty of the same intolerance?

Her beliefs aside, Besant's most admirable qualities were courage, humility and open-mindedness. She suggested as her own epitaph, 'She tried to follow truth.' That is all any of us can hope to do, isn't it?

> 'Art takes life as part of her rough material, recreates it, and refashions
> it in fresh forms, is absolutely indifferent to fact, invents, imagines,
> dreams, and keeps between herself and reality the impenetrable
> barrier of beautiful style, of decorative or ideal treatment'
> OSCAR WILDE 1854–1900
> *The Decay of Lying*

Oscar Wilde was an Irish playwright, writer, and proponent of *aestheticism*. Reacting against *Romanticism's* love of nature, realism – embodied in the novels of Balzac, Zola, or George Eliot – and desire for art to reflect life, aestheticism considers art to have no purpose but its own: 'art for art's sake'.

However, flashes of wit and elegantly crafted aphorisms disguise a serious purpose. Imagination elevates human consciousness. Faced with everyday life's drab and onerous conditions, art erects an 'impenetrable barrier of beautiful style'. So, aestheticism's emphasis on decoration, fantasy, fashion and pleasure doesn't reflect deeper truths, but *hides* them. Survival requires adopting a 'cultivated blindness' to life's unpleasantness: in short, one must cultivate the *art of lying*.

Whilst there are elements of courage, intelligence and creativity that set this apart from mere escapism, there's also an aristocratic disdain for the hardships of those not privileged enough to flee into a world of mannered frivolity. Aestheticism cannot resolve this tension, but must eventually bow to the inevitable – as happened to Wilde himself, where reality came calling in the form of the scandal that ruined him, and the imprisonment that broke his spirit. In *De Profundis*, written in jail, he realizes this:

> 'I wanted to eat of the fruit of all the trees in the garden of the world . . . My only mistake was that I confined myself so exclusively to the trees of what seemed to me the sun-lit side of the garden, and shunned the other side for its shadow and its gloom.'

Aestheticism, then, is a fair-weather philosophy; but what do we do when the clouds gather?

'In the past the man has been first; in the future
the system must be first'
FREDERICK W. TAYLOR 1856–1915
The Principles of Scientific Management

Frederick W. Taylor was an American engineer who introduced scientific management principles into industrial manufacturing. His ideas, known as *Taylorism*, have been hugely influential, and led to the development of the assembly line of American car manufacturer Henry Ford.

Taylorism's main principles address the perceived need for stricter organization, time management and more directed training. In traditional working environments, Taylor argued, there was too much room for individual innovation: three different people approaching the same job would not only take different amounts of time, but approach each aspect of the task in a different way. Thus, in analyzing jobs, breaking them down into their component tasks, and organizing the work process according to the most effective and time-efficient methods, overall productivity could be increased greatly.

Obviously, this is laudable merely from the point of view of profit, but, from the perspective of the worker himself, it has numerous harmful effects. Firstly, both Taylorism and Fordism de-skill the workforce. Where once a worker would learn a trade and gradually acquire expertise over many years, scientific principles dictated it more efficient to embed the skills in the productive process itself: the skill was reflected in the design of the system, not any individual. This made workers expendable and replaceable, for anyone could (with a little training) do any job. But being a replaceable part in the 'machine' of production also has its dehumanizing effects – on self-esteem, on sense of purpose and value.

Arguably, Taylorism also underestimates the social by-products of work. People don't just work to earn money, but to fraternize and form social bonds. Isolating individuals, reducing the time allowed between tasks, timing breaks, etc., therefore ultimately erodes social cohesion. It might be argued that modern companies have pioneered ways to address this – team building exercises and company picnics, for example. But doesn't singing the company song become one more time-bound duty the worker performs to keep the machine running?

'The ego is not master in its own house'
SIGMUND FREUD 1856–1939
A Difficulty in the Path of Psycho-Analysis

When psychology was still a burgeoning field not wholly distinct from either philosophy or medicine, the development of *psychoanalysis* by Austrian psychologist Sigmund Freud helped establish it as a separate discipline with its own concerns. Partly, this was because psychoanalysis appealed to the popular imagination: in its focus on dreams, symbolism, sexuality, and its concern with personal experience, it reached out to a public that, even if it did not fully understand its doctrines, at least felt able to engage with them. This is true even today, where although the psychoanalytical star is on the wane, its terms still crop up in common usage.

Psychoanalysis can be seen as a reaction against Enlightenment thinking. Whilst Newton, Locke, and Descartes may have differed on details, they all shared a belief that nature, society and the individual were – or should be – rationally ordered. However, Freud argued that the mind's rational, conscious veneer hides *irrational, unconscious* motivations that society wants us to *repress*. The self is not actually unified at all, but consists of potentially competing aspects: the *id*, the source of basic desires; the *ego*, the rational, decision-making self; and the *superego*, the internalization of the moral dictates of society and upbringing. Since an uncontrolled *id* would be nothing less than an amoral beast, the *ego's* role was to facilitate those desires which the *superego* told it were acceptable, and to repress those it said were not.

Nevertheless, this three-way relationship often resulted in conflict, and an individual could develop disruptive psychological symptoms, requiring a sort of coming to terms with the source of unconscious disruption. However, for Freud, repression itself was not 'bad'. Just as the job of a steam valve is not to let *all* the pressure escape, merely the required amount to avoid disaster, so the job of psychoanalysis was not to overcome repression *completely*, but merely to regulate it: we should be not too much, and not too little, but *just the right amount* of uptight.

> 'The interpretation of dreams is the royal road to a knowledge
> of the unconscious activities of the mind'
> SIGMUND FREUD
> *The Interpretation of Dreams*

Freud believed the central means of understanding a patient's psychological symptoms lay in analyzing unconscious material, which was therefore outside of conscious control and censorship. So, a psychoanalyst might look to a patient's dreams or fantasies to discover the problem that consciousness was trying to repress. However, such analysis requires a degree of subjective evaluation and symbolic interpretation. There is therefore a common ground between the artist or poet seeking inspiration and the intuitive leap of the analyst interpreting a dream: both are thinking creatively. However, whilst this may be fine for the creative type, it signals a problem for the scientist: how can such methods provide reliable and objective results?

Aside from subjectivity, a more serious charge, made by philosopher Karl Popper, is that psychoanalytic theory is *unfalsifiable*, and therefore unscientific. For instance, Freud argued that all dreams are expressions of wish fulfilments: you dream of winning the lottery because you'd like to be rich. However, what of nightmares? What wishes do *they* fulfil? Freud responded that the wishes are still there, they're just veiled or repressed – perhaps, secretly, you want a rich relative to die and leave you money, but since this is a dastardly desire that you cannot admit to yourself, you have a 'nightmare' where the relative dies. But how can we prove that this is a correct theory of dream interpretation? A dream which clearly expresses the wish supports the theory; but so does a dream which *doesn't* explicitly express the wish. But if both outcomes prove the theory, then it is no theory at all, for it can't be tested!

This is a serious problem for psychoanalysis. Discussing his theory that repressed sexuality often expresses itself in *phallic symbolism*, even Freud admitted that cigars, skyscrapers and rockets are sometimes just that. But if so, when is a symbol *not* a symbol? When, it seems, the analyst says so.

> 'God is the exalted father, and the longing for a father
> is the root of the need for religion'
> SIGMUND FREUD
> *The Future of an Illusion*

When we're born we are literally helpless. As we grow, mother becomes the source of nourishment and love, and father the figure of authority and protection, the great lawmaker and the vanquisher of external threat. As adults, whilst we learn to fend for ourselves, we never really overcome this inner psychological vulnerability, for we are all helpless in the face of the unknown (a fact we realize more fully than children). It is therefore this continuing vulnerability, Freud argues, that sows the seed for religious belief: God is the external manifestation of our need for protection.

In psychoanalytic terms, God is the result of *psychological projection*, whereby we externalize or 'project' our subjective needs onto the world. This can work in different ways: I might project my own unacknowledged feelings about myself onto another person to avoid dealing with them ('that person is *so* disorganized!'). Or – as in the case of religion – I may create the image of a loving, caring God to offset my anxiety about my own and my family's safety, my general fears about the future. Projection, then, is a defensive mechanism driven by desire for wish fulfilment.

Is God merely the product of wishful thinking? Firstly, the fact that we project our feelings onto God does not necessarily disprove his existence. I might think of a friend as trustworthy, ignoring contrary evidence, because I need a friend; however, the projection of my feelings does not determine whether or not my friend exists! Secondly, we may question the mechanism of projection itself. If God is an expression of a need for a father figure, then what about polytheism, or mother goddess religions, or even more philosophical belief systems (such as Buddhism) which seem not to involve any god at all? At best, then, projection represents a mere possibility, and one that doesn't seem to apply in all cases.

> 'Ere many generations pass, our machinery will be driven by a power
> obtainable at any point of the universe . . . Throughout space there is
> energy . . . it is a mere question of time when men will succeed in
> attaching their machinery to the very wheelwork of nature.'
>
> NIKOLAI TESLA 1856–1943
> 'Experiments With Alternate Currents of High Potential
> and High Frequency'

If Croatian scientist and inventor Nikolai Tesla had succeeded in his
vision, we would now have no gas or electric bills, and no unsightly
pylons trailing swathes of wires across the countryside: we would all
receive our energy directly through the atmosphere (see Keith Tutt,
The Scientist, the Madman, the Thief and their Lightbulb).

Tesla was undeniably a genius. His inventions are too numerous to
list, but he was the first to develop AC current for widespread use
(replacing Thomas Edison's less efficient DC supply). His innovative,
bladeless turbine was used to generate hydroelectric power from
Niagara Falls. And – most famously – he invented the means to convey
information via radio waves (Guglielmo Marconi, who is often mis-
credited with this achievement, merely used Tesla's designs to make
the first recorded radio broadcast). However, Tesla's invention of radio
transmission was just a start, for his plan was to utilize this to send
electricity through the atmosphere: instead of a radio, you would have
an energy receiving device. However, since this would be almost
impossible to monitor and thus charge for, his backers pulled out.

But Tesla's ultimate dream was even more radical than this: to use
the natural energy and motion of the universe itself – to attach
'machinery to the very wheelwork of nature'. This would be *truly* free
energy: no suppliers, no need for central generators. Who wouldn't
want that? The problem is that, whilst there is much talk of 'solving
the Earth's energy crisis', in reality this generally boils down to 'finding
a way to continue making money which doesn't destroy the planet'
(that is, for those who look that far ahead). Therefore, even if Tesla had
succeeded, it's unlikely that investors would support it – where's the
money in *free* energy?

'Every day, in every way, I am getting better and better'
ÉMILE COUÉ 1857–1926
How to Practise Suggestion and Autosuggestion

French pharmacist Émile Coué noticed that his clients seemed to respond better to treatment when their cures were accompanied by words of positive affirmation – how good the cure was, how quickly it would work, and so on. What Coué had really chanced upon was the *placebo effect*, which proposes that the attitudes and expectations of patients play a significant role in their recovery. Of course, Coué's cures were not mere 'sugar pills' (placebos), but the better-than-expected improvement suggested to him that a key part of health consisted in *healthy thinking*.

Coué's method was simply to repeat a positive phrase a number of times each day in the manner of a meditative mantra (our main quote being his most famous example). In this way, Coué realized that the patient could influence his own *unconscious* attitudes – which were the things that really shaped health and feelings. Coué termed this process *autosuggestion*.

For science and medicine, the placebo effect is something of a conundrum. It's one thing to train oneself by repeated suggestion to *feel* differently, perhaps, but quite another to use this process to affect the body's health. However, it is well-documented, and modern drug trials need to account for the percentage of patients who get better of their own accord. However, it need not be seen as a mystical phenomenon: the process of healing is something which the body mostly undertakes itself, and many medical treatments merely work to encourage or supplement natural processes. So, if the brain can be *tricked* into kick-starting a certain healing process through suggestion (rather than chemically, via the administration of a drug), then the result is still the same.

However, whilst it would be dangerous to take this too far – a cancer patient would be foolish to reject chemotherapy in favour of autosuggestion – it does suggest that modern medicine still has much to learn regarding the mind-body relationship. Should we blame Descartes?

'The connection between the signifier and the signified is arbitrary'
FERDINAND DE SAUSSURE 1857–1913
Course in General Linguistics

Structuralism originated with Ferdinand de Saussure, a Swiss linguist. Language is a system of written or spoken *signs*, and each sign has two aspects: *signifier*, the sound or shape of a word; *signified*, the accompanying concept. Independent of these is the *referent*, the thing to which the sign refers. So, the word 'dog' (the signifier) consists of written letters (d-o-g) and corresponding sounds; the meaning of the word (the signifier) is the *concept* of a dog; and the word may refer to an actual dog (the referent).

But words aren't merely labels for ideas: whilst the sounds that make up a word are initially arbitrary (they could have been *any* sounds), once convention has established them, they become a fixed part of the sign. There's nothing dog-like about the sound 'dog', but once linked, sound and idea become inseparable.

Why is this important? The fact that signifier and signified are inseparable suggests that they have evolved *together*. So, we don't just create concepts, and then label them; rather, concepts evolve alongside language, a system of signs that develops within a particular culture. Therefore, the meaning of a word consists not in its *content*, or what it *refers* to, but its role in the *structure* of the language (what Saussure termed *langue*). So, if we want to know what 'good' means, we should look at its opposite ('bad'), or what it's similar to ('right'), for it's these structural relationships that determine meaning. To understand a language is therefore to understand the culture that produced it, and how these structures evolved.

Later thinkers would export Saussure's ideas into other areas – anthropology, literary criticism, and of course philosophy – thus developing structuralism far beyond its linguistic origins. However, these origins were important, for it is from these and similar approaches that philosophy at this time takes what has been termed 'the linguistic turn': language becomes a clue to the nature of reality itself.

'. . . all suicides of the insane are either devoid of any motive or determined by purely imaginary motives. Now, many voluntary deaths fall into neither category; the majority have motives, and motives not unfounded in reality. Not every suicide can therefore be considered insane, without doing violence to language.'

ÉMILE DURKHEIM 1858–1917
Suicide

Émile Durkheim was a French philosopher commonly considered – along with Karl Marx and Max Weber – to be a founder of *sociology*. Following in the *positivist* steps of Auguste Comte, Durkheim attempted to evolve a rigorous method that would allow the identification of the key forces and laws that determined social structure and change.

Durkheim's most famous work on suicide was intended to show the effectiveness of *quantitative* methods of analysis. So, rather than considering suicide from a *qualitative* standpoint – e.g. what typical feelings accompanied or led to suicidal thoughts – Durkheim took a statistical approach, and compared suicide rates between different social groups (between Catholics and Protestants, men and women, different ages, etc.). From this he concluded that suicide was not always 'insane', but could have one of four causes:

Egoistic: resulting from weakened social bonds, leading to isolation and lack of social purpose (being an 'outsider').
Altruistic: being prepared to die for some greater cause (e.g. in war).
Anomic: where society lacks a purposeful social ethic (e.g. consumerist).
Fatalistic: where society oppresses the individual and allows no meaningful self-expression (e.g. totalitarian).

How true is this picture? Leaving aside Durkheim's statistical reasoning (which some have questioned), we see that, underlying his reasons for suicide, is the idea that individuals fulfil a role in society, and that suicide is generally related to the denial of that role. But is this the case? Are social forces always to blame for suicide? Statistics don't help us here, for, as existentialist Albert Camus argues, 'The worm is in man's heart', and the true cause may be well hidden. By denying the qualitative, personal aspects of suicide, Durkheim therefore commits an error positivists seem prone to: he leaves out the human.

> 'A moral ideal can exist nowhere and nohow but in a mind; an absolute
> moral ideal can exist only in a mind from which all Reality is derived.
> Our moral ideal can only claim validity in so far as it can rationally be
> regarded as the revelation of a moral ideal eternally existing in the
> mind of God.'
>
> HASTINGS RASHDALL 1858–1924
> *The Theory of Good and Evil*

The theory that true morality owes its existence to God, and therefore God must exist, perhaps finds its first modern expression in Kant. Since then, many philosophers have taken it up and adapted it into a more general form – as evidenced here by English philosopher Hastings Rashdall – that simply argues: morality exists; man cannot have created morality; therefore, God exists.

Rashdall argues that we can give *some* meaning to morality in natural or human terms, but not its *fullest* meaning. This is a common complaint against *naturalistic ethics* (as it's called), for defining morality as 'enlightened self-interest', 'the happiness of the greatest number', or 'will to power', is – the argument goes – to distort the nature of morality. If 'the good' is merely 'pleasure' or 'happiness', don't we lose much of what is characteristic about moral action, such as moral obligation or duty?

However, whilst this may be true, it seems to sidestep the issue slightly: the question surely is not whether we lose what is characteristic of morality in adopting a natural explanation, but simply whether such an explanation is true or not. If it turns out that morality *is* merely a matter of enlightened self-interest, and there is no 'absolute moral ideal', then it's *right* that we lose the notion of moral obligation, for *there's nothing* that we have an obligation *to*.

So, to say – as Rashdall does – that 'A morality which is not absolute or unconditional is not Morality' is in reality no argument at all, for just because something fails to live up to our ideal does not mean that our ideal must be true.

Consciousness is always of something. Asked what you're thinking, you might reply 'nothing', but actually – if conscious – there would have been *some* mental content: an idea, a perception, a feeling, etc. Thus, as German philosopher Franz Brentano suggested, consciousness has *intentionality*: our thoughts always have purpose and direction.

Edmund Husserl, who studied under Brentano, adopted this idea as a founding principle of *phenomenology*. Husserl believed, as had previous philosophers (Berkeley, Hume, Kant), that we only directly perceive our own ideas. But rather than fret about the existence or nature of a world beyond perception, Husserl proposed we study experience itself; we're certain our *ideas* exist, so analysis of mental *phenomena* will tell us not only about reality (as much as we're capable of perceiving, anyway), but how we *shape* it. Let's therefore set aside or 'bracket' the question of the 'real' world's existence (a process Husserl termed *epoché*), and study the structure of perception itself.

Husserl's work signals a shift from the traditional idea that philosophy and science study independent reality. It also marks a philosophical divide, with European philosophers mostly following his phenomenological lead, whilst Anglo-American philosophers mostly ignore it. Things are changing, and boundaries are blurring, but phenomenology is still essential to understanding later European philosophy.

However, some see phenomenology as leading to scepticism: since we cannot access reality, how do we know it exists, or that our ideas accurately represent it? This is a problem for Husserl, as is the notion that consciousness has a determinate structure. Later philosophers have therefore taken phenomenology in more radical directions, arguing, for instance (as does Jacques Derrida) that any supposed structure will only ever reflect cultural and personal bias. However, this is a long way from Husserl's original project: phenomenology would provide knowledge with a firmer foundation, not undermine it.

'"But the Solar System!" I protested. "What the deuce is it to me?" he interrupted impatiently; "you say that we go round the sun. If we went round the moon it would not make a pennyworth of difference to me or to my work."'

ARTHUR CONAN DOYLE 1859–1930
A Study in Scarlet

Arthur Conan Doyle was a Scottish doctor and author, best known as the creator of Sherlock Holmes. The eccentric, exasperating but brilliant protagonist, accompanied by his more prosaic, long-suffering sidekick, has become a template of crime fiction (even influencing modern medical TV drama *House, MD* – for 'House' and 'Wilson', read 'Holmes' and 'Watson'). It also presents an interesting attitude to knowledge.

Holmes flabbergasts Watson with his ignorance of *heliocentrism*: how can anyone *not* know that the Earth orbits the Sun? Holmes' defence is twofold: such knowledge makes no difference to his work; the brain has finite storage capacity, and by ignoring 'irrelevant' facts he makes space for useful ones: 'Depend upon it, there comes a time when, for every addition of knowledge, you forget something that you knew before' (obviously, Holmes is paraphrasing Homer Simpson here).

However, taking Holmes' second point first, whilst the brain does 'dump' what it deems useless, there may not be strict limits to human memory capacity. It's true that *short-term* memory is limited, and doesn't store information for very long, yet *long-term* memory – especially if efforts are made to organize it – has a potentially vast capacity. The key factors are therefore *organization* and *use*.

But what defines 'useful'? The phone number you had as a child is – arguably – a waste of memory space, but how does Holmes' know that information about the solar system is useless? What if, investigating some magical cult, he were to require knowledge of planetary order in order to interpret some clue? Can we therefore draw a strict limit between *useful* and *useless* knowledge? Holmes seems to have a very *positivistic* definition of knowledge: given enough relevant 'facts', any case can be solved. The truth, however, seems not so elementary.

> 'Mechanism . . . holds that nature has worked like a human being by
> bringing parts together, while a mere glance at the development of an
> embryo shows that life goes to work in a very different way. Life does
> not proceed by the association and addition of elements, but by
> dissociation and division.'
> HENRI BERGSON 1859–1941
> *Creative Evolution*

French philosopher Henri Bergson argued that there were two forces: the *material* and the *vital*. Material force (matter itself) was restraining and structuring, tending towards stasis and stability. Vital force – *élan vital*, as he termed it – was dynamic, free-flowing, and spontaneous, forever overflowing its bounds in a joyful dance of self-expression. Bergson therefore rejected Darwin's steady mechanical process of Natural Selection, whereby small changes accumulate over time, picturing instead the interplay between an irrepressible life force and the constraining forms of matter. Evolution's drive to greater complexity and diversity was therefore an expression of creativity, of life at play.

Bergson also thought these forces shaped perception and understanding: *intellect* represented material force, always straining to order and categorize experience, to give it definite form; *intuition* was its irrational brother, directly grasping reality's constantly changing flux in a non-conceptual form (this echoes Nietzsche). Furthermore, since intellect can only ever grasp an aspect of reality (an abstraction), then, without intuition, all intellectual endeavour is incomplete. Bergson therefore belongs to a tradition of anti-intellectualism that seeks to undermine the traditional philosophical assumption that reason alone can arrive at a clear understanding of reality.

Today, Bergson's *vitalism* is out of favour with evolutionary biologists, who argue that Darwin's *mechanist* account of natural selection provides a complete understanding of evolution without the need of some mysterious vital force. Bertrand Russell has also criticized Bergson's anti-intellectualism, arguing that it seizes on such occasional problems as rational enquiry faces to conclude that intellectual enquiry is fundamentally problematic. And yet, Russell argues, the mere presence of problems does not undermine the whole endeavour, and if we were to 'declare every momentary difficulty insoluble', then there would never be any progress in *any* field of knowledge.

> 'Education is a social process. Education is growth. Education is, not a preparation for life; education is life itself.'
> JOHN DEWEY 1859–1952
> attributed

American *pragmatist* philosopher and psychologist John Dewey had perhaps his greatest impact on the field of education. Influenced early on by the psychology of fellow pragmatist William James, Dewey's psychological theories developed an emphasis on practical application, an attitude that he was later to carry over into his writing on democracy and education.

In fact, for Dewey, the keyword for both political and educational life was *involvement*. The school was a microcosm, a representation of society in miniature, and so the doctrines that drove education could also be found in the world at large. However, as Dewey's own education revealed, the schooling of the time was authoritarian and repetitive, providing a passive experience for pupils that often failed to engage their interest. This was because subjects were delivered in a dry, abstract form that failed to highlight their practical application or their eventual social function. So, he argued, in teaching maths, why not get a child to make, build, or cook something, thus encouraging arithmetical skills through use of weights and measures? Dewey also argued that school curricula should reflect the needs of society, and not some elite notion of 'culture' or 'learning'. So, for instance, aside from teaching academic skills, schools should help immigrants to acclimatize to their new language and culture (*acculturation*), thus easing their passage into society.

This *progressive* attitude to education, as it's known, is now very much ingrained in Western education. It's now common, for instance, for pupils to undertake class projects, or to go on field trips. Of course, individual emphasis differs from school to school, but it's now well established that children learn better through listening *and* doing. However, Dewey didn't believe that education should be 'child-centred', in the sense that the teacher took a back seat: the teacher isn't a facilitator, a nanny, or a dictator, but simply a group leader, an experienced guide to society's knowledge.

> 'The physicist can never subject an isolated hypothesis to experimental
> test, but only a whole group of hypotheses'
> PIERRE DUHEM 1861–1916
> *The Aim and Structure of Physical Theory*

Homeopathy claims to work by the principle of 'like cures like'. This isn't in itself unscientific: vaccination, which allows antibodies to develop in response to weakened forms of disease, works along similar lines. However, homeopathy applies this principle broadly, claiming that minute quantities of a substance which would normally cause certain symptoms can in fact alleviate them. Also, homeopathic medicines contain only trace amounts of the medicinal substance, sometimes none at all, yet claim that greater dilution provides *increased* potency.

Incensed by these claims, and considering alleged cures merely psychosomatic, certain scientific sceptics recently 'overdosed' on homeopathic remedies, arguing that since overdose should be harmful, surviving *unharmed* proves that 'there's nothing in it' (literally, since homeopathic pills are mostly sugar). Shouldn't it?

Whilst well-founded scientific principles argue against homeopathy, the above 'experiment' doesn't itself falsify it. It's actually very difficult to falsify a single assertion – e.g. 'homeopathic overdose is harmful' – because it's hard to separate it from its background assumptions. So, homoeopathists might claim that the experiment merely shows remedies are ineffective in massive doses, or in public, or for sceptics, etc.

Whilst the observations of French philosopher Pierre Duhem initially concerned only physics, they apply equally to scientific experiment in general. Physicists may fail to find a predicted particle, but does that mean it doesn't exist? Can't be detected? Can't be detected *under those conditions*? In other words, theories must be tested *as a whole*.

Regarding homeopathy, we can begin by looking at evidence for its supporting assumptions. Whilst never conclusive, weight of evidence is most important. Also, some homeopathists claim no single dose – however large – can have adverse effects (40 pills at once is still only 'one dose'). Perhaps, then, rather than overdosing on enthusiasm, it might have helped the sceptics to do a little more research.

'. . . we must work into the depths of the students' souls through what is revealed to our individual insights. In this way we prepare them to grow into religious adults.'

RUDOLF STEINER 1861–1925

The Child's Changing Consciousness As The Basis Of Pedagogical Practice

German philosopher Rudolf Steiner was an innovative thinker in numerous fields – religion, agriculture, medicine – but most intriguingly in education. Originally drawn to Goethe, Nietzsche and Schopenhauer, Steiner also pursued spiritual interests, which eventually drove him to *Theosophy*. However, always his own man, he took a splinter group of theosophists with him to form his own creed, which he termed *Anthroposophy*.

Waldorf Schools (as they're called) apply Steiner's principles to education, resulting in freedom of curriculum, educational method and structure. Steiner believed in soul and spirit, in reincarnation, and *karma*, subscribing to a doctrine of conscious *spiritual* evolution, the key to which was independent development and creative self-fulfilment. Waldorf students are therefore encouraged to develop different aspects of themselves (artistic, scientific, physical, moral), to question and investigate, and there's a flexibility of approach that aims at accommodating individual differences and fostering independence.

There are now hundreds of Waldorf schools, kindergartens and special educational establishments worldwide (mainly in Europe). With their child-centred methodology, integration of the arts, and creative involvement, some studies suggest that they make a positive difference. On the downside, however, students wishing to progress to further education may have to patch gaps left by non-standard curricula (as, perhaps, with the Montessori method). Also, more seriously, some claim the existence of non-disclosed spiritual doctrines which underlie the central Waldorf methodology – e.g. development of clairvoyance – which parents may not be aware of, or agree with. This isn't a point *against* such doctrines – people are free to believe what they want, and even mainstream religion contains beliefs that sceptics may find eccentric or irrational – but about *transparency*. If the goal is to create independent and free-thinking 'religious adults', shouldn't this be based on free and informed choice?

> '... when asceticism was carried out of monastic cells into everyday life, and began to dominate worldly morality, it did its part in building the tremendous cosmos of the modern economic order'
> MAX WEBER 1864–1920
> *The Protestant Ethic and the Spirit of Capitalism*

Unlike Marx, German philosopher and sociologist Max Weber did not see the economic relationships as determining culture; rather, culture and belief shaped economic and social activity. By reversing this influence, Weber therefore emphasizes the importance of understanding the subjective meaning that individuals within society attach to their actions. Accordingly, Weber rejected Comte's *positivism*, which attempted to create sociology in the mould of the natural, empirical sciences: sociology was distinct from physics or chemistry because, in understanding society, *meaning* was more important that *empirical fact*.

Thus, in his work on the sociology of religion, Weber sought to understand the influence of religious attitudes on culture and society. Weber looked at Confucianism and Taoism in relation to Chinese society, and Hinduism and Buddhism in Nepal, and – most famously – the relationship between Protestant Christianity and capitalism. Noting the disproportionate representation of Protestants among Europe's wealthy capitalists, he wondered how a religion which traditionally turns its back on worldliness, business and finance, should seemingly support such things.

Weber observes that Protestantism – unlike Catholicism – made a virtue of work and 'busy-ness', perhaps summed up in the proverb, 'The devil finds work for idle hands.' This is an offshoot of Protestantism's *asceticism* (self-denial), where leisure was a form of indulgence or temptation. It's a short step, then, from this 'Protestant work ethic' (as, following Weber, it's become known), to the capitalist pursuit of profit. Money was not evil, because it was a by-product of work, and, furthermore, economic activity contributed to the general good.

Of course, Weber's analysis of how religions shape societies allows us to question the 'virtues' each ideology promotes. A life of industry leaves little time for contemplation, and even less for questioning the *status quo*.

> '. . . it is because the distinctions of past, present and future seem to
> me to be essential for time, that I regard time as unreal'
> J. M. E. McTAGGART 1866–1925
> 'The Unreality of Time'

J. M. E. McTaggart was an English idealist philosopher who argued that time is an illusion. McTaggart proposed that events within time can be arranged in two ways: as an *A series* and a *B series*. The *A* series organizes events into 'past', 'present' and 'future', whilst the *B* series merely sees events as 'earlier' or 'later'. So, if we only had the *B series*, then there could be no sense of change. The Battle of Hastings was *earlier than* the Battle of Waterloo; the French Revolution was *later than* the American War of Independence. This order gives a sense of sequence, but not a sense of *change*. Like the individual stills of a movie, each moment would be eternal and unchanging, for whilst the *B* series has a fixed order, unless those events are related to the present, there is no sense of the passage of time. The *A* series is therefore essential to our notion of time, and since 'earlier' and 'later' are temporal terms, the *B* series relies on the *A* series.

However, whilst essential, the *A* series leads to self-contradiction. An event cannot simultaneously be past, present and future. To avoid this, couldn't we say an event *is* present, *was* future, and *will be* past? Hence, there is no contradiction: before making it, breakfast is in the *future*; when eating it, in the *present*; after it's finished, in the *past*. So, breakfast possesses these different qualities at different times; no contradiction.

However, in saying that breakfast possesses these qualities at *different times*, we're using the *A* series to explain time – but if the *A* series *is* time, then we're using the notion of time to prove that time exists, thus arguing in a circle. Thus, if the *A* series leads to circularity, and the *B* series isn't sufficient for time, then time doesn't exist.

> '. . . the truly "mysterious" object is beyond our apprehension and comprehension, not only because our knowledge has certain irremovable limits, but because in it we come upon something inherently wholly-other, whose kind and character are incommensurable with our own, and before which we therefore recoil in a wonder that strikes us chill and numb'
>
> RUDOLF OTTO 1868–1937
> 'Religion as Numinal Experience'

Rudolf Otto was a German philosopher and theologian, most famous for *The Idea of the Holy*, which views God in terms of religious experience, rather than as a rational concept, thus adopting a *phenomenological* approach. In doing this, Otto highlights what he considers essential *non-rational* characteristics of religious experience that have been largely ignored.

As well as love, faith, admiration, etc., Otto argues that religious attitudes and experience are characterized by less definable feelings, notably religious fear, terror and awe – as reflected in Jacob's experience in Genesis (28.17): 'And he was afraid, and said, How dreadful is this place!'

Initially, Otto argued, the 'holy' designated *only* such feelings, whereas now it's primarily associated with ethical and rational meanings: God is good, and holy things are distinguished from profane ones. However, Otto argues, such primal irrational feelings aren't only central to our experience of the divine, but represent a *unique category* of feeling – the '*numinous*' – that cannot be reduced to any other.

The basis of this reaction is what Otto calls 'creature feeling', which is 'the emotion of the creature, submerged and overwhelmed by its own nothingness in contrast to that which is supreme above all creatures.'

So, whilst we admire and love God, we also feel inadequate, intimidated and even afraid. Of course, these emotions can also occur in more natural settings – in seeing the Grand Canyon, or meeting a famous or renowned individual. But the point isn't that we simply feel small, but that what we experience is so *other* we're shaken to the core of our being.

> 'We may reasonably draw the conclusion that religion is just as much a unique characteristic and interest of humanity as love of truth, love of beauty, love of country, and that the saint's "experience" is no more to be dismissed as an illusion than the thinker's, the artist's, or the patriot's'
>
> A. E. TAYLOR 1869–1945
> 'The Vindication of Religion'

It seems natural to give greater credit to beliefs which are formed by personal experience. When we come to religious matters, we would therefore prefer to establish our opinions first-hand. However, how are we to tell whether such experiences are genuine?

English idealist philosopher A. E. Taylor saw religious experience as a fundamental part of life. Therefore, when we evaluate it, we should not assume that religion is a special case. Just as the artist learns to appreciate composition, beauty, and light, etc., so the religious person's view of life is shaped by key experiences, such as gratitude, awe or even religious terror. But such experiences aren't necessarily isolated visions or revelations (though they may be), but form part of religious life taken as a whole. As such, genuine or illusory experiences, immature or sophisticated conceptions of the divine, are things that distinguish the experienced spiritual traveller from the beginner, the enlightened from the deluded. Furthermore, just as mistaken sensory experiences shouldn't make us doubt the 'real' world, so false religious experiences shouldn't rule out the possibility of true ones. We may therefore evaluate experiences not by consulting a 'little aristocracy of special persons' (e.g. priests), but – as with experience of everyday reality – through living, learning and growing.

However, does this prove the existence of God? If we accept Taylor's argument, then certainly false religious experiences are as much a part of religious life as mistaken sense perceptions are to everyday reality. And yet, there *is* a difference: there is no great divide between believers and non-believers as to the existence of the physical world, and we don't generally look to sense experience to prove it.

'Suffering is the badge of the human race, not the sword'
MAHATMA GANDHI 1869–1948
Young India

Pacifism **traditionally denotes** the belief that violence is absolutely wrong. However, there are various forms and degrees, both religious and non-religious, and we may distinguish between the use of non-violent protest in achieving some social or political end, and the broader pacifistic ideal.

In its absolute form, pacifism stems from recognition of fundamental spiritual truths: we should not harm one another because, at some level, we *are* one another. There is also a sense in which violent actions, and all forms of immorality, spring from ignorance and lack of development. This view, embodied in Jesus' forgiveness of his persecutors ('Forgive them Father, they know not what they do'), also underlies Plato's assertion that it's better to suffer wrong than to do wrong, for the wrongdoer is both ignorant and 'sick'. So, the roots of pacifism go back millennia, appearing in various traditions.

For Mahatma Gandhi, with whom non-violent protest has become inextricably linked, pacifism is both absolute doctrine *and* means to social change. Trained as a lawyer, Gandhi recognized that legal change was slow and often ineffective, but that violence was not only harmful but also counter-productive, for it effectively alienated those you wished to influence. Where social change was concerned, violence made it easier for the ruling powers – in Gandhi's case, the British rulers of India – to dismiss civil unrest as the irrationally motivated discontent of dangerous extremists. However, by adopting non-violent protest, Gandhi garnered the sympathy of both liberals and neutrals, and helped to show that the cause (Indian independence) was a rational, serious and determined one.

Consequently, non-violent protest is now often adopted by non-pacificists. In the age of global media, nothing is so affecting as witnessing a non-resisting protester beaten mercilessly in the name of 'social order'. Perhaps, though some philosophers contend we are basically aggressive apes, the fact that we empathize with suffering more than aggression suggests that empathy is a more fundamental human drive. Is there hope after all?

> 'The striving for significance, this sense of yearning, always points out to us that all psychological phenomena contain a movement that starts from a feeling of inferiority and reach upward. The theory of Individual Psychology of psychological compensation states that the stronger the feeling of inferiority, the higher the goal for personal power.'
>
> ALFRED ADLER 1870–1937
> 'Progress in Individual Psychology'

Austrian psychologist Alfred Adler was a co-founder of psychoanalysis with Sigmund Freud, but, like other psychoanalysts – Jung, Reich – he disagreed with Freud on key issues, and left to pursue his own path.

Adler's approach, which he termed *Individual Psychology*, shares with Nietzsche a belief that the person is fundamentally driven by a 'will to power'. However, he interpreted Nietzsche as saying that what this actually meant was that we all seek to realize ourselves fully – to feel *whole* (thus, the 'individual' of 'Individual Psychology' actually means 'indivisible' or 'complete'). Often, this feeling is frustrated, and we feel inferior, which in turn leads us to try to compensate for this, and occasionally to *over-compensate*. Therefore, Adler might argue, Hitler sought to compensate for his small stature, for his career frustrations, etc., by attempting to conquer Europe (an *overcompensation* – to say the least).

A key contrast with Freud, which Adler shared with Reich, was that psychological neurosis was not merely the fault of the individual, but that of society. So, like Reich, Adler argued that society should do everything it can to prevent the origin of neurotic behaviour. He saw the key to this in the establishment of genuine democracy and equality. Thus, he supported feminism, increased equality within family relationships, etc., in an attempt to minimize the harm that social restriction could inflict upon the development of the individual. This attitude was reflected in practice: Adler rejected the superiority of the analyst, seated above the supine analysand, in favour of two chairs. Thus, he reinforced the central message of therapy: equality is not an enemy of self-expression and fulfilment, but the means whereby it is achieved for all.

'. . . the greatest sign of success for a teacher . . . is to be able to say,
"The children are now working as if I did not exist"'
MARIA MONTESSORI 1870–1952
The Absorbent Mind

The *Montessori Method* of education was developed by Maria Montessori, an Italian doctor and educator. From early work with children with special needs and forms of challenging behaviour, Montessori discovered that provision of an environment furnished with materials for self-teaching and discovery produced more effective results than traditional teaching approaches. In subsequent observation of young children in day care, Montessori noted children's capacity for absorption in tasks of their own choosing, resulting in meditative contentment. So, left alone, and supplied with a choice of interesting activities and materials, a child will educate itself.

The key to Montessori's theory is the idea that a child's play is not frivolous or unstructured, but an expression of serious engagement with the world: intense interest and exploration is the child's 'true normal nature' (as Montessori terms it). The job of the teacher – who is, rather, a guide or facilitator – is therefore to help the child to *normalize* (to rediscover this natural absorption). Traditional educative approaches disrupt this, forcing the child's attention away from its natural interests, resulting in boredom, disruption, and eventual aversion to education.

There are some quite startling success stories associated with the Montessori method – tales of self-taught geniuses and precocious talents. Many self-starters and innovators have come through Montessori schools – for instance, Jeff Bezos, who founded Amazon, and Larry Page and Sergey Brin, founders of Google – and it certainly seems to foster creativity and self-expression. However, whilst it arguably benefits self-motivated types, how would it serve the rank and file? Traditionalists might worry that such an approach would not provide the general standard of rounded education that society requires. Of course, even if the Montessori method can address this worry, and therefore be applied more broadly, there is still the question of whether it *should*: after all, some people *like* rules, discipline, and being told what to do.

'There lies before us, if we choose, continual progress in happiness, knowledge, and wisdom. Shall we, instead, choose death, because we cannot forget our quarrels? We appeal as human beings to human beings: Remember your humanity, and forget the rest.'

BERTRAND RUSSELL 1872–1970
The Russell-Einstein Manifesto

The English philosopher Bertrand Russell was born into a family of wealth, privilege and influence (his paternal grandfather was 1st Earl Russell, Prime Minister under Queen Victoria, and John Stuart Mill was his godfather). However, aside from his philosophical and intellectual contributions, Russell was keen to prove that he was not content to sit on his family's laurels, and no one could have done more to involve himself in the political and social issues of the time.

Accordingly, Russell is perhaps better known by the general public for his championing of social causes – pacifism, nuclear disarmament – than for his philosophy. During the First World War, he was dismissed from Trinity College Cambridge for his anti-war activities, and even imprisoned for six months. He travelled to China and Russia (meeting Lenin), thereby evaluating at first hand the development of the new communist states. In the Second World War, he modified his pacifism in recognition of the genuine threat to freedom that Hitler posed, but later reasserted it in opposition to the Vietnam War. Perhaps his most notable cause was the Campaign for Nuclear Disarmament (CND), during which he published the *Russell-Einstein manifesto* (from which our quote is taken), signed by Albert Einstein and other prominent intellectuals and scientists.

What is most interesting about Russell's anti-war activities is the flexibility of his views combined with his idealism. In true accord with the principles of civil disobedience, he did not deviate from the stance that led to his imprisonment; however, later, he was not so absolutist as to reject the only means of opposing Nazism. Such actions attest to the quality of his mind and character as much as, or even more than, his contributions to logic, epistemology and philosophy in general.

> 'The essential characteristic of philosophy which makes it a study
> distinct from science, is criticism. It examines critically the principles
> employed in science and in daily life; it searches out any
> inconsistencies there may be in these principles, and it only accepts
> them when, as the result of a critical inquiry, no reason for rejecting
> them has appeared.'
>
> BERTRAND RUSSELL
> *The Problems of Philosophy*

It is always interesting when someone – especially a mind such as
Russell's – attempts to characterize philosophy, a subject as full of controversies as it is empty of certainties, not the least of which being an
account of what it actually is. Consequently, any attempted definition
tends to tell us as much about the philosopher who provides it as
about the true nature of the subject.

Russell, level-headed and socially-minded, saw it as making slow
but steady progress towards underpinning the sciences and knowledge in general. Wittgenstein, however, more enigmatic and tormented
by far, saw it almost as a sort of non-problem – a puzzle – that just
wouldn't let him alone. Sartre, and *existentialists* in general, viewed it
in much more subjective terms as a response to the absurdity of life,
calling not just for intellectual but also emotional involvement.

The delightful irony, of course, is that philosophers will no doubt
take issue with all my characterizations of the above philosophers.
Will there never be an end to controversy? Possibly not, which perhaps
supplies a clue to its true nature: philosophy is primarily concerned
with *doubt* – of opinions, theories, experiences, procedures – of just
about anything at all. Without this process of destruction, we couldn't
analyze things, see what they consist of, and thereby understand
them. However, having broken them down, and placed them in the
crucible, the philosopher is now left with a shifting mass of amor-
phous forms, which then calls into play the complementary process:
that of establishing truth. It is these two forces that – like the warring
dragons underneath Merlin's tower – are forever unsettling the foundations. No wonder nothing ever gets built.

> 'You can define the barber as "one who shaves all those, and those only, who do not shave themselves." The question is, does the barber shave himself?'
>
> BERTRAND RUSSELL
> *The Philosophy of Logical Atomism*

If a barber only shaves those who do not shave themselves, then he cannot shave himself; however, in not shaving himself, he becomes someone he must shave! Of course, the problem can be avoided if we simply define 'barber' as 'someone who shaves other people *and* himself' (perhaps), for there is no necessary reason to accept the definition that causes the paradox.

However, what is known as 'Russell's paradox', on which this example is based, is actually much more problematic. It originated in the search for a fundamental theory of mathematics. Russell and Gottlob Frege had thought that maths was reducible to logic, and had tried to develop a theory of number using 'set theory', seeing numbers as sets or classes of things. So, the meaning of '2', for instance, was 'the set of all pairs'; the meaning of '3', 'the set of all triples'; and so on. This seems fine, until you apply the notion of sets more generally.

Suppose 'red' refers to 'the set of all red things', and 'not red' to 'the set of all not-red things'. Now, since sets are themselves things (ideas) that can therefore be classed, we can ask whether a set is a member of itself. 'The set of all red things' is not (the set – the idea itself – is not red), but 'the set of all things that are not red' *is* (for it includes all not-red things – such as itself). However, is 'the set of all things that is not a member of itself' a member of itself? Here comes the paradox: a set that is *not* a member of itself should be in 'the set of all things which is not a member of itself', thereby becoming a member of itself – and ceasing to belong!

I think I need to lie down.

> 'By the law of the excluded middle, either "*A* is *B*" or "*A* is not *B*" must be true. Hence either 'the present King of France is bald' or "the present King of France is not bald" must be true. Yet if we enumerated the things that are bald, and then the things that are not bald, we should not find the present King of France in either list. Hegelians, who love a synthesis, will probably conclude that he wears a wig.'
>
> BERTRAND RUSSELL
> *On Denoting*

Given that France is a republic, and has no monarch, is the statement 'the present King of France is bald' false or meaningless? Being false would imply that its opposite ('the present King of France has hair') is true – and it isn't. But nor does it seem to be meaningless: we can perfectly well understand what it says. How then do we resolve the issue?

The problem is that such statements would seem to contravene a well-established law of logic called the *law of excluded middle*: a meaningful statement must be either true or false. So, we either abandon this law, or else find a solution.

Opting for the latter, Russell proposed, in what is now termed his *theory of descriptions*, that the statement about the King of France can be unpacked into three separate assertions (roughly put):

1. There is a King of France.
2. He is the only King of France.
3. He is bald.

Since the first assertion is obviously false, then we needn't worry about the other two. By analyzing the statement in this way, Russell therefore avoids the problem and preserves the law of excluded middle (and philosophy students can all sleep more soundly at night – or, in fact, in the day – during logic lectures perhaps . . .).

(Incidentally, the reference to Hegel is a quip: Hegel thought history progresses through opposition and synthesis: e.g. religion, atheism, humanism. So, a wig is a sort of 'compromise' between being bald and having hair.)

> 'We must not, therefore, be frightened by the assertion that a thing is natural into the admission that it is good; good does not, by definition, mean anything that is natural; and it is therefore always an open question whether anything that is natural is good'
>
> G. E. MOORE 1873–1958
> *Principia Ethica*

G. E. Moore was an English philosopher, contemporary with Bertrand Russell, and an early influence upon Wittgenstein. His most famous work, the *Principia Ethica*, argues for a form of *non-natural ethics*, where 'good' is seen as a 'non-natural property' of certain actions. Moore thereby opposed what is commonly termed *ethical naturalism*, which defines the good in natural terms. So, if – as traditional utilitarianism proposes – goodness can be equated with pleasure, we can never ask whether pleasure is 'good' (which there may be occasions to do). This is termed the *open question argument*, for it must always be an open question as to whether something is good or not (and not, as when we define 'good' as pleasure, a closed one).

Utilitarianism therefore commits what Moore terms *the naturalistic fallacy*: equating pleasure with good, it mistakes a property that moral actions *might* sometimes possess (pleasure or happiness), with a *defining* property. On the contrary, Moore argues, 'good' should itself be *unanalyzable*. When we call something 'good', this is not a term that can be broken down into component parts; good is good, and that's an end to it. Such concepts must rather be seen in terms of their relationship with other concepts. Understanding ethics is therefore more like understanding the rules of a game, as opposed to analyzing the chemical composition of a substance.

But Moore's solution has its own problems, for his notion of 'good' seems somewhat vague and mysterious. How do we know when we have arrived at a clear understanding of the good? Perhaps, however, Moore was not proposing some Platonic realm of pure ideas, but merely pointing out that for moral concepts to make sense, there must always be a point beyond which we cannot go.

'Gladly would I embrace Spiritualism if it could prove its claims, but I am not willing to be deluded by the fraudulent impositions of so-called psychics, or accept as sacred reality any of the evidence that has been placed before me thus far'

HARRY HOUDINI 1874–1926
A Magician Among the Spirits

Following his mother's death, driven by grief, renowned magician and escape artist Harry Houdini turned to *Spiritualism*. The movement originated in mid 19th century America, expressing a growing public fascination with spirit contact and associated phenomena, and involving *mediums* acting as conduits for the nearly departed, relaying messages and producing apparitions, manifestations and other supernatural effects.

As a stage magician well-schooled in the deceptive arts, Houdini quickly spotted that the alleged 'spirits' were the products of the very same methods employed in his own shows. Infuriated by the fraud perpetrated on the vulnerable and grieving, he became an arch sceptic, and set about systematically exposing their deceptions and debunking their counterfeit claims.

And yet, strangely, throughout this, Houdini never actually gave up hope of finding genuine evidence of life after death. In a pact with his wife Bess, it was agreed that whoever would die first would, if possible, relay a message in the same secret code they used in their 'mind reading' act. When, eventually, Houdini died, Bess started the tradition (continued by magicians to this day) of holding a yearly séance in an attempt to make contact with Houdini's spirit. In 1929, professed medium Arthur Ford relayed a coded message to Bess spelling out 'BELIEVE'. However, whilst Bess believed only she and her husband knew the code, it had in fact been revealed in a biography of Houdini the previous year.

The problem with spirit messages, and supernatural phenomena in general, is that – as Hume argued – more mundane explanations always seem more likely. Just as with stage magic, no matter how 'magical' the trick appears, it's always just that – a trick, with a boringly mundane explanation. And yet, probability never quite rules out possibility: we still want to believe.

'Do what thou wilt shall be the whole of the law ... Love is the law,
love under will'
ALEISTER CROWLEY 1875–1947
The Book of the Law

Edward Alexander Crowley, English writer, philosopher and magician, was born to a family of *Plymouth Brethren*, but rebelled. At university, he changed his name to Aleister (the Gaelic form of Alexander), and was eventually drawn to the *Golden Dawn*, an organization dedicated to the study and practice of religion and mysticism, and which attracted such celebrities as W. B. Yeats, Irish revolutionary Maud Gonne, and author Arthur Machen. However, as it disintegrated in feuds and infighting, Crowley struck out on his own, spending the next half-century travelling widely, writing, indulging his passion for mountaineering, and developing his unique philosophy.

On one such visit to Egypt, Crowley experienced a revelation, resulting in the composition of *The Book of the Law*, the central statement of his moral and spiritual philosophy, of which our quote – the so-called 'law of *Thelema*' (Greek, 'will') – is its central tenet. Superficially, it suggests a *libertarian* approach, stressing the supreme rights of the individual over society, yet underlying this is a religious concern with the 'true will'. The French satirist François Rabelais had pictured an 'Abbey of Thélème', where 'Do what thou wilt' is inscribed over the door, its members living according to the dictates of their own conscience. St Augustine had given similar advice: 'Love, and do what you will'. Thelema, then, doesn't describe personal whim or grant licence for moral anarchy, but rather to seek out the path of one's highest conceivable purpose, and to ensure that the means of achieving it are not contrary to the law (love).

Against this, we have the popular caricature of Crowley. Like Nietzsche, he set himself up against what he saw as harmful aspects of religious orthodoxy, styling himself 'The Great Beast 666' (after the book of 'Revelations'). This has made him a controversial figure, and, like Nietzsche, unjustly reviled, helping to distract attention from his main ideas.

'The dream is the small hidden door in the deepest and most intimate
sanctum of the soul, which opens to that primeval cosmic night that
was soul long before there was conscious ego and will be soul far
beyond what a conscious ego could ever reach'
CARL JUNG 1875–1961
The Meaning of Psychology for Modern Man

For Freud, everything was about sex. The id, the individual's instinctive drive, was primarily sexual, and the key to understanding a
patient's problems could therefore be found in his sexual practices,
desires and attitudes. However, for Swiss psychologist Carl Jung,
Freud's foremost pupil, not every problem was sexual in origin, and
some conflicts involved other forces.

Freud and Jung both saw the conscious mind as a small part of a
larger whole. However, unlike Freud, Jung split the unconscious into
two parts: the *personal unconscious* and the *collective unconscious*. The
latter is a vast storehouse of ancestral forces, what Jung termed *archetypes*, which have shaped the development of mankind, finding
expression in stories, myths and religions. Consequently, each individual develops in relation to their influence, and life is a path whereby
these various psychic forces are met and engaged with. In this way, the
self gradually moves toward integration, each conflict representing a
stage of psychic development towards wholeness. For instance, if I
grow up without a father, part of my development might involve
coming to terms with the 'father' archetype – through problems with
authority, perhaps. Furthermore, since these archetypes are shared,
this conflict will likely be echoed in others' experiences, or more generally in stories, myths and religious rites of passage.

Jung's theory is perhaps no more scientific or verifiable than
Freud's. However, like psychoanalysis – and unlike the more objective
forms of psychology – it appeals to us on a non-rational level. This
does not make it any more or less true, but does allow us to draw subjective meaning from it, engaging with it as we would a fairy tale or a
myth, for which 'true' and 'truthful' may have different senses.

Once, I finished reading a book that was part of a series, then went to visit a friend. On the way, I took a different route to the normal one, passing a second-hand furniture shop, which – on a whim – I entered: there, amidst a small selection of books, was the next in the series. Furthermore, I'd forgotten my money, and on asking the price, was told – after not being able to locate a price – that I could simply have it. The book? Jung's *Synchronicity*.

Well, actually, that last part's a lie – but the rest is true! The incident would still rank as a synchronistic event. Jung argued that modern man's emphasis on the rational scientific perspective as the only true source of knowledge was harmful and distorting – especially in terms of *self-knowledge*. Synchronicities therefore alerted us to the fact that the world isn't *just* that of the physicist, but also one of *meaning*.

For Jung, synchronistic events happen at the same time (are *synchronous*), but have no causal connection (are *acausal*). So, it's not 'weird' if you're thinking about your friend and then he appears, *if you're expecting him*; but it is if you're not, haven't seen him for 25 years, and haven't thought about him in the meantime. Furthermore, Jung saw synchronicities as trying to tell us something – that we're on the right track, or else need to change – and they were, he believed, our guide on our journey to wholeness.

But what is to differentiate synchronicity from mere coincidence? Well, nothing, strictly speaking – except perhaps, Jung would argue, its *meaning* for *us*.

'We have too long been occupied with the developing series of our own philosophical systems, and have taken no notice of the fact that there is a world-philosophy of which our Western philosophy is only a part. If, however, one conceives philosophy as being a struggle to reach a view of the world as a whole, and seeks out the elementary convictions which are to deepen it and give it a sure foundation, one cannot avoid setting our own thought face to face with that of the Hindus, and of the Chinese in the Far East.'

ALBERT SCHWEITZER 1875–1965
Philosophy of Civilization

Alsatian philosopher Albert Schweitzer is most remembered for his philanthropy (having been awarded the Nobel Peace Prize in 1952), and his attempt to found a universal ethics on Christian compassion, a doctrine which he termed 'Reverence for Life'. However, he was also a physician, noted music scholar, and theologian.

As Schweitzer recognized, if we are to alleviate global problems, we need to transcend those cultural, national and ideological differences that currently separate us. However, this mustn't involve the imposition of one culture onto another, but rather identification of that which cultures have in common. Schweitzer concluded therefore that, underlying each ideology were the seeds of a universal ethics. Thus, in identifying and promoting these unifying 'elementary convictions', we establish a means of leading people away from indifference or antipathy, and toward compassion and mutual respect.

Schweitzer argued that *Reverence for Life* springs from our recognition that all life possesses a 'will to live'. As such, suffering provokes our sympathy because we recognize the desire to live in ourselves. Yet, animals do not refrain from causing suffering and death, so why should we? Schweitzer countered that humans are different: our empathy distinguishes us.

A universal ethics is very appealing, but must we conclude that recognition of another's 'will to life' will lead us to one? We might, as Nietzsche did, conclude that therefore life is struggle ('will to power'). Perhaps, then, compassion isn't a necessary logical conclusion, but a choice.

'Man is born without a soul, but it is possible to make one'
G. I. GURDJIEFF C.1877–1949
Views from the Real World

Georges Ivanovich Gurdjieff was an Armenian-born mystic and religious philosopher whose complex metaphysical system and innovative brand of self-development aimed at the 'harmonious development of man'. Gurdjieff's main contention is that man is 'asleep', and his actions represent the automatic processes of an organic 'machine'. Therefore, as such, he possesses neither will nor soul, but rather, many selves, each of which works to an independent and sometimes contrary purpose. However, through unifying these disparate selves into a single entity, via a process which he termed 'work on oneself', man possessed the potential to 'create' a soul, which would in turn allow him the capacity of will.

Gurdjieff's methods were unconventional and represented what he saw as a critique and improvement upon traditional schemes of religious aspiration. The Buddhist monk works to still and control the mind through meditation; the *fakir* (an Indian 'wonder worker') to master pain and bodily discomfort through feats of physical endurance; whilst the Christian aims to master emotion through fostering an attitude of faith through prayer and contemplation. However, the *cunning man* can develop a *fourth way* (as he termed it), whereby he could work on each of these three aspects in turn, or even at once, and so develop the whole individual harmoniously (Gurdjieff's centre in Paris was named *The Institute for the Harmonious Development of Man*). Thus, through specially designed exercises, Gurdjieff's students were tasked to develop themselves physically, mentally and emotionally. Accordingly, Gurdjieff discriminates between mere intellectual knowledge and genuine knowledge, the former being an almost automatic and uncritical ingestion of opinion, the latter the result of an integrated response of all aspects of the individual working together.

Gurdjieff remains a controversial and fascinating figure. The origins of his system remain untraced – Gurdjieff himself claimed to have gathered ancient and neglected knowledge on his travels, but some commentators claim that his source was in fact *Sufism* (the mystical tradition of Islam).

ALFRED KORZYBSKI 1879–1950
Science and Sanity

Philosophers mostly agree that we do not perceive the world directly. The straight stick that appears bent in water, the mirage suggesting water on the desert floor, and other similar illusions, all indicate that our perceptions often lead us astray, so must be interpreted. So, once we understand how water refracts light, making the stick appear bent, we have a basis for knowledge. But this is not always easy, and we still often mistake illusion for reality.

Polish philosopher Alfred Korzybski took a more psychological perspective on this old philosophical chestnut. He argued that there were different levels of abstraction – a sort of hierarchy of ideas that we draw from experience – and that we frequently mistake a shallower level for a deeper one. For example, if I call you an idiot, I may mean either that something you have done is idiotic, or more generally that you are in fact a stupid person. However, Korzybski argued, the latter claim is too strong, for it assumes that you cannot behave otherwise, and therefore always will be an idiot. Furthermore, if you accept my assessment, then you too have chosen to believe the illusion: you have mistaken the map (an occasionally useful but limited generalization) for the territory (things as they actually are or could be).

There is an interesting anecdote about Korzybski which illustrates this. Whilst giving a lecture, he reached into his briefcase and proceeded to eat from a packet of biscuits. Apologizing for the interruption – he had missed lunch – he offered some to students in the front row. Some accepted, and after a while he revealed the name on the packet – 'Dog Cookies' – provoking a number to rush for the nearest toilet. We don't know whether they were actually dog biscuits, but it doesn't really matter: the students' reactions were based on what they *thought* they were, thus revealing that to change one's reality, it is often enough simply to change one's map.

'Subtle is the Lord, but malicious He is not'
ALBERT EINSTEIN 1879–1955
attributed, visit to Princetown University, 1921

If a philosopher is someone whose ideas alter the way we think about the world, then German-born physicist Albert Einstein can justly be considered one of the greats. Many of Einstein's breakthroughs stemmed from *thought experiments*, and he was – as much as any philosopher – primarily concerned with the deepest questions about reality and truth.

In his *special* and *general* theories of *relativity*, Einstein revealed the shortcomings of Newton's theories, replacing them with something more elegant and comprehensive. In doing so, he contradicted Newton's assumption that space and time were absolute – a sort of *film set* against which everything took place. In a famous thought experiment, Einstein envisages running alongside a light beam: everything would appear motionless or 'frozen' (just as, if I'm on a train, the train appears stationary relative to me). However, this means that, for me, time stops. So, time cannot be absolute (applying uniformly everywhere), but must be *relative* to the speed of the observer. But this also makes space (motion and position) relative – I may be motionless sitting on the train, but to you, standing on the platform as I pass, I am moving at 70 mph. Whose perspective is correct? Neither, according to Einstein, for, contrary to Newton's assumptions, there's no absolute point of rest according to which we can measure an object's position or motion. Furthermore, because time is linked to speed and motion, it cannot be separated from space, but must be thought of as part of the same thing – *space-time*.

However, Einstein's approach is simply rooted in a *different* set of assumptions to Newton's. Both have faith that Nature's laws are *determinate* (unchanging) – we just have to be patient and clever enough to find out what they are. However, even if God isn't 'malicious' enough to make the laws of physics variable, why can't they evolve over time, or – as quantum physics would go on to argue – depend upon the presence of an observer?

> 'Nothing is precious except that part of you which is in other people, and that part of others which is in you. Up there, on high, everything is all one.'
>
> PIERRE TEILHARD DE CHARDIN 1881–1955
> *Hymn to the Universe*

Teilhard de Chardin was a French philosopher and scientist who combined devout religious faith with a keen interest in evolution. However, he was not merely a passionate amateur who dabbled in scientific matters, but a prominent palaeontologist and geologist who moulded his scientific and religious beliefs into a startling vision of human spiritual evolution.

What makes his ideas fascinating, however, also made them controversial. As a Jesuit priest, Teilhard's theories were criticized by the Catholic Church, which did their best to marginalize his influence. As a scientist, his theory that evolution moves toward a preordained purpose contradicts Darwin, who saw natural selection as a blind, goal-less process.

Teilhardian evolution has two stages: *diversification*, where life multiplies and 'colonizes' the physical Earth; and *convergence*, where human beings, the apex of the evolutionary process, move towards unification. The Earth was initially a *geosphere* of physical matter, which biological diversification turns into a *biosphere*, teeming with life; finally, convergence produces the *noosphere*, unifying individual consciousness into one collective mind. This ultimate stage is possible because each human is *already* part of an extended consciousness, which is what actually allows human beings to communicate. Therefore, global consciousness will result when each individual soul recognizes this fact. So, as life becomes increasingly complex, consciousness moves in the other direction, towards unification. In this way, all creation is drawn toward the *Omega point*, a state of maximum complexity of life/unity of consciousness: God.

Some see Teilhard's theories as an uncanny predication of the Internet and the creation of *cyberspace*. As the ease and speed of global communications technology increases, so does our awareness of ourselves as part of a globally conscious network. However, Teilhard goes further: not only are we becoming closer to one another, we are realizing the fact that *we are one another*.

> 'What quality is common to Sta. Sophia and the windows at Chartres, Mexican sculpture, a Persian bowl, Chinese carpets, Giotto's frescoes at Padua, and the masterpieces of Poussin, Piero della Francesca, and Cézanne? Only one answer seems possible – significant form.'
>
> CLIVE BELL 1881–1964
>
> *Art*

Plato banished artists from his ideal republic on the basis that all art had a corrupting influence, reproducing subjects with insufficient concern for the message that should be conveyed. Underlying this attitude was therefore an assumption that art was mainly concerned with *representation*: making things look like other things. So, a successful portrait is one that manages to look like its subject, and, perhaps, also suggests something meaningful or insightful about it.

However, English philosopher and art critic Clive Bell argued that representation was irrelevant. In a view similar to Kant's, Bell proposed that it wasn't whether something *looked* like something else, or possessed certain biographical, historical or symbolic meaning, but how it arranged line, shape, and colour that made it art. If it did this successfully, then we might say that it possessed 'significant form', which in turn might lead us to what Bell termed an 'aesthetic emotion'. So, no matter whether a piece of visual art was a collection of abstract shapes, a detailed landscape, or a group portrait, each was to be judged on the strength of its 'significant form' and the quality of the corresponding emotional/aesthetic reaction that it produced in the viewer.

This approach is known as *formalism*, for understandable reasons, and there are some quite obvious objections to it. For instance, what if a work has significant historical resonances, such as Delacroix's 'The Raft of the Medusa', or Picasso's 'Guernica'. These may or may not possess 'significant form', but surely it is not that which makes them great paintings. Of course, this doesn't mean that significant form *isn't* important – many paintings, especially from the more classical periods of art history – also pay great attention to composition and arrangement. However, we would seem to miss out on a lot if we were *only* to consider a work's formal features.

> 'We are like sailors who on the open sea must reconstruct their ship but are never able to start afresh from the bottom. Where a beam is taken away a new one must at once be put there, and for this the rest of the ship is used as support. In this way, by using the old beams and driftwood the ship can be shaped entirely anew, but only by gradual reconstruction.'
>
> OTTO NEURATH 1882–1945
> *Empiricism and Sociology*

Austrian philosopher, sociologist and economist Otto Neurath was a founding member of *logical positivism*. However, he later rejected its central tenets (which had been influenced by the early ideas of Ludwig Wittgenstein) and adopted a new approach.

Wittgenstein initially believed that there must be, at some level, a direct connection between language and reality. So, to make sense, the structure of language must correspond in some way to the structure of reality – otherwise, how could we speak about the world? If our concepts are not, in some way, a reflection of actual facts, then they may as well be complete fiction or nonsense.

But what *are* facts? If I say, 'Jim is old', what facts does this sentence point to? I can see Jim has grey hair, etc., but this doesn't necessarily lead me to the fact that he is old. If someone else saw Jim, would they come across the same 'facts'? Not necessarily – it's partly a matter of interpretation. The problem is that there doesn't seem to be a neutral world of facts to which my concepts correspond.

Neurath recognized this, as his ship metaphor illustrates. Whereas Descartes, for instance, hoped to build up knowledge of reality from fundamental truths, Neurath saw that this is impossible. Language is like a boat that we use to navigate reality. We can no more build a completely rational basis for knowledge than build a ship whilst sailing it. We might occasionally manage to *improve* certain concepts (a plank or two), but we can't get out and start again. Language *is* reality.

> 'For at least another hundred years we must pretend to ourselves and to everyone that fair is foul and foul is fair; for foul is useful and fair is not. Avarice and usury and precaution must be our gods for a little longer still. For only they can lead us out of the tunnel of economic necessity into daylight.'
> JOHN MAYNARD KEYNES 1883–1946
> 'The Future'

Unlike Adam Smith, English economist John Maynard Keynes did not believe that an unregulated (*laissez-faire*) economy would naturally distribute wealth to the benefit of all. So, whilst he promoted capitalist principles, he also thought that there were times when the economy needed a little help in order to avoid the occasional crashes that the system seemed (and still seems . . .) prone to, and to avoid the hardships that such downturns caused to the less privileged. Thus, with judicious injections of public spending, the market can be kept stable and healthy.

Whether or not this is an effective *economic* theory isn't really within the province of the philosopher. However, what is interesting is Keynes' attitude to capitalism itself, which (at least in the essay quoted from) he sees as a necessary evil rather than (like Smith or Hayek) a virtue in itself. For Keynes, the love of money is 'one of those semi-criminal, semi-pathological propensities which one hands over with a shudder to the specialists in mental disease'. So, in supporting capitalist principles he is basically saying: don't worry, utopia is on its way, but we need to engage in some less than ideal activities in order to get there.

Of course, all but a (semi-pathological?) few would agree that money is a means to an end – to security, health, leisure, power. However, in fostering economic greed as a means to these ends, we are riding the crocodile across the river. Greed, by its nature, has difficulty in recognizing 'enough' – in the words of Epicurus, 'nothing is enough for the man to whom enough is too little'. So, we *may* reach the other side, but there's every chance we won't.

'We cannot, however, manage to make do with such old, familiar, and seemingly indispensable terms as "real" or "only possible"; we are never in a position to say what really is or what really happens, but we can only say what will be observed in any concrete individual case.'
ERWIN SCHRÖDINGER 1887–1961
'The Fundamental Idea of Wave Mechanics'

Since splitting the atom, physicists have tried to understand the sub-atomic world. Niels Bohr and Werner Heisenberg's *Copenhagen interpretation* considered the properties of certain sub-atomic particles as fixed only at the moment of measurement. So, reality isn't decided by fixed laws, but by the fact of observation: perhaps such laws are *indeterminate* or only *probable*. Einstein disagreed, but was aware he was in the minority – writing to fellow physicist Max Born:

'You believe in the God who plays dice, and I in complete law and order in a world which objectively exists ... though I am well aware that your younger colleagues interpret this as a sign of senility.'

Austrian physicist Erwin Schrödinger, siding with Einstein, high-lighted the Copenhagen interpretation's absurdity by a thought experiment. Imagine a cat in a sealed box, within which a poisonous gas is released if a particle is emitted. However, we cannot know this (and whether the cat is poisoned) until we open the box and observe it (fixing the outcome); until then the cat is *neither* alive *nor* dead – or *both*.

Ironically, weight of evidence is now so against him that *Schrödinger's cat* has become a popular illustration of the strangeness of *quantum physics*, its interesting consequences fuelling science-fiction. If, by observing the cat, I 'fix' one outcome, what happens to other possible outcomes? So, the *many worlds interpretation* argues that there are many 'alternative' realities, each of which represents a different fork on the quantum path.

Was Einstein's dream of discovering definite laws simply wishful? Many now think so, and yet, perhaps, all is not lost: the universe is nothing if not unpredictable.

> 'By creating for ourselves an imaginary experience or activity, we
> express our emotions; and this is what we call art'
> R. G. COLLINGWOOD 1889–1943
> *The Principles of Art*

When most people – the 'general public' – see a sheep preserved in formaldehyde, a painting made with elephant dung, or an unmade bed, claimed as a work of art, they often react with disbelief and derision: '*That's* not art!' However, ask them what art is, and they would probably cite the 'Mona Lisa' or Michelangelo's 'David'. But examples are not a definition, and beyond that they would probably have a problem – but they are not alone.

R. G. Collingwood, English philosopher and historian, was also deeply interested in this question. Firstly, he argued, art should be distinguished from craft or skill. Though a person who weaves a basket or builds a wall may be very skilled, they are not *artists*, but *artisans* (tradespeople). Of course, craft may occasionally go far beyond mere usefulness – a Fabergé egg, perhaps – and thereby acquire artistic value, but what marks the boundary?

The idea that the value of art is independent of any usefulness it might have – 'art for art's sake' – is a relatively modern view. Even Leonardo and Michelangelo were only considered (and considered themselves) craftsmen. However, art eventually begins to acquire a separate purpose, and becomes valued for something other than its usefulness, skill, amusement potential, any moral lessons it might convey, or symbolic meaning. Gradually, Collingwood argues, whilst it may still possess these aspects, art comes to be valued primarily for its ability to create emotional and imaginative experiences. This is slightly vague, but Collingwood's main purpose here is to be true to artistic experience, and to suggest what all the things we call art have in common.

Of course, modern art disagrees, and is more concerned with clever 'concept art' and self-commentary. But Collingwood is closer to what people would generally recognize as art, most of whom would agree with the janitor who inadvertently threw away one modern 'exhibit': modern art is just rubbish.

'What we cannot speak about we must pass over in silence'
LUDWIG WITTGENSTEIN 1889–1951
Tractatus Logico-Philosophicus

Born into a wealthy Austrian family, Ludwig Wittgenstein grew up surrounded by genius and power. His father, Karl, a great patron of the arts, threw musical parties attended by Brahms and Mahler, and commissioned Gustav Klimt to paint his daughter's wedding portrait. However, in family terms, Karl's love of excellence translated into parental expectation, and – whilst some children did indeed show signs of brilliance – two sons committed suicide. Ludwig himself was highly strung, and this intensity, combined with wilful independence of spirit, ultimately drew him toward philosophy. Presenting himself to Bertrand Russell, he so impressed the world-renowned philosopher that he was adopted as his protégé. Within a year, Russell declared to Wittgenstein's astonished sister, 'We expect the next big step in philosophy to be taken by your brother.'

However, completed in the trenches of WWI, Wittgenstein's first publication – *A Treatise in Philosophical Logic*, or more simply, the *Tractatus* – was also intended to be his last. For Wittgenstein, philosophy was a puzzle that left fundamental problems – ethical, spiritual, aesthetic – untouched. Solving it, therefore, freed him for the real challenge of living.

It begins cryptically: 'The world is all that is the case', and proceeds – in tightly ordered, numbered propositions (reminiscent of Spinoza's *Ethics*) – to set philosophy on a different footing. We live in a world of facts (propositions), not of things, and so 'the limits of my language mean the limits of my world'. Language is a picture of the world, and so philosophy really only involves working out which pictures are possible. However, sometimes we try to describe things that – due to the limits of logic and language – we cannot speak about directly without getting in a muddle. There are limits to what we can say, and some things are just too fundamental to our way of seeing the world to be the subject of enquiry. On these occasions, therefore, it is best to keep quiet.

> '. . . the meaning of a word is its use in the language'
> LUDWIG WITTGENSTEIN
> *Philosophical Investigations*

Wittgenstein repeatedly attempted to escape philosophy, but was always drawn back. He may have dabbled as an architect, school teacher, and hospital orderly, but there was always a sense in which philosophy was what his meticulous mind was best suited to, and its puzzles would simply not leave him alone.

He first returned some ten years after the publication of the *Tractatus*. Asked to explain it to a group of philosophers who had become influenced by it (the 'logical positivists', as they became known), he began to discern serious flaws. The *Tractatus* proposed that sentences consist of 'logical atoms' – things so 'small' that they have no individual meaning, but whose existence was essential if the sentences themselves were to have an overall sense. In other words, without such 'atoms', a proposition could have no 'logical structure', and therefore no determinate sense at all: there would be semantic anarchy!

However, Wittgenstein gradually realized, such atoms couldn't exist, and just as, decades before, Heisenberg, Bohr, and Einstein had begun to unravel Rutherford's model of the physical atom, so Wittgenstein began to unpick its logical equivalent.

So, rather than possessing an internal 'logical structure', a sentence has meaning because of the role it plays in our shared lives and experiences – not because a particular 'atomic' structure specifies its sense, but because each sentence has a role in the 'game' of language. Each utterance ('move') involves rules which have evolved communally, and therefore each 'move' has a public significance.

A good illustration of this is the case of 'Ayer's Crusoe'. A. J. Ayer argued that a man stranded on a desert island from birth (a variation on Defoe's *Robinson Crusoe*) could evolve his own private language. But Wittgenstein disagreed: he would possess no language without a community for his words to acquire sense in – he would not even, in fact, evolve the ability to think verbally. *Friday*, then, would remain nameless.

> 'Suppose everyone had a box with something in it: we call it a "beetle".
> No one can look into anyone else's box, and everyone says he knows
> what a beetle is only by looking at his beetle.'
>
> LUDWIG WITTGENSTEIN
> *Philosophical Investigations*

This peculiar thought experiment throws light on an old problem. For Descartes, I have *privileged access* to my own thoughts, because they are private mental experiences only I can possess. I may *infer* your thoughts based on actions or speech, but I cannot know directly. This gap – between my mind and yours – leads to a problem: if I can never know what others experience, how do I know their experiences are similar, or even that they have any? Perhaps they are 'zombies' or 'robots'. This is therefore known as the *problem of other minds*.

However, if we can never experience another's mind ('look into anyone else's box'), what is important is not what mental experience is actually like (what someone's beetle looks like), but how we describe it publicly (what 'beetle' means). Perhaps 'beetle' is a poorly chosen example, because anyone could simply compare beetles with those in the world and identify similarities or differences (thus establishing an objective measure). But Wittgenstein actually means something for which there is no objective measure (one's own subjective experience).

Consider colour. My experience of 'red' is – partly – private, so it's possible (if unlikely) that you experience 'red' as 'purple' or 'green'. However, the only way to find out is with a public test – if our identification of colours differ, we will realize; if not, then perhaps *no* test can decide the question – and it therefore doesn't matter. In Wittgenstein's analogy, that I cannot see your beetle and you can't see mine cancel each other out, for 'beetle' *cannot* mean 'what is in my box' – we would *never* understand one another; 'beetle' must have a public meaning. So, it really doesn't matter if your beetle is actually an ant – or if your box is empty . . .

Is Dr Doolittle, then, a fraud, or merely self-deluded? Philosophers such as Descartes and Francis Bacon saw animals not just as representing more rudimentary forms of life, but as actually representing a completely different *kind* from humans. The proof of this, for Descartes at least, was that humans possess speech, whilst animals only make instinctive and expressive sounds. Perhaps animals don't possess evolved-enough speech organs? But mocking birds and parrots can imitate sounds better than humans. Furthermore, we know that they are not simply less advanced than humans, for even children outperform animals linguistically. Perhaps they have their own language? But then, surely, we could learn such a language, or they could even learn ours.

This latter possibility might be termed the 'Dr Doolittle Hypothesis', though it is one that Descartes rejects: there is no suggestion that animals can learn anything as sophisticated as human language, and our analysis of theirs seems to confirm that it is largely behavioural and expressive. A number of modern studies with dolphins and primates would seem to challenge Descartes's conclusions – or at least soften them – but by and large there seems to be general agreement that human language represents a quantum leap beyond anything that most animals are capable of.

Wittgenstein's objection however is different. Even if animals *did* possess a language as sophisticated as ours, we wouldn't understand it because we couldn't share their experiences and outlook. 'Understanding' here means more than just translating the words, but possessing a similar biology, culture, and linguistic community. The objection therefore also applies to human communication: in understanding someone's words, we give them our own sense, but if that person is sufficiently different from me – in terms of education, experience, outlook, etc. – then I may have difficulty in truly understanding him – in 'knowing what makes him tick'. The difference is less extreme than that between a human and a talking lion, but the principle is the same.

> 'When I am furious about something, I sometimes beat the ground or a tree with my walking stick. But I certainly do not believe that the ground is to blame or that my beating can help anything. "I am venting my anger". And all rites are of this kind.'
>
> LUDWIG WITTGENSTEIN
> 'Remarks on Frazer's Golden Bough'

The Golden Bough by **Scottish anthropologist** James Frazer (1854–1941), is a monumental comparative study of religion and mythology across culture and history. Its influence has been immense, not only within its own and related fields, but upon the literature and thinking of the twentieth century.

Frazer's main thesis is that religion is based in magic. So, rituals were originally forms of primitive science: kings were sacrificed to appease the gods, ceremonial dances to bring the rains in times of drought, and effigies of enemies burnt to inflict harm. So, whilst 'primitives' believed in scientific causation, they lacked the knowledge or methodology to effect it. In short, they were mistaken.

However, Wittgenstein sees Frazer as coarsely misinterpreting primitive customs: '*His* explanations of primitive practices are much cruder than the meaning of these practices themselves.' Defending such practices, Wittgenstein points out that the rain dance only took place during the rainy season; it's not a *call* for rain to come, but a *celebration* of the rains *to* come. In other words, it's an *expressive* act, similar to (for instance) punching the air in joy, or defacing a picture of a person I dislike.

This interpretation of religious ritual as expressive is undoubtedly true in some cases, but it does present a problem: many 'primitives' don't share this understanding of their practices. The witch doctor who makes a doll of his enemy to curse him does not see it as some form of therapeutic expression; and, where practices are intended to ward off bad luck (throwing spilt salt over one's left shoulder), it's seen as risky *not* to perform them. So, in 'rescuing' primitive beliefs from Frazer's clumsy misunderstanding, does Wittgenstein misinterpret them? Was Frazer right all along?

> 'What is peddled about nowadays as philosophy, especially that of
> National Socialism, but has nothing to do with the inner truth and
> greatness of that movement [namely the encounter between global
> technology and modern humanity] is nothing but fishing in that
> troubled sea of values and totalities'
> MARTIN HEIDEGGER 1889–1976
> *Introduction to Metaphysics*

The philosophy of Martin Heidegger, as influential as it is complicated, has suffered through association with Nazism. This is
particularly perplexing given Heidegger's indebtedness to Jewish
mentor Edmund Husserl (whose anti-Semitic exclusion from academic life he did not even protest), and his affair with Jewish student
Hannah Arendt (who fled Germany, but remained a life-long friend).
But, while friends suffered, Heidegger prospered: Nazi party mem-
bership paved the way to rectorship of the University of Freiburg
– even praising the Führer in his inaugural address as 'the present and
future of German reality, and its law'.

Despite this, Heidegger was apolitical, yet shared with National
Socialism – albeit for more sophisticated, philosophical reasons – the
völkisch ideal of the German people's organic connection to the land. The
main quote is from a lecture given in 1935; but asked to revise it for publication in 1953 – to remove his praise for 'that movement' (the National
Socialists or *Nazis*) – Heidegger merely clarified it (the insertion in
square brackets): Hitler's racist, nationalistic, pseudo-messianic claptrap
wasn't what had attracted him, but the idea of a popular national movement that sought to preserve its 'folksy' culture against the advance of
technology and capitalism. Recognizing this common outlook, Heidegger
therefore seized the opportunity to promote his philosophy in real terms
– little realizing, perhaps, what those terms might ultimately involve.

This interpretation is more plausible if we consider that Heidegger's
masterwork, *Being and Time*, concerns how human *being* – what he
termed *Dasein*, 'being there' – is not separate from, but *embedded into*
the world, a truth that technological progress disrupts by distorting
the individual's understanding of nature.

Should we, then, forgive a philosopher on account of his unworld-
liness, or judge his moral failings *more* harshly? He has, after all,
thought on these things more than most.

'We do not know what "Being" means. But even if we ask, "What is
'Being'?", we keep within an understanding of the "is", though we are
unable to fix conceptionally what that "is" signifies.'

MARTIN HEIDEGGER

Being and Time

Whilst *Being and Time* never discusses Husserl's philosophy, it couldn't
have been written without it. This isn't because it agrees with it – in
large parts, it doesn't – but because Heidegger's approach owes much
to Husserl's phenomenology. However, whereas Husserl hoped to
explain reality in terms of the experience of a conscious subject,
Heidegger thought that this was an inadequate way of thinking about
our existence.

Heidegger's main focus is on *being*. He notes that philosophers
throughout history have been primarily concerned with *epistemological*
questions – what knowledge is, how we acquire it, how we can guarantee it. However, such puzzles ignore the more fundamental question
of what *existence* is. For instance, Descartes is so concerned with
proving his existence – that he's a thinking thing, that he's separate
from his body, etc. – that the *nature* of existence is barely touched on.

In contrast, Heidegger applies a *phenomenological* analysis to the
question of being. We find ourselves more profoundly *embedded* in
existence than Descartes's account suggests. But when we try to
understand what 'being' is – what 'is' is – we have only the faintest
notion: our being (*Dasein*), the thing with which in many ways we are
most familiar, is paradoxically the *least* known.

It's tempting – as some philosophers have – to dismiss all this: isn't
this really a *non-problem*? Can't we just say that we exist, and that's
that? Well, we *could*, but that would miss the true significance of
Heidegger's philosophy. Unlike previous philosophers, Heidegger
identifies the deep puzzlement and disquiet we feel on finding ourselves 'thrown into the world' (as he puts it). In directly addressing it,
thus paving the way for *existentialism*, he therefore proposed that the
most profound question was not *who* we are, or *what* we are, but *that*
we are: why is there existence at all?

> 'The conscious and intelligent manipulation of the organized habits and opinions of the masses is an important element in democratic society. Those who manipulate this unseen mechanism of society constitute an invisible government which is the true ruling power of our country ... We are governed, our minds are molded, our tastes formed, our ideas suggested, largely by men we have never heard of.'
>
> EDWARD BERNAYS 1891–1995
> *Propaganda*

The American Edward Bernays was a nephew of Freud, and applied his uncle's ideas to advertizing and the burgeoning field of public relations. Like Freud, Bernays saw society as governed by hidden, irrational forces. Thus, choices were often influenced by factors of which the individual was unaware. Bernays' insight lay in realizing that, by appealing to these unconscious instincts, people could be manipulated and controlled.

Bernays transformed advertising from a form of bragging, presenting exaggerated and even false claims, to an art of subtle persuasion, relying on insidious appeal. One famous campaign enticed women to smoke by linking in sexual equality (women were forbidden from public smoking in much of the US), branding cigarettes 'Torches of Freedom'.

Bernays' ideas are most influential – and controversial – in public relations, or *propaganda*, as it was once more plainly known. In a series of books, he outlined how public opinion could be manipulated, what he termed 'the engineering of consent' – a phrase echoed by Noam Chomsky's *Manufacturing Consent*. For Bernays, manipulation was not only compatible with democracy, it was essential: how could democratic society work unless opinions were harmonized? Of course, critics point out, this isn't the spirit of democracy, which involves rational and conscious consent. Bernays' views are therefore closer to *tyrrany* – which, depending on your view, is either benign or oppressive, for persuasion itself necessarily moral or immoral; it's merely a technique. This is perhaps best illustrated by the fact that Bernays' theories were very influential upon Joseph Goebbels, the architect of Nazi propaganda.

'To be shaken out of the ruts of ordinary perception, to be shown for a few timeless hours the outer and inner world, not as they appear to an animal obsessed with survival or to a human being obsessed with words and notions, but as they are apprehended, directly and unconditionally, by Mind at Large – this is an experience of inestimable value to everyone and especially to the intellectual'

ALDOUS HUXLEY 1894–1963
The Doors of Perception

English writer Aldous Huxley, grandson of T. H. and brother of Julian (both evolutionary biologists), is most remembered for *Brave New World*. However, as a broad-ranging thinker and prolific essayist he had interesting things to say on eugenics, religion, and hallucinogenic drugs. Given his social background, he seems an unlikely advocate of the latter, but it was its potential to enhance our intellectual and aesthetic faculties that interested him.

Huxley wasn't the first intellectual to try drugs for this purpose. Psychologist William James claimed that only on nitrous oxide did Hegel become intelligible, and American writer Oliver Wendell Holmes famously reported that, after having used ether, he wrote down the secret to the universe, only later to discover it to be, 'A strong smell of turpentine prevails throughout'. Such examples are often cited to prove that drugs provide an untrustworthy form of revelation (e.g. by Bertrand Russell, who actually seems to conflate these two anecdotes in his *History of Western Philosophy*). Is Huxley's position therefore mistaken, or even irresponsible?

There are separate issues here (health risks, public danger), but Huxley seems only concerned with whether such drugs provide *deeper* insight into reality. Certainly, they may change brain chemistry and even reorder neural pathways (as Timothy Leary argued). However, this is as likely to disrupt *useful* mental organization as it is negative thought patterns, and there's no guarantee that such intense experiences will respect sanity, or are even genuine. Weighed against these dangers, we might therefore temper Huxley's enthusiasm with caution, for even if genuine benefits exist, what use is a philosopher who cannot tie his shoelaces?

> '. . . the social system is an organization like the individual, that . . . is bound together by a system of communication, and that . . . has a dynamics in which circular processes of a feedback nature play an important part'
> NORBERT WIENER 1894–1964
> *Cybernetics*

Cybernetics is, broadly speaking, the study of systems, and as such can apply to anything – biological organisms, business organizations, machines. However, more specifically, it's concerned with how goal-oriented systems work, function to achieve their goals, and monitor themselves. Accordingly, cybernetics assumes a common basis to the way that different systems work, and has therefore had considerable influence on many different fields.

As a distinct area of study, it was founded by American mathematician Norbert Weiner, who proposed that goal-oriented systems worked by reacting to *negative feedback* in order to maintain what he called *homeostasis*. The simplest illustration of this is the humble thermostat: if the temperature drops below a certain point, the heating comes on; if it goes above, the heating goes off. Thus, negative feedback (too hot/cold) helps to maintain ideal conditions (homeostasis). Therefore, as Wiener put it, everything is simply information: 'Information is information, not matter or energy.'

These principles are hugely important for computers, or for anything designed to act independently or automatically. Thus, once we realize that all systems aim at homeostasis, we can apply this understanding to society, to systems of thought, to education, to politics – the applications are endless. Or are they? Whilst cybernetics *can* be used to model anything, there's a temptation to assume that the thing being modelled *is just* a cybernetic feedback system. However, when we apply these principles to more sophisticated human activities – such as learning, or problem solving, or even consciousness itself – then cybernetics (arguably) starts to fall short. The reason for this is that, despite its modern approach and terminology, it is merely a development of the old mechanistic view. But whilst such things as the human mind may have mechanical or systematic aspects, can we really say that it's *merely* a goal-driven system? What is the goal of consciousness?

'We keep inventing jobs because of this false idea that everybody has to be employed at some kind of drudgery because, according to Malthusian-Darwinian theory, he must justify his right to exist. So we have inspectors of inspectors and people making instruments for inspectors to inspect inspectors. The true business of people should be to go back to school and think about whatever it was they were thinking about before somebody came along and told them they had to earn a living.'

R. BUCKMINSTER FULLER 1895–1983
quoted in 'The New York Magazine Environmental Teach-In',
New York Magazine, 1970

American architect, designer and inventor R. Buckminster Fuller is most famous for his *geodesic dome*, a disproportionately strong design structure given its lightness and the amount of material used. Fuller christened his architectural approach *tensegrity* (short for 'tensional integrity'), which utilized the structural properties of certain geometric shapes and configurations. So, if the struts supporting a bridge also support *one another* (e.g. forming a triangle or a hexagon), the *tension* between them will create great *integrity* (structural soundness). This principle allows for construction using not only less, but cheaper and lighter materials, the known weaknesses of the material being offset by the overall arrangement of parts.

It's an unlikely step from here to solving the world's food and energy needs, but the principle underlying *tensegrity* – doing more with less – can also be applied to systems in general (what Fuller termed *synergetics*). Fuller proposed that many problems can be solved by thinking *holistically* and *cooperatively*. For instance, creating a global electrical network using renewable energy sources could supply everyone's needs, and similar cooperative solutions could address food scarcity and other forms of want.

But Fuller also hoped to revolutionize attitudes to survival. Work proves our usefulness to a society that doesn't tolerate 'freeloaders', but technological advance has made such 'drudgery' theoretically redundant. Life need no longer involve a Darwinian and Malthusian battle over resources, for selfishness is no longer necessary for survival. But if the game has changed, why are we still playing by the old rules?

'I maintain that Truth is a pathless land, and you cannot approach it by any path whatsoever, by any religion, by any sect'

JIDDU KRISHNAMURTI 1895–1986

speech dissolving the Order of the Star, 1929

Jiddu Krishnamurti was an Indian-born philosopher and writer. For over 50 years, he travelled worldwide, giving lectures and fielding questions on how to live, what to believe, and how to be happy, influencing such as Aldous Huxley, Alan Watts, and Joseph Campbell. Thus, he ironically fulfilled a role which he'd once rejected, and for which he'd been chosen by the leaders of the *Theosophical Society*, namely Annie Besant and C. W. Leadbeater, the latter having spotted his potential and plucked him from a life of modest means.

Theosophy proposes that spiritually evolved beings periodically reincarnate to usher in new stages of human development. Leadbeater and Besant were therefore on the lookout for the next World Teacher, whom Buddhist prophecy referred to as *Lord Maitreya*. Convinced that Krishnamurti would be his next 'vehicle', Besant and Leadbeater groomed him for the purpose. However, growing in stature and confidence, Krishnamurti became increasingly uncomfortable with the expectations and organizational paraphernalia surrounding him, and – in a famous speech – abdicated, claiming that 'truth is a pathless land', and that we should look to ourselves for guidance. As Leadbeatter noted, 'the coming had gone wrong'.

Freed from his role of global messiah, Krishnamurti stripped his message of inessentials, shunning methods and metaphysical trappings, and challenged all who would listen to change themselves – not by mantras, rituals, or secret techniques, but simply through self-observation. True meditation is the constant struggle for self-awareness, and, through understanding, to rein in the ceaseless tendency to seek comfort and consolation in illusion.

As liberating as this iconoclasm is, it's a hard and Spartan path, which few want or possess the capacity to follow with the intensity Krishnamurti required. Perhaps this isn't surprising: having dissected our weaknesses, and exposed our delusions, is it any wonder that our primary response to our liberator falls somewhat sort of gratitude?

> 'It is with children that we have the best chance of studying the
> development of logical knowledge, mathematical knowledge, physical
> knowledge, and so forth'
>
> JEAN PIAGET 1896–1980
> *Genetic Epistemology*

Swiss psychologist, Jean Piaget, greatly shaped modern attitudes to child development and education. Noticing that, when tested, children of a certain age made almost identical *types* of mistake, he theorized that children's cognitive abilities progressed according to developmental stages, of which he identified four.

Firstly, from birth to 2 years old – the *sensorimotor stage* – the child explores the world of physical movement and sensory impressions, and is naturally egoistic (self-centred). The second or *preoperational stage* (2 to 7) continues the development of movement whilst ushering in symbolic *thinking* (something *stands for* something else – a toy car for a real one), but the child still egocentrically assumes everyone sees things from his own viewpoint. In the *concrete stage* (7 to 11), the child begins to reason; thought and language increasingly becoming the main tools for understanding. Finally, the *formal operational stage* (11 up) develops reasoning using abstract concepts, and logic in the fullest sense.

Accepting Piaget's scheme (which we need not apply rigidly) has great implications for education, parenting, and other aspects of child development. For instance, it seems pointless to teach subjects requiring rational thought, or assume capacity to see things from another's point of view, before the age of seven. Realizing this, certain forms of inappropriate behaviour toward others become a temporary developmental issue: literally, *they'll grow out of it*. Also, the ability to read should not presuppose the ability to conceptualize, and age-specific educational texts should reflect this.

However, critics observe that Piaget's focus is primarily intellectual: he wants to know when a child *knows*. But what about emotion, self-esteem, or other important aspects of personality? This may be true, but it is perhaps offset by Piaget's rediscovery of the importance of *play* in education. A child learns by discovery: before we *know*, we must *explore*.

'SURREALISM, n. Pure psychic automatism, by which one proposes
to express, either verbally, or in writing, or by any other manner, the
real functioning of thought. Dictation of thought in the absence of all
control exercised by reason, outside of all aesthetic and moral
preoccupation.'
ANDRÉ BRETON 1896–1966
The Surrealist Manifesto

André Breton was a French poet and writer who helped found
Surrealism, a philosophical movement that has found expression in
art, literature, photography and film. However, as Breton makes clear
in the first *Surrealist Manifesto*, surrealist principles can apply to anything at all.

Surrealism is fundamentally opposed to *rationalism*, or the view
that human behaviour should be primarily based upon the dictates of
reason. However, Surrealism argued, it was precisely such 'rationalism' that lay behind the carnage of the First World War. Thus, in
combining a generally anti-establishment spirit with Freud's view of
the unconscious, it hoped to undermine the traditional concept of the
rationally motivated conscious individual, and free society from rigidly harmful thought patterns. In doing this, it employed a wide
variety of methods to release unconscious content, including hypno-
tism, automatic writing, and free association, seeking to express, like
a waking dream, something that disrupted traditional and expected
responses. By liberating the non-rational self, it therefore sought to
reintegrate emotion and imagination into society and personal
experience.

Naturally, this very general statement of Surrealist principles isn't
necessarily representative. Due to its anarchic and chaotic nature,
Surrealism is difficult to clearly define – which, of course, is partly
intentional. The same goes for Surrealists themselves, a diverse group
more united in their opposition to rationalism than in their conception of what Surrealism should be. However, in looking for meaning
in Surrealist works, we face a problem: are *all* attempts to find meaning
to be resisted as another expression of rationalism, or does Surrealism
simply aim at disrupting tradition and establishing a deeper meaning?
Can Surrealism mean anything *at all*?

> 'We cut nature up, organize it into concepts, and ascribe significances
> as we do, largely because we are parties to an agreement to organize it
> in this way – an agreement that holds throughout our speech
> community and is codified in the patterns of our language'
>
> BENJAMIN WHORF 1897–1941
> 'Science and Linguistics'

It's a fact well known to visitors of foreign lands that much can be achieved by speaking slowly, pointing, and – occasionally – resorting to mime. However, things may not be as simple as the linguistically challenged assume. Suppose you're at a fruit stall. You point out an unknown specimen – 'javani' the vendor responds.

However, 'javani' doesn't refer to the fruit as a whole, but only part of it, there being a custom to eat only the top third and discard the rest. As a linguistic and cultural outsider, you don't know this – in fact, may *never* know it. Furthermore, 'javani' may only be one of countless ways in which you will forever be excluded – not just from their language, but from their whole *view of the world*.

Associated with linguists Edmund Sapir (1884–1939) and Benjamin Whorf, and the philosophy of W. V. O. Quine (who uses a similar example to the above), the *Sapir-Whorf hypothesis* proposes that languages are tied to their communities; just as cultural practices and values differ, so does linguistic meaning. In a study of the language of the Hopi Indians, for instance, Whorf claimed they possessed a completely unique concept of time. This would be a nightmare for dictionary makers, who mostly seem to assume that words are simply labels for common ideas. You say 'zucchini', I say 'courgette', but we mean the same thing. However, Whorf argued, there may be concepts in the other language which may be completely alien to you, and untranslatable.

Of course, 'indeterminacy of translation' (as Quine calls this) can also apply to speakers of the *same* language: our diverse experiences, the different ways we've acquired words, may cause us to have subtly different understandings. Perhaps we should stick to pointing.

> 'The pleasure of living and the pleasure of the orgasm are identical.
> Extreme orgasm anxiety forms the basis of the general fear of life.'
> WILHELM REICH 1897–1957
> *The Function of the Orgasm*

Austrian psychoanalyst Wilhelm Reich studied under Freud, but rebelled. Reich agreed that sexual energy (*libido*) was the basis of psychic processes, but became dissatisfied with Freud's account of self-destructive acts – e.g. suicide or self-harm. If all behaviour is governed by the *pleasure principle*, what purpose could such acts serve? This led Freud to posit a *death drive*, whereby the rational self (*ego*) defended itself against its own unconscious forces. So, overwhelmed by feelings of guilt, someone might self-harm in order to 'push away' the guilty thoughts.

Reich saw this as a step backwards: the 'death drive' was merely the result of society's denial of the natural drive to seek pleasure. Unlike Freud, Reich thought that, faced with conflict between social codes and full sexual expression, *society* should change, not the individual. Human nature is basically good, and *sadism* and *masochism* stem from constraint and frustration. If sexual attitudes change, if people overcome their 'hang-ups', then common psychiatric problems would disappear, as would many social ills. The key to this was the orgasm. Most individuals did not experience full orgasm because – physically, mentally and emotionally – they had been disfigured by repressive attitudes.

Reich's theories, rejected and reviled by the establishment, nonetheless helped fuel the 1960's 'sexual revolution', and influenced other therapies (e.g. *Gestalt*). However, Reich later claimed that sexual energy was a universal material (which he termed *orgone*), and could be isolated, stored, and used to treat illness (even cancer). The American government seized on the cancer claim (though Reich never claimed a *cure*), and sadly his last years were spent in prison. Was Reich persecuted? Certainly, the extraordinary step of burning his books and papers more resembles totalitarian censorship than concern for scientific truth – and since when is government the arbiter of scientific truth? Also, given Reich's views on society, it also encourages conspiracy theory: was he onto something?

> 'Try to exclude the possibility of suffering which the order of nature
> and the existence of free-wills involve, and you find that you have
> excluded life itself'
> C. S. LEWIS 1898–1963
> *The Problem of Pain*

English writer and literary scholar C. S. Lewis is best known for his *Narnia* chronicles, a collection of fantasy books written for children (and, as Michael Ward plausibly argues in *Planet Narnia*, as a vehicle for religious allegory employing the medieval symbolism of the seven planets). However, Lewis is also duly renowned for his theological writing, and, following his conversion, as a *Christian apologist* (defending and explaining Christian belief against its detractors).

It's in this latter role that Lewis seeks to account for the problem of suffering, which is an aspect of the problem of evil: why, if God loves us, does he allow seemingly needless suffering? Lewis contends that if human beings were without free will, or the universe was one in which there was no ill consequence for any decision, life would be all but meaningless. If I can *never* suffer for my choices, how can I be truly good or moral? God's love therefore isn't that of a cuddly and indulgent grandfather, but a stern but caring father, who guides us toward the good ends we *should* be aiming for. Furthermore, because we have chosen a path independent of God (as the original sin of Adam implies), pain becomes God's way of teaching us, and reminding us of our transgression.

Lewis's approach contains elements of St Augustine, St Irenaeus, and, to an extent, Leibniz. God creates a world which contains suffering, but this is the best possible if we are to grow in our knowledge and experience of his love. And yet, as with these other approaches, we are left to wonder: in what way is the suffering of infants, or those incapable of learning justified? Is this too a consequence of Adam's sin? Therefore, whilst Lewis is sincere, insightful and persuasive, his solution is a partial one.

German philosopher Herbert Marcuse fused Marxism with
Freudianism to generate a critique of modern society. Like Reich,
Marcuse thought that it was the over-repressiveness of society that created psychological problems. Freud had argued that we are forced to
repress our desire for instant gratification (*the pleasure principle*) in
accordance with the requirements of work, social responsibility, etc.
(*the reality principle*). Therefore, in a sense, repression is a natural part
of growing up and existing in society.

However, Marcuse argued that modern society had taken this too
far, for whilst it is natural for gratification to be deferred in the achievement of 'higher' goals through *sublimation* (such as sexual energy
channelled into artistic creativity), capitalist society required the sublimation of instinctual gratification in the name of 'progress'. However,
such 'progress', whereby we sacrifice our current happiness for a long-
term goal, is actually the exploitation of the working classes for
financial profit. Ultimately, then, the cause of repression is not the
reality principle, but what Marcuse termed the *performance principle*,
whereby natural, biological instincts are repressed in pursuance of an
illusory ideal, which benefits the wealthy elite and oppresses the
proletariat.

In place of the performance principle, Marcuse proposes a Marxist-
inspired utopia founded not by the need to produce, but by the need to
express our natural desire for purposeful activity. Work is therefore a
form of 'free play', where workers aren't *alienated* from the product of
work (having no direct meaning except as 'work'), but are rather
engaged in a meaningful part of life.

It is easy to see, therefore, how Marcuse's utopian ideals were a
driving force in the cultural revolution of the 1960s. Whilst he did not
coin the slogan 'Make love not war', he did endorse and use it, and it
can therefore be seen very much in the spirit of his ideas: the natural
biological energies that constitute life should serve meaning and purpose, not profit and death.

'The people recognize themselves in their commodities;
they find their soul in their automobile, hi-fi set, split-level home,
kitchen equipment. The very mechanism which ties the individual
to his society has changed, and social control is anchored in the new
needs which it has produced.'

HERBERT MARCUSE
One-Dimensional Man

Whilst Marxism suffered from the gradual revelations of Soviet totalitarianism, Marcuse argued that more subtle but equally pervasive forms of social control were at work in apparently 'free' and 'liberal' Western democracies. We shouldn't, he argued, mistake consumer choice for actual freedom: ability to choose from a range of luxury items isn't itself a sign that we are not manipulated or controlled. Far from it, for through advertizing and media, desire to possess unnecessary commodities is fostered in society's members, so that they become wage slaves to these artificial needs.

Furthermore, capitalist consumerism generates an increased disrespect for the products themselves, which become temporary satisfactions that are quickly disposed of when superseded by the latest 'must-have' novelty. Thereby, the capitalist industrial machine is kept running, and the public are 'stupefied' by overwork and meaningless greed, genuine social relations are undermined, and society disintegrates into boxed-off individuals divorced from any sense of true community or purpose.

Obviously, this is an extreme view, but anyone who has ever sighed with dismay over their child's birthday list will empathize: you don't need to be Marxist or even socialist to recognize that consumerism has gone too far. But what are we to do? Marcuse's answer involves what he termed the *Great Refusal*: capitalist consumerism is so ingrained in our culture, our way of thinking and being, that, like the mythological multi-headed hydra, which grows another head with each one severed, we may despair of ever uprooting it completely – and yet, we must try, opposing capitalism in all its forms, at every turn.

But this is a hard demand, and we may also question its motive: isn't Marcuse's project in danger of becoming a puritan ideal, an *opposing* form of intolerance and oppression?

'We must face the fact that the preservation of individual freedom is incompatible with a full satisfaction of our views of distributive justice'

FRIEDRICH HAYEK 1899–1992

Individualism and Economic Order

Friedrich Hayek, Austrian-born economist and political theorist, saw society's ills as resulting from government attempts to organize everyone's life 'for the best'. Even where these ideals were benevolent – e.g. socialist concern for *distributive justice* (everyone gets a fair share) – history teaches that such attempts at control inevitably constrain individual freedom, often leading to *totalitarianism*. Thus, presented with the sobering horrors of Stalinist Russia and Nazi Germany, Hayek chose freedom.

Classical liberalism argues that government should be limited, only upholding law and protecting legitimate freedom. This allowed free trade and an unregulated market economy – *laissez-faire capitalism* – where government doesn't intervene to protect certain economic interests over others. This was a reaction against the so-called *post-war consensus*, where John Maynard Keynes argued that capitalism should be constrained by various safeguards, such as public welfare, health care, and nationalization of key industries. This outlook obtained until the 1980s, where it gave way to the modern *libertarian* view – based on the theories of those such as Hayek – where the individual's economic and ideological liberty was paramount.

As I write, many argue that this philosophy has run its course. Those who consider its effects wholly negative point to the increasing gap between rich and poor, the scandals of corporate corruption, and the global crash occasioned by the unrestrained greed endemic in the banking system. And yet, citing Adam Smith, the libertarian's response is to call for *still less* government involvement, as if car crashes are caused by brakes. Underlying this is Hayek's belief (like Smith's 'invisible hand') that an unregulated economy will somehow produce a 'spontaneous order'. As taxpayers bail out the banks to the tune of billions, we may feel entitled to question this article of faith, and wonder whether we're enabling individual liberty, or merely subsidizing irresponsible gamblers in a highly destructive and costly habit.

'The original is unfaithful to the translation'
Jorge Luis Borges 1899–1986
'Sobre el *Vathek* de William Beckford'

It's tempting, perhaps, to define philosophy as that which is pursued in university departments and academic books and journals. However, in doing so, we risk losing a deeper sense of what is significant about philosophy. A good illustration of this is the work of Argentinian writer and poet Jorge Luis Borges.

Most famous for his short stories, Borges combines elements of surrealism and fantasy into an approach known as *magical realism*. Thus, things happen which form part of a coherent narrative, but which may not be possible in everyday life: a man meets himself from the future (*The Other*); a book in which, once turned, no page can ever be found again (*The Book of Sand*); a 3rd century Roman soldier discovers immortality (*The Immortal*). In this way, Borges explores philosophical and artistic themes – infinity, death, time, knowledge – and his stories are often rich sources for the illustration of philosophical problems. Also, Borges often explicitly discusses the ideas of certain philosophers – Hume, Plato, Spinoza – and in '*Tlön, Uqbar, Orbis Tertius*', he even imagines a world where the idealism of Berkeley is accepted as true.

However, some would argue that this still doesn't qualify Borges as a serious philosopher, merely an author who utilizes philosophical themes – as plot devices, or points of interest. This is partly true, but this very fact reveals something interesting about Borges: ideas, systems, ideologies, theories – all are merely methods for transforming reality. In a late interview, Borges asserts that 'The task of art is to transform what is continually happening to us ... The poet never rests.' In other words, whilst philosophical ideas and theories may be interesting and important, they are just another means of changing our reality. It is in this spirit, then, that he can suggest (in our quote) that a translation *surpasses* the original. As the *aesthetes* proposed, and Korzybski agreed, we should not be constrained by 'reality' – or even, perhaps, by philosophy itself.

> 'Man need not be degraded to a machine by being denied to be a ghost in a machine. He might, after all, be a sort of animal, namely, a higher mammal. There has yet to be ventured the hazardous leap to the hypothesis that perhaps he is a man.'
>
> GILBERT RYLE 1900–1976
> *The Concept of Mind*

Descartes claimed the mind is an immaterial spirit, and the body a mindless automaton: the twin doctrines of *immaterialism* and *mechanism*. English philosopher Gilbert Ryle famously attacked this view, terming it 'the dogma of the ghost in the machine', and arguing that it stemmed from what he called a 'category mistake'.

Suppose you visit Oxford University (using Ryle's example), and someone shows you around: you see the libraries, academic buildings and departments, etc. On finishing your tour, when your guide asks if you wish to see anything else, you complain, 'But where is the University? I haven't seen that yet.' Obviously, there is a simple misunderstanding here: you don't realize that 'University' isn't a term for another *building*, but rather a collective way of referring to the various faculties and buildings that *make up* the university. However, just because it isn't any one building doesn't mean that it is some mysterious immaterial entity – that might carry on existing when all buildings were no longer there, perhaps; it's just another way of describing the same things. The mistake is explained, the 'problem' vanishes.

Relating this to Cartesian dualism, the same solution applies: mind is not something 'separate and distinct' from the physical body, but rather a way of referring to certain processes, actions, etc., that involve the body.

Having made this point, Ryle also wished to avoid *mechanism*: Man was not a machine, but a conscious living organism. We might *simulate* certain physical processes (an artificial heart or limb), but the organism is not itself mechanical.

But if human beings are not spiritual entities, then what would make them different (for instance) from an exact mechanical copy? Is there something *else* special about us?

'. . . the man who is born into existence deals first with language; this is a given. He is even caught in it before his birth. Doesn't he have a civil status? Yes, the child who is to be born is already, from head to toe, caught in this language hammock that receives him and at the same time imprisons him.'

JACQUES LACAN 1901–1981

Interview, 1957

Lacan was a French psychoanalyst whose ideas blended a range of influences – Freud, Hegel, structuralism, linguistics – and in turn helped shape European philosophy from the 1960s onwards. Consequently, he can be quite forbidding reading, and – like many 'postmodern' writers – it sometimes feels you're wading through a sea of labels, theories and jargon before even beginning to consider the ideas themselves.

One such idea concerns the role language plays in structuring experience. It's tempting to believe, with Descartes, that I possess a distinct 'I' that, when I'm born, is thrust into the world of experience, and gradually learns labels for the various objects and relations that make up reality. However, Lacan argues, it's the other way around: 'I' am actually a structure that exists *in language itself*, which when I'm born 'clothes' me in concepts, like a 'babygrow' I never remove. So, 'I' don't merely learn the structure of language; language structures 'me'.

There are pre-echoes of this idea in earlier philosophers (e.g. Nietzsche), but Lacan does much to elaborate on the detail of this process. For example, during the 'mirror stage', the infant identifies with his reflected image, which becomes more 'real' than his bodily sensations. Thus is the 'ego' or self formed: 'I' am therefore a construct, a choice made in the process of interacting with the world.

We can see here the influence of *structuralism*: we may understand reality through analyzing how language is structured. However, as with structuralist approaches in general, this reveals a disquieting possibility: there are no 'structures' – self, other, reality – independent of language. Perhaps, then, only in the mirror of language do 'I' exist: I *blink* therefore I am?

> 'In so far as a scientific statement speaks about reality, it must be falsifiable: and in so far as it is not falsifiable, it does not speak about reality'
> KARL POPPER 1902–1994
> *The Logic of Scientific Discovery*

The *problem of induction* suggests the impossibility of logically proving certain general statements based on experience: 'James always eats ice cream after lunch', might change any day; even 'the Sun always rises' may eventually prove false (and the problem of induction will be the least of our concerns . . .).

However, Austrian philosopher Karl Popper proposed a novel solution: instead of *verification* of theories, why not *falsification?* 'All cows are vegetarian' is unverifiable; we may search forever only encountering vegetarian bovines, which doesn't mean there aren't *non*-vegetarian ones somewhere. However, the first carnivorous cow we discover, the observation becomes false. The resulting negative statement – 'some cows are *not* vegetarian' – is less encompassing than its positive cousin, but at least seems certain.

Scientific progress, Popper argues, therefore requires being *wrong*, and continually revising and refining hypotheses to rule out false assertions. Furthermore, this helps us characterize science, and distinguish it from *pseudo-science*. If the weatherman says 'Today, there will be weather', he cannot be wrong (unless the Earth's atmosphere gets sucked into space, perhaps . . .). Similarly, when your astrology forecast predicts, 'Today, your sensitive Cancerian nature makes you mull over past events', it's difficult to see how such a general prediction could be false: is there ever a day when we *don't* think about the past? Even just, 'Now where did I put my keys . . .?'

However, falsification is problematic. Firstly, it's not generally the way that science proceeds. Conclusively falsifying theories can be as difficult as verifying them: was the machine properly calibrated? Have all variables been accounted for? Many successful theories are therefore grand conjectures that it would be difficult to conclusively falsify – the theory of Natural Selection, for instance. The success of such insightful 'guesses' therefore suggests that science does not progress by little, rational baby-steps, but by large intuitive strides.

> 'It was intended that when Newspeak had been adopted once and for all and Oldspeak forgotten, a heretical thought – that is, a thought diverging from the principles of IngSoc – should be literally unthinkable, at least so far as thought is dependent on words'
>
> GEORGE ORWELL 1903–1950
>
> *1984*

George Orwell was the pen name of English writer Eric Blair, famous for *Animal Farm* and *1984*. The latter's bleak vision of a futuristic police state employing constant surveillance, censorship and indoctrination, represents Orwell's warning as to the ultimate consequences of *totalitarianism*. The brutality of Stalin-backed communists in the Spanish Civil War convinced Orwell that state control – even for supposedly benign ends – could only ever curtail freedom.

1984, set in a post-revolutionary Britain, details the dictatorship of 'Big Brother', the shadowy figurehead of an oppressive state machine. As in Stalinist Russia, even *Ing-Soc* ('English Socialist') party members live in constant paranoia and fear of displeasing the ever vigilant powers-that-be.

However, as well as round-the-clock surveillance ('Big Brother is Watching You!'), members are more subtly controlled by language itself. 'Newspeak' attempts to rewrite English ('Oldspeak'), eventually making it impossible to even *think* 'incorrectly'. Thus, Newspeak reverses traditional meanings: 'War is Peace. Freedom is Slavery. Ignorance is Strength.' What was good is now bad; what was bad, good.

Some liken *political correctness* (PC) to Newspeak in that it attempts to restrict and replace terms that embody negative attitudes and associations – 'native American' for 'Indian', 'differently abled' for 'handicapped'. Whilst sometimes noble, this can go too far – 'least best' for 'worst', 'unpaid sex worker' for 'wife' – and is easily mocked: the dead are 'terminally inconvenienced'; a serial killer, 'someone with difficult-to-meet needs'.

But does vocabulary control thought? Given the constant need to replace terms that re-acquire negative associations, perhaps not as much as Orwell thought; ultimately, whether or not we call a spade a spade, we still dig with it.

'All animals are equal, but some animals are more equal than others'
GEORGE ORWELL
Animal Farm

Animal Farm, originally subtitled, *A Fairy Story*, was actually no such thing, but a biting political satire on Stalinist Russia and the corruption of the communist ideal. Whether or not, as some argue, communism is by nature flawed, Orwell chooses to focus on the role played in its demise by corrupt leadership.

On a literal level, the animals on Mr Jones' farm, led by the pigs, rebel against their human master and, adopting the creed of *Animalism*, rename it 'Animal Farm'. Gradually, however, the ideals of the revolution are lost as self-interest and power-lust cause the pigs to become more and more human, until finally – all trace of Animalism lost – the faces of Napoleon and the other pigs become indistinguishable from their human counterparts.

Whilst efforts have been made to trace exact historical parallels to the events and characters of the book, and intentional allusions undoubtedly exist, it is perhaps best to view it as a commentary on the human factors that undermined communism. Chief of these, of course, is the inequality that crept into the system, as the need for greater and more centralized control (supposedly to better effect communist goals) led to the creation of a power elite, eventually dwindling to the one-man dictatorship of Stalin himself. Thus, just as Napoleon ultimately adopts the attitudes, practices, dress, and even two-legged gait of a man, so – Orwell implies – in its treatment of workers and the general populace, Stalinism merely presents a variation upon conditions under capitalism, not a liberation from them (the neighbouring farmers congratulate Napoleon on having the hardest-working animals!).

Orwell originally wrote a preface, detailing his difficulties in obtaining publication for a book critical of Russia (which was still a war ally with the UK and US), and also highlighting the absence of such criticism in the press. However, this was withheld from final publication (and only first restored in the 50th anniversary edition) – a neat irony, given that one of the defining characteristics of totalitarianism is censorship.

'It is curious, but till that moment I had never realised what it means to destroy a healthy, conscious man. When I saw the prisoner step aside to avoid the puddle I saw the mystery, the unspeakable wrongness, of cutting a life short when it is in full tide. This man was not dying, he was alive just as we are alive. All the organs of his body were working . . . his brain still remembered, foresaw, reasoned – even about puddles.'

GEORGE ORWELL

'A Hanging'

Whilst serving in the British Imperial Police in Burma, Orwell witnessed an execution, recounted in his essay, 'A Hanging'. Whilst not directly involved, he describes the circumstances in detail – the prisoners whose cells resemble 'animal cages', the brusque impatience of the jail superintendent, the nervous conversation. At one point, a dog even appears, mistaking the guards' attempts to catch it as a game. And yet, amid the mundane events and low-key tension, there's a growing realization that a man is about to die.

On his way to the gallows – as described in the quote – the man sidesteps a puddle. This single event seems to have produced in Orwell a kind of epiphany: why should a condemned man be concerned with keeping his feet dry? Orwell therefore takes this one act as a quintessential expression of the conscious human life which the hangman's noose was about to end. Surely, this is wrong?

But this is not a rational appeal. Orwell doesn't attempt to provide a reasoned argument against capital punishment – that it can lead to injustices, or that it doesn't really deter crime, perhaps – but simply cites a recognition of common humanity: we too, who will live on, would have sidestepped that puddle. Of course, the man may have been a murderer, a rapist, or committed any number of terrible crimes – Orwell doesn't say, preferring to let the occasion speak for itself. In doing so, however, he is perhaps making a deeper point: it's not just *this* or *that* life which is worth preserving, but all.

> 'Only a humanity to whom death has become as indifferent as its
> members, that has itself died, can inflict it administratively on
> innumerable people'
>
> THEODOR ADORNO 1903–1969
>
> *Minima Moralia*

Born Theodor Wiesengrund, German philosopher Theodor Adorno
adopted his mother's less-Jewish-sounding maiden name whilst
fleeing Nazi persecution to America. From the haven of the New
World, Adorno was free to meditate on the oppression he had escaped,
diagnosing the totalitarian Nazi regime as the expression of rationalism taken to its extreme – as, in fact, the ultimate consequence of
the Enlightenment. Ironically, then, the very force that had risen in
opposition to the dogma and authoritarianism of the Catholic Church
had become the most severe manifestation of intolerance.

But how did this happen? Influenced by Kant, Adorno argued that
we can never access true reality, and there will always be aspects of the
world that escape rational comprehension and conceptualization.
However, in its extreme form, rationalism denies this: it values only
reason and order, rejecting everything that disrupts its fixed, black-
and-white understanding of the world. In social terms, this leads to
totalitarianism, absolute respect for authority, and prejudice against
minorities, which become scapegoats to its pure vision of an ordered
society. So, Hitler's persecution of Jews, communists, homosexuals,
etc., was as much an attempt to rid the world of irrational elements –
those things that did not fit – as it was for any moral or political reason.

However, totalitarianism was not just a form of society, but a personality type and way of thinking (a *person* might be totalitarian in his
attitudes to education, sex, or work). In *The Authoritarian Personality*,
Adorno and Max Horkheimer devised an *F-Scale*, whereby the precise
degree of fascist tendencies could be measured. A useful interview
tool for school governors, perhaps: a child forgets his maths home-
work – what do you do? Cut the school lawns with *just* his teeth?
Indeed. Forgets to stand for the national anthem? Oh! *Literally* suspended! I see. I think we have all we need, thank you.

'... the "self" as ordinarily understood is only a small part of a much larger trial-and-error system which does the thinking, acting, and deciding. This system includes all the informational pathways which are relevant at any given moment to any given decision.'

GREGORY BATESON 1904–1980
Steps to an Ecology of Mind

In applying cybernetics to anthropology, English-born philosopher Gregory Bateson sought to understand social groups as complex human systems controlling and regulating the flow of *information*. However, by 'information', Bateson is proposing a different meaning from our everyday understanding; it is 'any difference which makes a difference in some later event.'

Bateson argues that what we commonly think of in mental terms (we possess *information* if we *know* something), can also be thought of in a *physical* sense. So, for instance, if a branch on a tree has a weak spot, so that it will snap under a certain amount of strain, we can consider this a piece of 'information' that exists in the physical world. Therefore the *difference* present in the branch (its weak spot) would make a *difference* (cause something different to happen) given certain future conditions.

Thus, Bateson undermines traditionally opposing concepts: mind and body, self and other, cause and effect – all are just 'information'. So, the self isn't a limited and defined entity (such as Descartes thought), but forms part of a much larger God-like super-system which Bateson termed 'the Mind': in fact, 'large parts of the thinking network are located outside the body' – that is, in cultural traditions, friends and advisors, or in any form of 'information' which influences how we think of ourselves and choose to act.

How convincing is this perspective? In one sense, it's interesting, and might help to account for cultures and traditions where notions of self are different from ours. However, it also seems questionable whether 'information' can exist separately 'in the world'. Doesn't 'information' presume an individual self that's *informed*?

'We knew the world would not be the same. A few people laughed, a few people cried, most people were silent. I remembered the line from the Hindu scripture, the *Bhagavad-Gita*. Vishnu is trying to persuade the Prince that he should do his duty and to impress him takes on his multi-armed form and says, "Now I am become Death, the destroyer of worlds." I suppose we all thought that, one way or another.'

J. ROBERT OPPENHEIMER 1904–1967
Interview, 1965

J. Robert Oppenheimer was an American physicist, and head of the scientific team tasked with developing the atom bomb, an operation codenamed the *Manhattan Project*. His words, now famous, are a reaction to the success of the *Trinity test*, the prototype bomb's first experimental outing in White Sands, New Mexico. A few weeks later, its success resulted in two such bombs being dropped, on the Japanese cities of Hiroshima and Nagasaki respectively, thus provoking the Japanese surrender and the end of World War II.

Immediate deaths from the bombs are estimated at around 170,000, rising over subsequent years to a total death toll – due to burns, injuries, radiation sickness, and cancers – of around 340,000. However, estimates differ widely as most of the information required to arrive at more precise totals was destroyed in the bombing.

Oppenheimer would later become an influential figure in post-war politics, but whilst his experience with the bomb and its human cost made him keen to steer governments towards the peaceful use of atomic energy, it seems not to have turned him against military technology altogether. His attitude was basically, 'If we don't develop it, the Russians will'. As such, then, whilst he opposed aggressive militarism, he embodies the dilemmas and compromises of the man of knowledge caught up in political affairs.

In the *Bhagavad Gita*, Vishnu's assumption of his horrific aspect has a benign purpose: in developing the bomb, Oppenheimer likewise sought good ends. And yet, as he discovered, politics offers no neat and clean decisions, only dirty compromises; and knowledge, once released, cannot be put back in the box.

'In the absence of an effective general mythology, each of us has his private, unrecognized, rudimentary, yet secretly potent pantheon of dream. The latest incarnation of Oedipus, the continued romance of Beauty and the Beast, stand this afternoon on the corner of Forty-second Street and Fifth Avenue, waiting for the traffic light to change.'

JOSEPH CAMPBELL 1904–1987
The Hero with a Thousand Faces

American mythologist Joseph Campbell was particularly influenced by psychoanalysis, especially Carl Jung's notion of psychological *archetypes*, and married these ideas with his own interests in religion, myth and literature.

Each individual is a variation of an old theme, for the same life forces that have shaped man in all ages and cultures continue to mould the modern psyche, the difference being that modern man has a much poorer mythological apparatus with which to understand these processes. This, for Campbell and Jung, accounted for the popularity of psychoanalysis and dream interpretation, which provided for the lack of a 'general mythology'. Campbell therefore saw his role as reintroducing and interpreting ancient mythology and culture for our times.

Interestingly, Campbell's ideas were extremely influential upon George Lucas, who perhaps has created one of the great modern myths of popular culture in the *Star Wars* films. The permeation of these ideas is so great that, in the 2001 census of England and Wales, 390,127 people described their religion as 'Jedi', thus making it the fourth largest religion. However, since the Jedi religion is itself a distillation of Eastern philosophy and religion – notably Taoism and Zen – then *Star Wars* is basically a vehicle for the reintroduction of ancient mythological, philosophical and religious ideas.

However, as this connection has become known, Campbell's ideas have become a new orthodoxy in Hollywood, representing a sort of ideal narrative pattern for film plots (see, e.g., *The Writer's Journey*, by Chris Voegler). Obviously, this has detracted from the effectiveness of these mythical structures, which have become seen as a formula for financial success. Obi-wan would turn in his grave.

'Education is what survives when what has been learned has been forgotten'

B. F. SKINNER 1904–1990

'New Methods and New Aims in Teaching'

Whilst psychoanalysis did much to advance psychology as a separate discipline, its ideas also provoked much criticism: introspection and personal interpretation were simply not scientific methods. A new approach therefore developed which focused on objectively measurable data. Since we cannot see inside another's mind, and we shouldn't perhaps trust our own mental processes as evidence, we should only study external behaviour. However, since this is what is important to us anyway – thoughts and feelings require expression and action to be understood – then we lose nothing by ignoring internal processes. *Behaviourism*, then, proposed that the mind is a 'black box', the contents of which we could not, and did not need to, enquire into.

Building on the work of Ivan Pavlov and J. B. Watson, American psychologist B. F. Skinner proposed that education merely involved provoking the desired response to a certain stimulus, what he termed *operant conditioning*. So, where Pavlov had rung a bell when feeding his dogs, until eventually the bell was enough to make them salivate, Skinner saw that the food could be seen as a sort of 'reward' for the dogs' salivation at the bell; thus, good behaviour is merely that which is done in expectation of reward. Applying this principle more broadly, he showed that much could be achieved by rewarding or *reinforcing* desired behaviour, and punishing, ignoring or withholding reward from undesired behaviour. Through this simple method, Skinner claimed, any animal *or* human could be 'educated'.

The philosophical implications of this are quite bleak. Man has no free will, and morality is determined by the desire to fulfil instinctive desires and avoid pain. However, perhaps the most dehumanizing effect of Skinner's theories is that it treats education as a form of indoctrination: there is no room for creativity, or spontaneous innovation, but merely a correct or incorrect response – which may be fine for learning one's times tables, but who could learn philosophy by rote?

'The history of cosmic theories can be called, without exaggeration,
a history of collective obsessions and controlled schizophrenias,
and the manner in which some discoveries have been made
resemble the conduct of a sleepwalker, rather than the
performance of an electronic brain'
ARTHUR KOESTLER 1905–1983
The Sleepwalkers

As already seen with such scientific luminaries as Newton and
Copernicus, the popular picture of the rationalist champion of scientific progress smiting the dragon of ignorance, dogma and superstition
is perhaps not the true picture. However, whilst many have strived to
minimize focus on their heroes' 'irrational' interests (alchemy, hermeticism, numerology), Hungarian-born philosopher and novelist
Arthur Koestler highlighted them: 'Why should we allow artists, conquerors and statesmen to be guided by irrational motives, but not the
heroes of science?'

In analyzing the traditional portraits of such figures as Newton,
Galileo, Copernicus and Johannes Kepler, and by placing them in a
broader historical context (stretching back as far as ancient
Mesopotamia), Koestler does two things. Firstly, he attacks the modern
scientific rationalist attitude that tries to free itself completely from
irrational forces. Secondly, he argues that some of the greatest
advances in science have actually stemmed from *irrational* influences.
Truth, then, is not necessarily the waking goal of a rational mind, but
the unconscious destination of a 'sleepwalker'.

One of Koestler's central aims is to undermine the traditional
opposition between reason and faith, behind which lies 'a common
source of inspiration'. Aspects of the Catholic Church, he argues, were
actually *supportive* of Galileo, and it was actually the reaction of his
fellow *scholars* that he feared. Similarly, Copernicus and Kepler both
received orthodox support for their ideas. Some of these points are
obviously contentious, but Koestler's main assertion is interesting and
valid: there is no firm divide between the rational and the so-called
'irrational'. The origin of such a division is therefore an interesting
question: could it be that modern science has created its own
mythology?

> 'Man is condemned to be free; because once thrown into the world, he
> is responsible for everything he does'
>
> JEAN-PAUL SARTRE 1905–1980
> *Existentialism is a Humanism*

Young men looking to impress ladies at parties will be heartened to
hear that Existentialism is a bleak, yet romantic and manly philosophy
that comes with its own specialist vocabulary. It is a form of *humanism*,
a way of seeing the world that places man at its centre. Because there
is no God, we must come to terms with this *abandonment*, and the
anguish this causes when faced with absolute responsibility for our
lives. Everything therefore springs from the fact that we have no ultimate essence or human nature, and must not only justify our own
decisions, but also select our own values – or, in some cases, create
them (either way, we are responsible). The *authentic* person faces
these truths head on, whilst the *coward* who denies or ignores them
lives in *bad faith* (a form of wilful self-delusion).

Existentialism is therefore tough on responsibility. There are no
excuses. We either accept responsibility for all our actions and choices,
or else hide away in self-deception. This is what French philosopher
Jean-Paul Sartre calls the 'paradox of freedom': we do not have absolute choice, for presumably that would allow us to choose *not* to be
free; we are, rather, 'condemned to be free', in that freedom is a fact
about ourselves that we are forced to accept and live with.

This seems harsh, and perhaps unsustainable. Schopenhauer
argued that, 'Man can indeed do what he wants, but he cannot want
what he wants.' In other words, there will always be aspects of ourselves which are beyond conscious control, our own desires being a
case in point. Sartre would say that we can choose whether to act on
them or not, but such things can also exert an unconscious influence
– on what we wear, the people we like, our hobbies and interests.
Existentialism therefore seems to argue that we can choose the basis
for our own choices – which is impossible!

'Existence precedes essence'
JEAN-PAUL SARTRE
Existentialism and Human Emotions

There once was a TV game show which involved guessing the original function of certain strange and now-obsolete household objects. 'A Victorian toe-warmer?' 'A device for mending spiders' webs?' The programme was based on a single premise: however eccentric, bizarre, or self-indulgent, each object was nonetheless designed with a single use in mind, prescribed by its inventor. In philosophical terms, we would say that its *essence* (its reason for being) precedes its *existence* (its *coming into* being).

When we consider found objects, the situation is slightly different: a certain-shaped rock is a handy paperweight, a long stick can clear a blocked drain; neither of these uses is *inherent* in the objects, but rather assigned to it by its user.

However, with organic objects – such as animals, flowers, and human beings – the case is more controversial. When we look at a heart beating, for instance, it seems strange to think of its purpose as something that we impose upon it, like the paperweight or the drain-unblocking stick; rather, we want to say that the *purpose* of the heart is to pump blood. But who made it so? The religious answer is obviously 'God', but most modern science rejects this answer – it is, well, not scientific enough! An alternative is that such purposes arise through natural selection and evolution, but this gives us a different problem: can we call those things 'purposes' which arise through blind unconscious forces?

One solution proposed by Sartre is that there are no purposes – no 'essences' – except those that are prescribed by human agents. As regards man himself, the designer who would endow us with purpose – if we share Sartre's atheism – is absent. But, unlike the Victorian toe-warmer, we are conscious, and therefore feel the full weight and expectation (*anxiety*) of our purposelessness. Our existence precedes our essence; we *are* before we know why or to what end. What are human beings for? We must, it seems, decide for ourselves.

As any student of the *Big Brother* TV show will know, there is no greater torture than the long-term close proximity of strangers (well, apart from *watching* it, maybe). Stuck in an elevator, on a delayed train, or in any number of other mundane situations, we quickly recognize the truth of this: eventually, the veneer of politeness wears thin, the strained smiles snap, and if that guy doesn't stop whistling that stupid tune I'm going to . . .

The problem is that strangers have not generally been vetted according to our personal tastes and values. We have not, by long acquaintance, come to overlook their annoying habits in light of their other wonderful qualities. This is why, ultimately, most cultures practise respect of personal space, observe social etiquette, and have locks on toilet doors.

However, in typically cheery fashion, Sartre extends this observation to include people in general. In his play *Huis Clos* ('No Exit' or 'Dead End'), he pictures Hell as a hotel, where the punishment consists merely in the presence of the other 'guests'. The three characters constituting the main cast spend the whole play in one room. At first, they assume they are in some sort of ante-room, awaiting the torture that will eventually begin. As they wait, they gradually reveal their 'sins' (all have, directly or indirectly, caused the death of another), which are in turn scrutinized mercilessly by the other characters, employing the same lack of sympathy and callousness that caused them to sin in the first place. And so, ultimately, they come to realize that *this* is their punishment: hell is other people.

As secular alternatives to spiritual damnation go, this is quite poetic: the greatest punishment for wrongdoing is self-awareness. This dovetails neatly with the other tenets of existentialism, which stress the central importance of personal choice and responsibility: we may be free to choose our own morality, but we must also accept its consequences. Hell is of our own choosing.

'I had been playing with matches and burned a small rug. I was in the process of covering up my crime when suddenly God saw me. I felt His gaze inside my head and on my hands.'

JEAN-PAUL SARTRE

Words

The extract is from a short memoir detailing the first ten years of Sartre's life. It is interesting for two reasons. Firstly, it marks the point at which he claims to turn his back on God: 'He never looked at me again.' But it also echoes Sartre's notion of 'the Other', whereby we come to have an awareness of self in relation to others, and therefore the significance of our actions.

Imagine, Sartre said, spying on someone through a keyhole: whilst you are undiscovered, you are unselfconscious, merely an eye engrossed in its spectacle; however, the moment you hear a creek on the floorboard behind you, you are consumed with shame and embarrassment. This reaction is caused by your awareness of others as conscious entities like yourself.

Sartre used this realization to address a traditional problem in the philosophy of mind. Descartes argued that it is self-contradictory to doubt our own existence as conscious beings. However, we have no proof that there are other minds than ourselves: we can reasonably assume that others have similar mental experiences, but this is not immune to sceptical doubt. But, Sartre argued, our experience of shame is not a rational argument built up from premises, but rather a direct experience of the Other; my experience of shame *includes* an awareness of being observed, which could not be the case if there were no observer.

Sartre's argument is interesting and original, but flawed, and the extract illustrates this. When he feels the 'gaze of the Other', it is proof of the existence of other minds; but when he feels the 'gaze of God', he rejects it as illusory. But, to be consistent, shouldn't he either accept or reject both? Either atheism is wrong, or the experience of 'the Other' is not proof of anything.

'A man who becomes conscious of the responsibility he bears toward a human being who affectionately waits for him, or to an unfinished work, will never be able to throw away his life. He knows the "why" for his existence, and will be able to bear almost any "how".'

VIKTOR E. FRANKL 1905–1997
Man's Search for Meaning

Having endured the horrors of the Nazi concentration camps, Austrian psychotherapist Viktor Frankl emerged with an understanding of the most fundamental human drive. Whereas Freud proposed the *pleasure principle*, and Adler a Nietzsche-influenced *will to power*, Frankl saw that, in the direst circumstances, it was meaning that kept people going. The view of life as meaningless was a sign of what Frankl termed *existential neurosis*, and therapy should therefore aim at helping people to find that which gave them a sense of purpose and direction (what he termed *Logotherapy*).

Obviously, for each person this meaning will be different. Not everyone is struck by Sartre's *existential angst*, and some loss of meaning springs from situations which are easily resolved: loneliness and isolation may be addressed by finding friends with common interests, or doing voluntary work. Therefore, many people don't need to grapple with the deepest philosophical issues of existence in order to be happy. However, for those who have experienced the deepest forms of trauma, their very appreciation of the value of life has disappeared.

In answer, Frankl cites his own experience. Faced daily with death, disease, hardship and suffering, he realized that the deepest meaning that can be found in life is *love*. As Sartre argued, a gun to our heads, in the midst of dreadful suffering, we're still free to choose how we react. So, Frankl's love for his wife, parents, friends, what they stood for, was what drove him on, and, even after the war and the discovery that many of them were murdered, continued to give his life meaning. Such a love – for others, for an ideal, for God – gives solace when even hope of survival is gone.

'Civilization is the progress toward a society of privacy. The savage's whole existence is public, ruled by the laws of his tribe. Civilization is the process of setting man free from men.

AYN RAND 1905–1982
The Fountainhead

Russian-born writer Ayn Rand advocated what she termed *Objectivism*. Like Stirner, and to an extent Thoreau, she espoused a form of *individualism*, arguing that moral and social evolution involves abandoning communal ideals in favour of *personal* ones. Rand was therefore a proponent of *ethical egoism*, the idea that morality should foster self-interest – where helping someone must always, in some way, benefit *me* (whether directly and immediately, or indirectly and in the long term).

However, Objectivism takes this to an extreme. Bringing together various strands – unfettered capitalism, rationalism, atheism – it is united by the themes of self-interest and the pursuit of productive goals (*objectives*). In this she was particularly influenced by Aristotle, Plato and – early on – Nietzsche, but moved away from the latter in light of his criticism of the rationalism of the former. She was also highly scathing of Kant, whose attempt to found a selfless morality on rational principles stands in diametrical opposition to egoism.

Assessing Rand's work, it's perhaps churlish – as some have done – to argue that she was neither a first-rank philosopher nor a novelist, but there is perhaps a sense in which her work isn't rigorously reasoned or systematically developed, rather an attempt to popularize certain personal ideals. Her main contention – that both society and individual are better off from fostering self-interest – isn't original, and her 'individualism' seems simplistic. In her novel *Altas Shrugged*, the world's creative and intellectual elite reject society to form their own community (freed from all the 'spongers' and hangers-on), thus making a point: it is such individuals (and the individual *per se*) which make things tick. Maybe – but tick *for whom*? Doesn't a large part of our sense of purpose, happiness, even self, reside in doing things for *others*?

'The trouble with Eichmann was precisely that so many were like him, and that the many were neither perverted nor sadistic, that they were, and still are, terribly and terrifyingly normal'

HANNAH ARENDT 1906–1975
Eichmann in Jerusalem

Like Mussolini, but to a much more sinister end, Adolf Eichmann made the trains run on time. Charged with the logistics of transporting thousands of Jews to the concentration camps, Eichmann's infamous defence – at his trial in Jerusalem, 1960 – was that he was 'just following orders'.

Covering the trial, Jewish philosopher Hannah Arendt – who had herself been forced to flee Germany during the Nazi's rise – was struck by what she termed 'the banality of evil'. Eichmann was a liar, a coward, a hypocrite, mired in self-deception, and blind to the full impact of the evil he facilitated. But he was not a monster or a psychopath. In fact, he was distressingly normal. Like many prominent Nazis, he was an opportunist rather than an idealist, and his rise within the ranks outweighed any qualms of conscience his work occasioned. For Arendt, therefore, he was not an anti-Semite with a personal animus against the Jewish people, but merely an amoral bureaucrat – in fact, we may take his claims to have been on 'good terms' with prominent Jews at face value (at least from his own perspective). It was 'too bad' that this or that individual should die, and – you know – he *really tried* to do his best to save them. His 'best' though, certainly when compared to other Germans like Oskar Schindler and Karl Plagge, amounted to very little indeed.

Arendt's assessment is controversial. Doesn't it diminish the evil perpetrated during the holocaust, as if it were merely an unfortunate turn of events? However, Arendt's account is unsettling because it forces us to entertain an unwelcome possibility: we are all capable of evil. Without lessening Eichmann's guilt, we should therefore perhaps look to understand evil differently: 'monsters' can turn out to be ordinary, and ordinary people can perform monstrous acts.

'. . . there are even relatively easy problems in the theory of ordinary whole numbers that can not be decided from the axioms'

KURT GÖDEL 1906–1978

'On Formally Undecidable Propositions of *Principia Mathematica* and Related Systems'

The search for the foundations of mathematics had been dealt a heavy blow by Russell's paradox, but mathematicians and philosophers had not completely given up hope. This search was important because, without such foundations, maths remained *incomplete*. However, in 1931, Kurt Gödel, a 25-year-old Austrian mathematician, proposed a series of arguments that sounded the death knell of these ambitions.

Theories require *axioms* – traditionally, basic, self-evident and unquestionable truths. A mathematical axiom would therefore be something like, 'the sum of even numbers is always even'. The goal of a complete theory of maths was therefore to identify such axioms, and show how all mathematical truths could be derived from them. However, Gödel argued that this was not possible, for even quite simple mathematical procedures involving natural numbers (1, 2, 3, etc.) require rules that are 'undecided' (neither provable nor disprovable). In short, maths requires rules which cannot be derived from axioms, thus rendering any theory forever *incomplete* (Gödel's proofs are therefore known as the 'incompleteness theorems').

Why is this of interest to anyone other than a mathematician? The proofs turn out to have far-reaching and profound consequences. Since any system or theory has its axioms and procedures, we can argue that none is ever completely provable. So, incompleteness applies not only to maths, but to science and knowledge in general. Basically, there will *always* be hidden assumptions that make your theory work that are not themselves provable using your theory. For instance, Descartes claimed 'I think therefore I am' as an axiom, implicitly assuming that there is an 'I', that it is the same 'I' as five minutes ago . . . and so on.

Some philosophers resist this general application of Gödel's ideas, but similar conclusions have been advanced by other philosophers (e.g. Quine). Disquieting as it is, incompleteness, it seems, is inescapable.

> 'If one could possess, grasp, and know the other, it would not be other.
> Possessing, knowing and grasping are synonyms of power.'
>
> EMANUEL LEVINAS 1906–1995
> 'Time and the Other'

Emanuel Levinas, born a Lithuanian Jew, became a French citizen, and was drafted to fight against the Nazi forces. Made a prisoner of war, he was lucky to avoid the concentration camps, yet the holocaust was still a formative influence upon him.

Central to Levinas' philosophy is the notion of *the Other* (which greatly influenced Sartre). Instead of criticizing Descartes's traditional notion of the self (as did contemporary philosophers), Levinas tried to show how the self is formed in response to the existence of things which are 'not me': other beings, the world in general, or even God.

Out of respect for the Other, we learn which actions and attitudes are morally appropriate. A person isn't an object, but a desire for 'possessing, knowing and grasping' him treats him as such. This is the foundation of Levinas' ethical and religious views: the Other is always separate, and its 'Otherness' should be respected; the Other is prior to the notion of the self, and provides a non-rational basis for morality (the Other isn't a rational hypothesis or subject to proof; it just *is*).

Similarly to Adorno, Levinas saw the intolerance and violence of totalitarianism as an attempt to dominate or eradicate the Other. The authoritarian self seeks *totality* (to be everything), and in doing so ceases to respect the Otherness of things that it is not. Furthermore, without respect for the Other, morality breaks down, producing the inhuman horrors of the holocaust.

However, whilst Levinas' ideas are original and interesting, as an ethical system it is somewhat vague: if the Other is something that we sense, and has no clear definitions, it would seem to be a subjective basis for ethics. Secondly, Levinas' approach seems to advocate pacifism, even masochism. If the Other is what defines us, how should we react to those who don't respect *our* 'Otherness'? Shouldn't we fight back?

> 'We stand now where two roads diverge. But unlike the roads in Robert Frost's familiar poem, they are not equally fair. The road we have long been traveling is deceptively easy, a smooth superhighway on which we progress with great speed, but at its end lies disaster. The other fork of the road – the one less traveled by – offers our last, our only chance to reach a destination that assures the preservation of the earth.'
>
> RACHEL CARSON 1907–1964
> *Silent Spring*

In 1962, **American environmental biologist** Rachel Carson published her grim vision of the decimation of our natural habitat by chemical agriculture, where she chillingly imagined a 'silent spring', devoid of birds, animals, and human life itself. The message was clear: if agriculture continued to use pesticides with total disregard to the long-term consequences to the natural environment, we ring our own death knell.

Silent Spring is often credited with sparking the environmental movement, but its central thesis – that use of such pesticides as the scarily-long-named dichlorodiphenyltrichloroethane (DDT) is ecological suicide – remains controversial. Carson considered such chemicals so virulent that they're not just pesticides, but 'biocides', killing all life, friendly and unfriendly. Accordingly, DDT was eventually banned worldwide. However, critics argue this has only forced adoption of less effective chemicals, with resulting reduced crop yield and increase in pests, including disease-bearing insects such as mosquitoes.

The problem here lies in assessing the motives of the respective parties. As with the current controversy over global warming, many industries with vested interest have clandestinely funded 'independent' scientific research, some of which calls for a reinstatement of DDT. Furthermore, it should be borne in mind that the use of chemicals as pesticides and domestic cleaning products was a direct result of a production surplus from their use in chemical weapons in WWI (see *Secrets of the Soil*, Peter Tompkins and Christopher Bird). Of course, I'm all in favour of balanced debate, and whilst I *hope* that even profit-driven mega-corporations would not be so colossally irresponsible as to endanger all our futures simply to line their pockets . . .

Willard Van Orman Quine was an American philosopher who attacked the foundations of *empiricism*. From Locke to Ayer, empiricists considered sense experience to be the foundation of knowledge. However, in doing so, they assumed that experience comes with some ready-made guarantee of its own trustworthiness. However, Quine didn't reject empiricism, but *purified* it of what he saw as *non-empirical* 'dogmas'.

One problem stems from the notion that we can arrive at a fundamental understanding of reality. If, for instance, as science proposes, the true picture of reality lies in a physical description of the world, then the world ultimately consists of sub-atomic particles. However, this is only true *relative* to the viewpoint of physics, for the existence of such things (their *ontology* or 'being') is a supposition of the overall theory. In other words, quarks, muons, etc., only exist from a physicist's point of view, and other viewpoints are *possible*. Perhaps it's even possible to explain physics using a *different, more fundamental* 'SuperTheory'. However, even the fundamental truths of the *SuperTheory* will only be true relative to the theory itself. *All* truths are relative to a theory.

Quine isn't being sceptical here, merely pointing out that, since knowledge comes from experience, this leaves room for interpreting that experience differently. So, beliefs are correct not because they are built on independently fundamental truths, but because, together with others, they form a coherent *web of beliefs*. Thus, whilst some beliefs are more fundamental to the overall 'web', none is independent of it.

One interesting consequence of Quine's view is that it leaves open the possibility of *other*, equally fundamental views of reality. If what defines truth is whether it's coherent with experience and other beliefs, then mightn't it be possible for two or more theories to be equally 'true' in this way? Or for all to be equally *false*?

> 'A musician must make music, an artist must paint, a poet must write, if he is to be ultimately at peace with himself. What a man can be, he must be.'
>
> ABRAHAM MASLOW 1908–1970
> *Motivation and Personality*

In *Psychoanalysis*, humans skate the thin ice of rationality over dangerous depths of antisocial and irrational desire; *behaviourism* ignores the person altogether, but focuses on conditioning desired behavioural outcomes. However, beginning in the 1950s, *humanist psychology* began to see happiness and well-being in terms of achievement of self-potential.

American psychologist Abraham Maslow, through analysis of prominent individuals, claimed to identify key criteria for self-fulfilment. Einstein, for instance, was seen to have achieved 'self actualization' by following his personal goals to a point where they made him happy, spontaneous, and spiritually satisfied. Such people were also marked by what Maslow termed 'peak experiences', or moments of great creative expression, insight or performance, which – in a more humble form – were available to everyone. The goal of life was therefore to realize this self-potential.

But what of ordinary people who have to earn a living, or raise children? Maslow argued that full *self-actualization* cannot occur until more basic needs are met. His famous *hierarchy of needs* is a 'ladder' of self-development, where lower needs must be met before higher ones. These are (in order): physiological (food and water, sleep, sex), safety (shelter, health, employment), love and belonging (family, relationships, friends), and esteem (self-respect, reputation, achievement). So, once the four primary needs are met, the individual seeks self-actualization through pursuing creativity, interests and hobbies, questioning the nature of existence, and so on.

But does self-development work like this? It explains, perhaps, why rich people get bored, or artists endure hardship. However, it also seems to represent an *ideal* of balanced development: what we *should* do, not what often happens. True artists don't wait for financial security before creating. And would a suffering genius really be happy in a *well-furnished* garret? Also, of course, what of those seemingly happy with fulfilment of basic needs? Are they self-deluded?

'One is not born, but rather becomes, a woman'
SIMONE DE BEAUVOIR 1908–1986
The Second Sex

In her most famous work, *The Second Sex*, French philosopher Simone de Beauvoir argues that women often receive their identity from their relationship to men – as wife or lover, daughter or mother – and must therefore strive hard to carve out their own distinct persona. It is highly ironic, then, that as much as she is remembered for her contribution to feminism, she is equally as well-known for her long-term relationship with Jean-Paul Sartre.

The notion of 'the Other' in existentialism springs from the idea that I define others in relation to myself, and not always through any distinct characteristics that others possess. Sometimes, this leads us to distort or ignore others' qualities: a talented artist might tend to deny or belittle others' artistic efforts (*they* are not really artists). This is especially the case when one person in a relationship is more powerful than the other, which is precisely Beauvoir's point: men, physically stronger and more aggressive, follow their instincts and chosen interests – science, politics, the military – and designate them 'male' domains, thereby leaving females – the 'second sex' – to adapt themselves in relation to men, and to be defined by male desire.

This is now a familiar argument, and the fact that many traditionally male domains are opening up to women might be seen as a sign that feminism is working. However, underlying this is a more complex and interesting debate: if it's getting easier for a woman to choose career and identity, independent of male desire, what is it that she wants? Whilst it's increasingly common for women to occupy powerful social roles, what of the woman who *wants* to be a housewife and a mother? Or the woman who consciously cultivates her role as a sex object? Are such women still living in 'bad faith', as Sartre would say, defined by another, or is theirs too an authentic free choice?

> 'The curse which weighed upon Sade ... was this "autism" which prevented him from ever forgetting himself or being genuinely aware of the reality of the other person ... his instincts drove him toward outside objects with which he was incapable of uniting, so that he was forced to invent singular methods for taking them by force'
>
> SIMONE DE BEAUVOIR
> 'Must We Burn Sade?'

Beauvoir initially agreed with Sartre that freedom is absolute: at gunpoint, facing death or imprisoned, freedom lies in choosing our reactions – not 'looking on the bright side', but accepting responsibility for how we face the inevitable. However, later, in an essay on the Marquis de Sade, the infamous literary pornographer and origin of the word *sadism*, she begins to question whether freedom is really immune to outside influence.

In part, Sade is an existentialist hero, rejecting conventional morality, Church and State, and defining himself through his choices. However, he's also problematic, for his own pleasures come at the expense of others; his morality is founded on cruelty. But on what basis can existentialism complain? Sade doesn't blame anyone or anything for how he is, so his choice isn't an act of *bad faith*. Therefore, whilst celebrating Sade's existentialism, Beauvoir must also show how he went wrong.

Beauvoir sees 'sadism' as compensation for aloofness ('autism'), a surrogate for genuine intimacy where 'one is freed of his own presence and achieves immediate communication with the other'. Incapable of this, Sade verifies himself through cruelty ('I whip therefore I am', perhaps ...). Consequently, the only way for the victim to be free is to become *like* Sade – which, by nature or opportunity, may not be possible for him. Thus, Sade's main failing lies in generalizing from his own case: cruelty makes *everyone* feel alive and free.

In criticizing Sade, Beauvoir accepts freedom isn't absolute: 'social injustice affects the individual even in his ethical potentialities'. Thereby, she moves away from the Cartesian self toward an *embodied* self, vulnerable and subject to external restriction – a self which Sade didn't recognize, and therefore failed to respect.

> 'One must be very naïve or dishonest to imagine that men choose their beliefs independently of their situation'
>
> CLAUDE LÉVI-STRAUSS 1908–2009
>
> *Triste Tropiques*

What is the opposite of 'grey'? 'Colourful'? Or, perhaps it's 'clear' – 'the sky was *grey* but now it's *clear*'? But in which case, I could just as well say 'blue'. The point I'm making here is that which answer we choose depends on viewpoint and context. In a sense, there is no fixed opposite.

French anthropologist Claude Lévi-Strauss borrowed from Saussure's structural linguistics to explain certain features of human society. In comparing various cultures, especially their myths, Lévi-Strauss argued that the same underlying *structure* was present. In fact, one didn't actually need to know anything of the language that the individual myth appeared in, for it was obvious from its *structure* what sort of work it was doing.

For Lévi-Strauss, this work was to separate *nature* from *culture*, the process of civilization. For instance, in studying various cultures, he came across very common oppositions: male/female, raw/cooked, hot/cold, tame/wild, and so on. However, if, as this seems to suggest, humans are driven to categorize things into opposites, then surely it becomes a secondary concern as to *what* those actual things are. So, whilst individual oppositions might be unique to the place in which they occur, categorization into opposites seems itself to be universal.

This is quite a startling idea, really, especially when we apply it to philosophy. When we think of traditional philosophical problems – cause and effect, mind and body, free will and determinism – we can see that they too can be seen to spring from a sort of innate desire to 'separate things out'. But if this process is just some sort of inbuilt natural instinct, then aren't we deluding ourselves in trying to solve these problems rationally?

So, Lévi-Strauss and other *structuralists* argue, we should abandon traditional philosophical problems, and instead analyze them simply in terms of their structure. However, in doing this, aren't we abandoning philosophy in favour of an empty, purely *formal* exercise?

> 'Two prisoners whose cells adjoin communicate with each other by knocking on the wall. The wall is the thing which separates them but is also their means of communication. It is the same with us and God. Every separation is a link.'
>
> SIMONE WEIL 1909–1943
> *Gravity and Grace*

Simone Weil was a French philosopher, Christian mystic, and social activist. In her relatively short life, ignoring physical frailty and ill health, she repeatedly sought out arduous and even dangerous environments – voluntary work, hard manual labour, war – both to show solidarity with the suffering of others, and thereby to get closer to God.

This link between suffering and salvation is common in Christian thought, suggesting a possible solution to the problem of evil. Since God is a perfect being, the only way he could create anything separate from himself – that anything else could exist *at all* – was to *withdraw* from it. But if the world is *not* God, but his absence, doesn't that make it *evil*? In a sense, yes, but this explains all the *natural evil* in the world (earthquakes, tsunamis, famines). Suffering is a sort of divine cattle prod, provoking us into seeking God: 'Evil is the form which God's mercy takes in this world.'

This startling and unsettling view lies on the fringes of Christian theology. It resembles *Gnosticism*, the heretical view that the world was created by a *demiurge*, an imperfect creator deity identified with the God of the Old Testament, to be distinguished from the New Testament's supreme God of love and compassion. Whilst Weil did not explicitly go this far, her emphasis on suffering as a means of salvation seems to similarly verge on denying the positive value of the world.

Like Schopenhauer (who influenced her), Weil sees life as something to be endured, a scourge to whip us back to God. It is, certainly, one answer to the problem of evil, but it also disturbs us: what sort of God would consider evil to be a form of mercy?

> 'The principal claim which we think we have on the universe is that our personality should continue. This claim implies all the others. The instinct of self-preservation makes us feel this continuation to be a necessity, and we believe that a necessity is a right.'
>
> SIMONE WEIL
> *Waiting On God*

In the *New Testament* (Matthew 22:23–32), the Sadducees pose a problem to Jesus: a man dies childless, so, as commanded by Moses, his brother takes his wife; this happens six times, so that by the time the woman dies, she's had seven husbands. Which will be her husband in heaven?

Jesus neatly sidesteps the conundrum: there *are* no husbands or wives in heaven. The problem illustrates the sort of muddle religious believers encounter by assuming the afterlife to be more or less a continuation of *this* one. Actually, exploiting these confusions is a common method employed by atheists wishing to show that religion is a mixture of confused thinking and superstition: if Heaven is a place, where is it? If your grandfather dies when you're a child, and your mother dies when you're an adult, when you die, will you appear to them as a child or an adult? More importantly, without a body, how will anyone recognize one another? And so on.

Simone Weil accepts these criticisms. It is wishful thinking, she argues, to assume our personality will continue after death, and – as the above problems show – such expectations lead to all sorts of contradictions and confusions. Rather, she argues, we should understand immortality in terms of 'selflessness' and of 'dying to the self'. By letting go of our mundane personality, our ego, we reach a state of impersonal transcendence; 'immortality' is therefore achieved in the way that we *live* life, not after it.

Many – atheists and believers alike – are disappointed by this denial of literal immortality; former atheist Antony Flew famously remarked that such 'survival' would be as much consolation as 'the news that my appendix would be preserved eternally in a bottle'. That is, no consolation at all.

> 'I saw a Divine Being. I'm afraid I'm going to have to revise all my
> various books and opinions.'
> A. J. AYER 1910–1989
> attributed

For years, English philosopher A. J. Ayer was the poster boy of atheism
and a strident critic of all things religious and metaphysical. Early on,
he aligned himself with *logical positivism* and the view that if a statement could not be verified by experience, and was not mere tautology
('all bachelors are unmarried'), then it was literally nonsense. In effect,
this rubbished whole libraries of traditional philosophy, leaving
modern philosophers with little to do other than quibble over the
foundations of epistemology and tidy things up for science.

As logical positivism declined, Ayer's views softened, but he maintained his antagonism toward spiritual matters. Then, in 1988,
admitted to hospital with pneumonia, he choked on some food, suffered cardiac arrest, and was technically 'dead' for four minutes. Ayer's
resultant experience, reported in 'What I Saw When I Was Dead', is
strikingly similar to other accounts: he converses with 'higher beings',
experiences a new perspective on life, tries to cross a 'river' (as the
dead in antiquity were ferried across the river Styx), and is finally
drawn towards a distant light . . .

What shall we make of this, philosophically speaking? As Ayer
points out, after-death survival provides no guarantee of the existence
of God, for if 'there is no good reason to believe that a god either created or presides over this world, there is equally no good reason to
believe that a god created or presides over the next world'. The afterlife *may* give us such proof, but – in typically logical-positivist fashion
– he concludes that 'we have no right to presume on such evidence,
when we have not had the relevant experiences'.

However, comparing the above with his words to the attending
physician shortly after the event (our main quotation), Ayer has back-
tracked. Is it just intellectual caution, or, as a lifelong atheist – and
philosopher to boot – did Ayer simply find his experience to be . . .
embarrassing?

'The presence of an ethical symbol in a proposition adds nothing to its factual content'

A. J. AYER
Language, Truth and Logic

The boxer, who was allegedly plying his persuasive charms on the supermodel, was asked by Ayer to desist:

'Do you know who the [expletive deleted] I am? I'm the Heavyweight Champion of the World,' the then reigning Heavyweight Champion of the World informed the philosopher. 'And I am the former Wykeham Professor of Logic,' replied Ayer. 'We are both pre-eminent in our field. I suggest that we talk about this like rational men.'

What's interesting here is that Ayer *didn't ultimately believe* that ethical debates could be settled 'like rational men'. *Emotivism* holds that moral statements are not factual. 'Violence is wrong' is not a statement of fact – unlike 'Apples are fruit' – but an expression of personal preference: 'I don't like violence'. Convincing someone of this doesn't therefore involve an appeal to rational principles, but rather to emotion – 'Boo! for violence', 'Hurrah! for pacifism.' Accordingly, this has become known as the 'Boo-Hurrah' theory of ethics.

However, standing opposite 200+ lbs of peak-condition physical ferocity, a man with growing notoriety in *and* outside of the ring, who'd famously told one opponent that he'd 'eat his children', simply expressing distaste for inappropriate behaviour towards women seems a somewhat weak and dangerous gambit. However, Ayer appeals to the boxer's rationality, cleverly tying together the notions of pre-eminence, rational behaviour, and gentlemanly conduct.

Then isn't Ayer appealing to reason after all? Not necessarily. Ayer thought that moral arguments work either when shared values are involved, or when you can *persuade* someone to share them. Accordingly, one may appeal to supporting facts – 'People will disapprove of this' – but only if the values they suggest are (or become) shared. If the boxer hadn't cared about public reputation, Ayer's words would have fallen on deaf ears; their *emotional* appeal would have proven unpersuasive.

In this sense, both heavyweights (in their field) shared one value: they believed in the power of persuasion.

'The medium is the message'
MARSHALL McLUHAN 1911–1980
Understanding Media

This much quoted mantra of technological progress seems to sit comfortably alongside other slogans of the 1960s. However, whereas LSD guru Timothy Leary urged people to 'turn on, tune in, and drop out', Canadian philosopher Marshall McLuhan was more interested in observing and analyzing cultural change than provoking it. So, the 'slogan' is less a piece of advice than an insight into the relationship between technology and culture – for, McLuhan observed, technology causes as many problems as it solves.

Society advances in technological leaps, but the *forms* that new media take are more important than the content they serve. The printing press was not just a handy labour-saving device, but also a catalyst for social revolution. Whereas previously, trained scribes had copied a small number of exclusive texts for an educated social elite, printed books made knowledge increasingly affordable and available to society in general, thus encouraging literacy and the spread of ideas. The printing press is therefore a tool of democracy, for as studies of totalitarian regimes show, the first sign of tyranny is the 'book burning' (restriction of information). Curiously, it therefore doesn't really matter *what* is printed, for it is the form itself that dictates social change.

Technology also alters our sense of self. What would you save if your house were on fire? A medieval yeoman might be content to escape with his life, a Victorian carpenter with his toolkit, whilst a modern businessman might brave the flames to save his Blackberry. In other words, technology is an extension of self, tied in to my idea of who I am, my purpose in life, and my place in society. However, whilst enabling us in new ways, media and technology also 'amputate' – both limbs and senses: the foot on the car pedals is less likely to walk, the hands which type less likely to write, the filmgoer less likely to read or listen to the radio, and so on. Is this also progress? The message, it seems, is double-edged.

'The new electronic interdependence recreates the world in the image of a global village'
MARSHALL MCLUHAN
The Gutenberg Galaxy

The effect of the industrial revolution was to 'detribalize'. Tribal or village society ties skills and occupations to particular individuals – growing up in a Welsh village, I was particularly aware of this: Dai-the-Farm, Mary-the-Shop. However, industrialization changes this by creating 'the labour force', where each individual is a faceless unit of potential work. Whilst this does foster individuals, these are not psychologically unique characters, but rather isolated and relatively similar parts in the overall machine of capitalist enterprise, cut off from their former sense of individual purpose and community.

But whereas industrialization isolates, electronic technology reunites. The speed and ease with which electronic media transfer information reduces distances and connects people. Nothing is a greater illustration of this – or a better fulfilment of McLuhan's uncanny predictions – than the Internet, but it applies equally to telephone, television, or anything that in effect brings far things near. This has the ultimate consequence of encouraging a sense of global identity: 'In the electric age we all wear mankind as our skin.'

But before we are carried away to Coca-Cola Land by a vision of love and world harmony, there is a flipside to this metaphor. In 1990, Donella Meadows imagined the world as a village of one thousand people (*The Global Citizen*): one third would not have access to clean and safe drinking water, 335 adults would be illiterate, and only half the 330 children would be immunized against preventable infectious diseases; 200 people would earn 75% of the income, and another 200 only 2% of it; there would be one doctor.

The electronic age, McLuhan argues, also makes information the chief commodity. This means that all forms of employment become 'paid learning', and all forms of wealth result from the movement of information.

However, as British journalist, Mike Holderness, has argued ('Down and Out on the Electronic Frontier'), this means that those without the skills or opportunity to utilize the new technology – 'the information-poor' – may find themselves out in the cold – literally.

'I believe that at the end of the century the use of words and general educated opinion will have altered so much that one will be able to speak of machines thinking without expecting to be contradicted'

ALAN TURING 1912–1954

'Computing Machinery and Intelligence'

Since machines developed, people have dreamt of artificial life. If, as *mechanism* proposes, nature is an organic machine, won't we one day replicate life? Printed-circuit boards and microchips seemed to bring this dream closer, suggesting that intelligence was merely a complex form of mechanical *computation*. If so, we might not only create life, but *intelligent* life.

In the 1950s, when computers were still embryonic, English mathematician Alan Turing proposed a thought experiment – the 'Turing Test': if, in appropriate circumstances, a machine could fool someone it were human, wouldn't we consider it intelligent? Intelligence is difficult to define. Does it involve skill? Animals can solve quite complex problems, but we'd hesitate to call a squirrel 'intelligent'. Does it require consciousness? The solution to a puzzle sometimes just 'appears' in our minds, suggesting the steps involved were not conscious. Sidestepping such difficulties, Turing adopted a *behaviourist* approach: if a machine *behaved* in a way we'd consider intelligent were it a human, then it is. 'If it walks like a duck, and talks like a duck, it's a duck!' This is a 'black box' model of intelligence: it is what happens 'outside', not 'inside', that matters.

In 1997, the 'Deep Blue' computer defeated world chess champion Gary Kasparov. Had it passed the Turing Test? Not necessarily. Pocket calculators can outperform humans, and a computer that fools someone that it is human, or intelligent, may only be good at fooling people (you can fool your boss you're ill, it doesn't mean you are!). The Turing Test, with its behaviourist assumptions, therefore seems flawed: something that walks like a man, and talks like a man, may be a mechanical man, which, like the Tin Man in the *Wizard of Oz*, might just be missing that essential something . . .

'. . . instead of coming to have a concept of something because we have noticed that sort of thing, to have the ability to notice a sort of thing is already to have the concept of that sort of thing, and cannot account for it'

WILFRID SELLARS 1912–1989
Empiricism and the Philosophy of Mind

Any philosophy which concentrates on sense impressions – or 'sense data', as they are sometimes called – assumes that such impressions tell us about reality. *Empiricism*, for instance, sees all knowledge as coming through the senses, whilst *phenomenology* tries to identify what it takes to be the structure of experience itself.

However, such approaches assume what American philosopher Wilfrid Sellars called the *myth of the given*, involving the tendency to believe that experience possesses a certain objective form: faced with a certain circumstance, it says, we would all experience the same thing. But imagine that a blue pen rolls behind a chair and out the other side – how do you know that it is the *same* pen? Well, judging merely from the 'sense data', you don't; all you see is a blue shape that disappears and reappears. In fact, even calling it 'blue', 'pen' or 'shape' would seem to be putting an interpretation on it: other cultures might have a different way of categorizing 'blue' (classing it with 'green', for example) or possess other categories of shape, and a pen can have many different uses.

This doesn't mean we should be sceptical about pens, or doubt their shape or colour, but merely realize that our knowledge of such things is not 'given' directly to us from sense experience, and so we shouldn't assume that there is just one way of interpreting it. Sellar's point is similar to that of Kant, who argued that the form of experience is not something we find ready made in the world, but something that we impose upon it in order to make sense of it. However, unlike Kant, Sellars does not see such concepts as fixed. Your blue pen, perhaps, is another's green backscratcher.

'. . . in a universe suddenly divested of illusions and lights, man feels an alien, a stranger. His exile is without remedy since he is deprived of the memory of a lost home or the hope of a promised land. This divorce between man and his life, the actor and his setting, is properly the feeling of absurdity.'

ALBERT CAMUS 1913–1960
The Myth of Sisyphus

Similar notions to the Absurd existed before Albert Camus, but the French existentialist philosopher made it his own. Its basic tenet is that life is essentially meaningless. We may *give* it meaning, but we cannot hope to find any 'ready made' – there is no God, no human nature, no standard of right and wrong, no ultimate goal that we can appeal to. We spring from nothing, exist to no purpose, and return to oblivion.

The Absurd is at once a description of this fact, and the realization that greets us when we recognize it. This can happen at any time: 'At any street corner the feeling of absurdity can strike any man in the face.' Our daily routines, with their often boring and relentless repetition, are therefore rich soil for this epiphany – especially when things go wrong. Certain experiences – a broken car jack when changing a flat tyre, the bare foot that finds the lost needle – emphasize the futility of our endless struggle, and question its purpose. *Sod's Law* ('If anything can go wrong, it will'), whilst not an essential element of the Absurd, can often be in play at the point of realization, when the camel's back breaks and the penny drops: what is the point of any of this?

Camus's favourite metaphor for this employed the Greek myth of Sisyphus. After angering the gods in numerous ways, he was ultimately consigned to Tartarus (the Greek hell), forced to push a boulder up a hill for all eternity; every time the boulder approached the top, it would roll back down to the bottom. This was quite dispiriting. We each have our own boulder, our own hill, our own hell. Tiring, isn't it?

> 'There is but one truly serious philosophical problem, and that is suicide. Judging whether life is or is not worth living amounts to answering the fundamental question of philosophy. All the rest – whether or not the world has three dimensions, whether the mind has nine or twelve categories – comes afterward. These are games; one must first answer.'
>
> ALBERT CAMUS
> *The Myth of Sisyphus*

If life is an absurd, meaningless pantomime, don't we owe it to ourselves to do the logical thing, and end it? Camus is not being morose here; he was, by all accounts, a warm and amiable individual who relished life. Rather, he asks us to be dispassionately logical. Many have taken their lives from despair or despondency, but who has done so from the necessary conclusion of a logical chain of reasoning? We must also distinguish between having a reason to kill oneself, and suicide motivated by the ultimate meaninglessness of life. The former may be a rational option – as it was for the Stoics – even for those who retain a sense of life's meaning, but whose dignity, or quality of life, has permanently dropped below a level acceptable to them. However, suicide based on the absurdity of life would be different, more fundamental: it is *philosophically justified* suicide, which says 'no' to life *whatever the circumstances.*

So, philosophically speaking, is life worth living? Sisyphus' task is pointless, and even what is achieved is consequently undone. However, pointlessness is different to meaninglessness, a distinction that Camus stressed, for acceptance of the Absurd is merely the first step to a higher philosophy. If we overcome our disappointment and despair, avoiding the false lures of hope and illusory dreams, then we can achieve a new clarity and strength. At the end of Sophocles' *Oedipus Rex*, the tragic hero finds himself blind, desperate, and exiled, yet accepts both his choices and absurd fate. Could we not similarly conclude that, despite our absurd existence, and all that life throws at us, 'all is well'?

'I had only a little time left and I didn't want to waste it on God'
ALBERT CAMUS
The Outsider

In Camus's novel *The Outsider*, the protagonist Meursault is imprisoned for murder, having shot a man in what appears to be cold-blood.
The court sentence to death an amoral, remorseless killer, but, Camus
suggests, whilst Meursault is undoubtedly an uncommon man – an
'outsider' – his crime is principally one of not fitting in or playing the
role expected of him: he doesn't cry at his mother's funeral, and never
displays regret for the killing. Living only for the present, his actions
are unplanned and spontaneous, concerned with simple, sensuous
enjoyment. He is, then, an Existentialist hero, but also a caricature,
exaggerated to highlight the hypocrisies of a society living in 'bad faith'
(to use Sartre's term); which pays lip-service to religious convention,
whilst hiding from life's true absurdity.

Meursault's attitude to religion follows orthodox Existentialism: he
rejects the approaches of the chaplain offering to hear his confession,
for even the little time remaining to a condemned man is wasted on
religion. However, unlike Sartre, Camus' attitude to religion was
ambiguous. Whilst never explicitly abandoning atheism, Camus
increasingly recognized the role God played in believers' lives – one
that, perhaps, Existentialism could not fulfil. In a later novel, *The
Plague*, a town is beset by a deadly epidemic. Set in the 1940s, it recalls
the Nazi occupation of France, as fear and imminent death reveal people's true nature. Father Paneloux, an outspoken Jesuit priest, warns
the town that the plague is sent by God to test their faith. Shortly after,
he himself dies, but examination of his body reveals no signs of
plague, and his death is therefore considered a 'doubtful case'.

In these words, does Camus reveal a change of heart regarding religion? His premature death at 46 robs us of answers, but it's intriguing
to consider how he might have reconciled religious belief with his
earlier views, where 'If there is a sin against life, it consists . . . in
hoping for another.'

'Nothing fails like success'

ALAN WATTS 1915–1973

The Book on the Taboo Against Knowing Who You Are

Alan Watts was an English philosopher and author who settled in America, becoming a key spiritual influence on the counter culture of the 1960s. Watts is best known for his popularization and transmission of Eastern philosophy to the West. In this, he was both prolific and precocious, writing over 40 books (many published posthumously), the first of which – *The Spirit of Zen* – was written when he was only 21.

Whilst some have criticized Watts' interpretation of Eastern philosophy, his role in disseminating its ideas to European and American readers cannot be underestimated, nor can his sincerity and intensity. In his writing, he aimed (like his friend Joseph Campbell) to re-spiritualize a culture that he saw as stressing independence and individuality at the expense of a more holistic approach to life: that saw man as 'an independent agent – *in* the universe, but not *of* it – saddled with the job of bending the world to his will'. His success in isolating himself was therefore his biggest failure, a victory which led to his growing dissatisfaction and unhappiness, which saw human life in terms of the existence of 'a separate ego enclosed in a bag of skin'.

For Watts, however, the *ego* or 'I' is a false construct which fools us into accepting our separateness; whereas, in reality, we are *part* of life, not *apart* from it. The reason for this was because we are joined to all living and inorganic things by a unifying and universal spirit, or cosmic self. Such a God-like being, which Watts simply called IT, is in truth 'so much more myself than I thought I was'. In other words, when we look at the world, we look at IT, but – since IT is *also* us, we are in effect IT looking at IT-self! Existence is therefore a sort of cosmic game of hide and seek that IT plays with IT-self, and where the 'I' is no more than a temporary place to hide.

> '. . . the birth of the reader must be at the cost of the death of the
> Author'
> ROLAND BARTHES 1915–1980
> *Image-Music-Text*

Literary critics traditionally saw the author as God, and their task as a type of theology, explaining and interpreting the great writer to the reading flock. A text's meaning therefore lay in deciphering the author's intentions, which were held to be sacrosanct.

French philosopher and literary theorist Roland Barthes criticized this picture, proposing that the true significance of a work lay in the hands of its readers, and not in the revered message of an 'Author-God'. Authorship was actually an intermediary process: an author was himself the product of cultural and social processes, an uncreative 'scriptor', who recombined and disseminated these influences in the process of writing: 'it is language which speaks, not the author'.

Barthes' theory can be traced ultimately to the influence of psychoanalysis. Freud had argued that the conscious control of the individual was an illusion, and that the conscious agent was at the mercy of unconscious forces. But Barthes went further: the author's control was illusory, for – in opposition to Descartes – he believed that there was no central 'I' or ego to which intentions could be attributed.

Once we relinquish this idea of the Author-God, the meaning of any text becomes subject to an analysis of the cultural forces that produced it. However, since we ourselves are also just the products of such forces, our interpretation is no truer than any other. Meaning therefore becomes a dynamic and shifting thing that cannot be pinned down by any one perspective.

Barthes argued that writing should therefore move away from traditional 'readerly' texts, where the reader expects to find, and the author relies upon, a set of conventional and fixed meanings, and toward 'writerly' texts, which treat the reader not as a passive consumer, but an active producer and fellow collaborator in the generation of meaning. Of course, you do wonder how a dead author can aim to produce *anything* – even 'writerly' texts.

'The fluttering of a butterfly's wing in Rio de Janeiro, amplified by
atmospheric currents, could cause a tornado in Texas two weeks later'
EDWARD LORENZ 1917–2008
'Predictability: Does the Flap of a Butterfly's Wings in Brazil Set Off a
Tornado in Texas?'

Edward Lorenz was an American mathematician and meteorologist,
whose idea that very tiny factors can have large and unpredictable consequences on overall systems – the *Butterfly Effect*, as he called it – was
a founding influence upon *Chaos Theory*.

Whilst rerunning a computer weather simulation, Lorenz saved
time by rounding down one of the variables: so, for example, instead
of inputting 1.23456 (as he'd done previously), he entered 1.234.
However, the result was a completely different weather pattern. From
this, Lorenz realized that tiny changes in conditions could, over time,
result in drastically different results – as illustrated by the butterfly
analogy. The reason such behaviour is termed 'chaotic' is that – like
the renowned unpredictability of the weather – it *seems* to be so.
However, as Lorenz proposed, such 'chaotic systems' are actually ruled
by ordered principles, but which, due to influence of factors too small
to measure, can sometimes behave unpredictability.

Lorenz's findings (as well as the contributions of others) have great
consequences not only for physical systems, but also for the study of
human behaviour and society. So, for instance, it's useful for police to
be able to understand the principles that govern the behaviour of
crowds (e.g. to ensure safety at concerts, sporting events, etc.).
However, whilst we may arrive at a rule of thumb that seems to work
in many, even most situations, there'll always be the possibility that
one or more individuals will influence group behaviour in unpredictable ways. Such outcomes are not strictly unpredictable, for we might
foresee them if we knew the determining factors – but, sometimes,
these factors are just too small to be measurable.

Some therefore see Chaos theory as undermining *determinism*: but
this is not strictly true. The fact that we cannot predict things doesn't
mean that they're *undetermined*, but merely that they're
– unpredictable.

'Ideology (as a system of mass representations) is indispensable in any society if men are to be formed, transformed and equipped to respond to the demands of their conditions of existence'

LOUIS ALTHUSSER 1918–1990
For Marx

Althusser was an Algerian-born French philosopher who, in a parallel way, did for Marxism what Lévi-Strauss did for anthropology and Lacan for psychoanalysis, by bringing *structuralist* ideas to bear on political theory. One of Althusser's most influential ideas is that of *Ideology*, meaning the underlying beliefs, roles and concepts that we accept as part of society, and which we are indoctrinated in by society's various social institutions – such as the Church, schools, and family – which Althusser termed 'Ideological State Apparatuses'.

It's possible here to see links with Foucault, who was in fact taught by Althusser at the École Normale Supérieure in Paris. Both see institutions as not only telling us what to do, or how to think, but also *who we are*. Althusser terms this 'interpellation', the process which creates subjects of authority in support of the underlying ideology.

But how, if we're 'created' in terms of this ideology, are we to escape it? As a communist and Marxist, Althusser therefore saw any change in revolutionary terms: to uproot the prevailing ideology and replace it with a communist one. Interestingly, however, this process, which seems to merely replace one ideology with another, does not change the way in which the subject is seen. In other words, Althusser's revolutionary ideology is just as controlling as the regime which it replaces. The reason for this is that structuralism shares with Marx a belief in the power of society over the individual. But, structuralism goes further than this, for it basically assumes that without society *there would be no individual*.

However, in terms of achieving revolutionary change, the fact that structuralism sees the individual as effectively illusory undermines this: without individuality, we have no free will or choice; without choice, society is effectively a machine. But machines don't change; they either work, or break down.

'. . . Raoul Francé put forward the idea, shocking to contemporary natural philosophers, that plants move their bodies as freely, easily, and gracefully as the most skilled animal or human, and that the only reason we don't appreciate the fact is that plants do so at a much slower pace than humans'

PETER TOMPKINS 1919–2007 AND CHRISTOPHER BIRD 1928–1996
The Secret Life of Plants

Are plants sentient? In *The Secret Life of Plants*, a bestselling but controversial book published in 1973, American journalists and researchers Peter Tompkins and Christopher Bird presented a host of evidence that seemed to suggest that they were.

The authors recounted experiments where plants responded to music – they preferred Mozart and Bach to Hendrix, but classical Indian sitar music most of all. Human thought and emotion was also claimed to affect plants, and studies allegedly showed that plants spoken to and encouraged verbally responded with more luxuriant growth than those who were merely fed and watered. Furthermore, Bird and Tompkins reported that there were suggestions that plants could even 'remember' those who had mistreated them in the past, registering distress signals (measured by an EEG machine, such as is used to measure the electrical activity of the brain) in the presence of the abuser – detecting even the *intention* to harm (thus suggesting a form of telepathic ability).

But is there anything in this? Firstly, attempts to replicate some of the experiments described have met with mixed results, which leaves the status of the claims – scientifically at least – controversial. However, from a more general philosophical standpoint, the possibility of plant sentience is highly unsettling. If true, it not only questions our understanding of what consciousness and sentience are, but also raises awkward ethical issues: have we then a duty to treat plants humanely, or even to refrain from eating them at all? Obviously, the latter position is untenable for most people, for it would require an almost impossible shift in attitudes to agriculture, ecology, nutrition, etc. Just as well then, perhaps, that the experiments are inconclusive.

> 'The climate and the chemical properties of the Earth now and throughout its history seem always to have been optimal for life. For this to have happened by chance is as unlikely as to survive unscathed a drive blindfold through rush hour traffic.'
>
> JAMES LOVELOCK b.1919
> *Gaia: A New Look at Life on Earth*

Aside from convincing all but hardened 'flat-Earthers' that the world is round, the first pictures from space suggested to English scientist James Lovelock a more radical possibility. Earth isn't a battleground of natural and material forces, existing in precarious balance; it's a living system, a *superorganism*, which not only regulates life, but atmosphere, planetary temperature, and even subterranean processes. Earth is alive.

Whilst *Gaia theory* shares the name of the Greek Earth goddess, it's not some woolly, New Age, pseudo-scientific nature worship, but an increasingly recognized and influential field of scientific study. Lovelock argues that the conditions required to foster and maintain life are too fortunate to have arisen by chance. For instance, the atmosphere contains exactly the right composition of chemical gasses for life – a fact so unlikely (for it to have reached this point *at all*, and for this balance to have been maintained) that it represents almost a 'violation of the rules of chemistry'. Instead, Lovelock proposes, *life itself* has constructed and managed Earth's atmosphere in order to produce its own optimum conditions. The result is a *biosphere*, an environment created by – and including – all living organisms and material processes that life manipulates to sustain itself.

If the biosphere *is* a global 'feedback system', maintaining its own balance, the consequences are enormous. Firstly, efforts to address climate change must complement whatever Earth already does to maintain equilibrium; if there are in-built coping mechanisms to sustain life in response to such changes, then we need to work *with* them, not in ignorance of – and therefore possibly *against* – them. Secondly, however, we must realize that there's a difference between maintaining *life*, and maintaining *human* life: we may not be essential to Nature's plans.

The famous advice of American psychologist Timothy Leary, the
'High Priest of LSD' and guru of 1960s counter culture, has become
synonymous with 'the hippies' and everything they stood for – peace
and love, sexual revolution, spiritual reawakening. However, behind
the often-misinterpreted slogan lies a serious message concerning
personal change, society and human potential.

A respectable Harvard University psychologist, Leary's life was
drastically altered when he experimented with *psilocybin* mushrooms.
This led, at first, to his pioneering of psychological trials involving a
then-legal equivalent, *lysergic acid diethylamide* (LSD), aimed at
assessing its use for clinical purposes. But its recreational and mind-al-
tering potential quickly attracted Leary's more hedonistic and
creatively-minded acquaintances, and he was increasingly drawn into
a world of personal exploration and revolutionary ideals.

Leary's progressive involvement with LSD, his subsequent championing of drug-fuelled liberation, and his resulting conflicts with law
and authority – detailed in his aptly-named autobiography *Flashbacks*
– make fascinating and entertaining reading. However, his message
wasn't primarily chemical. 'Turning on' consisted of exploring alternative ways of experiencing the world, and increasing mental and
physical engagement with life (for which LSD was an ideal catalyst).
'Tuning in' meant harmonizing yourself with the natural rhythms that
society drowns out. And 'dropping out' involved rejecting the destructive models of behaviour, belief systems, institutions, etc., that
constituted your adherence to your previous mindset.

However, Leary admits, 'my explanations of this sequence of personal
development were often misinterpreted to mean 'Get stoned and abandon
all constructive activity.' But, in aiming at liberation, 'Drugs were only one
way to accomplish this end', and his threefold process is reflected in traditional asceticism: the monk withdraws from society (*drops out*), practises
prayer and meditation (*turns on*), and attempts to focus solely on God
(*tunes in*). But, like other radicals (e.g. Reich), Leary thought individual
change shouldn't involve withdrawal from society, but itself result in *social*
change. The ultimate goal was revolution.

'I have set out to design my own death, or de-animation as I prefer to call it . . . Even if you've lived your life like a complete slob, you can die with terrific style. I call it "Designer Dying," and it involves two basic principles by which I've lived my life: think for yourself and question authority.'

TIMOTHY LEARY (WITH R. U. SIRIUS)
Design for Dying

In 1995, Leary was diagnosed with inoperable prostate cancer. From then on, in typically provocative fashion, he faced the inevitable with a combination of philosophical calm, faith in technology, and his trademark humour and irreverence. Initially, Leary's head was to be cryogenically frozen, awaiting reanimation when scientific technology was suitably advanced (on condition, he quipped, that he wouldn't 'be brought back during a Republican administration').

However, in line with the mental flexibility he always valued – 'You're only as young as the last time you changed your mind' – something turned Leary against this, deciding instead to be cremated and have his ashes sent into space. Perhaps he concluded that by trying to cheat death he wasn't actually changing our *attitude* to it; it was still something to be feared and avoided. Therefore, the more profound response was to change the way we thought about death, and what we conceived it to be: 'I'm gonna give death a better name, or die trying.'

Design for Dying, and the detailed public documentation of his final months, were therefore an attempt to do that. Leary questions our distinctions between 'living' and 'dead', between 'self' and 'other': doesn't part of us live on in our friendships, our possessions, our actions? In the blurred line between 'me' and 'mine', isn't there a sense in which I am more than the little Cartesian conscious self? There's a similarity here with Derek Parfit's impersonal view of personal identity. However, true to form, Leary isn't dogmatic about such options, but rather toys with them as whimsical possibilities, content merely not to rule any of them out – for, as his final words put it, 'Why not?'

'The presence of voices which had to be obeyed were the absolute prerequisite to the conscious stage of mind in which it is the self that is responsible and can debate within itself, can order and direct, and that the creation of such a self is the product of culture. In a sense, we have become our own gods.'

JULIAN JAYNES 1920–1997
The Origin of Consciousness in the Breakdown of the Bicameral Mind

Looking back over human evolution, we assume the main things that have changed are our knowledge and ability to reason. Early man was much like us – similar in mental, emotional and physical experience – differing only in the sophistication and content of his experiences.

However, in 1976, American psychologist Julian Jaynes proposed a radically different possibility: consciousness, as we now think of it, was not a facet of the internal experience of early man, but only developed some 3,000 years ago (around the time of Homer's *Iliad* and *The Old Testament*), mainly as a result of the development of writing. Until this point, humans had experienced 'consciousness' as an *auditory hallucination*: they *heard* their gods, spirits, ancestors, etc., as 'external' sources of advice (whereas you or I would simply be aware of our own thoughts as a sort of 'internal commentary'). Over time, this 'bicameral' mentality (i.e. split in two) broke down, the 'external' voices became internalized, and consciousness was born (specifically, *introspection*, or awareness of one's own mental states).

Jaynes' theory represents an intriguing possibility, and has attracted much popular and academic attention. On the one hand, it's given credence by *schizophrenia*, which displays similar symptoms and is taken by Jaynes to represent a throwback to the bicameral mentality. It also provides a tempting atheistic account of the origins of religion. However, whilst plausible, the theory is difficult to prove, for it concerns the mental experience of people who existed 3,000 years ago. In addition to this problem, can we accept that people could walk and talk like us, produce literature, etc., and *not* be conscious in the same way?

'The principles of justice are chosen behind a veil of ignorance'
JOHN RAWLS 1921–2002
A Theory of Justice

The theories of American moral and political philosopher John Rawls have become central to modern notions of justice and equality. In his landmark work, *A Theory of Justice*, Rawls argues that the principles of justice are those that fair-minded and rational individuals would choose from an impartial perspective (what he terms the *original position*).

Along with Locke and Hobbes, Rawls advances a form of social contract theory: individuals agree to give up self-interest in exchange for justice and equality. However, the only way to ensure the fairness of the social contract would be if it's formulated behind a *veil of ignorance*. In other words, principles of justice and fairness should be arrived at in complete ignorance of the type of individuals they might apply to. For instance, if I'm the strongest, or the smartest, or possess certain advantages in terms of property or wealth, then (assuming I'm a typically selfish person) I would want those principles to benefit me. However, from behind a 'veil of ignorance', I do not know I'm strongest or smartest, so to protect myself – since I do not know what advantages others possess – I would favour principles which fostered equality. Furthermore, since there is every chance in this unseen society that I may suffer at the hands of fate, then I would also want to safeguard against poverty or similar disadvantage. Therefore, following what is known as the *maximin strategy*, I would choose principles that 'maximized the minimum', thereby ensuring that the worst thing that could happen represents the best of all alternatives (e.g. if I became homeless, there would be some support for me).

However, whilst it's been hugely influential, Rawls' *justice of fairness* also arguably strips morality from its cultural roots, and privileges a very Western notion of the rational individual (see, e.g., MacIntyre). In framing justice and fairness in terms of the enlightened self-interest of the individual, don't we lose a deeper sense of community?

> '. . . civil disobedience [is] a public, non-violent, conscientious yet political act contrary to law usually done with the aim of bringing about a change in the law or policies of the government. By acting in this way one addresses the sense of justice of the majority of the community.'
>
> JOHN RAWLS
>
> *A Theory of Justice*

Like Thoreau, Gandhi and Martin Luther King, Rawls thought *civil disobedience* acceptable, but only when certain conditions are met.

Firstly, acts must be *public*, for the primary intention is to highlight injustice. Secretly liberating chickens from the local battery farm doesn't qualify because it's not clearly distinguished from a private act of theft or sabotage. Also, a public, publicized act shows that protestors otherwise respect the law, and aren't seeking to undermine the state as a whole – if protest results in imprisonment, they should accept this. Secondly, disobedience should be *conscientious*, possess a political aim, and seek to change the law for the betterment of everyone. This rules out acts of self-interest or personal preference. Driving whilst over the legal limit for alcohol, just because you believe you've a higher tolerance than most, doesn't count. Thirdly, it must be *non-violent*, proportionate and reasonable. Protesting about the lack of parking facilities near my home by wrecking the cars of non-locals is disproportionate vandalism. Non-violence, as Gandhi recognized, distinguishes civil disobedience from actions with other motives – such as criminality or terrorism. Fourthly, it should appeal to society's sense of *justice*. The campaigns for sexual and racial equality both sought to highlight the irrational injustice of treating these groups differently by appealing to deeper shared values. Above all, of course, it must actually be illegal – peaceful, legal protest is not civil disobedience – and a last resort when all legal avenues have been exhausted.

But are Rawl's conditions too narrow? Some actions are necessarily secret – think of Greenpeace's protests – because publicity would allow authorities to safeguard against them; others aim not at changing laws, but merely attitudes, decisions or practices (e.g. deforestation). Are such actions therefore illegitimate?

> 'Under normal conditions the research scientist is not an innovator but a solver of puzzles, and the puzzles upon which he concentrates are just those which he believes can be both stated and solved within the existing scientific tradition'
> THOMAS KUHN 1922–1996
> *The Essential Tension*

Beginning as a theoretical physicist, American philosopher Thomas Kuhn developed an interest in the philosophy and history of science, which eventually led him to a radical and sceptical account of scientific progress.

Traditionally, science sees itself progressing toward truth. So, each crisis and revolution of thought brings it closer to understanding how the world is. However, Kuhn came to reject this view. Focusing mainly on Copernicus and Galileo, though his ideas apply equally to any period of scientific history, Kuhn argued that science goes through *normal* and *revolutionary* periods. In *normal science*, the central concern is on solving puzzles and tidying up how the overall theory fits the available evidence. During this period of stability, the underlying assumptions go unchallenged, and anything which does not fit the world view is ignored or explained away as an anomaly. However, over time, if enough of these anomalies occur, discontent will grow, until eventually a crisis will result, and a new *paradigm* (theoretical view) will emerge. This period produces *revolutionary science*, during which the new theory is established (a *paradigm shift*), eventually settling down once more into normal science. But the new paradigm is not progress – there is no sense of logical progression from the old to the new paradigm, for they are built on different assumptions, and are therefore *incommensurable* (cannot be compared).

Kuhn's view is obviously controversial, but not implausible. At the time of writing, an ancient temple has been discovered in Turkey, built some 11,500 years ago, which completely disrupts the accepted history of ancient man's development. Its discoverer found it using the notes of a previous archaeologist, who had stumbled across it 50 years before, but had simply found it too big an anomaly to deal with. Was this an example of *normal science* at work?

> 'What would have to occur or to have occurred to constitute for you a
> disproof of the love of, or the existence of, God?'
> ANTONY FLEW b.1923
> 'Theology and Falsification'

Picture two explorers travelling through a jungle. Coming upon a clearing containing both flowers and weeds, one explorer believes that someone tends the spot, whereas the other one isn't so sure. So, they keep watch, but no gardener ever appears. Undismayed, the first explorer suggests that, perhaps, he is an invisible gardener. Therefore, they erect an electrified fence, set trip wires, use bloodhounds, and generally employ all possible means to detect the gardener, with no success. But the first explorer continues to hold out hope, suggesting further excuses – at which point the second explorer finally loses patience: 'What is the difference between your undetectable, invisible gardener, and no gardener at all?'

This is a parable for religious belief. Many believers, argues English philosopher Antony Flew, adapt their beliefs to account for problems and objections. Thereby, what start as assertions – 'God loves us', 'God has a plan' – undergo what Flew terms 'death by a thousand qualifications', eventually becoming meaningless: if *nothing* counts against their assertions, are they really asserting anything?

A similar point is made in psychology. *Cognitive Dissonance Theory* describes the different ways in which individuals adapt their views to accommodate conflicting beliefs. A cult expecting the end of the world will continue to exist when the end doesn't arrive, by choosing to think that God has spared them. Is this what Flew's believers are doing? Faced with – for instance – the problem of evil, and the apparently conflicting beliefs that 'God loves us', is omnipotent, etc., are they choosing to *adapt* their cherished beliefs rather than relinquish them?

In a fascinating and controversial twist, Flew himself – a lifelong scourge of religion – has recently converted to 'deism' (the belief that the world was created by, and is therefore proof of, God). Having so long criticized religion for its *irrationality*, has Flew found *new* reasons, or finally decided that *reason* is not enough?

> '... there is only *one* principle that can be defended under *all* circumstances and in *all* stages of human development. It is the principle: anything goes.'
> PAUL FEYERABEND 1924–1994
> *Against Method*

Bothered by some of the wilder theories of psychoanalysis, Karl Popper had proposed that there must be definable characteristics that separated science from not-science: scientific theories, he argued, could be *falsified*, but pseudo-scientific theories could not. However, philosophers such as Thomas Kuhn argued that this gives a falsely rationalistic picture of how science progresses, creating the impression that it moves forward as old theories are falsified and new, better ones take their place.

Austrian philosopher Paul Feyerabend agreed with Kuhn, but argued more radically that 'irrational' forces played as key a role in scientific change as 'rational' ones, and it is the tension between many different competing theories that pushes science forward. So, for instance, conventional science had rejected the ideas of *Hermeticism*, *Gnosticism*, and *Neoplatonism* as mystical claptrap, but it is these very ideas which were to form a secret influence upon Isaac Newton and Copernicus. No idea was therefore to be rejected, and no method preferred to any other: anything goes.

Of course, modern science pales at the idea that there isn't a secure rational basis to scientific progress, and most would reject out of hand Feyerabend's anarchic approach. And yet, Feyerabend's idea isn't that we should abandon method, but that we shouldn't reject marginal or fringe theories out of hand. There's hardly a theory that exists that wasn't initially rejected by some. Furthermore, since successful science is all the less likely to question its own assumptions, a constant openness to opposing views is the only way that we can test those assumptions: for, 'how can we possibly examine something we use all the time and presuppose in every statement?' In other words, the more different an approach is from ours, the more likely it is to identify those assumptions we don't notice: sometimes, what is furthest from our notice is right in front of us.

> '**Clouds are not spheres, mountains are not cones, coastlines are not circles, and bark is not smooth, nor does lightning travel in a straight line**'
>
> BENOÎT MANDELBROT b.1924
> *The Fractal Geometry of Nature*

Studying the fluctuation of cotton prices on the 1960s stock exchange, French mathematician Benoît Mandelbrot realized that market prices didn't always behave in the way that contemporary economists predicted. *Gaussian* or *normative distribution* (the 'bell curve') seems to account for general behaviour, but often fails to predict extreme market behaviour – such as *crashes* (dramatic stock-price decline) and *bubbles* (rapid stock-price inflation). Instead, Mandelbrot argued that such fluctuations followed *fractal* principles.

Fractal principles can be represented visually as a complex non-regular shape that, at some point of magnification, eventually 'repeats' itself, thus mirroring the overall shape at a smaller level (what's known as *recursion* – where something includes or refers to itself). Thus, in analyzing cotton price patterns, Mandelbrot claimed to discern fractal principles at work. As such, fractal mathematics is a central strut of *chaos theory*, for it provides a means of understanding complex and irregular systems, which – as our main quote suggests – whilst *appearing* rough or random, are actually determined by extremely intricate *fractal* principles.

So, can we get rich on the stock market? Well, not necessarily. Because behaviour or systems can display fractal qualities, this doesn't mean we can fully understand the *factors* that influence the overall behaviour. Whilst fractals are ordered, they are also infinitely complex, thus – since we can never base our predictions on an infinite amount of data – there'll always be some (possibly vital) piece of information that we miss.

However, this doesn't mean that there is no use for fractals. Firstly, knowing the fractal behaviour of weather, stock markets, etc., should lead us to place less trust in standard models of prediction (and make provisions for things going wrong). Also, knowing a process is fractal, we may even take it as a sign of trouble when it becomes *regular* (such as natural rhythms and cycles – the human heartbeat, bird migration patterns). Chaos isn't all bad – and it sure is pretty!

'Play is obviously very serious to its participants; they strive very earnestly and with great effort at their play and sports, and their efforts produce important personal and social outcomes that cannot be gotten easily in any other way. In addition, there are many societies in which play is an integral part of religious and work ceremonies; where the duality of work versus play, so often taken for granted in Western eyes, is simply not valid.'

BRIAN SUTTON-SMITH b.1924
The Ambiguity of Play

New Zealand academic and play theorist Brian Sutton-Smith considers play of central importance to the wellbeing of people of all ages. Play fulfils an important educational and developmental role – consider the play-fighting and hunting games young animals engage in – and allows us to practise and acquire skills of use elsewhere. However, Smith-Sutton argues, play is more than just a preparation for adulthood, and children take play very seriously *on its own terms*: therefore, understanding play must involve close scrutiny of *all* its manifestations throughout life.

'Play' has diverse meanings: *playing* a game, watching a *play, playing* for points or fun, *playing* hooky, *playing* up, and so on. Thus, play is difficult to pin down. Sutton-Smith identifies seven traditional ways of seeing (or *rhetorics* of) play. For example, the rhetoric of *progress* sees the play as developmental (e.g. pretend hunting) – this is currently the dominant model; however, the rhetoric of *the self* sees play as consolidating individuality – providing 'me' time, and switching off from work and duty; the rhetoric of *power*, as a means of expressing conflict and resolving status struggles peacefully.

Sutton-Smith doesn't reject these or other rhetorics, but notes that – individually – none of them completely describes play. Instead, he proposes that, underlying these different emphases, play represents an attempt of the human organism to make itself more *viable*: nature (and Natural Selection) may have made you small, slow or weak (relatively), but play helps you to find ways of surviving – socially, emotionally, intellectually. So, play is flexible and non-rigid because these are key survival tools. We play to live.

'I've had enough of someone else's propaganda. I'm for truth, no matter who tells it. I'm for justice, no matter who it's for or against. I'm a human being first and foremost, and as such I am for whoever and whatever benefits humanity as a whole.'

MALCOLM X 1925–1965
The Autobiography of Malcolm X

Unlike Martin Luther King, African-American rights activist Malcolm X did not believe that non-violence was the only valid response to the racial problems faced by black people in America. Rather, he thought that violence in the name of self-defence was a valid response to the often life-threatening violence aimed against blacks by whites.

This was always a sticking point between the two great activists, and can perhaps be traced to a difference in life experience. Born Malcolm Little, he had joined the *Nation of Islam* whilst serving time in prison for theft-related offences, changing his surname to 'X' (like other members) to reflect the unknown original surname that his enslaved ancestors had been deprived of. Having had three uncles, and possibly his father, die from racially motivated violence, Malcolm X took to the Nation's extremist message of black separatism (a separate homeland for black people), and their teachings that blacks were the original, superior race, and that whites were 'devils'. Also, importantly, its principles – whilst not *pro-violence* – were not pacifist, and Malcolm X appears never to have completely renounced them. As he observed in his famous 'The Ballot or the Bullet' speech: 'What's good for the goose is good for the gander.'

However, following an acrimonious break with the Nation (members associated with which were eventually to assassinate him), Malcolm X became a Sunni Muslim, and undertook the *Hajj* (the holy pilgrimage to Mecca made at least once in a Muslim's lifetime). His experiences there changed his attitude to race, marking the beginning of a realization that the path to change was an international, not a domestic issue: it wasn't just about how whites treat blacks, or even how races treat each other, but how *humans* treat each other.

> 'Education, with its supporting system of compulsory and
> competitive schooling, all its carrots and sticks, its grades,
> diplomas and credentials, now seems to me perhaps the most
> authoritarian and dangerous of all the social inventions of mankind.
> It is the deepest foundation of the modern slave state, in which most
> people feel themselves to be nothing but producers, consumers,
> spectators, and "fans," driven more and more, in all parts
> of their lives, by greed, envy, and fear.'
>
> JOHN HOLT 1923–1985
> *Instead of Education*

American educational theorist John Holt was a fierce critic of standard educational practices. However, unlike previous theorists, it wasn't a particular emphasis that he was critical of, but education *itself*. Thus, rather than improve it, we should 'end the ugly and antihuman business of people-shaping' (as he called it), and facilitate the means to let people shape themselves.

Holt's solution was *homeschooling*. School is a foreign environment where children are often too afraid to express themselves, and forced to study subjects they don't necessarily possess any interest in. However, if an environment conducive to learning were created at home, the child could continue to develop its early curiosity in a natural way. But merely being kept at home isn't enough: a child also needs to be presented with a range of learning opportunities that are neither too guided nor too open-ended, but a mixture of life experience and more abstract knowledge acquisition (an approach Holt termed *unschooling*, to emphasize its difference).

This approach has obvious parallels with Montessori, with its similar reliance upon natural curiosity and desire to learn. However, there are also similar concerns, for it would seem difficult for a child to independently master a curriculum that might fit him out for later education or employment. But perhaps a greater concern is social integration: school may not be ideal, but it at least allows children to mix with others in a way that prepares them for society. It would be nice, of course, to acquire all we need to know merely from living, but isn't this idealistic?

'Does this path have a heart? If it does, the path is good; if it doesn't, it is of no use. Both paths lead nowhere, but one has a heart, the other doesn't. One makes for a joyful journey; as long as you follow it, you are one with it. The other will make you curse your life.'

CARLOS CASTANEDA 1925–1998
The Teachings of Don Juan

Carlos Castaneda was a Peruvian anthropologist and writer, famous for his series of books detailing his apprenticeship to Don Juan Matus, a Mexican (*Yaqui* Indian) shaman. An anthropology student at the University of California, Castaneda's first book – *The Teachings of Don Juan: A Yaqui Way of Knowledge* – was accepted as his master's thesis. It became a bestseller, hailed by anthropologists for providing unique insight into a heretofore secret culture. What's more, it unexpectedly revealed, in Don Juan's world view, a metaphysical system as sophisticated and complex as any.

In Don Juan's words, 'all paths lead nowhere', but – in a curiously *existentialist* world, seemingly devoid of inherent meaning or God – some paths are better than others. What shapes the shaman is his awareness of the true, inhuman infinity which our day-to-day constructed personality keeps at bay. The shaman lifts this mask, and faces the inevitability of death with clear-sighted courage.

As the initial enthusiasm died down, however, sober-eyed commentators began to spot inconsistencies, and with each contradiction, the likelihood that Castaneda's account was literally true correspondingly receded. The deathblow came when Richard de Mille (*Carlos Castaneda: The Power and the Allegory*) checked Castaneda's university library record: not only was he in the library when supposed to be taking *peyote* with Don Juan, but actually reading *someone else's* account of such a ceremony. Was it all fiction?

Perhaps Castaneda changed details to protect sources, but there's also evidence that certain events were 'borrowed' from elsewhere. What then did the books represent? Castaneda's personal philosophy? Something cobbled together from other sources? A disguised but genuine tradition? Whatever the case – debate continues – perhaps only Castaneda knows: did he choose a path with heart?

> 'Prison continues, on those who are entrusted to it, a work begun
> elsewhere, which the whole of society pursues on each individual
> through innumerable mechanisms of discipline'
> MICHEL FOUCAULT 1926–1984
> *Discipline and Punish*

In 1785, Jeremy Bentham proposed a design for a revolutionary new type of prison, which he christened the Panopticon. Owing to its ingenious design, all prisoners would be potentially visible at any time, whilst the observers themselves would remain unseen. This would provide the constant *sense* of being surveyed, even if it were not the case. In fact, no guards need be present: effectively, the prisoners watch themselves.

French philosopher Michel Foucault takes this as a metaphor for society in general. We are, he says, monitored, disciplined, controlled and punished by the very structure of society itself. This is increasingly the case with the pervasiveness of technological means of surveillance and monitoring – the use of CCTV, greater reliance on electronic communication and media, all of which can be easily tracked. If, as Marshall McLuhan said, 'The medium is the message', then, concludes Foucault, the message is, 'We are watching you!'

However, this is much more than some sort of technology-driven 'Big Brother' style paranoia. Foucault thought that knowledge, power and language were all intimately interrelated. The purpose of prison is not reform, but control, which takes place also in schools, churches, factories and hospitals. The increasing amount of information that is held about people, the growing tendency toward categorization and labelling, and the mounting rules and regulations that govern what we can, should, or mustn't do, are all subtle extensions of state power. Even the so-called 'free' merely live in an open prison, a vast 'Panopticon' where all our thoughts and actions are monitored and controlled – by our attitudes, by the very labels we use and by which we are categorized.

Consequently, prison is only a step in the gradual move toward self-policing. Conscience – as Sartre's account of shame suggests – is a response to the sense of being watched – even, perhaps, when no one is there.

'... if you are not like everybody else, then you are abnormal, if you are abnormal, then you are sick. These three categories, not being like everybody else, not being normal and being sick are in fact very different but have been reduced to the same thing.'

MICHEL FOUCAULT

interview, 1975

Foucault's views on power, knowledge and language are best understood through his work on madness. The modern notion of insanity, he argues, began with the Enlightenment, which first saw the exclusion of mental illness in a systematic way. Until then, whilst the insane were still pushed to the fringes of society, they weren't singled out for this exclusion, sharing it with beggars, orphans, the jobless, and other outsiders. However, the Enlightenment created the expectation that humans should behave wholly rationally, and 'madness' became a blanket term for anyone who did not meet society's increasingly exacting standards. Thus, those classified 'irrational' received increased attention, ultimately producing what Foucault calls 'the Great Internment', where, from this point onwards, such individuals were isolated, incarcerated, studied and treated.

Psychiatry therefore does a comparable job to other social functions, defining individuals in relation to a rational norm, and 'treating', 'punishing' or 'educating' them either to fit, or be *misfits*. This use of madness as a tool of social control can be seen in the alarmingly recent practice (1960s) of institutionalizing unmarried mothers in the UK for 'moral deficiency'.

But if knowledge is merely a tool of power, objectivity becomes impossible – everyone shapes the world in their own image (effectively, Nietzsche's concept of 'will to power', which greatly influenced Foucault). We may reject this, but there's still something in what Foucault says. Before the Enlightenment, madness might be a sign that something was wrong with society: a symptom of a deeper problem. Now, we prescribe Prozac like jelly beans, treating only the symptoms by staving off irrationality with a chemical straightjacket. But what if madness isn't just the malfunctioning of a delicate machine? What if it's trying to tell us something – that, perhaps, there is something wrong with the norm?

> 'Briefly, my aim is to examine the case of a society which has been loudly castigating itself for its hypocrisy for more than a century, which speaks verbosely of its own silence, takes great pains to relate in detail the things it does not say, denounces the powers it exercises, and promises to liberate itself from the very laws that have made it function'
>
> MICHEL FOUCAULT
> *The History of Sexuality*, Vol.1

It's become commonplace to see the Victorians as repressing sex; an animalistic act that didn't square with man's spiritual dignity, providing at best brutish pleasures, but occasionally necessary for procreation. An act which, if it must, should happen infrequently, in the dark, and with one foot on the floor.

We, however, having finally realized that sex *isn't* a sin, are still struggling out from under their shadow. Freud helped somewhat, as did the 1960s, but we've still a way to go before we can speak about this most natural of acts without embarrassment and shame.

That is the official story – but is it true? In one sense, no. The last two centuries have seen a great *increase* in *talk* about sex, which the Victorians did nothing to arrest – in fact, were instrumental in promulgating. Far from silence and avoidance, there has been a flood of discourse. But how does this square with the so-called *repression* that was supposed to exist?

Foucault's point is that we should not confuse any frustration or negativity we feel about sex with an injunction against speaking or thinking about it. Rather, we're *encouraged* to communicate – and this is how we are controlled. It's through this sort of confessional approach to sexuality – now agonizing over it, wringing our hands; now becoming indignant – that sex becomes a public concern. Through increased discussion, sex grows to be a greater component of our identity; we worry about it: are we 'normal'? Are we getting a sufficient amount? Is it good enough? Like madness and crime, talk about sex is therefore just another means whereby authority exerts control.

> 'The mad things said and done by the schizophrenic will remain essentially a closed book if one does not understand their existential context. In describing one way of going mad, I shall try to show that there is a comprehensible transition from the sane schizoid way of being-in-the-world to a psychotic way of being-in-the-world.'
>
> R. D. LAING 1927–1989
> *The Divided Self*

What is it to be rational? Perhaps the simplest definition is to say that *rational* beliefs have *reasons* – they may not be *good* reasons, but they are reasons nonetheless. It is in this spirit that Scottish psychiatrist R. D. Laing approaches the problem of mental illness: the 'mad' are not completely 'irrational' – they have 'reasons' – but they are simply not ones that we accept or condone.

In its most extreme form, it's tempting to see illnesses such as schizophrenia as a complete break with reality – as madness, something which has been traditionally viewed externally, as something that by its nature we cannot understand or share. For, as Polonius argues in Shakespeare's *Hamlet*: 'to define true madness, what is't but to be nothing else but mad?' However, Laing disputes this, seeing 'madness' as a term used to distance us from something that scares us.

To illustrate this, Laing attempts to trace the progress from the *schizoid* personality – a sane but extreme attitude of alienation and emotional isolation – to the *schizophrenic* – someone beset by hallucinations and often bizarre delusions. As his use of the phrase 'being-in-the-world' suggests, Laing is influenced by Heidegger and his *existential phenomenology*. This approach attempts to see the experience of the schizophrenic in terms of his own experience and values (*phenomenologically*, or what it means for him), and as a reaction to the existential choice that faces us all: how to *be*. Furthermore, once we open this previously 'closed book', we see the true nature of the condition, and achieve a better understanding of how to truly help them. Of course, we also recognize an uncomfortable fact: madness is much closer to sanity than we'd hoped.

> 'There are situations in economics or international politics in which, effectively, a group of interests are involved in a non-cooperative game without being aware of it; the non-awareness helping to make the situation truly non-cooperative'
> JOHN NASH b.1928
> 'Non-Cooperative Games'

Mathematics is a foreign language, but occasionally evolves broad applications that speak to the layman. Such an example is *game theory*, which applies mathematical models to real-world scenarios to identify the best strategies. It's no surprise, therefore, that game theory crops up in politics, business and military strategy.

Early game theory, associated with John Von Neumann and Oskar Morgenstern, was successful in dealing with two-person *zero-sum* games, where one's loss is another's gain (I eat everything; you get nothing). However, this has limited real-world application, for real situations often involve *non zero-sum* games, where many players can mutually benefit. For such games, Neumann considered the best strategy to be cooperation, for one person can't second-guess the motives of so many people. Or could he?

American mathematician John Nash argued that multiplayer *non-cooperative* games (with no agreements between players) possess an 'equilibrium point': if each player must make a simultaneous decision (without cooperating) which affects all others, my best strategy is to choose that which will work best *given an expectation* that others will do the same. The most famous illustration of this is the *prisoner's dilemma*. Two people are arrested on suspicion of a crime: if one confesses, he goes free and the other serves 5 years; if both confess, they both serve 3 years; if neither confesses, they both serve 1 year. The *Nash equilibrium* therefore advocates ratting on your partner, for – whilst not the *best* option (that would be to stay quiet) – it maximizes gain relative to risk.

This has countless applications, from economics to traffic management, but its importance lies in understanding how people behave according to strategic self-interest. As such, it's a good model of the 'social contract' view of morality: we don't 'win' as much as if we behaved immorally, but we don't 'lose' either. Is morality, then, just a game?

'Colorless green ideas sleep furiously'
Noam Chomsky b.1928
Syntactic Structures

With the rise of modern science, rationalism seemed to be finally losing the age-old debate with *empiricism* concerning innate ideas. Science favours the empirically provable, and the notion that certain ideas were inbuilt – with, perhaps, a divine origin – seemed increasingly implausible, outdated and insupportable.

However, in other respects, the empiricist approach was equally problematic. In considering how we acquire language, the 'blank slate' model of the mind seems inadequate. There is what American philosopher and linguist Noam Chomsky calls a 'poverty of stimulus': our experience is insufficient to account for our linguistic skills. Chomsky argued that our grasp of grammar has nothing to do with the *meaning* of words, but represents an *innate* ability to recognize and utilize the *structure* of language. Compare our main quotation with the similar sentence 'Furiously sleep ideas green colorless': both are nonsensical, but only the former is grammatical. Chomsky concluded that we can only know this because everyone possesses a *universal grammar* that is 'hardwired' into the brain. So, whilst we may learn the *names* of types of words – noun, verb, adjective – we already know how to apply them.

This is supported by various studies. For instance, a child will apply a rule – such as adding *ed* in the past tense (I *waited*, he *asked*) – *even when* this is incorrect, as with irregular verbs (he *runned*, she *digged*). Since these children weren't simply copying these incorrect words from their parents, they must have created them according to an unconscious rule. So, adding *ed* is something they recognized as correct for most cases (regular verbs), but they had never been taught these rules, nor even been told that rules were involved.

Nativism, as it's called, is still controversial. Some argue that we *don't* all learn correct grammar, others that children are corrected more often than the theory assumes. However, some version of nativism would help account for the fact that we don't seem to learn *how* to learn, or find out *how* to find out: we already know.

> 'You never need an argument against the use of violence, you need an argument for it'
>
> NOAM CHOMSKY
>
> *Hegemony or Survival*

It seems natural to move from the notion of innate universal grammar, to the possibility that, underneath our apparent differences, we also share an innate morality. This is an attractive proposition, but – as Chomsky observes – linking the two is a problem that is 'still very much on the horizon of enquiry', and, of course, extremely contentious.

Various philosophers have argued for an innate universal morality. For instance, Kant contended that certain moral notions are determined by the limits of human reason: that there is a *categorical imperative* to perform certain actions, because it would be a contradiction in terms not to (if *everyone* lied, truth couldn't exist). Conversely, David Hume thought there could never be an all-compelling *rational* motivation to do something, for choosing an action will always be optional (*x* might be considered morally right, but that doesn't mean that I *ought* to do *x*). Hume therefore argued that morality has a basis in emotion and feeling, which allows us to form bonds of empathy with others, appeal to their compassion and sense of justice, etc. So, if basic emotional reactions are universal (as argued by psychologist Paul Ekman, the inspiration for the TV series *Lie to Me*), then so might moral sentiments be.

These approaches are controversial, but Chomsky takes a more pragmatic line. Whilst holding out hope for a theoretical basis for universal moral rights, he simply observes that, in the real world, there is already a surprising amount of general consensus: people want to be safe, healthy, and free; they want hospitals and schools, not guns; they want discussion, not aggression. The development of the United Nations is a sign of this consensus, and the increasing role of the UN in agreeing conventions on torture, human rights, children's rights, and other issues, indicates that, whilst the philosophers squabble, and governments wrangle, the people themselves are agreed.

'. . . the democratic postulate is that the media are independent and committed to discovering and reporting the truth, and that they do not merely reflect the world as powerful groups wish it to be perceived . . . If, however, the powerful are able to fix the premises of discourse, to decide what the general populace is allowed to see, hear, and think about, and to "manage" public opinion by regular propaganda campaigns, the standard view of how the system works is at serious odds with reality.'

NOAM CHOMSKY AND EDWARD S. HERMAN b.1925
Manufacturing Consent

With co-author Edward Herman, Chomsky advances 'the propaganda model' of the media. Modern newspapers, television stations, etc., are *primarily* businesses, and cannot be assumed to possess a disinterested approach to truth. 'News' is therefore propaganda, promoting the vested interests of wealthy advertisers and political parties over a duty to inform the public.

So the purpose of the media is, as American political commentator Walter Lippman (1889–1974) states, 'the manufacture of consent'. Like Edward Bernays, Lippman considered the public a 'bewildered herd' whose opinions needed 'guidance'. Thus, the modern media, in compliance with Lippman's advice, is shaped by the policies of government and business, where each can exact telling punishment for disobedience: newspapers can be denied access to information which its rivals remain privy to, major advertisers can threaten withdrawal, and so on.

Critics argue that Chomsky's anti-establishment views get sufficient press, and there is adequate evidence of disagreement with government policies in news and media. However, the point is not that dissenting views exist, but that the coverage they receive is drowned out by the chorus of state- and business-sponsored orthodoxy; what's more, 'anti-government' criticism tends to be very narrow, reflecting minor divergence in the range of opinion within the establishment itself. Thus, *truly* divergent opinion is once again ignored.

Isn't this conspiracy-mongering? Chomsky's claim doesn't rely on far-fetched theories and leaked secret memos, but is (as Lippman illustrates) an open fact, ascertainable by anyone who cares to look: the truth is there, in black and white.

'One may well ask: "How can you advocate breaking some laws and obeying others?" The answer lies in the fact that there are two types of laws: just and unjust. I would be the first to advocate obeying just laws. One has not only a legal but a moral responsibility to obey just laws. Conversely, one has a moral responsibility to disobey unjust laws.'

MARTIN LUTHER KING JR. 1929–1968
Letter from Birmingham Jail, 1963

Inspired by Gandhi, American clergyman and black-rights activist Martin Luther King, Jr. considered non-violent protest the most effective spur to social change. This places him firmly within a tradition of *civil disobedience* that aims to target unjust laws whilst respecting the rule of law *in general*.

Malcolm X had presented a robust justification of a black man's right to self-defence, but its more aggressive tone was arguably less effective in garnering white sympathy. However, King's Christian-based pacifism was *inclusive*, reaching out to white, Christian, middle-class America, and drawing parallels with acts of martyrdom, insubordination and direct action central to the American liberal ideal – the death of Socrates, the crucifixion of Jesus, the Boston Tea Party. In this way, King linked black civil rights with the central tenets of Christianity and the principles of democracy.

The quote comes from an open letter written whilst imprisoned for his part in non-violent protests in Birmingham, Alabama. Responding to the call of local clergymen to seek change through legal means, King argues, in typically eloquent and impassioned manner, that legal action wouldn't only be slow, with no guarantee of success, but would present their case too meekly. Injustice, violence and discrimination were a daily fact of black American life, requiring *immediate* redress, not at some convenient future point (which might never come).

But isn't this 'extremist'? So be it, he says, for all such challenges to majority intolerance have come from 'extremists'. 'So the question is not whether we will be extremists, but what kind of extremists we will be. Will we be extremists for hate or for love?'

> 'A feature of utilitarianism is that it cuts out a kind of consideration which for some others makes a difference to what they feel about such cases: a consideration involving the idea, as we might first and very simply put it, that each of us is specially responsible for what *he* does, rather than for what other people do'
>
> BERNARD WILLIAMS 1929–2003
> 'A Critique of Utilitarianism'

In a famous thought experiment, English philosopher Bernard Williams describes Jim, a botanist on an expedition, who finds himself in a South American town where twenty Indians are waiting to be executed for anti-government protests. However, to honour Jim's visit, the captain in charge offers him an option: kill one Indian, and nineteen go free; refuse, they all get shot.

The scenario highlights difficulties for two ethical approaches: *consequentialism*, the best-known representative of which is *utilitarianism*, argues that Jim should choose based on *outcome* (e.g. actions which maximize happiness or pleasure). *Deontology*, as represented by Kant, argues that Jim's duty is to absolute principles – in this case, 'killing is wrong'. Faced with Jim's dilemma: consequentialists would kill one man to save nineteen; deontologists wouldn't kill anyone, thus resulting in the death of all twenty, but whose blood (arguably) would be on the psychotic captain's hands, not Jim's.

Williams' main target here is utilitarianism, but his conclusions apply also to Kantianism. Arguably, there's no 'correct' solution to this horrible situation. Morality isn't an impersonal rational 'calculation' that favours the 'common good', nor a strict adherence to a set of inflexible rules. Influenced by Nietzsche, Williams argues that ethics are coloured by personal experience, by the *person* we are, and our individually formed concept of integrity; from *internal* feelings and desires, not an *external* abstract code. Some argue this leads Williams to a subjective position: 'each to his own'. However, I think his purpose is merely to make morality *personal* again – a choice based on values arrived at in the course of life, not imposed from outside by some artificial system (whichever one it is).

> 'What we possess ... are the fragments of a conceptual scheme, parts
> which now lack those contexts from which their significance derived.
> We possess indeed simulacra of morality, we continue to use many of
> the key expressions. But we have – very largely, if not entirely – lost our
> comprehension, both theoretical and practical, of morality.'
> ALASDAIR MACINTYRE b.1929
> *After Virtue*

In *After Virtue*, **Scottish moral philosopher** Alasdair MacIntyre argued
that modern ethical philosophy sits in ruins. Having turned its back
on tradition, it has also lost the true notion of the good. However, he
argues, the answer lies in returning to Aristotle's notion of telos.

The *telos* is the purpose, or *final cause*, of a thing. The *telos* of a heart
is to pump blood; of a stone, to fall to earth. In ethics, the *telos* of moral
action is therefore what we aim at: 'the good'. The good isn't absolutely
fixed (we learn to be moral, leaving room for trial and error), but is
independent of individual desire or viewpoint.

Yet, just as Galileo rejected Aristotle's physics, so Enlightenment
thinkers – such as Hume and Kant – rejected his ethics, creating a
moral philosophy that centred on the individual. Kant, recognizing
that by this move morality was in danger of becoming subjective, tried
to argue that moral notions are *universal*, reflecting rational limits that
moral judgements impose upon us: some attitudes are just self-contradictory, whilst others imply a rational duty. However, thinkers such
as Nietzsche saw the flaw in 'rational' proofs for morality, for they
were merely wishful attempts to justify *irrational prejudices*: we'd *like*
murder to contradict certain rational principles, but it just doesn't.

Where then does this leave us? MacIntyre agrees with Nietzsche's
criticisms, but rejects his conclusions. Morality isn't individual, but
communal: 'good' is learnt as a member of a *community* (a view known
as *communitarianism*). Thus, moral rules aren't rational calculations
(Kant), or non-rational commands (Nietzsche), but stem from a shared
perspective: for, just as society helps craft our identity, so we look to it
for our values, and the very meaning of moral terms.

'. . . it is by no means enough to show that the fetus is a person and to remind us that all persons have a right to life – we need to be shown also that killing the fetus violates its right to life, i.e., that abortion is unjust killing. And is it?'

JUDITH JARVIS THOMSON b.1929
'A Defence of Abortion'

The issue of abortion is not just an ethical one, but involves conceptual questions regarding what we conceive the fetus to be. A mere collection of cells with no inherent rights? A human soul whose termination equates to murder? A person whose future happiness must be respected? However, American philosopher Judith Jarvis Thomson argues that whatever a fetus *is*, its rights often don't outweigh those of the mother.

In a famous thought experiment, Thomson imagines waking up one morning to discover that you've been kidnapped by a society of music lovers, who – to save a famous violinist dying from kidney disease – have 'plugged' him into your body (the only one with the necessary blood type to help him). If you stay 'attached' for nine months, he'll live and can be unplugged; if not, he'll die. What should you do?

The situation is analogous to that of a pregnancy caused by rape: you didn't give your consent to the violinist being 'plugged in', just as a woman who is raped doesn't consent either to sexual intercourse or the resulting pregnancy. Therefore, whilst it would be 'nice' of you to save the violinist, you have no obligation: it is *your* body. Thomson also makes a similar point in relation to an unplanned pregnancy where contraception has failed: the baby is an uninvited visitor, and the rights stay with the mother.

Or do they? Even if we reject the 'right to life' approach (which, perhaps, we needn't), mightn't we argue that – whether it arrived via failed contraception or rape – the fetus isn't to blame? And should an innocent life be denied life due to events outside of its control?

JACQUES DERRIDA 1930–2004
Of Grammatology

No one perhaps illustrates the divide in modern philosophy better than Jacques Derrida. The Algerian-born French philosopher stands at the forefront of *postmodernism*, chief exponent of a view he terms *deconstruction*, wherein every view of 'reality' is taken to have its own inherent biases and assumptions, and ultimately to be no more valid than any other – famously, Derrida has claimed that we cannot effectively distinguish between truth and fiction.

Deconstruction therefore attempts to 'deconstruct' these different perspectives, each of which – using writing as a metaphor for all forms of communication and thought – is a 'text'. However, when we examine the 'text', we find that it doesn't mean what the 'author' intended it to. For instance, philosophy has traditionally assumed that we experience the world as distinct subjects; however, Derrida argues that it is impossible to clearly distinguish between 'subject' and 'object', between 'self' and 'other', for both are merely constructions of the text. Writing and thought therefore suffer generally from this inability to refer to anything outside of the text: we think that language 'points' to reality, but in actuality, 'reality' is merely another construction: there is only the text.

Characterizations of *postmodernism* often identify 'self-reference' as a key feature. Anything which doesn't take itself seriously, or that's aware of its own artificiality or 'constructed' nature – a film or novel which comments upon the conventions of film-making or authorship – is therefore said to embody 'postmodern irony'. Applied to philosophy, however, this approach undermines everything that is significant about what philosophers have traditionally tried to accomplish. If there is 'nothing outside the text', then notions of 'reality' or 'objectivity' become irrelevant – what is the point of looking for truth if there's no such thing?

For this reason, whilst some idolize him, others reject Derrida's work as inconsequential: a clever but ultimately meaningless game. We might also argue that deconstruction undermines itself: if there's no determinate meaning, truth, or reality, there would seem to be no point in studying philosophy – even Derrida's.

'Remain in wonder if you want mysteries to open up for you. Mysteries never open up for those who go on questioning. Questioners sooner or later end up in a library. They end up with scriptures, because scriptures are full of answers. And answers are dangerous, they kill your wonder.'

OSHO 1931–1990
The Book of Wisdom

Osho was an Indian religious philosopher and *guru*. Born Chandra Mohan Jain, he studied and eventually taught philosophy, but, never able to refrain from speaking his mind, he acquired a reputation for troublemaking and unorthodox opinion. Claiming to have achieved spiritual enlightenment at 21, his spiritual ambitions gradually supplanted philosophical ones, eventually abandoning academic life and setting himself up as a guru. In this role, he repeatedly reinvented himself – as 'Acharya Rajneesh', 'Bhagavan Sri Rajnessh', and finally 'Osho' – his controversial opinions earning him increasing notoriety, and his advocation of sexual liberation leading the popular press to christen him the 'sex guru'.

Osho seems to have a *syncretic* philosophy, combining aspects of different schools of thought – Indian *Tantra* (spiritual – especially sexual – practices), meditation, Buddhism, Taoism, Zen. But in reality saw himself as a spiritual Master or *Bodhisattva*, a representative of the unified spiritual tradition of mankind (as, for instance, envisaged by Madame Blavatsky). However, he was also highly critical of many traditions – notably ascetic Christianity and Hinduism – and sought to foster his disciples' self-reliance, sense of wonder, and independence from all organized systems of thought and belief (which, since they were his *disciples*, reveals perhaps a tension in his approach!).

The most controversial aspect of his teaching, perhaps, is his attitude to wealth. Renowned for his love of luxury – Rolls-Royce cars (93 of them!), expensive watches and clothing – he claimed renunciation to be of no real benefit, and thus wealth, like sex and other forms of enjoyment, was no barrier to spirituality. In fact, wealth was central to what might be called *spiritual hedonism*: if the riches of spirituality consist of pleasure and selfless ecstasy, don't we all want to be rich?

'Sous les pavés, la plage!'
ANONYMOUS GRAFFITI
Paris, 1968

Towards the end of March 1968, at Paris University at Nanterre, students and cultural figures held a sit-in protest over issues of class discrimination and funding. As the situation escalated, it drew in students and workers' unions country-wide, culminating in disruptions that brought France to a halt and its government to near collapse.

'May 1968', as it is known, marked a turning point in French culture, uniting France's youth and intellectual elite in opposition to the dominant power structures, which they saw as fostering mindless consumer-capitalism as a means of social control. Many slogans from this time, splashed on posters and scrawled as graffiti, drew on the ideas of the *Situationists*, a loosely affiliated international group of Marxist-inspired revolutionary thinkers, writers and artists. The foremost of these was French philosopher Guy Debord (1931–1994), whose book, *Society and the Spectacle*, published the previous year, brilliantly dissected the capitalist agenda. France was in economic boom, nonplussing many commentators as to the cause of the unrest, but Debord argued that prosperity was simply a by-product of another means of authoritarian control. Since survival is, in most Western countries, no longer an issue, and technology gradually liberates the labour force, the populace must be persuaded to work to achieve 'higher' standards of living. Do you *really* need the latest gadget or novelty? If *you* don't, then your children's Christmas lists will take care of it. However, even should you *not* wish to be your darlings' wage slave, you have little choice, for society is geared towards consumerism *in general* – the 'spectacle', as Debord terms it – and to opt out is risky (check out shop doorways after midnight).

As protests continued, becoming more heated and confrontational, protestors noticed that beneath the uprooted paving blocks that they cheerfully hurled at Parisian riot police, there was sand. And thus, the slogan was born: 'Beneath the paving-stones, the beach!' Beneath the contrived world of consumer capitalism and social control, lay the real, natural world – and freedom?

'... if you find yourself a slave, do not accept your masters'
descriptions of the real; do not work within the boundaries of
their moral universe. Instead, try to create a reality of your
own by selecting aspects of the world that lend themselves
to your judgement of the worthwhile.'

RICHARD RORTY 1931–2007
Truth and Progress: Philosophical Papers Volume 3

Richard Rorty was an American philosopher who sought to dismantle
philosophy. Wittgenstein, perhaps, held similar attitudes, but Rorty
sees the *whole* of Western philosophy as founded on a misconception.
Traditionally, philosophy holds a mirror up to nature: there's a 'real',
separately existing world distinct from our descriptions and conceptions of it, and the job of philosophy is to show how a true understanding
of it is possible – a project which, Rorty argued, is profoundly
confused.

However, Rorty isn't arguing that the 'real' world doesn't exist,
merely that we can only ever have *descriptions* of it, where – since
there's nothing for these descriptions to correspond *to* (only other
descriptions) – each is as 'valid' as the next. What's to choose between
them? Rorty adopts a *pragmatist* attitude to truth: instead of 'that
which best corresponds to reality', truth is 'that which works best' – or,
as he says, that which is 'good to steer by'. But 'steer' to where? As our
quote suggests, people adopt descriptions which serve their own ends
– which they deem 'worthwhile'. But, even if he's right, doesn't this
lead to *relativism* (all perspectives are equal)? Also, don't we lose any
notion of progress? Is science no 'better' than superstition?

But Rorty neither rejects progress nor embraces *relativism* (all views
are equal), merely the claim that we gradually work towards absolute
truth and reality; we can still think in terms of moving toward goals
that the community shares. But what defines the majority or consensus opinion as 'right'? There seems to be a tension here between
Rorty's notion of 'truth' and progress: he can't *both* define progress in
terms of 'what most people want', whilst also claiming that we must
create a reality of our own – can he?

> 'If thinking is just carrying out a computation of some kind, then it
> might seem that we ought to be able to see this most clearly in our
> mathematical thinking. Yet, remarkably, the very reverse turns out to
> be the case. It is within mathematics that we find the clearest evidence
> that there must actually be something in our conscious thought
> processes that eludes computation.'
>
> ROGER PENROSE b.1931
> *Shadows of the Mind*

In *The Emperor's New Mind*, and its sequel, *Shadows of the Mind*,
English physicist and mathematician Roger Penrose argues – against
the tide of opinion – not only that computers can't be conscious (a
position known as *Strong Artificial Intelligence*, or *AI*), but also that
they cannot replicate human thought (*Weak AI*). If Weak AI is false,
then Strong AI must be, so Penrose's strategy aims to scupper the
whole debate before it gets off the ground.

Using ideas similar to Gödel's concerning the incompleteness of
mathematics, Penrose argues that, since computers use mathematical
algorithms (rule-based operations), such arguments must apply to
them. To illustrate this, he cites the famous *halting problem*. To sim-
plify Penrose's argument greatly, imagine that we asked a computer to
search for an odd number that's the sum of two even numbers.
Obviously, a human quickly realizes there's no such number, but a
computer won't – it will never *halt* the operation, but simply continue
searching through an infinite series of numbers.

Has Penrose proven that computers will never model human
thought? Not necessarily. John Searle, whilst sharing Penrose's opposition to Strong AI, thinks Penrose makes the mistake of assuming
that a successful computer model of the mind must be based on provable mathematical theorems. However, it needn't: whilst the machine
will never 'realize' that it should halt the procedure, we can programme in that realization. Also, of course, there may be procedures
that a human mind doesn't yet realize are pointless.

And yet, Penrose seems to be on to something. Perhaps there are
certain capacities of the mind which aren't rule based: is there an algorithm for insight?

'He alone is aware of the truth, and if all men were aware of it, there would be an end of life. In the country of the blind, the one-eyed man is king. But the kingship is kingship over nothing. It brings no powers and privileges, only loss of faith and exhaustion of the power to act. Its world is a world without values.'

COLIN WILSON b.1931
The Outsider

Colin Wilson is an English writer, none of whose prolific output – covering psychology, philosophy, religion, crime, literature – has yet to overshadow the impact of his very first book, *The Outsider*, written when only 24. In it, he focuses on the significance of the misfit and the rebel, whom, he argues, is often the type from which the great creative and innovative figures of history have been drawn.

Through case studies of various figures – Nietzsche, Sartre, Camus, Gurdjieff, Dostoevsky, Kafka – he claims that the basis of their value to society lies in their isolation and alienation: because they don't think and feel as others, they're in a better position to evaluate what others are blinded to. I think he's right in this, especially as concerns the great philosophers: the ability to philosophize has always assumed a prior capacity to *disengage* from life, to step back and to judge dispassionately (or at least, *more* dispassionately).

The problem, however, is that such disengagement and alienation leads to disenchantment. Ordinary meaning and purpose are denied to the outsider. What, then, is he to do? Wilson's outsiders have developed 'lopsidedly' – intellectually, physically, or emotionally – at the expense of other aspects (which is partly what estranges them from others). Like Gurdjieff, then, Wilson sees the outsider's alienation as a starting point: he must work towards integration, towards the building of a new ideal, and a new man.

Wilson's philosophy is therefore a curious blend of *existentialist* nihilism, Gurdjieff's emphasis on change, and Nietzsche's pursuit of a self-created ideal – the latter considered by Wilson to have been, in effect, 'a religious mystic'. Does this then also describe Wilson?

> '... there is in us a disposition to believe propositions of the sort *this flower was created by God* or *this vast and intricate universe was created by God* when we contemplate the flower or behold the starry heavens or think about the vast reaches of the universe'
> ALVIN PLANTINGA b.1932
> 'Is Belief in God Properly Basic?'

Foundationalism argues that beliefs are rational when they're well-founded, and either so obvious that we cannot doubt them, or else based on such beliefs. However, the problem here – as Descartes illustrates – is that we can always question *how* we know that a foundational belief is beyond doubt (and thus open up a can of worms).

So, certain philosophers therefore argue for what's termed 'reformed epistemology', which, whilst maintaining that claims to knowledge should be based on *basic* beliefs, rejects the claim that such beliefs should themselves be beyond doubt. This has the benefit of allowing us to consider our day-to-day beliefs rational, even though they may not be absolutely certain.

American philosopher Alvin Plantinga argues that belief in God may be considered in this way. If 'the real world exists', and 'I exist' can both be basic beliefs (though open to doubt), then why not 'God exists'? So, this isn't a proposition that requires evidence, but rather a basic, foundational belief that sits alongside the other tenets of my faith, such as 'God has created all this', or 'God disapproves of what I have done'.

But if basic beliefs needn't be beyond doubt, couldn't I choose to believe *anything*, such as that the Great Pumpkin returns every Halloween? No, because general standards of rationality still apply, just as they would if I claimed the 'real' world didn't exist, or that 'I' am a figment of a dream.

Plantinga's point about foundationalism seems fair: if no beliefs are beyond doubt, we must relax the criteria. However, what if I *don't* feel that 'this vast and intricate universe was created by God'? Doesn't this make choice of belief subjective? Why believe in God?

> 'The reason that no computer program can ever be a mind is simply
> that a computer program is only syntactical, and minds are more than
> syntactical. Minds are semantical, in the sense that they have more
> than a formal structure, they have a content.'
>
> JOHN SEARLE b.1932
> *Minds, Brains and Science*

You're in a room with two hatches. Through one hatch come tiles with Chinese symbols. You look them up in a book, which tells you which tiles to select from a stack of similar tiles. You then send these out the other hatch. You have no idea what the symbols mean, and are merely following rules. Are you speaking Chinese?

Most people would answer 'No'. Knowledge of a language requires more than blindly following rules without understanding what is said. But, says Searle, this is what computers do. Computer processes are *syntactical* (involving *syntax* or rules). So, computers can't 'understand', because understanding is *semantical* (involving *semantics* or meaning); computers deal with *form*, not *content*.

Searle's argument targets *Strong AI* (*Artificial Intelligence*), which argues that a computer perfectly mimicking human brain function would possess intelligence, understanding, and even consciousness. Searle disagrees, pointing out that – whilst machines can, in a sense, 'think' (the *Weak AI* view) – they'll always lack human understanding and awareness.

If Searle is right, this isn't just a problem for AI enthusiasts and Hollywood scriptwriters, but also the computer model of the brain. If brains do more than computers can, then – surely – brains *are more* than mere computers.

Some dismiss Searle's objections: the man in the room may not understand Chinese, but nor do individual neurons in the brain (which is the level at which the analogy must be understood); but taking processes as a whole (*lots* of men in Chinese *rooms*, perhaps), *then* we have understanding. However, this misses the point: understanding relies on *consciousness* and the fact that things *mean* something *to you*. You could put the *whole population of China* in 'Chinese rooms' and they still wouldn't *truly* understand Chinese. Oh – hang on . . .

> '. . . the only significant test of the existence of extraterrestrial intelligence is an experimental one. No *a priori* arguments on this subject can be compelling or should be used as a substitute for an observational program.'
> CARL SAGAN 1934–1996
> 'The Abundance of Life-Bearing Planets'

There is much that is of philosophical interest in the search for extra-terrestrial life, not least of which is the question of whether such expensive programmes don't simply siphon off money that would be much better spent on schools, hospitals, etc.

American astrophysicist and astronomer Carl Sagan was a prominent and vocal advocate for programmes aimed at searching for alien life, and was instrumental in the promotion of SETI (the programme for the Search for Extra-Terrestrial Intelligence). His argument was basically that, whilst there are long odds against the development of humanoid life on any planet, the odds shorten when we consider (a) the size of the universe, and (b) the strong possibility that life may develop to intelligence-supporting levels in *non-humanoid* forms. Thus, basically, *Star Trek* or *Star Wars* might be right, and rationally intelligent life may develop at numerous places using (for instance) reptiles as a basis, or slugs, or whatever.

The problem with this is obviously (as Hume argued) that we have only the one instance of a life-supporting planet to base our analysis on (our own). We assume that life will take a broadly similar evolutionary course, but we just don't know. Also, given the vast size of even our own solar system (which, using current technology, would take many years to cross), it is likely that any alien civilization, even if it were to arise in the nearest possible place, is far beyond our means of visiting. Unless, of course, such a civilization had evolved vastly superior technology to ours, so that crossing the immense reaches of space did not represent the barrier to exploration that it currently does to us (and even this is wishful thinking). So, even *if* we could determine that life exists, does it leave anything for us to do but stare longingly at a distant star?

> 'When deep religious believers pray *for* something, they are not so
> much asking God to bring this about, but in a way telling him of the
> strength of their desires. They realize that things may not go as they
> wish, but they are asking to be able to go on living whatever happens.'
>
> D. Z. PHILLIPS 1934–2006
> *The Concept of Prayer*

Dewi Zephaniah Phillips, often just D. Z., was a Welsh philosopher
prominent in philosophy of religion. Influenced by Kierkegaard,
Simone Weil and especially Wittgenstein, Phillips promoted an alternative perspective on religious faith, which he claimed to rescue from
common misunderstandings.

In *The Concept of Prayer*, Phillips provides an account of what he
considers religious believers attempt to achieve when petitioning
God. Resisting what he views as shallow misreadings, he claims that
true believers don't use prayer to 'change God's mind', but rather pray
not to change events (though they might wish that), but *to have the
strength* to cope with whatever happens. Thus, fearing someone may
die, I *pray* that they don't, but in doing so I seek to make peace with
God's will. Thus, the purpose of prayer is to change *us*, or that which
would make us unhappy should things go other than as we wish –
namely, our own desires.

However, some think Phillips a *pious atheist*, his apology for religion pleasing neither traditional religious believers nor non-believers.
The reason for this is that Phillips essentially argues that religious
language is *non-referential*. That is, in using terms like 'God' and
'spirit', etc., we don't present a scientifically testable hypothesis, and
nothing that can settle the matter for sceptic or devout. In this, he
echoes Wittgenstein's attitude to the primitive's rain dance, which isn't
a superstitious appeal for divine favour, but a merely expressive act.
Similarly, then, Phillips sees prayer – and all religious belief – as constituting a particular emotional and attitudinal approach to life, which
can never, in itself, contradict science or accepted knowledge. But is
this what the faithful *really* believe? Is Phillips *rescuing* or *misrepre-
senting* religion?

'Many women do not recognize themselves as discriminated against;
no better proof could be found of the totality of their conditioning'
KATE MILLETT b.1934
Sexual Politics

With the publication of her freshly completed Ph.D. thesis at Columbia University, American feminist philosopher Kate Millett created a runaway bestseller, transforming its author into the 1970s' spokeswoman of the second wave of feminism. Whilst 'first wave' feminism, exemplified by the *suffragettes*, concentrated on establishing equal voting and property rights, the second wave, whilst it also addressed legal issues, focused more broadly on women's status in society: are women seen as equal, and treated with the same degree of respect as men? The answer, for Millett, was no.

Most human societies, Millett argued, possess a *patriarchal* structure: families, businesses, institutions, and society itself, defer to a male authority figure (*patriarch*). The father, director, headmaster, governor, are therefore symbolic expressions of male dominance, their continued presence in supposedly democratic societies showing that, fundamentally, nothing has changed. Women still do men's bidding – bear and raise children, keep house, service sexual needs. Furthermore, these roles – mother, lover, maid, mistress – are *culturally* (not *biologically*) assigned, yet so ingrained that women often fail to recognize the fact, and frequently dismiss attempts to point this out: they're happy. But being content under certain conditions doesn't make those conditions right: a caged animal may be 'happy' if fed and not mistreated, but it's still caged.

However, whilst Millett's book reinvigorated feminism, and inspired others such as Germaine Greer, Andrea Dworkin and Gloria Steinem, it's also been criticized (e.g. by Camille Paglia) for 'institutionalizing negativity toward men' by creating a stranglehold of fear over the expression of traditional manliness. Of course, Millett and other feminists would respond that such manliness is only really sexist bigotry, and such men dinosaurs fearing change and loss of power. Whatever the case, feminism is no longer unified in its simple opposition to *patriarchy*; as Paglia's backlash shows, modern feminism – its *third* wave – is now as likely to be found fighting itself.

'. . . strictly speaking, *traits* don't get selected at all; traits don't either win competitions or lose them. What wins or loses competitions are *the creatures that have the traits.*'

JERRY FODOR b.1935

'Against Darwin'

When Jimmy got 'flu, Granny made her famous restorative cordial. Jimmy liked it so much, he told friends – Granny drafted helpers to meet demand. Her secret ingredient? Not, as she thinks, rosehip, but cocaine. The bag of white powder in the cupboard (belonging to her elder grandson with the rock-star lifestyle) wasn't sugar. Restorative indeed.

For 'Granny' read 'Natural Selection'; for 'secret ingredient' read 'significant trait' (this is similar to, but slightly different from the example that Fodor uses, incidentally). Darwinists think creatures are 'selected for' significant traits, just as Granny believes in rosehip. However, selection involves creatures (cordial), *not* individual traits (ingredients).

Are cheetahs selected for speed? Perhaps they're just in the right place at the right time. If Noah had two arks, and one was sunk by a typhoon, are the creatures on the surviving ark selected because of their *traits*? No. Similarly then, explanations of how animal *x* was 'selected for' trait *y* are actually historical or *post hoc* explanations (after the fact). But historical explanations don't identify natural laws, merely detail events: that mud mired his cavalry was a factor in Napoleon's defeat at Waterloo, but there is no 'law of battles' involving mud. The danger is that natural selection becomes a 'just so' story: how the peacock got its tail. Since it's the *peacock* that was selected, the tail may have *no* evolutionary significance. Because a story fits the facts doesn't make it a *lawlike explanation* of the facts.

But Fodor, an American philosopher, isn't advocating creationism, design, or even theism, merely being sceptical about natural selection. There's *some* natural explanation why traits survive, but it isn't as neat as Darwinists assume. Such laws, if they exist, might not be the ones we think, or be infinitely complex; perhaps, for instance – the biologist's worst nightmare – evolution is determined by quantum mechanics.

> 'Fundamentally an organism has conscious mental states if and only if
> there is something that it is to *be* that organism – something it is like
> *for* the organism'
>
> THOMAS NAGEL b.1937
> 'What is it like to be a bat?'

Whilst neuroscientists try to figure out how the brain produces consciousness, philosophers are more concerned with how consciousness fits into our understanding of the physical world. This is the *mind-body* problem: is consciousness separate from the physical, produced by it, or identical with it? All answers to this question have to account for the fact that *we* appear to be subjectively aware, whilst *other* things aren't: stones aren't (as far as we know), and even forms of life lower down the evolutionary chain may not be (molluscs, plants, etc.). American philosopher Thomas Nagel therefore argued that what decides the question of whether creatures are conscious or not is whether *there is something it is like* to be that creature.

In a famous article, 'What is it like to be a bat?', Nagel argued that knowing the physiological properties of a creature wasn't enough to tell us about the subjective qualities of its experience (what later philosophers term *qualia*). Presumably, there is something it is *like* to be a bat, but its sensory apparatus is so different from ours that we can't even guess what its subjective experience is like. We could *imagine*, but that would simply be based on *our own* experiences (linked to our own brains and senses) and therefore likely to be wrong.

However, if we can't know a bat's *qualia* from its physical properties, then perhaps subjective experience is a distinct aspect of reality. Nagel is not necessarily proposing that consciousness is a special type of 'soul stuff', but merely pointing out that subjective experience may not be reducible to objective properties: the taste of sugar is *more* than just an account of how our taste buds are triggered in certain ways, sending messages to our brain, etc. The *qualia* of sweetness is something that brain science can never capture.

'Ultimately, nothing or almost nothing about what a person does
seems to be under his control'
THOMAS NAGEL
Moral Luck

An assassin, lining up his target from a grassy knoll, has his bullet intercepted by a passing bird; simultaneously, from the book depository across the street, his accomplice's bullet finds its mark. When they are both caught, one is tried for murder, whilst the other is tried for the lesser crime of attempted murder.

Unfair? Kant thought so. We should be judged primarily according to our intentions, not their consequences. Actions motivated purely by duty (what Kant termed the 'good will') are moral; those motivated solely by inclinations, however noble – a desire to be liked, affection for someone – are not. You see someone starving, feel pity, and give them money for food. But unless you also help them out of a rational recognition of your moral duty, you have the wrong motivation. Kant has a point: pity also motivates immoral acts ('Aw! The poor psychopath's lost his axe! Here, have mine.'). So, both assassins should be judged equally, for only chance separates them.

However, chance plays a role in any number of situations: you are impressionable, fall in with a bad crowd, and end up a criminal; if you had fallen in with a *good* crowd, you might not have. Such examples suggest that both good and bad deeds are heavily determined by what Bernard Williams terms 'moral luck' – by things outside of our control: our upbringing, our genetic makeup, the circumstances surrounding our actions. Perhaps, then, intentions aren't as relevant as we think. As Thomas Nagel puts it:

> '. . . there is a morally significant difference between rescuing someone from a burning building and dropping him from a twelfth-storey window while trying to rescue him.'

Consequences do matter. However, whilst, as Nagel and Williams argue, moral luck upsets utilitarianism and Kantianism alike, taken to its extreme it also seems to undermine moral responsibility itself. If the Nazi concentration camp guard was simply 'unlucky', then can't we apply that to *every* immoral action?

> 'We all ask the big why occasionally. I wanted to know why our society
> was willing to pauperize a man of such integrity. I thought I would do
> something about it.'
>
> NOEL RILEY, SPEAKING OF JULIUS TOMIN b.1938
> *New York Times*, Nov. 7, 1988

Julius Tomin is a Czech philosopher who fled to Britain in 1980 as a political dissident. Initially invited by academics at Oxford University, he allegedly fell out of favour when he proposed an alternative chronology of Plato's dialogues (horror of horrors . . .). Forced to claim welfare benefit, this was stopped when – though seeking academic work – he refused to consider any other form of employment except street sweeper (which would at least allow him to think). Commenting on the failure of his appeal, he said:

> 'My work is the best contribution I can make to society but it demands full-time commitment . . . Society should be prepared to give a philosopher elementary support . . . In Prague it was the police who tried to silence me and here it is the DHSS [Dept. of Health and Social Security].' (*The Age*, Sept. 19, 1988)

However, the situation took an unexpected but delightful turn when Noel Riley, the landlord of the Beehive pub, Swindon, offered the philosopher three years' financial support in return for delivering occasional lectures at his pub.

> 'I was horrified to read about his plight . . . I'd been thinking about buying a new car, then I thought: sod it, I'll have a philosopher instead.' (*The Age*)

This whimsical story made the papers internationally, but most ignored the underlying issues. Since then, despite occasional work, Tomin has claimed continued academic neglect – both in the UK and Czechoslovakia. Certainly, it's true that, as philosopher Michael Dummett observed (*Independent*, Aug. 20, 1988), 'Before the war universities had the resources to create posts for refugee scholars escaping persecution in their own countries.' Now, there's dwindling funding for studies with less 'social impact' (philosophy especially). Perhaps, then, Tomin's plight is merely early warning of the exclusion of philosophy itself. One for the road?

> 'Suppose there were an experience machine that would give you any experience you desired. Superduper neuropsychologists could stimulate your brain so that you would think and feel you were writing a great novel, or making a friend, or reading an interesting book. All the time you would be floating in a tank, with electrodes attached to your brain . . . Would you plug in? What else can matter to us, other than how our lives feel from the inside?'
>
> ROBERT NOZICK 1938–2002
> *Anarchy, State and Utopia*

The 'experience machine' of American philosopher Robert Nozick is meant to show that human beings aren't just slaves to the *pleasure principle*; that is, we are not mere *hedonists*, who consider pleasure the chief and only good. However, to differentiate it from the headlong pursuit of sensual pleasure, philosophers talk of *ethical hedonism*, which has two aspects. Firstly, it argues that humans are basically pleasure-seeking machines; secondly, it prescribes that we ought therefore to maximize that pleasure. Freud can perhaps be cited as an example of someone who advocated the first, but not the second point (we chase pleasure, but shouldn't), whilst utilitarian Jeremy Bentham held both. However, if the first is false – as Nozick argues – then there would seemingly be no support for the theory in general: if we reject the experience machine, then we aren't merely concerned with maximizing pleasure, and aren't ethical hedonists.

We *hope* we're not mere pleasure junkies, that our lives possess purpose and meaning, but the machine supplies 'higher' and not just 'base' forms of pleasure (e.g. publishing a great novel), so its lure would be more subtle than we might at first suppose: effectively, it offers the chance to programme our own paradise, whatever that means.

But wouldn't the knowledge that the paradise was false eventually sour our experiences? It would be like the disappointment of waking up from a dream of winning the lottery. However, to say that the machine wouldn't satisfy us does not necessarily disprove ethical hedonism: perhaps desire for pleasure is simply not as straightforwardly satisfied as we might think.

'. . . an unspecified number of monkeys on Koshima were washing sweet potatoes in the sea. . . . Let us say, for argument's sake, that the number was ninety-nine and that at eleven o'clock on a Tuesday morning, one further convert was added to the fold in the usual way. But the addition of the hundredth monkey apparently carried the number across some sort of threshold, pushing it through a kind of critical mass, because by that evening almost everyone was doing it. Not only that, but the habit seems to have jumped natural barriers and to have appeared spontaneously . . . in colonies on other islands . . .'

LYALL WATSON 1938–2008
Lifetide

Lyall Watson was a South African biologist, anthropologist and writer, best known for his book *Supernature*, a biological perspective on the supernatural, and for the concept of 'the Hundredth Monkey'. The latter is based on the research of Japanese scientists studying macaque monkeys, who – claimed Watson, who interviewed them – feared to report it for ridicule. The idea suggests that new social behaviour can spread through a whole group if it reaches *critical mass*, when the 'hundredth monkey' adopts it. Gaining popular acceptance, the idea has been more broadly applied to concepts and attitudes, thus becoming a general metaphor for hope: one person *can* make a difference, for you may just be the 'hundredth monkey' that tips the balance.

However, critics such as Ron Amundson have doubted Watson's claims. Firstly, there's no evidence of isolated monkeys on other islands adopting the practice – and even if there were, this may have occurred accidentally (as in the original group), or through 'migrant' monkeys swimming to other islands. Secondly, the 'critical mass' observation seems to have been Watson's invention – who, it turned out, hadn't interviewed the scientists, but merely relied on unconfirmed report.

I think this episode reveals more about *humans* than monkeys: we're desperate to make a difference, and eagerly seize upon any reason that suggests we can. Perhaps, then, the best evidence of the hundredth monkey is the idea itself – which has spread like – well, washing sweet potatoes in the sea! Will it reach critical mass?

'The meme for blind faith secures its own perpetuation by the simple
unconscious expedient of discouraging rational inquiry'
RICHARD DAWKINS b.1941
The Selfish Gene

Coined by English evolutionary biologist Richard Dawkins, the idea of
the *meme* has spread – well, like a meme! Inspired by the transmission
of hereditary information in *genes*, Dawkins rather whimsically proposed that cultural information spread in a similar way. So, the catchy
song you can't stop whistling, the joke you heard on the radio, the
latest piece of slang – all these are *replicators*, spreading by making
copies of themselves. Whilst genes self-replicate by bringing about the
means of their own survival – through reproduction, bacteria and
viruses, etc. – *memes* do a parallel job in society: a song spreads by
having a hummable melody, a meaningful message, or a backer who
knows radio station producers. So, whereas a gene is a unit of *genetic*
information, a meme is a unit of *cultural* information.

Culture and society is therefore a battleground where memes live
or die – are *culturally selected* or not. But what, then, marks the *fitness*
of a meme? This would seem to differ according to the type of meme:
a song can be catchy, but a joke must be funny, a hairstyle attractive –
but what about ideas? As our main quote suggests, to survive, an idea
need not be true (for Dawkins at least): as with its biological brother,
cultural evolution does not necessarily preserve the best or most
admirable examples, as can be seen from any cursory analysis of what
has been popular at any one time in history.

And yet, whilst musical tastes change, fashions come and go, and
humour varies, religion lives on. Dawkins – an ardent atheist – sees
this as a sign that people prefer irrational fantasy to sober reality, not
questioning to facing uncomfortable truths. Possibly. But since popularity is not a sign of truth, neither is it a sign of error, and, believers
would argue, a meme that spans human history must at least have
something going for it.

'What we can expect to observe must be restricted by the conditions
necessary for our presence as observers'
BRANDON CARTER b.1942
'Large Number Coincidences and the Anthropic Principle in
Cosmology'

Wondering at nature's complexity, or awestruck at images from the
Hubble telescope, we may catch ourselves questioning how all this
can have come about by chance. This is the *design argument*: the universe, more specifically life, is too complex and ordered to be randomly
caused.

But if the world *weren't* ordered in this way, and life *hadn't* arisen,
we wouldn't be here to wonder at anything. This is called the *anthropic
principle*, a term coined by Australian astrophysicist Brandon Carter,
though the idea is older, which basically argues that the things that
make us wonder – uniformity, order, function – are the conditions
necessary for life. So, observers merely discover those conditions necessary for observers to exist!

The argument has two forms, *weak* (outlined above), and *strong*.
The strong version, considers the existence of observers as somehow
built into the nature of the universe. So, whilst the weak version suggests that other, lifeless universes *could* have existed, the strong
version implies that capacity to support life is part of what makes a
universe viable, or even that observers are required in order for the
universe to exist (such as quantum physics might argue, perhaps,
where observers 'create' events). Whichever version we accept, the
conclusion is the same: the universe appears handily designed because
if it weren't there wouldn't be anyone to observe that fact.

The anthropic principle is a variant of an argument used against
supposed evidence for psychic phenomena: you dream about something before it happens; but what of all those other occasions when
you *didn't*? So, both arguments highlight the danger of concluding
from limited experience: there were, or are, for all we know, many
'failed' universes, that don't support life. If so, the design argument
seems less convincing; if not, more tempting. But since we may never
know, don't both alternatives cancel each other out?

> 'Since the brain stem, not the heart, is recognized as the specific area which regulates all vital processes, it follows that after brain-stem death the heart and other organs can never again function naturally. At most the heart and lungs can be mechanically operated for two weeks. But during this period one would be merely ventilating a corpse. There are no reversals of brain-stem death.'
>
> DAVID LAMB b.1942
> 'Diagnosing Death'

Whether after uttering some last immortal words, or clutching, gasping and choking in agony, the portrayal of death in TV or film is often an all or nothing affair: you're alive; you're dead. But as anyone familiar with medical emergencies and critical care knows, death isn't as clear-cut as that.

The problem is comparatively new. Prior to modern resuscitation techniques and other forms of 'heroic' measure (as they're called), it was simpler: without heartbeat or breath, you were dead. However, since we're now able to bring people *back* from this state – through CPR (cardiopulmonary resuscitation), for instance – then we can no longer call it 'death'. This has resulted in the demise of the so-called *cardio-pulmonary* (heartbeat/respiration) definition of death. But what do we replace it with?

In the quote, Welsh philosopher David Lamb argues that, since the brain-stem controls and integrates all automatic activity (heartbeat, respiration, other *autonomic* function), then brain-stem death is death itself. But is it? The problem is that we have competing instincts as to what 'living' means. Is a 'brain-dead' body sustained by mechanical ventilators still 'alive', or are we – as Lamb puts it – merely 'ventilating a corpse'? Or, perhaps it's the absence of *consciousness*, not 'functional integration', which is significant? Thus, we can declare death merely when the *higher brain* (the cerebral cortex) is irreversibly damaged.

These controversies rage on, but the waters are further muddied by the continued advance of technology. Even if Lamb is right, and brain-stem death is sufficient for death itself, mightn't it one day be possible to develop an *artificial* brain stem? This would obviously make Lamb's definition redundant. Death, perhaps, isn't necessarily the end.

'There is no single, definitive "stream of consciousness," because there is no central Headquarters, no Cartesian Theatre where "it all comes together" for the perusal of a Central Meaner. Instead of such a single stream (however wide), there are multiple channels in which specialist circuits try, in parallel pandemoniums, to do their various things, creating Multiple Drafts as they go.'

DANIEL DENNETT b.1942
Consciousness Explained

We tend to think of the self as a little man (or woman) sitting in our head, looking out. He sits at a control desk, monitoring bodily function, emotion, etc., staring at the visual input from the eyes on a big display screen. Obviously, no one believes this *literally*, but it's a picture implied by the common notion of the 'I' or conscious self. American philosopher Daniel Dennett calls this the *Cartesian Theatre* model of the mind, which, stemming from Descartes, sees consciousness as taking place in a definite, central place in the brain, where the 'self' resides.

However, this *homunculus* view, as it's also called, presupposes what it tries to explain: how does the 'little man' *see* or *hear* things? Does he have a little man inside *his* 'head' too? Obviously, this is not a criticism of the belief in pixies, but of the idea that consciousness has a specific location where experiences are presented to a central point of awareness. This model is based on our daily experience: we experience the world from a central point (our physical bodies), so when we try to explain consciousness itself, this seems the most obvious model – but it's completely wrong.

Dennett's alternative is called the *Multiple Drafts model*. Rather than a unified point of consciousness, there are multiple neurological circuits that provide different perspectives (*drafts*) – spatial awareness, touch, emotion, movement – that experience constantly edits and updates. However, the notion of a central 'I' is a myth, an idea imposed upon experience when we 'interrogate' these different channels: in the many stories the brain writes, there's no single author, and no unifying plot.

The existence of subjective mental states or *qualia* suggests that consciousness isn't merely another physical property of the brain, like its weight or consistency. This seems to raise the question of whether a neurological account of brain processes 'leaves anything out'. In other words, are objective descriptions of brain processes necessarily incomplete because they cannot account for what it is like to be conscious?

Australian philosopher David Chalmers attempts to prove this with *zombies*. Imagine that zombies exist – not the *I'm-going-to-eat-your-brain* variety, but zombies identical to us in terms of behaviour, ability to communicate and think, etc. – with one important difference: they have no *qualia*. If we *can* conceive of such zombies, then *qualia* are real, and consciousness cannot be accounted for merely in physical terms.

Dennett and other *physicalists* disagree: since we *are* only physical beings, then zombies that are *physically* identical to us would be identical *full stop*. So, either zombies *aren't* conceivable, or *we're all zombies*! Dennett therefore effectively denies that *qualia* exist. Accordingly, his position is consistent with *strong artificial intelligence*: an artificial brain would be conscious.

This is a startling claim. Dennett isn't just saying that consciousness isn't some extra *spiritual stuff*, or that there's no 'I' with which to *be* conscious – which many philosophers would concur with – but actually that subjective experience is *illusory*: we think we have *qualia*, but it's all just smoke and mirrors. However, as John Searle points out, this *explains consciousness away*. To be illusory, there must be *something the illusion is like*. If I'm mistaken about seeing something, it's still true that I'm having an illusory experience; but how can I be mistaken about being conscious? Having an illusion *implies* being conscious.

Elsewhere, Dennett criticizes 'greedy reductionism': science *reduces* surface explanations to fundamental ones (e.g. colour to light waves), but sometimes goes too far, attempting to reduce *irreducible* things. But, ironically, isn't this what Dennett does with consciousness?

> 'The regularities of nature are not imposed on nature from a
> transcendent realm, but evolve within the universe. What happens
> depends on what has happened before. Memory is inherent in nature.
> It is transmitted by a process called morphic resonance, and works
> through fields called morphic fields.'
>
> RUPERT SHELDRAKE b.1942
> *A New Science of Life*

How do seeds become flowers? Conventional biology proposes that genetic instructions cause strings of amino acids to form protein molecules, in turn forming cells, etc. But how do these instructions produce the *form* of the flower? Controversial English biologist Rupert Sheldrake argues that they can't; there must be other factors which guide *morphogenesis* (the unfolding of structure and shape).

Each living thing has a *morphic field*, Sheldrake argues, an energy template or 'memory' that shapes genetically programmed processes. Without such fields, organic life would be an unassembled mass of molecules, for assuming that organic life simply assembles itself is like saying that 'if all the materials were delivered to a building site at the right times, the building would automatically assemble itself in the right shape as a result of blind physical forces' (*The Sense of Being Stared At*).

Yet morphic fields don't just guide morphogenesis, but also development of instincts, behaviour, social organization, and even concepts. Thus, such ideas can be used to account for seemingly 'uncanny' things – the social structures of bee hives or ant colonies, the flocking behaviour of birds, and so on.

Critics accuse Sheldrake of 'pseudoscience'. Morphic fields suppose the existence of a *vital force* that can exist separately from organic substance. Thus Sheldrake opposes the orthodox *mechanistic* view, placing himself with other scientific 'heretics' (e.g. Wilhelm Reich) whom academia would prefer to dismiss than engage with critically. The problem, of course, is that to take Sheldrake seriously science would have to question the cherished principle of *mechanism* – and is there really *sufficient reason* to do that?

'When I believed that my existence was such a further fact, I seemed imprisoned in myself. My life seemed like a glass tunnel, through which I was moving faster every year, and at the end of which there was darkness. When I changed my view, the walls of my glass tunnel disappeared. I now live in the open air.'

DEREK PARFIT b.1942
Reasons and Persons

A famous thought experiment, proposed by English philosopher Derek Parfit, imagines that future scientists invent a *teletransporter* that allows travel to other planets. It works by disassembling your physical cells, scanning their configuration, and sending that information via radio waves to your destination, where you are *reassembled*. Since, Parfit argues, you *are* no more than your physical body, then it doesn't matter that your 'old' body is destroyed, or that the 'new' one is built from fresh atoms, because it is the configuration – specifically, the memories and personality encoded in your physical brain – that matters.

However, one day the teletransporter malfunctions: instead of destroying your 'original' body, it merely produces a duplicate version of 'you'. To make matters worse, affected by the malfunction, your original body will soon die. Therefore, as you sit on Earth, watching 'yourself' on Mars on the video-phone, should you be content that 'you' will live on, or distraught at your approaching death?

This is a test of our intuitions concerning personal identity: if you're content, you share Parfit's view (your memories and personality are what's important); if you're distraught (probably the majority view), then you believe you're *more* than strings of memories – there is what Parfit terms a 'further fact' about yourself that makes you 'you'. However, aside from undermining the traditional notion that there's only one 'you', is Parfit's view *depressing* or *liberating*? Parfit argues that, by rejecting the 'further fact' notion of self, we gain a new freedom: death merely ends the illusion of a unique, unified self. Whilst 'I' die, things that were 'me' live on: physical processes, others' memories of me, possessions, etc. Don't you find this . . . reassuring?

> 'If aliens visit us, the outcome would be much as when Columbus
> landed in America, which didn't turn out well for the Native
> Americans . . . We only have to look at ourselves to see how intelligent
> life might develop into something we wouldn't want to meet.'
> STEPHEN HAWKING b.1942
> interview, *The Discovery Channel*, 2010

Setting aside the question of *whether* alien life exists, there's the problem of how we might communicate with it, or even whether we should. In 1972, NASA launched the *Pioneer 10*, a spacecraft designed to pass through the asteroid belt beyond the orbit of Mars, and relay back information about Jupiter – all of which it did successfully. However, aware that this would be a one-way trip, and thus that *Pioneer* would eventually pass out of our solar system, NASA took this opportunity to equip the craft with a message to any alien life forms that might be passing by.

Tasked with composing the message, Carl Sagan and fellow astrophysicist Frank Drake decided on representations of the solar system (indicating the *Pioneer*'s trajectory), the Sun's relation to the centre of our galaxy, some information concerning hydrogen (the most common universal element), and depictions of a nude man and woman – a thing which, in later versions of the message (on *Voyager* 1 and 2), was removed due to complaints. However, the end result is a highly cryptic, cosmic crossword puzzle that most humans would fail to decipher – what chance, then, have aliens? The mistake is to assume that the more abstract and scientific the knowledge, the more common a denominator it will be. Personally, I would have gone with more pictures.

English astrophysicist Stephen Hawking, who agrees with Sagan as to the likelihood of the existence of extra-terrestrial life, nevertheless argues that perhaps we shouldn't even be trying to make contact. Since any alien life capable of reaching us is likely to be more advanced, we're as likely to attract aggressive space-plunderers as enlightened beings. However, I don't think we should worry too much: given the directions, it's highly unlikely that they could find us anyway.

'. . . in the nineteenth and twentieth centuries, science became too technical and mathematical for the philosophers, or anyone else except a few specialists. Philosophers reduced the scope of their enquiries so much that Wittgenstein, the most famous philosopher of this century, said, "The sole remaining task for philosophy is the analysis of language." What a comedown from the great tradition of philosophy from Aristotle to Kant!'

STEPHEN HAWKING
A Brief History of Time

In *A Brief History of Time*, Stephen Hawking bemoans the path modern philosophers – 'the people whose business it is to ask *why*' – have taken, rejecting the 'big questions' in favour of 'the analysis of language'. This 'linguistic turn' in philosophy (as it's called) still characterizes much of Western philosophy in both its *Anglo-American* and *Continental* strains. Has philosophy therefore abdicated its true role?

In one sense, Hawking is right: modern philosophers *are* mostly shy of – even embarrassed by – the big questions. Of course, this doesn't imply that their work isn't meaningful, or even occasionally *useful* to society in general, but merely that – like the mathematical formulae of scientists such as Hawking himself – it's often too specialist for the layperson. And yet, what Hawking rues is merely part of a process that has seen science grow. Once dubbed 'Queen of the sciences', philosophy has seen its own fledglings flee the nest and set up on their own: mathematics, science, psychology, anthropology – all once sheltered under philosophy's 'wing'. Now – as Wittgenstein's quote reflects – to engage directly in any of these subjects seems like trespass.

But is this a wholly accurate picture? Whilst, in a sense, philosophy has retreated into narrower confines, it's also delved deeper into the question of knowledge itself. In lamenting the decline of philosophy, therefore, Hawking reveals an old-fashioned notion of what philosophy does – and a corresponding lack of awareness of what's its *currently* doing. For, whilst it seldom now walks hand in hand with science in search of knowledge, it increasingly questions the objectivity of the scientific world view itself – an approach perhaps which Hawking does not consider 'true philosophy'?

'. . . the basic units of human cognition are states such as thoughts, beliefs, perceptions, desires, and preferences . . . These assumptions are central elements in our standard conception of human cognitive activity, a conception often called "folk psychology" to acknowledge it as the common property of folks generally. Their universality notwithstanding, these bedrock assumptions are probably mistaken.'

PAUL CHURCHLAND b.1942
The Engine of Reason, The Seat of the Soul

The *mind-body* problem aside, philosophers also debate how physical systems (human brains) possess *intentionality* (beliefs, intentions, desires). Some argue that the mind *isn't* just a physical system. When your phone battery runs low, the phone doesn't 'feel a little run down' (as a human might). There's a difference, then, between physical and conscious systems: a mind has *intentional states*.

But if mind is just the brain, there are problems explaining belief, etc., in purely physical terms (e.g. how people will behave under certain circumstances): 'I believe it'll rain', doesn't necessarily mean 'I'll carry an umbrella' – I may *want* to get wet; similarly, I can think, 'I want to lose weight' and still eat a chocolate bar.

Given these and other difficulties, thinkers such as American philosopher Paul Churchland are more radical. Intentional states stem from 'folk psychology'; they don't really exist – no one *really* believes, perceives, or desires, just as the Sun doesn't *really* 'rise' or 'set' – they are just loose (mostly false) ways of speaking. Where such terms reflect the findings of science, we can keep them; where not, we should *eliminate* them. This approach is therefore called *eliminativism*.

However, apart from denying common sense (that I desire, believe, prefer), eliminativism treats 'folk psychology' as a primitive scientific theory. But is it? Admittedly, certain aspects of self-knowledge may be open to change or correction, or be culturally determined – what influences my choices, my sense of self – but such attitudes aren't *theories* as such: my belief in 'belief' isn't a working hypothesis! Furthermore, because something *can* be reduced to simpler elements, doesn't make its existence illusory. As John Searle argues, I'm not mistaken that cars and tables exist simply because they are made of atoms.

> 'It is not individual limitations, of whatever kind, which are the cause of the problem but society's failure to provide appropriate services and adequately ensure the needs of disabled people are fully taken into account in its social organisation'
>
> MIKE OLIVER b.1945
> 'The Individual and Social Models of Disability'

The medical model is still the basis of most public policy attitudes to disability, considering individuals 'disabled' by some personal limitation. This view, argues English disability rights activist Mike Oliver, stems from 'the personal tragedy theory of disability': it's very sad, but the whims of fate have determined that this or that person is born blind, suffers hearing loss, loses a limb, etc.

However, this situates the problem squarely with the disabled individual. Since the disabled are 'abnormal', there is, firstly, a pressure to achieve as close an approximation of 'normality' as possible – through physical rehabilitation, corrective surgery, drug treatments – thus going beyond merely helping the individual to cope with illness or suffering. Secondly, this 'medicalization of disability', leads to the view that the disabled individual must be treated, counselled, specially provided for, and otherwise patronized and disempowered. However, Oliver rejects the idea that this attitude is *purely* medical; rather, he suggests, it should be called the *individual model*, for medicalization is only an aspect of a more general discrimination against the disabled individual.

What, then, is the answer? Oliver proposes that we move from the *individual* to the *social model* of disability: society disables people, but it's not just 'disabled' people that it affects, but minorities of all types – and 'minority' here is defined by context. Steps not only 'disable' wheelchair users, but also pram-pushing mothers; awkward door handles are a struggle for children as well as those missing fingers. The social model therefore promotes *inclusivity*: not *special* provision for *special* cases (and the disempowerment this implies), but catering for *all* varieties of ability. Failure to adopt this approach merely highlights the fact that *social attitudes* are at the root of the problem: we are all only as able as society *enables* us to be.

'Empirically, all pornography is made under conditions of inequality based on sex, overwhelmingly by poor, desperate, homeless, pimped women who were sexually abused as children'
CATHARINE MACKINNON b.1946
Only Words

Catharine MacKinnon is an American lawyer, feminist and activist. She helped establish sexual harassment as a legal issue, and similarly sought (with Andrea Dworkin) to criminalize pornography as a form of sexual discrimination involving the exploitation of women. This latter issue became a *cause célèbre* when she attempted to obtain damages for Linda Boreman, star of pornographic film *Deep Throat*, for her alleged mistreatment by then husband Chuck Traynor, the film's production manager. Rare in its genre (possessing a plot and some production values), *Deep Throat* came close to mainstream acceptability and success, premiering, on its 1972 release, at the World Theater, New York, and advertized in the *New York Times*. However, public interest in 'porn chic' (as it became known) was short-lived.

MacKinnon contends that pornography causes harm, and isn't therefore protected by freedom of speech and expression. So, just as other forms of harm (theft, injury) merit damages, why not pornographic exploitation? However, harm – where not obvious – is sometimes a matter of personal perspective, involving notions of consent and free choice. If someone involved in pornography claims to be happy and freely consenting, what can be done? MacKinnon and Dworkin were therefore forced to argue that such women *don't know* what they're doing; they're harmed and exploited, but so brain-washed that they don't realize it.

But doesn't this undermine part of what defines morally acceptable action? Coercion is an issue for people with limited freedom (wage slaves) or immature or reduced rationality (children, drug addicts, the mentally impaired). But mature and rational adults are generally presumed to know what's good for them. It's a complex issue, but MacKinnon's cause is too broad: it's not just porn that harms women, she argues, but their *general* exploitation by men, thus diverting attention from the widely shared concern with morality and pornography. However, does rejecting MacKinnon's arguments force us to consider *some* pornography legitimate?

'If we can prevent something bad without sacrificing anything of
comparable significance, we ought to do it; absolute poverty is bad;
there is some poverty we can prevent without sacrificing anything of
comparable moral significance; therefore we ought to prevent some
absolute poverty'

PETER SINGER b.1946
Practical Ethics

Australian philosopher Peter Singer advocates *preference utilitarianism*:
instead of seeking actions that maximize happiness or pleasure (as
traditional utilitarianism does), we should seek to satisfy people's *preferences* or desires. This, ultimately, provides greater respect for
individual choice. For instance, your love of motor racing may result
in severe injury (or even death); therefore, in terms of risk of probable
injury, a traditional utilitarian might rule it out. However, preference
utilitarianism would say: it's legal, it's not harming anyone else, you
love it, so go for it!

Applying this to practical ethics often produces challenging results.
Singer's unflinching commitment to his utilitarian principles sometimes leads him into controversy – on abortion, on euthanasia, on
animal rights – and he's been accused of lack of respect for human
life, and even of advocating forms of genocide.

However, both Singer's first and his most recent books address the
question of poverty: if we can alleviate the worst forms of suffering,
shouldn't we, even to the point of causing *ourselves* hardship? For most
people, the question is not *whether* we should give, but *how much*. But
doesn't charity create a one-way dependency? Shouldn't we instead
seek long-term solutions to poverty, such as affecting political policy?
Well, says Singer, it's a gamble, for the benefits of immediate relief are
always much more tangible and certain than proposed long-term
solutions.

Perhaps, then, the answer isn't 'either/or', but 'both'? But even this
requires partly diverting efforts from immediate relief. And yet, isn't it
unrealistic to expect people to donate 25% of their earnings (as Singer
does)? Wouldn't such persuasive efforts be better focused on changing
the root causes of poverty? But we need to decide: are we to gamble on
human life?

'All the arguments to prove man's superiority cannot shatter this hard fact: in suffering the animals are our equals'

PETER SINGER

Animal Liberation

Peter Singer is most famous for his views on animal rights. His 1975 book, *Animal Liberation*, became the bible of the animal rights movement, arguing that treating animals differently from humans is actually 'speciesism' (prejudicial treatment based on belonging to a different species). If we believe that humans should not suffer needlessly, then why not animals? Furthermore, if we decide how beings should be treated based upon level of intelligence or conscious awareness, then certain large apes are more deserving than certain brain-damaged humans. Therefore:

'An animal experiment cannot be justifiable unless the experiment is so important that the use of a brain-damaged human would be justifiable.'

Obviously, most people would reject this – then shouldn't they also reject the use of animals?

Animal experimentation, like factory farming, represents something that most are dimly aware takes place, but prefer not to think about. And yet, whilst factory farming is a profit-driven evil, animal testing may be considered a necessary one. If we didn't test drugs and other substances on animals, we'd be severely hampered in terms of medical knowledge.

However, much animal testing – for cosmetics, shampoos and other beauty products – *isn't* absolutely necessary. Furthermore, humans can and do take part in drug trials, and something may even pass animal testing that is subsequently found to be harmful to humans, due to their different physiology.

But, to reiterate, Singer's point is more hard-line: it's not just that *some* testing is needless, but that it's *speciesist*. There *may* be cases where a greater good might result from animal testing, but this should also apply to the brain-damaged, etc. Is this callous? I think sometimes people miss Singer's true position: it's not that he's driven by love and respect for animals to treat them better (though this *may* be true); it's rather that he thinks animals should have an equal share in the utilitarian calculation – whatever the result.

'. . . the fact that a being is human, and alive, does not in itself tell us whether it is wrong to take that being's life'

PETER SINGER

Rethinking Life and Death

Some of Singer's most controversial views concern abortion. As with animals, Singer avoids the tricky question of rights, and concentrates instead on capacity to hold individual preferences and to feel pain or pleasure.

Firstly, fetuses have limited if any capacity for sensation, and therefore satisfaction or discontent. So, weighed against the fully conscious desires and preferences of its adult mother, the fetus loses out.

Secondly, even young babies don't possess the degree of *presonhood* (being a person) that adults do. Holding preferences requires certain capacities: *rationality*, the ability to formulate preferences and goals; *autonomy*, the power to make conscious choices; and *self-consciousness*, an awareness of oneself as an individual that benefits or suffers from living or dying. Other features might be suggested – being a conscious member of a community, possessing language, etc. – but reason, autonomy and self-consciousness would seem to represent the minimum needed for personhood. However, the baby seems to lose out here also, and so what chance does a fetus have?

Singer's views therefore seem to legitimize not only abortion, but even, in some cases, infanticide. There are also controversial consequences for euthanasia, conduct towards those with disability or brain damage, etc. However, are these uncomfortable consequences really the sign that we must accept the 'collapse of our traditional ethics' (as Singer argues)?

Not necessarily. Firstly, why not simply reject utilitarianism? If it leads to uncomfortable consequences, and has no room for ideas of the sanctity of life, then perhaps it actually distorts what ethics is. Secondly, we might adopt a different form of utilitarian calculation by considering the potential fulfilment involved in the fetus's *future* life. That would balance the scales somewhat. We need not adopt either of these positions, but they at least suggest the possibility that, even if something is not currently a person, it may still possess the right to life.

> 'Heterosexual intercourse is the pure, formalized expression of
> contempt for women's bodies. Rape is the primary emblem of
> romantic love.'
>
> ANDREA DWORKIN 1946–2005
> 'The Rape Atrocity and the Boy Next Door', Speech, 1975

The highly controversial reputation of American writer, radical feminist, and political activist Andrea Dworkin, continues to divide
opinion. Some see her as feminism's leading light, a campaigner for
sexual equality highlighting institutionalized oppression of women in
society; others, a deranged extremist, distorting sex itself into a crime
perpetrated on weak, passive women by a brutal patriarchal culture.
But who is right?

Analysis of key professions, political roles, wage structures, social attitudes, etc., suggests that, despite recent advances, male bias still exists.
However, Dworkin's arguments propose that *all* society, *all* heterosexual
relationships, even language itself, have a *patriarchal* structure.
Everything that men do is *phallic* – driven by masculine need to dominate and 'penetrate', symbolically and literally – creating woman as the
submissive object of his cruelty. Aside from rape, sexual abuse and
domestic violence, therefore, society's conventions of romantic love and
male notions of gender roles both provide a pretext for domination: the
hopeful date, brandishing his bottle of wine, is actually a 'rapist'.
Consequently, the only true sexual equality lies in the abolition of gender.

However, Dworkin's definition of traditional maleness itself as
sexual aggression isolates those otherwise sympathetic to the cause –
not simply 'normal' men, but gay men, and heterosexual women
seeking not just sexual equality but positive sexual expression. Some
critics therefore argue that Dworkin is *anti-sex*, distorting sexuality,
and high-jacking the equality movement to pursue her own man-
hating agenda. Dworkin's own personal experience of sexual violence,
and her advocacy of a *lesbian separatist*, independent, women-only
state with its own militia ('women need land and guns'), perhaps supports this interpretation. But apart from providing the bachelor party's
least likely holiday destination of choice, 'Womanland' reinforces the
satirical stereotype: sexual equality is merely the concern of a 'lunatic
fringe' who see the sexes as so fundamentally incompatible that they
cannot even occupy the same country.

'There is no female Mozart because there is no female Jack the Ripper'
CAMILLE PAGLIA b.1947
Sexual Personae

'Porn Wars' sounds like the sort of parody of mainstream culture that the pornographic industry is partial to, but it actually refers to an area of debate that began in the 1970s involving anti-pornography feminists, such as Andrea Dworkin and Catharine MacKinnon, and what has been termed *sex-positive feminism*, espoused by such as Ellen Willis and Betty Dodson.

Sex-positive feminism generally takes a liberal approach, arguing that in focusing on the oppression of women by men, and viewing sex as an expression of this relationship, traditional feminism failed to promote positive sexual values or show how a woman might find sexual fulfilment or freedom. Thus, sex-positive feminists number among them sex therapists and counsellors, sexual health workers, writers of feminist erotica (or *herotica*), and even workers in the sex industries.

Against this backdrop, American *third-wave* feminist Camille Paglia presents a radical alternative. Paglia highlights the irrational in human nature, and traces the darker aspect of sexuality not to *patriarchy*, but to the perpetual struggle between reason and passion, which – borrowing from Nietzsche – she characterizes as *Apollonian* and *Dionysian* respectively. Pornography is an expression of the Dionysian aspect of human nature, something that should be explored and selectively embraced, for to deny such forces – as Nietzsche himself claimed – is to deny life. So, the musical genius and the serial killer, like Apollo and Dionysus, are merely two inter-dependent sides of the same coin.

Paglia is provocative, controversial and not shy of weighing in on delicate topics with robust opinion – doubting the genetic basis of homosexuality, the truth of global warming. Following her criticism of traditional feminism, the backlash has been quite scathing: she's been compared to Hitler, accused of intellectual dishonesty and shock-tactics, and charged with glorifying male dominance. Guilty or not, Paglia represents a distinct third voice in the Porn Wars, which show no signs of a ceasefire.

> 'Just after the Second World War, in his series of lectures to the
> neo-Kantians of Paraguay, [Botul] proved that their hero was an
> abstract fake, a pure spirit of pure appearance'
>
> BERNARD-HENRI LÉVY b.1948
> *On War in Philosophy*

Bernard-Henri Lévy, Algerian-born French philosopher and journalist, is the founder of the 'New Philosophers' (*Nouveaux Philosophes*), a group aligning itself in opposition to Marxism and what it sees as other forms of totalitarianism. However, Lévy and its other members have become as much media celebrities as intellectuals, appearing regularly on TV and in popular magazines – even *Playboy*.

Such exposure has led some to question Lévy's intellectual integrity: isn't he more concerned with image and fame than with actually doing philosophy? Such critics were therefore gleeful when it emerged that in his latest book – a damning critique of Immanuel Kant – Lévy quotes from the work of Jean-Baptiste Botul to support his claim that Kant was a 'fake'. Unknown to Lévy, however, it was Botul that was the fake, a fictional philosopher invented by Frédéric Pagès (journalist at French satirical publication *Le Canard Enchaîné*) as a lampoon on the very sort of shallow and inadequately supported philosophy that some have accused Lévy himself of producing. Lévy however blustered through the ridicule: whether Botul or Pagès, the arguments were sound, and he stood by them.

Botul-ism, as we might term it, is an increasingly common danger. Even researching this story on the Internet, the same details, phrases and quotes are passed on and repeated uncritically. Is it any wonder, then, that even forefront intellectuals have succumbed to this culture of expediency? Faced with a broadening sea of information, even careful researchers must occasionally rely on broad generalization, or else trust in second-hand opinion: no one has the time to read everything. As human knowledge increases, therefore, *Botul-ism* becomes more likely. We might even formulate 'Botul's law': facing an exponential increase in information, all we know will either become too general to be accurate, or too narrow to be practical. Eventually, no one will know anything.

> 'In the world shown to us by Darwin, there is nothing that can be
> called progress. To anyone reared on humanist hopes this is
> intolerable. As a result, Darwin's teaching has been stood on its head,
> and Christianity's cardinal error – that humans are different from all
> other animals – has been given a new lease on life.'
>
> JOHN GRAY b.1948
> *Straw Dogs*

Modern humanism puts man at the centre of the universe, and points him on a path of progress, rationality, and moral self-improvement. In *Straw Dogs*, English philosopher John Gray undermines these cherished notions, arguing that, since we're merely semi-conscious, largely irrational animals, driven by instinct with little capacity for self-control and moral behaviour, there is no progress: we are what we are.

Humanism is therefore nothing more than a secular reworking of Christian themes: however, instead of 'salvation', we have progress – to improve society, to advance knowledge, to establish behaviour on rational grounds. However, such 'salvation' is illusory. Darwinism, to which modern humanists often appeal to bolster their faith in *human* evolution, can actually supply nothing of the sort: there's no 'progress' in nature, no long-term goal, merely adaptation and diversification.

Gray also attacks other humanistic holy cows. Invoking Hume and Buddhism, he argues that self is an illusion. Following Freud, that consciousness is a tiny, ineffectual part of self, which is driven by irrational unconscious forces; that rational morality is a sham, and – as Schopenhauer and Nietzsche argued – nothing more than the expression of instinctual drives. Therefore, we shouldn't try to improve humanity, but simply attempt to see life clearly for what it is, and which of the above illusions we can live without.

Bleak, isn't it? Gray's points are not new, but pull together already existing strands into a coherent vision. Underlying it all, however, is Schopenhauer's pessimism: hope, it says, is a meaningless indulgence. And yet, in attacking the tendency to divorce man from animal, hasn't Gray gone too far? Illusory or not, doesn't our distinction from animals lie in the very fact that we have such ideals?

> 'Cyberspace. A consensual hallucination experienced daily by billions of legitimate operators, in every nation, by children being taught mathematical concepts . . . A graphic representation of data abstracted from banks of every computer in the human system. Unthinkable complexity. Lines of light ranged in the nonspace of the mind, clusters and constellations of data. Like city lights, receding into the distance . . .'
>
> WILLIAM GIBSON b.1948
> *Neuromancer*

The term cyberspace first appeared in 1982 in 'Burning Chrome', a short story by American author William Gibson, and is a contraction of *cybernetic space*. Whilst most were struggling to get to grips with the first home computers, Gibson envisaged a *virtual reality* – a 'nonspace of the mind' – where human interaction, information exchange, and data access and manipulation took place using 'graphical representations'. Today, whilst the precise details of Gibson's vision remain an unrealized (but nearing) possibility, the notion of cyberspace – as a 'nonspace' where 'virtual' things happen – is an increasingly important one.

However, cyberspace *isn't* the Internet – the many interconnected computer networks spanning the globe – nor the World Wide Web – those networks publicly accessible via protocols pioneered by scientist Tim Berners-Lee. Rather, cyberspace is where you *go* when accessing the Internet or the Web. This might seem fanciful, for the 'going' is only metaphorical – we don't *actually* 'visit' or 'leave' a website. And yet, our day-to-day reality is also in a sense 'metaphorical': if I see my friend Ben, it's not so much 'him' I see as his body, his behaviour, etc. But he's not (or not *only*) these things, but a *construction* (a personality or identity) built upon them. Similarly, if I talk on the phone, the conversation isn't 'in my head', or somewhere along the phoneline, but in a sort of *nonspace* which does and doesn't exist.

These are slippery issues, but the point is that public or shared space is virtual in the same way that cyberspace is; neither *really* exist – at least, not separately from their human users: they are, in Gibson's words, 'a consensual hallucination'. You didn't realize you're living in the matrix, did you?

'When you are put into the Vortex you are given just one momentary glimpse of the entire unimaginable infinity of creation, and somewhere in it a tiny little mark, a microscopic dot on a microscopic dot, which says, "You are here".'

DOUGLAS ADAMS 1952–2001
The Restaurant at the End of the Universe

In his bestselling *A Hitchhiker's Guide to the Galaxy* series of books, English author Douglas Adams allowed his fertile and quirky imagination free play over many of the central problems of philosophy. The beauty of this is that it's not done in a systematic way – there is no underlying 'philosophy' to Adams' books – but rather out of love of the perplexing and often absurd nature of philosophical problems. With humour, insight and clarity, Adams illustrates what many academically trained philosophers have struggled to put into a popular form.

However, if there is an underlying theme to the books, it's that our perspective on life is only one among many, and that human knowledge and values often distort reality into an *anthropocentric* (human-centred) form. So, throughout the books, Adams has great fun in overturning the assumption that humanity is central to the development of the universe: the Earth is demolished to make way for an 'interstellar bypass', dolphins are discovered to be a more-evolved and intelligent form of alien life, and the Earth and humanity itself is revealed to be part of an experiment conducted by 'hyper-intelligent pan-dimensional beings' that look a lot like mice.

The overall message is therefore that 'we're not as important as we think'. This is echoed in James' Lovelock's *Gaia* theory, and Adams' own concern with endangered species, for if human disrespect for the environment were to jeopardize the natural balance, then Nature might simply wipe us out. Perhaps the clearest illustration of our cosmic insignificance is provided by an imagined torture device called the 'Total Perspective Vortex', which presents a virtual reality mock-up of the universe, with a miniscule dot labelled 'you are here'. Against the backdrop of infinity, human concerns barely register.

'[Cow:] May I urge you to try my liver, it must be very rich and tender by now, I have been force feeding it for months?

[Arthur:] Is there any reason why I shouldn't have a green salad?

[Cow:] I know many vegetables who are very clear on that point, sir, which was why it was decided to cut through that whole problem by breeding an animal that actually wanted to be eaten.'

DOUGLAS ADAMS
The Restaurant at the End of the Universe

A central concern of animal rights is the question of suffering. If animals are sentient, philosophers such as Bentham argue, we have a duty to ensure their welfare, though not perhaps to refrain from eating them (it doesn't seem that Bentham was vegetarian). As Kant argued, animals aren't rational, and so their death doesn't frustrate any long-term plans they might possess. So, sentience isn't itself an argument against eating meat if animals are ethically reared and killed painlessly and without distress.

But does inability to think, 'I'd like to eat grass tomorrow', legitimize killing something? What about living or sentient *humans* who lack rational thought? Can we treat the mentally impaired or the irreversibly comatose in whatever way we please, terminating their lives and harvesting their organs, or using them for medical testing? Peter Singer might say so, but the majority will oppose it, thus leading to double standards.

But what if a man leaves a 'living will', permitting doctors to remove his organs, etc., should he enter irreversible coma? Similarly, if Adams' *Almegian Major Cow* is bred to *want* to be eaten, doesn't this sidestep the problem of killing a sentient or living being?

However, this raises the problem of *consent*, which is an enduring one for *liberalism*: if we allow acts based on the consent of all parties, then do we give up the notion that certain acts are *inherently* wrong (such as murder or torture)? Perhaps, however, we might doubt the mental health of someone consenting to be eaten. Is the cow *insane*?

> "Forty-two!" yelled Loonquawl. "Is that all you've got to show for seven and a half million years' work?"
>
> "I checked it very thoroughly," said the computer, "and that quite definitely is the answer. I think the problem, to be quite honest with you, is that you've never actually known what the question is."'
>
> DOUGLAS ADAMS
> *The Hitchhiker's Guide to the Galaxy*

Tasked by an ancient alien civilization with finding the answer to The Great Question of life, the universe and everything, supercomputer *Deep Thought* took seven and a half million years. Its answer, however – 'forty-two' – merely revealed that no one had really thought much about the question itself.

Many people coming to philosophy for the first time are disappointed by its apparent failure to answer such big questions: why are we here? who are we? what is the purpose of life? Instead, they get what seem to be inconsequential squabbles over the different approaches to knowledge, controversies concerning the interpretation of past philosophers, and narrow discussions of very technical and obscure issues. Does modern philosophy have any relevance to the average person, or any longer bear any resemblance to the 'love of wisdom' pursued by Socrates and Plato?

Perhaps, however, this complaint is based on misconceptions. Anyone who's read Plato will know that, whilst he's often concerned with 'big' questions – what is truth, goodness, etc. – his arguments involve very close and technical discussion of fine points and distinctions. Also, it might be argued that philosophy has *never* been of great appeal to the common man, but the preserve of academics, intellectuals and the educational elite. Therefore, modern philosophy is no different really to its ancient forbear.

But there *is* a modern tendency to ignore the big questions. Wittgenstein famously argued that philosophical problems stemmed – like Deep Thought's task – from a confused *questioning*. Furthermore, Wittgenstein is happy to leave the central questions of ethics and religion as personal matters – they're not really philosophy's domain. But it's one thing to clarify a philosophical question, and quite another to claim that philosophy can't answer it.

> 'By the way, anyone who believes that the laws of physics are mere
> social conventions is invited to try transgressing those conventions
> from the windows of my apartment. I live on the twenty-first floor.'
> ALAN SOKAL b.1955
> 'Transgressing the Boundaries: An Afterword'

In 1996, American Physicist Alan Sokal, annoyed by what he considered the nonsense that passed for philosophy of science in *postmodernism*, decided to test a theory: if an article containing impressive-sounding but ultimately empty waffle were submitted to a postmodern academic journal, would it be accepted? When his 'Transgressing the Boundaries: Towards a Transformative Hermeneutics of Quantum Gravity' was accepted by *Social Text*, a postmodern cultural studies journal published by Duke University Press, he had his answer.

The following controversy, which became known as the *Sokal affair*, divided commentators: did it reveal, as Sokal claimed, the intellectual bankruptcy of postmodernism? Some thought so, but others – including the journal editors themselves – felt that Sokal had behaved unethically: submitting an article implies that an author is serious in his opinions (which Sokal was not).

But the Sokal affair is merely part of a much larger controversy, going by the name of the *science wars*. Since postmodernism broadly argues that *all* forms of knowledge are merely social constructs, even science doesn't have the 'last word' on reality. Furthermore, science itself reveals the cultural bias of scientists – who are mostly white, male, bourgeois, and rationalist. In response, scientists point out that science is backed up by practical results (such as jumping from Sokal's twenty-first-floor apartment): certain types of truth are therefore simply not up for debate.

The truth may lie somewhere in the middle. Loathe as most scientists are to admit it, knowledge *is* to an extent 'socially constructed' – as with Bacon's 'idols', there *are* obstacles to objective knowledge that philosophy should help uncover. Arguably, however, postmodern philosophy is failing in this duty, seeing its role rather more destructively as exposing the underlying ideologies behind *all* forms of knowledge. The science wars, it seems, are destined to rumble on.

> 'But if there is a language instinct, it has to be embodied somewhere in the brain, and those brain circuits must have been prepared for their role by the genes that built them'
> STEVEN PINKER b.1956
> *The Language Instinct*

Steven Pinker, Canadian-American cognitive scientist and psychologist, argues that the ability to learn and use language is genetic (therefore innate). In this sense, he's close to Noam Chomsky, but unlike him, Pinker argues that linguistic ability isn't just a by-product of more general abilities (such as capacity for speech), but is a distinct ability in itself: we're genetically programmed to use language.

This general approach is known as *evolutionary psychology*, and proposes that cognitive abilities are *adaptations* that have occurred in response to evolutionary challenges. So, just as sea-dwellers' fins adapted to land by growing into legs, the human brain evolved 'modules' to deal with specific aspects of its physical and social environment: for instance, the dexterity required to make and use weapons evolved to meet the need to hunt. In this way, the mind can be seen as a toolbox of different components, each addressing different problems.

However, evolutionary biologist Stephen Jay Gould has argued that such an approach is guilty of *panadaptation*. That is, if we see the human mind as evolving separate adaptations to deal with specific problems, then we're in danger of having an adaptation for *everything* (like a Swiss army knife). So, if we see the capacity for language, not as a by-product, but as a direct adaptation, then what next? Innate capacity for sarcasm? Inherent ability to recognize business opportunities? Obviously not, but this is the danger of 'adaptationitis'.

A more general problem concerns *genetic determinism*: if we think and act the way we do because of the way our brains have evolved, then does that mean that we've no control over such things? Evolutionary psychologists deny this: the environment may have as much say over how we develop as do our genes. But this just seems to muddy the waters – *are* we genetically determined, or not?

'Once technology has fully teased out the constituent processes and structures of memory, cognition and personality, and given us control over them; once we are able to share or sell our skills, personality traits and memories; once some individuals begin to abandon individuality for new forms of collective identity; then the edifice of Western ethical thought since the Enlightenment will be in terminal crisis'

JAMES J. HUGHES b.1961

'The Future of Death: Cryonics and the Telos of Liberal Individualism'

Whilst traditional religious notions of immortality involve 'dying to the self', *transhumanism* sees science and technology as possessing the means to overcome the obstacles to *physical* immortality (thus *transcending* normal *human* limitations). Such potential takes many forms, ranging from humble vitamin supplements, to reprogramming of the genetic trigger for human ageing, to 'downloading' one's consciousness onto a computer. Accordingly, American philosopher James J. Hughes argues that we will 'soon' be in a position to choose from a range of possible forms of 'enhanced' or 'post-mortem' existence.

But Hughes doesn't just see technology as extending human existence, but as *challenging* the very notions that existence is built upon – as he puts it: 'Technology is problematizing death.' The reason for this is that technology seems to allow (at least theoretically) for possibilities which would undermine current notions of self, individuality, life and death. For instance, if your mind *could* be downloaded to a computer as some form of algorithm, then, since computer algorithms merely consist of formal procedures, it could be augmented by other programs; it could be transmitted, duplicated, or shared; or even, perhaps, deleted . . .

Such scenarios currently represent no more than sci-fi thought experiments. Should we take them seriously? Disciples of technology often cite *Moore's Law* (after the co-founder of computer-chip manufacturer *Intel*, George E. Moore), which states (roughly) that computer power doubles every 18 months. This is often linked to the belief that scientific knowledge will advance *exponentially*. But, even if currently true, will it *continue* to do so? And mightn't such increase in knowledge involve a realization that there are *limits* to what can be achieved?

'The phenomenology of fish and slugs will likely not be primitive but relatively complex, reflecting the various distinctions they can make. Before phenomenology winks out altogether, we presumably will get some sort of maximally simple phenomenology. It seems to me that the most natural place for this to occur is in a system with a correspondingly simple "perceptual psychology," such as a thermostat.'

DAVID CHALMERS b.1966
The Conscious Mind

In the ongoing debate concerning consciousness, Australian philosopher David Chalmers occupies a fairly unique position. Firstly, along with materialists such as Daniel Dennett, he argues that the mind is a sort of computer, where psychological states play a *functional* role in the system as a whole (a view known as *functionalism*). However, like John Searle and Thomas Nagel, he also argues there's an aspect of consciousness that can't be reduced to a description of the physical workings of the brain.

In defending these two positions, Chalmers ends up in strange territory. Since functional systems can be simple (a thermostat) or complex (a human), the difference is merely one of degree (we are more *functionally complex*). However, since there's 'something it's like' to be a complex functional system (a human), why not also 'something it's like' to be a thermostat? Certainly, Chalmers says, 'it will not be very interesting to be a thermostat', but it'll nonetheless possess some form of simple experience ('maximally simple phenomenology').

Like Bateson, Chalmers sees the world as consisting of 'information' (data embodied in physical states of affairs). So, if the physical brain is conscious due to its capacity to process 'information', then 'information' is all that's required to produce conscious awareness – and since 'information' exists everywhere, then . . . consciousness is everywhere!

There are many problems here, but the most perplexing question is why, given that *organic life* is the only thing definitely known to be conscious, Chalmers should argue that the most significant thing about the human brain is its capacity to process 'information'.

> 'You actually cannot sell the idea of freedom, democracy, diversity, as if it were a brand attribute and not reality – not at the same time as you're bombing people, you can't'
> NAOMI KLEIN b.1970
> interview, 2004

In *No Logo*, **Canadian writer** and opponent of *globalization* Naomi Klein traced the genesis of the brand. Once, people sold things; other people bought them. Even when advertizing employed increased psychological subtlety, the message was simple: buy this product; it's good. However, in the 1990s, a sea change took place. Brands, which had long been around – a sign of trust and quality – developed a life of their own. From hereon, products didn't *help* you experience freedom, satisfaction, or to be cool, they *were* freedom, satisfaction, coolness. This allowed brands to go far beyond the remit suggested by the product itself – to sell a lifestyle, an attitude, a dream.

However, Klein argues, this leaves a gaping spiritual hole – you buy the dream, but you go home with a pair of trainers, a carbonated drink, or a mobile phone, and a vague sense of belonging to, or ownership of, something nebulous and indefinable. So indefinable, in fact, that it dissipates, leaving you with your trainers/drink/phone, an empty feeling, and a gnawing impulse to buy something else to fill it.

Like the carnival games at which no one can win, we might just laugh at this and shake our heads at our own gullibility. However, the transition from product to brand, from concrete thing to idea, highlighted a tension: whilst companies were pushing brands conveying high ideals, these weren't principles embedded in their own business practices. Thus, big brands sold their own factories and outsourced manufacturing to third world countries with cheaper labour and laxer employment laws.

More unsettlingly, however, the principles of 'brand management' spread to politics. After the Afghanistan War, the US Government hired a brand expert to redress what it feared was growing anti-Americanism around the world. But, Klein observes, ideas aren't reality; 'freedom, democracy, diversity' aren't brands that you can sell, but words that must be backed up with actions.

INDEX